THE ACTING PERSON

CARDINAL KAROL WOJTYŁA

THE ACTING PERSON

Translated from the Polish by
ANDRZEJ POTOCKI

This definitive text of the work
established in collaboration with the author by
ANNA-TERESA TYMIENIECKA

for publication in the Reidel book series
Analecta Husserliana

D. REIDEL PUBLISHING COMPANY

DORDRECHT : HOLLAND / BOSTON : U.S.A.
LONDON : ENGLAND

Library of Congress Cataloging in Publication Data

John Paul II, Pope, 1920–
    The acting person.

    (Analecta Husserliana; v. 10)
    "Translated and revised from the 1969 Polish edition,
Osoba i czyn."
    "This definitive text of the work established in collaboration
with the author by Anna-Teresa Tymieniecka."
    Includes index.
    1. Act (Philosophy). 2. Personality. 3. Philosophi-
cal anthropology. 4. Phenomenology. I. Tymieniecka,
Anna-Teresa. II. Title. III. Series.
B3279.H94A129   vol. 10   [B105.A35] 142'.7s   78-31349
                   [128]
ISBN 90-277-0969-6 (library binding)
ISBN 90-277-0985-8 (cheaper cloth binding)

Published by D. Reidel Publishing Company,
P.O. Box 17, Dordrecht, Holland

Sold and distributed in the U.S.A., Canada, and Mexico
by D. Reidel Publishing Company, Inc.
Lincoln Building, 160 Old Derby Street, Hingham,
Mass. 02043, U.S.A.

Translated and revised from the 1969 Polish edition, *Osoba i Czyn*,
Polskie Towarzystwo Teologiczne, Cracow

*Also published in 1979 in a library binding
in the Reidel book series Analecta Husserliana,
Volume X, edited by Anna-Teresa Tymieniecka*

Cardinal Karol Wojtyła, later to become Pope John Paul II, giving a lecture on 'Participation or Alienation?' on 27 March 1975 in a follow-up session to the *Fourth International Phenomenology Conference* held in Fribourg, Switzerland, in January 1975. At the main conference, organized by the International Husserl and Phenomenological Research Society, the lecture had been read *in absentia*.

PREFACE

Now that the present work is going to emerge from the limited readership to which it has so far been confined by the original language of composition, I would like to preface it with several introductory remarks.

First of all, audacious though it may seem in the present day – in which philosophical thinking is not only nourished by, and based upon, history, but in which to "philosophize" often means to reflect upon theories about theories – the present work cannot be seen otherwise than as a personal effort by the author to disentangle the intricacies of a crucial state of affairs and to clarify the basic elements of the problems involved. I have, indeed, tried to face the major issues themselves concerning life, nature, and the existence of the human being – with its limitations as well as with its privileges – directly as they present themselves to man in his struggle to survive while maintaining the dignity of the human being: man, who sets himself goals and strives to accomplish them, and who is torn apart between his all too limited condition and his highest aspirations to set himself free.

These struggles of the human being are reflected by the struggles of the author himself, who has attempted in the present work to unravel the subjacent apparatus of man's operations as it may lead either to his victories or to his defeats; only as such should the present work be seen. May it contribute to this disentangling of the conflicting issues facing man, which are crucial for man's own clarification of his existence and direction of his conduct.

Our approach runs also counter to another trend of modern philosophy. Since Descartes, knowledge about man and his world has been identified with the cognitive function – as if only in cognition, and especially through knowledge of himself, could man manifest his nature and his prerogative. And yet, in reality, does man reveal himself in *thinking* or, rather, in the actual *enacting* of his existence? – in observing, interpreting, speculating, or reasoning (which are changeable, even flexible insofar as they are acts, and often futile when confronted with the facts of reality) or in the confrontation itself when he has to take an active stand upon issues requiring vital decisions and having vital consequences and repercussions? In fact, it is in reversing the post-Cartesian attitude toward man that we undertake our study: by approaching him through action.

Considering the enormous spread of issues confronting the philosopher who seeks a new approach to the human being and who attempts to apply it, it is only natural that our work must at this point be too sketchy. We are perfectly aware of both past and present literature sharing this approach, but it appears to us imperative to undertake it in our own way.

Granted the author's acquaintance with traditional Aristotelian thought, it is however the work of Max Scheler that has been a major influence upon his reflection. In my overall conception of the person envisaged through the mechanisms of his operative systems and their variations, as presented here, may indeed be seen the Schelerian foundation studied in my previous work.

First of all, it is Scheler's value theory that comes into question. However, in our times, when the differentiation of issues concerning man has reached its peak – introducing the most artificial cleavages into the heart of the issues themselves – it is the unity of the human being that it seems imperative to investigate. In fact, in spite of the fundamental Schelerian, and for that matter generally phenomenological, efforts conducive to the cognition of the complete man, this unity, its basis, as well as its primordial manifestation, are still missing in the present-day philosophical conception of man – whereas in traditional Aristotelian thought it was the very conception of the "human act" which was seen as the manifestation of man's unity as well as its source. It seems then that by introducing here this approach to man through action we may yield the necessary insights into the unity of the human being.

And it is certainly not necessary to emphasize the importance of an inquiry into the unifying factors of man for the present-day outlook upon life, sanity, culture and their prospects.

One more point must be mentioned. In the lapse of time between its first appearance in the Polish language and the present version of this work, not only the author's participation in the philosophical life, but also a numerous series of philosophical discussions have contributed to greater precision on many points. There were first discussions with a number of Polish philosophers (published in *Analecta Cracoviensia* 1973/74). Those with Professor Anna-Teresa Tymieniecka of Boston however were the most important for the present publication. They have added to the clarification of numerous concepts and consequently to an improved presentation. Professor A.-T. Tymieniecka, having consented to become the philosophical editor of this work, has proposed some changes which have been incorporated into the definitive version with the full approval of the author. The author is also pleased that this definitive version of his book appears in the distinguished *Analecta Husserliana* Series.

And last but not least, I would like to thank the translator, Mr Andrew Potocki, who has attempted most expertly and with great devotion and care to render this rather difficult Polish text into the English language.

CARDINAL KAROL WOJTYŁA

Facsimile of the Handwritten Draft of the Author's Preface

The definitive version of the author's preface given on p. vii was written and sent to the publisher, together with the first half of the manuscript of the book, in March 1977. The author might have given to it in the proofreading those additional personal touches which only he could make; but since these touches are of necessity missing now, we are giving on p. xiii an English translation of the original draft of the preface and are reproducing in facsimile the first and last pages of that handwritten draft.

A.-T. T.

(amerykańskiego)
autor (angielskiej)
Przedmowa do wydania „Osoba i czyn"
w „Analecta Husserliana"

Uważam za mój obowiązek zwrócić
1) do P. Prof. A. T. Tymienieckiej jako
wydawcy i naczelnego redaktora serii
„Analecta Husserliana" nie tylko z ser-
decznym podziękowaniem za inicjatywę
publikacji mej pracy „Osoba i czyn",
ale także z pewnym wyjaśnieniem.
Uważam, że wyjaśnić to powinno zna-
leźć w przedmowie do amerykańskiego wydania „Osoby i czynu" –
i tę przedmowę, która poprzedni
~~dwomy po~~ w niniejszym wstępie do polskiego wydania tego trudnem.

Koncepcja osoby, którą w studium
tym przedstawiam, zrodziła się na
gruncie moich osobistych prac,
w szczególności zaś na gruncie ana-
liz M. Schelera. powiem myśleniem
sego dzieła autorze. Wiadomo, że

Translation of Handwritten Draft of the Author's Preface

J M   *Totus Tuus sum et omnia mea Tua sunt*

AUTHOR'S PREFACE TO ENGLISH/AMERICAN
EDITION OF *THE ACTING PERSON* IN
ANALECTA HUSSERLIANA

I consider it my duty to turn to Professor A.-T. Tymieniecka not only with cordial thanks for her initiative in publishing my work, *The Acting Person*, but also with some explanation. I think that this explanation should constitute a preface to the English/American edition of *The Acting Person* and should precede the translation of the preface in the Polish edition.

The concept of the acting person which I am presenting was born from my previous works, especially from my analysis of M. Scheler, above all of his *Wertethik*. As it is known, Scheler built his concept of *materiale Wertethik* with the thought of challenging the aprioristic ethic of pure form, or rather, of pure duty, which, as Kant's heritage, dominated throughout the nineteenth century. Scheler's critique, irrespectively of his scholarly relations with Husserl, followed the line that had been charted by the master of phenomenology on the foundation of the principle *zurück zum Gegenstand*. This basic controversy, conducted in the name of the return toward that which is objective in ethics (and above all in morality), presents at its very root the problem of the subject, namely, the problem of the person, or of the human being as a person.

This presentation of the problem, completely new in relation to traditional philosophy (and by traditional philosophy we understand here the pre-Cartesian philosophy and above all the heritage of Aristotle, and, among the Catholic schools of thought, of St. Thomas Aquinas) has provoked me to undertake an attempt at reinterpreting certain formulations proper to this whole philosophy. The first question which was born in the mind of the present student of St. Thomas (certainly a very poor student) was the question: What is the relationship between action as interpreted by the traditional ethic as *actus humanus*, and the action as an experience. This and other similar questions led me gradually to a more synthetic formulation in the form of the present study *The Acting Person.*

The author of the present study owes everything to the systems of metaphysics, of anthropology, and of Aristotelian–Thomistic ethics on the one hand, and to phenomenology, above all in Scheler's interpretation, and through Scheler's critique also to Kant, on the other hand. At the same time, an individual attempt has been undertaken at reaching this reality which is the man-person as seen through his actions. ...

... I thank the editor, Professor A.-T. Tymieniecka, who, guided by her excellent knowledge of the philosophic environment of the West, gave to my text its final shape. In comparison with the first and only Polish edition, the text now published in *Analecta Husserliana* contains a number of changes, although the basic concept of the work has remained unaltered. Footnotes, which are lacking in the Polish edition, have been introduced; they partially reflect the debate which the author of *The Acting Person* carried on while groping for his formulation of the concept of the "acting person." Perhaps, the reader, after having surmounted all objections that may be put forward from the point of view of the splendid precision and inner logic of philosophical systems, will accept something from my broadened discovery of the person through his actions. In this the author sees a turn toward the most interesting "thing itself" (*zurück zum Gegenstand*) which is precisely the human being as a subject.

Written in Rome, March 1977 (Ed.)

(Translated from the Polish original by
Professor M. K. Dziewanowski)

TABLE OF CONTENTS

PREFACE   vii

FACSIMILE OF THE HANDWRITTEN DRAFT OF THE
    AUTHOR'S PREFACE   x

TRANSLATION OF HANDWRITTEN DRAFT OF THE
    AUTHOR'S PREFACE   xiii

EDITORIAL INTRODUCTION   xix

INTRODUCTION

1. The Experience of Man   3
2. Cognition of the Person Rests on the Experience of Man   8
3. The Stages of Comprehending and the Lines of
   Interpretation   14
4. The Conception of Person and Action to Be Presented in
   This Study   18

PART ONE: CONSCIOUSNESS AND EFFICACY

CHAPTER ONE / THE ACTING PERSON IN THE ASPECT
    OF CONSCIOUSNESS   25

1. The Historical Wealth of the Expression "Human Act"   25
2. The Attempt to Discern Consciousness in the "Human
   Act"   28
3. Consciousness and Self-Knowledge   35
4. The Twofold Function of Consciousness and the
   Experience of Subjectiveness   41
5. The Emotionalization of Consciousness   50
6. Subjectivity and Subjectivism   56

CHAPTER TWO / AN ANALYSIS OF EFFICACY IN THE LIGHT
    OF HUMAN DYNAMISM   60

1. The Basic Conceptions and Differentiations of Human
    Dynamism   60
2. The Definition of Efficacy   66
3. The Synthesis of Efficacy and Subjectiveness. The Person
    as a Basic Ontological Structure   71
4. The Person and Nature: Their Opposition or Integration?   76
5. Nature as the Basis for the Dynamic Cohesion of the
    Person   80
6. Potentiality and Its Relation to Consciousness   85
7. The Relation of Potentiality to Consciousness Expressed
    by Subconsciousness   90
8. Man in Becoming: The Manifestation of Freedom in the
    Dynamism of the Man-Subject   96

PART TWO: THE TRANSCENDENCE OF THE PERSON
                    IN THE ACTION

CHAPTER THREE / THE PERSONAL STRUCTURE OF
    SELF-DETERMINATION   105

1. The Fundamentals of the Personal Structure of Self-
    Determination   105
2. An Attempt to Interpret the Integral Dynamism of the Will   108
3. Free Will as the Basis of the Transcendence of the Acting
    Person   115
4. The Significance of the Will as the Person's Power of
    Self-Determination   120
5. Decision Is the Focus of the Activities of Free Will   124
6. Responsibility in the Acts of Will – Motivation and
    Response   128
7. The Moment of "Truth about Good" as the Basis for the
    Acting Person's Perception and Transcendence   135
8. The Cognitive Experience of Values as the Condition of
    Choice and Decision   139
9. The Creative Role of Intuition Is Undiminished by the
    Judgment of Values   143

CHAPTER FOUR / SELF-DETERMINATION AND
   FULFILLMENT 149

1. Performing an Action Brings Personal Fulfillment 149
2. The Reliance of Self-Fulfillment on the Conscience 152
3. Conscience Depends on Truthfulness 158
4. The Obligation to Seek Self-Fulfillment 163
5. Responsibility 169
6. Happiness and the Person's Transcendence in the Action 174
7. The Transcendence of the Person and the Spirituality of
   Man 179
8. The Unity and Complexity of the Man-Person 183

PART THREE: THE INTEGRATION OF THE PERSON
IN THE ACTION

CHAPTER FIVE / INTEGRATION AND THE SOMA 189

1. The Fundamentals of the Person's Integration in Action 189
2. The Integration in the Action Manifested in Disintegration 192
3. The Person's Integration in the Action Is the Key to the
   Understanding of Man's Psychosomatic Unity 196
4. The Integration and the "Integrity" of Man on the Basis of
   Interacting Psychosomatic Conditionings 199
5. The Person and the Body 203
6. The Self-Determination of the Person and the Reactivity of
   the Body 206
7. Action and Motion 210
8. Instinct and the Person's Integration in the Action 215

CHAPTER SIX / PERSONAL INTEGRATION AND
   THE PSYCHE 220

1. The Psyche and the Soma 220
2. A Characteristic of the Psyche – Emotivity 223
3. Feelings and Consciousness in the Experience of the Body 226
4. Sensitivity and Truthfulness 231
5. Desire and Excitement 234
6. "Stirring Emotions" and Emotivity 238
7. The Emotivity of the Subject and the Efficacy of the
   Person 242

8. The Emotivity of the Subject and the Experience of Value   246
9. Action and Emotion – The Integrating Function of Skill   250
10. Conduct and Behavior   254
11. The Person's Integration in Action and the Soul–Body
    Relation   255

PART FOUR: PARTICIPATION

CHAPTER SEVEN / INTERSUBJECTIVITY BY
    PARTICIPATION   261

1. Introduction to the Concept of Participation   261
2. The Personalistic Value of Action   264
3. A More Detailed Definition of "Participation"   267
4. Individualism and Anti-Individualism   271
5. Participation and Community   276
6. Participation and the Common Good   280
7. "Authentic" Attitudes   283
8. "Nonauthentic" Attitudes   288
9. Fellow Member and Neighbor   292
10. The Commandment of Love   295

POSTSCRIPT   299

NOTES   301

APPENDIX: THE UNREVISED TRANSLATION OF
    CHAPTER SEVEN   317

INDEX OF NAMES   358

ANALYTICAL TABLE OF CONTENTS   360

EDITORIAL INTRODUCTION

THE THEME

The volume which we here present to a philosophical audience for the
first time in its definitive form constitutes a further advance in an
investigation which the World Institute for Advanced Phenomenological Research and Learning has been conducting under the heading
'The Phenomenology of Man and the Human Condition.' The theme
of *action* has been present for some time in the joint efforts of our
collaborators published in *Analecta Husserliana*. First, it ran as an
undercurrent through our quest for the *Irreducible Element in Man*,
then rose to prominence in our inquiry concerning the basis of the
human condition – a basis we located in the correlation between *The
Self and the Other* (*Analecta*, vol. VI), of which *action* is a root
factor. In *The Human Being in Action* (vol. VII) we took a further
step and examined, within the perspectives of consciousness, body,
imagination, will, moral conscience, and creative action, the
phenomenologically observable articulations of human activity, tracing them in that functional and existential web within which each
human being, as individual and as person, finds himself enmeshed,
and from which personal, deliberate action arises.

In the program of inquiry hitherto pursued, we have left aside the
transcendental as well as the eidetic or hermeneutic approaches of
classic and current phenomenologies, and have focused on the human
being as an individual and as a person, directly and comprehensively,
in an attempt to bring out the various entanglements and knots in his
functioning. These revealed themselves precisely in the individual's
central existential expression as an *agent*, that is, as manifesting
himself in action.

In the present book Cardinal Karol Wojtyła treats the human being
directly as "acting person." He tries to cut through the web of
countless capillaries, as it were, that support a person's existence, to
reach the major arteries. The apparently confused network found in
nature must be differentiated and untied, then reknit in a clear

philosophical scheme. The guiding aim of this complex investigation is to elucidate the nature of the *specifically human being* insofar as he or she is capable of personal action: that is, interaction with another person, establishing a *life-world*, both communal and social, within which the full possibilities of human existence can be realized.

In his attempt to formulate adequately the intuitive glimpses gathered along the tortuous path where such a subject leads, the author leaves aside historical references, polemics, and conceptual conventions. His passionate faithfulness to the "state of things themselves" – worthy of Max Scheler, through whom he early initiated himself into the phenomenological radicalism of intuitively grasping "things in themselves" – brings this extremely personal investigation within the field of phenomenology. Indeed, has not all genuine philosophical reflection throughout history arisen through this same radical fidelity to intuitive perception?

To the student of phenomenology proper, my statements may appear surprising. Not without reason, neither transcendental genetic analysis, which focuses upon the genesis of human consciousness constitutive of the *life-world*, nor eidetic analysis of the structures of objectivity as such, has approached human agency directly. Human activity, which carries the first and enacts the second, escapes the immediacy of the inspection practiced by both. In his own approach, the author traces the inspiration of phenomenological intuition back through Brentano all the way to Aristotle; and the purely descriptive analysis of the given – of things in themselves – rejoins the explanation of their *causal-existential network*. (Did not Eugen Fink already emphasize that within the broad scope of phenomenological philosophy, descriptive analysis cannot be but the basis of philosophical reconstruction?) Hence the picture of the human agent and of human agency which emerges in this study fuses description and explanation, born of reasoning as well as direct intuition.

THE AUTHOR

Cardinal Wojtyła is well known to the readers of *Analecta Husserliana*. They doubtless recall his continuing contribution to our debates and explorations. His unbiased reflection on specific issues, blending "the modern with the ancient," harmonizes with our effort to steer a middle course between the extremes of contemporary philosophical thought. On the one hand, does not even the greatest ingeniousness amount to nothing more than breaking down doors already open if it ignores contemptuously the acquisitions of past genius? At the other extreme, do we ever attain the level of "the state of things in themselves" if we eternally dwell upon history as supposedly laid bare by the polemical dissection of concepts?

Though varied philosophers and trends of thought – Aristotle, Aquinas, Kant, contemporary philosophies of existence – appear as points of reference during the course of the book, the special attention paid to Max Scheler's phenomenological thought suggests the author's background. Questions regarding freedom and responsibility, the foundation of moral judgment, the relation between values and conduct, concerned the author from the start of his philosophical reflection. At that time, when the scientism and empiricism inherited from the last century were spreading into all areas of thought and when particularly in Poland positivism such as that espoused by the famed Polish school of logic reduced the human to the empirical, the phenomenological trend introduced there by Roman Ingarden came as an innovative breath of fresh air. The Cardinal's contacts with Ingarden, personal or intellectual, postdate the writing of the present study. But he had previously written a dissertation on Scheler, resulting in the first of his philosophical books: *The Possibility of the Foundation of Christian Ethics on the Philosophy of Max Scheler.* Themes tentatively treated there and in his subsequent studies are more fully developed in this, his central philosophical work.

THE BOOK'S SIGNIFICANCE

The author stresses that his study is strictly anthropological, not ethical. By means of an "ontological hermeneutics" it probes the functional dynamisms integrated by the "acting person." No mere creature of circumstances, conditioned and engulfed by his social milieu, the human agent alone, through self-possession and self-governance, can fashion a social life worth living. In its emphasis on the communal condition of man but at the same time on the *irreducible transcendence of the human person* with respect to the current of social life, the book counteracts the deviant, reductive tendencies we have noted, so prevalent in contemporary philosophy and culture.

It is however evident that such a study, though anthropological, also has significance for ethics, and in particular for the origin and foundation of moral judgment. The solvent influence of contemporary movements – deterministic, behavioristic, utilitarian; in psychology, psychoanalysis, and elsewhere – is well-known. And phenomenology, despite its massive investigation of the human subject, has provided no new, valid foundation. Yet Kant was right in viewing moral judgment as a knot tying together crucial issues of epistemology, ontology, cosmology, and metaphysics. The present study goes still deeper in this direction. Unraveling the network of man's constitutive tendencies and strivings, it reveals his status in the world, the meaning of freedom and of human fulfillment. There can be no doubt: *The Acting Person* shows man constituting himself through moral judgment and corresponding action.

THE PREPARATION OF THIS PUBLICATION

The present volume is essentially the English translation of the book written and published in Polish under the title *Osoba i Czyn*. This earlier version was printed from an original draft before the author had the opportunity to give it more careful attention and to edit it himself for publication. Consequently for the English edition it has been necessary to subject the work to the sort of careful scrutiny customary for scholarly publications and to revise it extensively. The revision work has been accomplished in a collaboration between the author and the editor. As the author states in his preface, he brought to the revision new reflection, new insights and new organization of his thought. A set of references added by him, which were missing in the original edition, as well as the division of the entire work into sections, show the depth of the renewed reflection that he has brought to this task. At the same time, the editor went through the specifics of philosophical expression and style, proposing thorough emendations for the author's approval. The definitive version thus emerged from an extensive consultation.

As editor of the *Analecta* series, I would like to thank the author for consenting to my editorial work. Thanks are also due Count Andrzej Potocki, for bringing all his talent and attention to the task of translation. I cannot forget also to thank Professor Gareth Hallett for his precious help, and Mr Webb Dordick, the copy-editor of our series, for his usual dedicated work. I wish also to thank with all my heart Monsignor Stanisław Dziwisz and Sister Eufrozyna Rumian, the author's secretary, without whose constant care and attention this complex enterprise would have been altogether impossible.

It remains for the reader to assess the book for himself. I think he may then sense that it provides some cornerstones of a novel foundation for the moral consciousness of our times.

Rome, 15 March 1977   ANNA-TERESA TYMIENIECKA

POSTSCRIPT

On 23 April 1978 I dispatched with the author's approval the second and last portion of the manuscript to the publisher. The thorough revision by consultation between the author and the editor had extended over the entire first half of the book and the Notes. This revision work began in fall 1975 and was carried on through the middle of April 1978. Although all the major emendations proposed by the editor to the author in the following part were also discussed and approved by the author, he gave only a cursory look at the details. In view of the fact that these details followed the previously established line of revision, it was considered sufficient for the author to give them more attention in the proofreading. The last chapter, 'Intersubjectivity by Participation', which had been only very slightly edited, was left by the author for reading in proof.

However, the obligations of his High Office prevented the author from proofreading, and particularly from reviewing this final version of the second half of the book. The editor takes responsibility for the philosophical consistency of the stylistic revisions of this portion of the book with the trend of revision set by the author and herself in the preceding portion.

The unrevised translation of Chapter Seven is included as an Appendix.

Belmont, 5 November 1978   A.–T. T.

INTRODUCTION

INTRODUCTION

1. THE EXPERIENCE OF MAN

The Meaning of "Experience"

The inspiration to embark upon this study came from the need to objectivize that great cognitive process which at its origin may be defined as the experience of man; this experience, which man has of himself, is the richest and apparently the most complex of all experiences accessible to him. Man's experience of anything outside of himself is always associated with the experience of himself, and he never experiences anything external without having at the same time the experience of himself.

Speaking of the experience of man, however, we are primarily concerned with the fact that in this experience man has to *face himself*; that is, he comes into a cognitive relation with himself. The experiential nature of this relation is, in a sense, continuous; but it is also renewed each time the relation is disrupted and then re-established. For the experience of the relation is not uninterrupted even when it refers to the ego. At the level of consciousness it stops, for instance, in sleep: nevertheless, man always remains in his own company and so his experience of himself is in one way or another continuing. There are in it some vividly expressive moments and also whole, dull sequences, but they all sum up to make the specific totality of experience of that individual man who is myself. The totality is composed of a multitude of experiences and is, as it were, their resultant.

The phenomenalistic standpoint seems to overlook the essential unity of the distinctive experiences and to attribute the unitary nature of experience to its allegedly being composed of a set of sensations or emotions, which are subsequently ordered by the mind. Undoubtedly every experience is a single event, and its every occurrence is unique and unrepeatable, but even so there is something that, because of a whole sequence of empirical moments, may be called the "experience

3

of man." The object of experience is the man emerging from all the moments and at the same time present in every one of them (we disregard here all other objects).

Moreover, we cannot say that experience as such exists only in the one moment of its occurrence and that subsequently there is only the work of the mind shaping "man" as its object on the basis of a unitary empirical moment or sequence of such moments. The experience of man, of myself (the man I am), lasts as long as there is maintained that cognitive relation in which I am both the subject and the object.

Intimately associated with the relation is the process of comprehension that also has its own distinctive moments and its continuity. Ultimately, our comprehension of ourselves is composed of many separate moments of understanding, somewhat analogous to experience, which is also composed of many distinctive experiences; it thus seems that every experience is also a kind of understanding.

Experience as the Basis of the Knowledge of Man

All that was said here applies in fact only to that man who is myself. But men other than myself are also the objects of my experience. The experience of man is composed of his experience of himself and of all other men whose position relative to the subject is that of the object of experience, that is to say, who are in a direct cognitive relation to the subject. Naturally, the experience of an individual does not encompass all men, or even all his contemporaries, but is necessarily limited to a certain, larger or smaller range. The quantitative aspect in this experience has some significance; for the more numerous are the people encompassed by man's experience, the greater and, in a way, the richer it becomes.

Digressing from the main trend of our discussion of experience, which is important not for its own sake but for the whole problem of understanding the human being, we should note that different people may mutually exchange the results of their experiences had in intercourse with their fellowmen even without direct communication. These results themselves are a quantum of knowledge contributing to what we *know* about man rather than to our *experience* of him – the knowledge that may be either pre-scientific or scientific and pertaining to different tendencies or domains of learning. It is, however, ultimately grounded in experience, and, consequently, the knowledge of man that people share in mutual communications appeals in one way or another to everyone's own experience. This knowledge not only springs from experience but somehow also influences it. Can it deform experience? In view of what was said about the relation of experience and understanding there is no reason to think it does. It seems more likely that having its source in experience this knowledge serves as a means of multiplying and supplementing experiences.

The Ego and Man in the Field of Experience

It becomes clear in our considerations that the need for explaining the meaning of experience in general, and the meaning of the experience of man in particular, is becoming increasingly evident, and we shall have to return to this point later. In the meanwhile, before proceeding to an explanation of this fundamental concept, we shall sketch in rough outlines the highly complex and intricate cognitive process, which we have here called the "experience of man." A point of great importance for the present, and even more for our future considerations, is that other men as objects of experience are so in a different manner than I am for myself or than every man is for himself. We may even ask whether both cases are rightly called the "experience of man," whether they are two different experiences and thus mutually irreducible. In one of them we would have the experience only of *man* and in the other only of the *ego*. It is however impossible to deny that in the latter case we are also dealing with a human being, and we are having an experience of him while having an experience of the ego. The two experiences differ but are not separable. For all the difference between the subject and the object of experience, in either case there is a fundamental unity of the experienced object. There are indubitable reasons to speak of a disparity in the experience, but, equally, there are reasons to assert the essential points of its inherent sameness.

The disparity occurs because I am given to myself as my own ego and thus more directly and differently than any other man who is not myself. Even when we assume the closest possible relation to another human being the difference will always remain. Sometimes when we are very close to another person we may find it easier to objectivize what there is in him or what he actually is, though this is not equivalent to "having an experience." Everyone is the object of his own unique experience and no external relation to any other human being can take the place of the experiential relation that the subject has to himself. An external experiential relation may contribute many cognitive insights that are unobtainable in the subject's experience of himself, and these will differ according to the closeness of the relation and the manner of his involvement in the other person's experience (or, so to speak, in the other person's ego). This, however, cannot lessen the essential disparity of that unique experience – the experience of the man who is myself – with any other experience of man.

Experience and Comprehension

The experience of oneself, however, is still the experience of man; it does not extend beyond the limits of an experience that includes all humans, that is, man himself. This is certainly the result of the participation of the mind in the acts of human experience. We cannot say what is the stabilizing effect of sense alone with regard to the object of an experience, for a human being has no way of knowing from his own human experience what is the nature and what are the limitations of a purely sensuous experience (which is found only in animals). Yet there must be some stabilization of this kind, even if, at the most, it is exercised by individuals, in which the particular sets of sense qualities converge. (It is in this way that a dog or a horse, for example, recognizes its master from a stranger.) The stabilization of experiential objects peculiar to the human experience is essentially different and is accomplished by mental discrimination and classification. It is owing to this kind of stabilization that the subject's experience of his own ego is kept within the bounds of the experience of man and that these experiences may be subsequently superimposed on one another.

Such interference between experiences, which results from the specific stabilization of the object, then constitutes the basis for developing our knowledge of man from what is supplied in both the experience of the man I am and of any other man who is not myself. Let us note that the stabilization of the object of experience by the mind is in itself no evidence of knowledge *a priori*; it only evidences in the whole process of human cognition the indispensable role played by the intellectual element in the formation of the experiential acts, those direct cognitive encounters with objective reality. It is to the intellectual element that we owe the inherent sameness of the objects in the experience of man both when the subject of this experience is the same as the object and when they differ.

Simultaneity of the Inner and Outer Aspects in the Experience of Man

The likeness, however, ought not to be concealed by the disparity, which results from the fact that the experience had from the inside is only possible in relation to the man who is myself, and that this inner experience can never be had in relation to any man but myself. All other men are included in experience had from the outside, termed "outer experience." There are of course other ways than an experience of communicating with them and obtaining access to what is the object of their own experience had from the inside, but the inner experience itself is untransferable by and out of the ego.

Nevertheless, in the totality of our cognition of man this circumstance does not produce any cleavage that would cause the "inner man," who experientially can only be the ego, to differ from the "outer man," who is always other than myself. Other human beings in relation to myself are but the "outerness," which means they are in opposition to my "innerness"; in the totality of cognition these aspects complement and compensate each other, while experience itself in both its inner and outer forms tends to strengthen and not to weaken this complementary and compensating effect.

Thus, being the inner and the outer object of either experience I myself am first of all for myself my own innerness and outerness. Although every man other than myself is for me only the object of experience had from the outside, he does not relatively to the totality of my cognition represent the outerness alone but also has his own peculiar interior. While I do not experience his interior directly, I know of it: I know about people in general, and in the case of individuals I may sometimes know very much. When based on a definite relationship this knowledge may occasionally develop into something similar to an experience of somebody else's interior; though this experience differs from the experience of my own ego had from the inside, it also has its peculiar empirical traits.

All this has to be taken note of when considering the experience of man. It is impossible to isolate artificially this experience from the whole range of cognitive acts having man as their object. It is also impossible to separate it artificially from the intellectual factor. The nature of the whole set of cognitive acts directed at man, both at the man I am and at every man other than myself, is empirical as well as intellectual. The two aspects interpenetrate, interact, and mutually support each other.

In this study we must keep in mind the total experience of man: the disparity in the experience of man, which was mentioned earlier, does not cause any cognitive disruption or irreducibility. In our cognitive exploration we may venture far into the structure of the human being without fear that the particular aspects of experience will lead us astray. We may even say that the complexity of the experience of man is dominated by its intrinsic simplicity. The complexity itself of this experience simply shows that the whole experience, and consequently the cognition of man, is composed of both the experience that everyone has concerning himself and the experience of other men, the experience had both from the inside and from the outside. All this tends to compose a whole in cognition rather than to cause complexity. Thus, this conviction of the intrinsic simplicity of the experience of man may be considered as an optimistic aspect of the cognitive aims that confront us in this study.

2. COGNITION OF THE PERSON RESTS ON THE EXPERIENCE OF MAN

The Empirical Standpoint is not Identifiable with Phenomenalism

In the course of the preceding argument it seemed necessary to define with greater precision the meaning of experience in general in connection with the experience of man. Naturally we do not interpret experience here in the purely phenomenalistic sense, as has often been the practice in the broad sphere of empiricist thinking. On the contrary, the empirical approach adopted by us must not, and indeed cannot, be identified in any way with the phenomenalistic conception of experience. To reduce the range of experience to the functions and the content of sense alone would lead to deep contradictions and serious misunderstandings. This may be vividly illustrated by considering the object of cognition (the main concern of this work). For once the phenomenalistic stand is adopted it becomes necessary to ask, what then is given directly in experience? Is it only some "surface" aspect of the being called "man," an aspect detectable by sense, or is it man himself? Is it my own ego as a human being and if so, to what extent is it given? It does not seem reasonable to believe that we are given only some more or less undefined set of qualities in, or rather of, man, but not man himself. Moreover, it seems most improbable that man with his conscious acting or action is not given as the object of experience.

The Argument Begins with the Assumption that "Man-Acts" Is Phenomenologically Given

An experience is indubitably connected with a range of data which we have as given.[1] One of them is evidently the dynamic totality of "man-acts." It is this fact that we take as the starting point, and on it we shall primarily concentrate in our argument. Acting is a ceaselessly repeated event in the life of every man, so that when we consider the number of living people we obtain innumerable facts and hence an enormous wealth of experience.

Moreover, experience is indicative of the directness of cognition itself, of a direct cognitive relation to the object. While it is true that the relation of sense to objects in the surrounding reality, to the range of different facts mentioned above, is direct, there is no reason, however, to assume that these objects or facts can be grasped directly only in a "sensuous" act. It would be difficult to deny that the intentional-intellectual act must play a part in the direct grasping of the object. Such directness as an experiential trait of cognition can abolish neither the difference of content between a complete act of cognition and a purely sensuous act nor the difference of their genesis.

But these are detailed problems from the theory of knowledge and need not be discussed here. At present we are concerned with that cognitive act as a whole to which we owe among other things our grasp of the fact of man's acting. It would be impossible to accept as true that in grasping this fact experience only reaches to the "surface," that it would be restricted to a set of sense data, which in every particular case is unique, while the mind is, so to speak, awaiting these data so as to make of them its objects, which it will then call either "action" or "acting person." On the contrary, it seems that the mind is engaged already in experience itself and that the experience enables it to establish its relation to the object, a relation also, although direct in a different sense.

Action as a Special Moment of Insight into the Person in the Experience of Man's Acting

Thus in every human experience there is also a certain measure of understanding of what is experienced. This standpoint seems contrary to phenomenalism, but fits very well with phenomenology, which stresses more than anything the unity in the acts of human cognition. To put the matter in this way has a vital significance for the study of the person and of action. For our position is that *action serves as a particular moment of apprehending – that is, of experiencing – the person.* This experience is, of course, inherently connected with a strictly defined understanding, which consists, as already mentioned, in an intellectual apprehension grounded on the fact that man acts in its innumerable recurrences. The datum "man-acts," with its full experiential content, now opens itself for exfoliation as a person's action. It is only in this way that the whole content of experience reveals the fact with characteristic manifestness. What in this case is the meaning of manifestness? First, it seems to indicate an essential ability of an object to manifest or visualize itself, which is its characteristic cognitive trait. But, at the same time, "manifestness" means that the interpretation of the fact that "man-acts," in terms of the person's action – or rather in terms of the acting-person's totality – find full confirmation in the content of experience, that is, in the content of the datum "man-acts" in its innumerable recurrences.

Earlier, however, we said that action was a particular moment in the apprehension of a person. This statement defines more accurately our approach to the points that are the basis of the whole argument in this study; it also shows with greater precision the direction we shall follow in discussing experiences and understandings. Indeed, the interpretation of the fact of man's acting in terms of the dynamic person–action conjunction is fully confirmed in experience. Neither is there anything in experience that would be opposed to this interpretation when the fact that "man-acts" is objectivized in terms of a person's action is confirmed. Within the frame of this expression, which could perhaps be put differently, there appears, however, the question of the appropriate relation of *person* and *action*. Their close correlation – their semantic homology and interdependence – becomes manifest in experience. Action is not a single event but a processlike sequence of acting; and this corresponds to different agents. The kind of acting that is an action, however, can be assigned to no other agent than a person. In other words, an action presupposes a person. This has been the standard approach in different fields of learning that have as their object man's acting, and is especially true of ethics, which treats of action that presupposes a person, that is, presupposes man as a person.

In our study, on the other hand, the aim is to reverse this relation. The title itself of this book, *The Acting Person*, shows it is not a discourse on action in which the person is presupposed. We have followed a different line of experience and understanding. For us action *reveals* the person, and we look at the person through his action.[2] For it lies in the nature of the correlation inherent in experience, in the very nature of man's acting, that action constitutes the specific moment whereby the person is revealed. Action gives us the best insight into the inherent essence of the person and allows us to understand the person most fully. We experience man as a person, and we are convinced of it because he performs actions.

The Moral Modality of Human Actions

But this is not all. Our experience and also our intellectual apprehension of the person in and through his actions are derived in particular from the fact that actions have a moral value: they are morally good or morally bad. Morality constitutes their intrinsic feature and what may be viewed as their specific profile, which is not to be found in acting that assumes agents other than a person. Only the acting, in which the agent is assumed to be a person – we have stressed earlier that only such acting deserves to be called "action" – has moral significance.

This is why the history of philosophy is the tale of the age-old encounter of anthropology and ethics. That branch of learning which has as its aim the comprehensive study of moral goodness and evil – and such are the aims of ethics – can never evade the state of affairs that good and evil manifest themselves in actions, and by actions they become a part of man. It is not surprising, therefore, that ethics, especially in the traditional approach, has always assiduously concerned itself with action and man. Examples can be found as early as in the *Nicomachean Ethics*. And though in modern philosophy, particularly in contemporary philosophical thought, there is a visible tendency to treat the problems of ethics somewhat apart from anthropology (this terrain is now being explored by psychology and moral sociology), the total elimination of anthropological conclusions from ethics is not possible. The more a philosophical reflection becomes comprehensive, the more the anthropological questions tend to appear. For instance, it seems their role is much more important in phenomenological than in positivistic thought – in Sartre's *L'Être et le Néant* than in the works of the Anglo-Saxon analysts.[3]

Moral Value Deepens Our Insight into the Person

Mention was already made that it is the rule in ethics to presuppose the person because of his actions, which are vested with direct moral value. In the present discourse we have adopted an opposite approach. We assume that actions provide the particular moments for apprehending and hence for experientially cognizing the person. Actions, therefore, are the most adequate starting point for comprehending the dynamic nature of the person. But moral value as the inherent property of actions leads in an even more direct way to the same result. We are not interested here in moral values as such, this being the domain of ethics, but we are very much concerned with their actual participation in actions, with their dynamic *fieri*. For their actual dynamic involvement gives us an even better and deeper insight into the person than into action itself.

This moral aspect – it could equally be termed "dynamic" or "existential" – allows us to reach a better understanding of the human being insofar as he is a person: this is precisely the aim of our inquiries. Hence, while deliberately relying on the total experience of man we can never avoid consideration of the experience of moral values. The latter experience in its dynamic or existential aspect is indeed an integral part of the experience of man, which as we already know provides firm ground for our understanding of the person. Moreover, it has to attract our special attention because moral values – good or evil – not only determine the inner quality of human actions, but they also never enter into a dynamic sequence of actions without leaving an imprint whereby man as a person, owing to his actions that may be good or may be evil, himself becomes either good or evil. Thus, assuming the dynamic or existential point of view, we may say the person stands at the origin of moral values just as much as in their final outcome. In them the person emerges into view more completely than in "pure" action. Indeed, to detach human action from moral values seems an artificial operation that would turn our attention away from its full dynamism.

Anthropology and Ethics Rest on the Unity of the Experience of the Moral Man

This book is not a study in ethics. The person is not presupposed, is not implied in it; on the contrary, all our attention is centered on possibly the most comprehensive explanation of that reality which is the person. The source of our knowledge of the reality that is the person lies in action, but even more so in the dynamic or existential aspects of morality. In this approach we shall rely on the real objective unity of the experience of moral value and the experience of man, rather than try to retain the traditional links of anthropology with ethics. This is the fundamental condition of exfoliating and then progressively comprehending the person.

Ethics as the Common Factor

As to the position of the relationship of anthropology and ethics in this approach it may be formulated – by analogy to operations used in algebra – as placing a term before brackets. We place outside brackets those factors of an algebraic expression which in one way or another are common to all the terms of the expression, that is, which are somehow common to everything that remains within the brackets. The aim is to simplify subsequent operations and not to reject what is withdrawn or to sever the relations of what is outside to what remains in brackets. On the contrary, the operation underlines and enhances the significance of the factor isolated from the expression. If it were not placed outside the brackets, it would remain hidden among the other terms of the expression; but it is now brought to light and given prominence.[4]

Similarly, the traditional problem in ethics of the person–action relation, when we look at it as if it were withdrawn from brackets, may reveal itself more fully not only in its own reality but also in that abundant reality which is expanded by human morality.

3. THE STAGES OF COMPREHENDING AND THE LINES OF INTERPRETATION

Induction and the Unity of Meaning

We said earlier that the person–action relation is grasped, or rather the person is revealed in action, on the ground of the experience of man. The experience of man is composed of innumerable data, the most important for our discussion being those of man's acting: it is in them that the person is especially revealed by action. All these data manifest – besides their multiplicity, that is, their quantitative complexity – the already mentioned complexity; this means that in all men other than myself they are given from the outside, and they are also given from the inside on the ground of my own ego. The transition from the multiplicity and complexity of "factual" data to the grasping of their essential sameness, previously defined as the stabilization of the object of experience, is achieved by induction. At any rate this is how Aristotle seems to have understood the inductive function of the mind.[5] This view is not shared by modern positivists, such as J. S. Mill, for whom induction is already a form of argumentation or reasoning – something which it is not for Aristotle. Induction consists in grasping mentally the unity of meaning from among the multiplicity and complexity of phenomena. In connection with our earlier assertions we may say that induction leads to that simplicity in the experience of man which we find in it in spite of all its complexity.

When the experience of man takes the form of apprehending the person through action, it is in this apprehension that experience in its whole simplicity is focused and the experience itself is expressed. Thus the transition from the manifold to the sameness of experiential elements is operated from the point of view of the apprehension of the person; it enables us to assert that in every instance of a person's acting there is the same person–action relation, that the same relation implies the manner in which a person becomes visualized through action. "Sameness" is understood here as equivalent to the "unity of meaning." Since experience as such cannot take us farther than the multiplicity of factual data, it becomes the task of induction to reach this unity. The whole wealth and diversity of "factual" data accumulated from individual details is retained in experience, while the mind disengages from their abundance and grasps only the unity of meaning. In order to grasp this unity the mind, so to speak, allows experience to predominate without, however, ceasing to understand the wealth and diversity of experience. The grasping by the mind of the unity of meaning is not equivalent to a rejection of experiential wealth and diversity (though sometimes this is how the function of abstraction is erroneously interpreted). While comprehending (say) the acting person on the ground of the experience of man, of all the "factual" data of "man-acts," the mind still remains attentive in this essential understanding to the wealth of diverse information supplied by experience.

Reduction Allows Us to Explore the Experience of Man

This is probably the reason why, concurrent with the understanding of the person–action relation, there appears the need to examine and explain it. Induction opens the way to reduction. It is precisely the need for examining, explaining, or interpreting the rich reality of the person, which is given together with and through actions in the experience of man, that has inspired this study. Thus we think it a waste of time to demonstrate or prove that man is a person and his acting is "action." We assume these to be irreducibly given in the experience itself of man: person and action are somehow contained in every instance of man's acting. Nevertheless, it is necessary to explain in detail the various aspects of the reality of the acting person on the ground of a fundamental understanding of person and action. The experience of man not only reveals this reality but also stimulates the need for discussing it and provides the basis for the discussion. The wealth and the diversity of experience somehow provokes the mind to the effort of grasping and explaining as fully as possible the reality of person and action when it has been apprehended. But this can be accomplished only by going deeper and deeper into the content of experience so as to bring the person and his actions out of the shadow and into full light for the cognizing mind to thoroughly examine and explore.

It is by an analytic argument and reductive understanding that experience is explored. We have to remember, however, the correct meaning of the term "reductive," which does not indicate here any reduction in the sense of diminishing or limiting the wealth of the experiential object. On the contrary, our aim is to bring it out more fully. The exploration of the experience of man ought to be a cognitive process in which the original apprehension of the person in and through his actions is continuously and homogenetically developed. At the same time, this first apprehension has to be enriched and consistently extended and deepened.

Reduction and Interpretation Lead to a Theory Issuing from Human Praxis

This, in broad outline, is our plan for the interpretation of the acting person. Induction makes possible the fundamental "intersubjectivation" proposed in the present approach to replace an "objectivation" of person and action, which stand out as an object for everyone to see, regardless of the subjective implications, in which the object is at least partly involved. "At least partly" is a necessary qualification, because a very important part of the experience of man consists in the experience of his ego. We may rightly say that for every one of us the person–action relation is first of all an experience, that is, it is a subjective event, a factual datum. Induction, however, makes of it a problem for and a subject of reflection, and it is then that it comes within the scope of theoretical considerations. For, being an experience, that is to say, an experiential factual instance, the person–action relation is also partaking of what in traditional philosophy was called "praxis." It is accompanied by that practical understanding which is necessary and sufficient for a man to live and to act consciously.

The line of understanding and interpretation that we have chosen here leads through a theoretical treatment of this praxis. The question thus facing us is not how to act consciously but what conscious acting or action really is, how the action reveals the person and how it helps us to gain a full and comprehensive understanding of the person. In this study an interpretation along these lines appears from the start to be self-evident. Nevertheless, it has seemed useful to include also the moment of the relation to the praxis, to the so-called "practical cognition," with which ethics has long-standing traditional links. We already noted that in ethics the person is only presupposed, while here our chief task is to examine and interpret the person.[6]

Issues Relevant to Adequate Interpretation

This is why in this study the argument is based on reduction. The term reduction, as here used, has no limiting or diminishing implications: to "reduce" means *to convert to suitable arguments and items of evidence* or, in other words, *to reason, explain, and interpret.* When reasoning and explaining we advance step by step to trace the object that is given us in experience and which directs our progress by the manner in which it is given. The whole wealth and diversity of experience together with all its complexity lie open awaiting our exploration, and they are not in the least overshadowed by induction and the associated intersubjectivation of person and action; indeed, they remain an inexhaustible source and unfailing help for the mind seeking for evidence and adequate arguments to explain fully and comprehensively the reality of person and action.

After all, we are not concerned with the abstract but seek to penetrate something that actually exists. The arguments explaining this existence have to correspond to experience. Thus also reduction, and not only induction, is an inherent factor of experience without at the same time ceasing to be, though different from induction, transcendent with respect to it.

Generally speaking, understanding is intrinsic to human experience but also transcends it, not only because experience is an act and a process, the nature of which is sensuous while the nature of understanding and interpretation is intellectual, but because of the intrinsic nature of one and the other. To experience is one thing and to understand and interpret (which implies understanding) is quite another.

The aim of interpretation is to produce an intentional image of the object, an image that is adequate and coincident with the object itself. This means that all the arguments relevant to the object must be grasped in their correct proportions. On this largely depends the correctness of the interpretation and this also increases the difficulty.

The Understanding and Interpretation of the Object

Similar difficulties beset the conception, that is to say, in this case the expression itself of the understanding, which matures gradually from the initial apprehension of the acting person to the final and complete interpretation. It is not only the question of an inner conviction that the man who acts is a person, but also of finding such a manner of expressing this conviction in both thought and speech, of giving it such an outward form (in this study) as would make it fully communicative. Such a conception develops parallel with the growing understanding of the object and takes on the form necessary to allow understanding – which should be as complete and as comprehensive as possible – to be expressible and effectively communicable to other people. For it is by the mutual communication and exchange of things understood that human knowledge, which is a social phenomenon, develops.

The difficulties besetting the interpretation and the conception of man are associated with the already mentioned disparity inherent in the experience of man, and thus also indirectly in that grasping of the person–action relation which issues from this experience. Evidently the manifestation of the relation with reference to the ego will be different within the range of the immanent experience than within the range of the outer experience, which extends to all men other than myself. In the course of the interpretation and in the conception of person and action the problem will unavoidably appear of integrating the manifold of singular understandings that emerge from the disparity in experience. The resolution of this problem by an attempt to integrate correctly the two aspects in the experience of man is one of the main tasks that face us in this study.

4. THE CONCEPTION OF PERSON AND ACTION
TO BE PRESENTED IN THIS STUDY

Attempt to Approach the Subjectivity of Man

Although the disparity in the experience of man that we have been stressing here is an obstacle to the arrival at an interpretation and conception of man, it does open new possibilities and wide vistas for investigation. On the ground of the integrated experience of man, unlike through the behavioristic approach, the person is revealed through action, because in this experience man is given us from the inside and not only outwardly. Just because he is given not as the man-subject but, in his entire experiential subjectiveness, as the ego, new possibilities are opened for such an interpretation of man which will at the same time allow us to reproduce in the right proportions the subjectiveness of man. This has a fundamental significance for the conception of person and action that we intend to present.

Perhaps we have the right to assume that the divergence of the two great currents in philosophical thought, separating the objective from the subjective and the philosophy of being from the philosophy of consciousness, has at its root the experience of man and that cleavage of its inner aspect from outerness which is characteristic of this experience. Admittedly, to attribute this divergence only to the double aspect of experience or to the duality of the data in this experience would unduly simplify the matter. At any rate, it is not in that direction that we intend to pursue our inquiries, all the more so as their subject matter is strictly defined. However, from the point of view of our subject matter itself, which is the acting person, and which we will try to interpret and understand on the ground of the experience of man (the experience of "man-acts"), we reach the conclusion that much more important than any attempt to attribute absolute significance to either aspect of human experience is the need to acknowledge their mutual relativeness. If anybody asks why, then the answer is that this relation lies in the very essence of the experience that is the experience of man. We owe the understanding of man precisely to the interrelation of these two aspects of experience, and this interrelation serves as the basis for us to build on the ground of the experience of man (of "man-acts") our conception of person and action.

The Aspect of Consciousness

Once the problem is put in these terms, it immediately becomes evident that the analyses in this study are not going to be conducted on the level of consciousness alone, though they will necessarily include also the aspect of consciousness. If action is, as already mentioned, the special moment of revealing the person, then naturally we are concerned not with action as the intentional content constituted in consciousness, but instead, with that dynamic reality itself which simultaneously reveals the person as its efficacious subject. It is in this sense that in all our analyses we will consider action; and it is in this sense that we intend to exfoliate the person through action. At the same time, however, we must keep clearly in mind that action as the moment of the special apprehension of the person always manifests itself through consciousness – as does the *person*, whose essence the action discloses in a specific manner on the ground of the experience of man, particularly the inner experience. Accordingly, both person and action have to be discussed under the aspect of consciousness. Nevertheless, it seems evident that the manifestation of action under the aspect of consciousness is not the only reason why action – the act of the person – consists in acting consciously.

Our first task, therefore – in Chapters 1 and 2 – will be to examine the interrelation of consciousness and the efficacy of the person, that is to say, of consciousness and what constitutes the essence of the dynamism pertaining to man's action. Going deeper into the wealth of that experiential whole in which the person reveals itself more and more fully through action we shall discover the specific transcendence disclosed by the person's action, and we shall then – in Chapters 3 and 4 – try to submit it to a thorough analysis.

Transcendence and Integration of the Person

The apprehension of the transcendence of the person in action constitutes in a way the main frame of the experience that we are always referring to throughout our conception, because it is in experience that we also find the fundamental evidence allowing us to assert that the man who acts is a person, and that his acting is really the act of a person. It would, of course, be possible to develop a more comprehensive and more elaborate theory of the person as a being, but in this study our first and chief concern is to educe from the experience of action (that is, of "man-acts") that evidence which shows man to be a person or "brings the person into view."

The basic intuition of the transcendence of the person in action allows us to perceive simultaneously that moment of the integration of the person in action which is complementary in relation to trans-cendence. For integration is an essential condition for the transcen-dence of the person in the whole of the psychosomatic complexity of the human subject. In Chapters 5 and 6 we shall analyze this complexity from the point of view of the integration of the person in action. In this part of our study our chief aim will be to place the basic intuition on sounder grounds rather than provide an exhaustive treatment of that extensive problem. Integration as a complementary aspect of the transcendence of the person-in-action supports our claim that the category of person and action adequately expresses the dynamic unity of the human being, which must have its basis in an ontic unity. In this study, however, we will not embark upon an analysis of the ontic unity, our aim being solely to approach as closely as possible the elements and issues that are essential to it. It is this approach, which, we believe, allows us to draw in the fullest way upon experience and to make use of the phenomenological approach to man, that we regard as the distinguishing trait of the conception of person and action to be presented here. The last chapter, 'Intersubjectivity by Participation,' brings us to a different dimension of the experience of "man-acts," a dimension that it is absolutely necessary to note but whose more complete analysis we shall not undertake.

The Significance of Personalistic Problems

The argumentation and analyses contained in this study reflect the tremendous significance that personalistic problems have today. Their vital import in the lives of all men as well as of the whole, always expanding, human family is undeniable. Ceaseless speculations about the various trends in the development of mankind – for example, the quantitative aspects of development, the progress of culture and civilization with all the resulting inequalities and their dramatic consequences – are a powerful impulse for the philosophy of the person. We cannot help feeling, however, that the magnitude of cognitive efforts spent in all directions is out of proportion to the efforts and achievements actually concentrated on man himself. It may be not merely a question concerning the cognitive efforts and accomplishments, which we know to be enormous and increasingly comprehensive. Perhaps the problem consists of the fact that man is still awaiting a new and profound analysis of himself, or rather, what is much more important, an ever-new synthesis, and this is not easy to attain. Having conquered so many secrets of nature the conqueror himself must have his own mysteries ceaselessly unraveled anew. In the absence of a definitive analysis, man must forever strive for a new – a more mature – expression of his nature.

Moreover, as already noted, man is the first, closest, and most frequent object of experience, and so he is in danger of becoming usual and commonplace; he risks becoming too ordinary even for himself. It is necessary that this be avoided; and it was precisely due to the need to oppose the temptation of falling into the rut of habit that this study was conceived. It was borne out of that wonderment at the human being which, as we know, initiates the first cognitive impulse. As a function of the mind, this wonderment – which is not to be confused with admiration, albeit they have something in common – manifests itself in a set of questions and then in a set of answers and solutions. In this way not only is an inquiry (our own inquiry) initiated in a train of thoughts about man, but, in addition, one of man's fundamental needs receives attention. Man should not lose his proper place in the world that he has shaped himself.[7]

The problem consists in coming to grips with human reality at the most propitious point, the point that is indicated by the experience of man and which man cannot abandon without a feeling of having abandoned himself. In embarking upon this work the author is fully aware that there are many who have already explored or will explore the domains of human experience. The reader himself will readily recognize all the influences and borrowings in this work – influences which form a part of man's great philosophical heritage and of which any new study of man must in one way or another take account.[8]

It has not been the author's intention to produce a historical or even a comprehensive, systematic study of the subject. It is merely his own individual endeavor to understand the object of his concern, an essay in analysis aimed at developing a synthetic expression for the conception of person and action. The essence of this conception has for its prime objective the understanding of the human person for the sake of the person himself; it is thus designed to respond to the challenge that is posed by the experience of man as well as by the existential problems of man in the contemporary world.[9]

PART ONE

CONSCIOUSNESS AND EFFICACY

CHAPTER ONE

THE ACTING PERSON IN THE ASPECT
OF CONSCIOUSNESS

1. THE HISTORICAL WEALTH OF THE EXPRESSION "HUMAN ACT"

The Act in Its Traditional Interpretation

Before embarking upon a discussion of the act and the person it is first necessary to look, however briefly, into a question that has but the semblance of purely terminological significance. It is only man's *deliberate acting* that we call an "act" or "action." Nothing else in his acting, nothing that is not intended and deliberate deserves to be so termed. In the Western philosophical tradition a deliberate action has been seen as the *actus humanus*, the human act, with the stress laid on the aspect of purpose and deliberateness; it is in this sense that the term is used, even if implicitly, throughout this book, since only man can act purposely and deliberately.[10] The expression "actus humanus" itself is not only derived from the verb *agere* – which establishes its direct relationship with action and acting because *agere* means to act or to do – but it also assumes, as it is traditionally used in Western philosophy, a specified interpretation of the action, namely, the interpretation found in the philosophies of Aristotle and St. Thomas Aquinas. The interpretation is realistic and objectivistic as well as metaphysical. It issues from the whole conception of being, and more directly from the conception of *potentia-actus*, which has been used by Aristotelians to explain the changeable and simultaneously dynamic nature of being.[11]

Here we are concerned with the concrete being that is man, with his own proper mode of acting. The specific mode of man's acting is precisely the reason why in Scholastic philosophy the action is defined as *actus humanus* or, more precisely, as *actus voluntarius*. Such action is the concretion of the dynamism proper to man, insofar as its performance is conformable with the free will. The feature indicated by the attributive *voluntarius* is the decisive factor in the inherent essence of action as well as for its separateness from the

25

acting of any other subject that is not a person. In the light of the
Aristotelian conception as interpreted by the Scholastics, the peculiar
aspect of the term *actus* is its close link with a corresponding
potentia. This points to the potential substratum of actualization; it
explains why *actus humanus* considers man as the subject who acts;
less directly, it accounts for his potentiality as the source of acting.
The same is accomplished with still greater precision by the expression *actus voluntarius*, which points directly to the power that serves
as the dynamic basis in conscious acting, the basis of action. The
power in question is the free will. The attribute *voluntarius* also tells
us how the action is accomplished, namely, that it is "voluntary" –
which means there is nothing to interfere with the actualization of the
free will.

Action as Peculiar to the Person

Nevertheless, the term "human act" or "action" as such contains a
definite interpretation of action as conscious acting, which is strictly
connected with the philosophy of being. In its own way this interpretation is correct. It accounts for the experiential facts as a whole
and brings out most meaningfully all that is essential in them. In a
sense we may even say no other interpretation of human action is
possible; for it seems there is no conception better suited for grasping
both the thoroughly dynamic nature of human actions and their
intimate association with the human being as a person. It seems,
moreover, that any attempt at dealing with this problem, any attempt
that strives to attain the full meaning of all its essential elements and
constitutive interrelations, must in one way or another acknowledge
the philosophical content hidden in the terms "human act" and
"voluntary act." The same philosophical content is assumed also in
the attempt undertaken in this study. Nevertheless, in the course of
our considerations we shall have to scrutinize and unfold these
assumptions further and reexamine them in their various aspects. For
the moment it suffices to say that the historical conception tends to
assume the human person as the source of action: whereas the
approach of this study is from the opposite side, and aims to bring
into full view precisely that which is only assumed in the classic
conception of the "human act"; for indeed, as we have pointed out
before, action may also serve as a source of knowledge of the

person.[12] Action as such – that is, as the human action – ought to be helpful in the cognitive actualization of the potentiality, which it takes for granted as its roots. But the potentiality is that of the personal being, so that action is to be interpreted not only as the human action but also as the action of the person. In approaching the person through his actions we shall have to retain that philosophical intuition which appears to be indispensable for the comprehension and the philosophical interpretation of any dynamism and thus also of the dynamism of action, that is, of conscious acting. Since, then, the fullest and most comprehensive interpretation of that dynamism is the only way of bringing into view the whole reality of the person, the provision of such an interpretation shall be our main objective.

When so defined, *action* is identical in meaning with human action; the noun *action* is related to the verbs *to act* and *to do*. "Action," in the sense it is used here, is equivalent to the acting of man as a person. While "human act" shows such action as a specific manner of becoming based on the potentiality of the personal subject, the terms *act* or *action* themselves tell us nothing about it. They seem to denote the same dynamic reality but, in a way, only as a phenomenon or manifestation rather than as an ontic structure. It does not mean, however, that they prevent us from gaining access to this structure. On the contrary, both *action* and *conscious acting* tell us of the dynamism proper to man as a person. It is owing to this intrinsic content that they comprise all that is meant by "human act"; apparently philosophical thought has so far failed to develop a more fundamental concept for expressing dynamism apart from the concept of *actus*.[13]

Voluntariness as Indication of Consciousness

By "action" is meant acting consciously. When we say "conscious acting" we implicitly refer to the kind of acting that is related to and characteristic of the will. Thus the phrase to some extent corresponds to the *actus voluntarius* of Scholastic philosophy, since any acting pertaining to the human will must also be conscious. We can now see even more vividly how condensed is the meaning of "action" or of the corresponding "conscious acting" of everyday speech. In it are contained the ontological meanings, which belong to the *human act*, as well as the psychological meanings, which are traceable in such

attributives as the Latin *voluntarius* or the English *conscious*. Hence
the notion of *action* contains a great wealth of implications, which
will have to be gradually extricated and explicated. Simultaneously,
our explication will gradually disclose that reality of the human
person; indeed, it is the object of this study to uncover and gradually
to expound the notion of action from the point of view of the reality
of the human person. That aim we shall strive to achieve step by step,
keeping in mind the organic integrity of the concrete action in its
relation to the person. This gradual approach is, indeed, the direct
consequence of the very conception of an "aspect"; an aspect may
never stand for the whole and may never put it out of view. If it is
substituted for a whole, it ceases to be but an aspect, and unavoidably
leads to errors in the conception we form of any composite reality.
But it is precisely such a complex reality that we have in the acting
person. We cannot for a moment forget the existence of this complexity and the ensuing epistemological principles when we embark
upon the analysis of the person and his action by examining first, the
aspect of consciousness and second, that of efficacy.

2. THE ATTEMPT TO DISCERN CONSCIOUSNESS IN THE "HUMAN ACT"

Is this Analysis Possible and Necessary?

The concept of "conscious acting" brings us to envisage the aspect of
consciousness in an action but does not precisely identify it. It is first
necessary to recognize the difference between conscious acting and
the consciousness of acting; the aspect of consciousness will then
come into view, as it were, in itself. The distinction, when we make it,
allows us to gain a direct access to consciousness, thus enabling us to
examine it in greater detail – though obviously we must continue to
take account of the function which it performs in the acting as well as
in the whole existence of the person. For man not only acts consciously, but also has the consciousness that he is acting and even
that he is acting consciously. This is apparent in the fact that
"conscious" and "consciousness" have two different applications: one
is used attributively, when reference is made to conscious acting; the
other is employed as a noun, which may be the subject, when the
reference is to the consciousness of acting. Our discussion will

henceforth concentrate on the consciousness of acting and consequently on the consciousness of the acting person; hence our aim will be to disclose its relationship with the person and the action. It is only in this connection that consciousness as such will be considered. When, on the other hand, we speak of conscious acting – without stressing the *consciousness* of acting – then we point only to action, to its constitutive feature that proceeds from cognition. What is implied here is the kind of cognition that makes the action also voluntary, which means that it is performed according to the will; for cognitive objectivation is assumed in the correct functioning of the will. It now becomes clear why the expression "conscious acting" says nothing directly of the consciousness of acting. It is, however, possible and even necessary to discern, in that dynamic whole, consciousness as such, and to examine it as a special aspect. Since we shall be concerned throughout this study with conscious acting an examination of the consciousness itself of acting, which is the theme of this chapter, may throw new light on the whole dynamic system of person and action.

At this point the question may, or even should, be asked why the aspect of consciousness is discussed in the first chapter, that is, why the discussion of the consciousness of acting precedes the discussion of efficacy, though it is efficacy that makes of conscious acting the *action* of the person. Why in our analysis do we first consider what is secondary and not what is fundamental in our conception of action? The question cannot be answered in advance; a possibly full and detailed explanation will emerge only in the course of our inquiry. At any rate, if we first undertake an analysis of the consciousness of acting, we shall be better able to disclose the ground for the analysis of efficacy, to extend, as it were, the range of the analysis, and at the same time to draw in sharper contour the image of action as the dynamism which best expresses the human person as such. Needless to say, even when considered in a position of priority, the analysis of consciousness refers also to efficacy – as well as to the whole human dynamism – and permanently presupposes it. I do not intend to enter here into an analysis of consciousness as such and in itself, but only in its strict association with the dynamism and efficacy of the human being, just as in the reality of the human experience the consciousness of acting is strictly associated with acting consciously. The singling out of consciousness as a separate object of investigation is only a methodical operation; it is like taking a term out of brackets in order thereby to gain a better understanding of what remains bracketed. That is precisely the reason why in the title of this chapter mention is made not of consciousness alone but of the person and his acting in the aspect of consciousness.

How Is Consciousness Implied in the Human Act?

The traditional interpretation of action as human act implies consciousness in the sense earlier defined as attributive: *human* is equivalent to conscious acting. It is in this sense that *consciousness* is, so to speak, completely merged in the *voluntarium*, in the dynamism of the human will. This interpretation neither isolates nor develops the aspect of consciousness. But consciousness as such, consciousness in the substantival and subjective sense, because it permeates deep into the whole person–action relation and because in itself it is an important aspect of this relation, may be perceived by itself in conscious acting. It is this aspect that not only reflects the existence of the person as well as his actions, but also fashions them in a specific manner. Let us note, however, that although in the traditional conception of human act this aspect was not entirely disregarded, its presentation was vague, and, as it were, only implied in it.[14]

The traditional conception of *actus humanus* was in fact, as we already remarked, a tributary, not only of an epistemologically realistic position, but also of a metaphysical standpoint. It conceived consciousness as something that was incorporated and subordinate, as if it was dissolved in man's actions and in his being, the being of the rational nature; though man existed and acted consciously, it was not in consciousness that his being and acting had their specific origin. In this connection we have to keep in mind that our own stand on that question is also clearly against any tendency to attribute absolute significance to consciousness. We want, however, to bring out and, so to speak, to expose the fact that consciousness constitutes a specific and unique aspect in human action. Whereas in the Scholastic approach, the aspect of consciousness was on the one hand only implied and, as it were, hidden in "rationality" (this refers to the definitions, *homo est animal rationale* and *persona est rationalis naturae individua substantia*); on the other hand it was contained in the will (understood as *appetitus rationalis*) and expressed by *voluntarius*. The task set out in this investigation is to go farther and to exhibit consciousness as an *intrinsic and constitutive aspect of the dynamic structure*, that is, *of the acting person*.

Indeed, man not only acts consciously, but he is also aware of both the fact that he is acting and the fact that it is he who is acting – hence he has the awareness of the action as well as of the person in their dynamic interrelation. His awareness is simultaneous with conscious acting and, so to speak, accompanies it. But it is also present before and after. It has its own continuity and its own identity separate from the continuity and the identity of any particular action.[15] Every action finds consciousness, if one may say so, already there; it develops and comes to pass in the presence of consciousness, leaving behind little trace of its passage. Consciousness accompanies and reflects or mirrors the action when it is born and while it is being performed; once the action is accomplished consciousness still continues to reflect it, though of course it no longer accompanies it. The accompanying presence of consciousness is decisive in making man aware of his acting rather than in making his acting conscious. Again, it is its presence that makes him act as a person and experience his acting as an action, the role of the aspect of consciousness being manifested most appropriately in the latter. This is precisely what we shall now strive to expound.

In What Sense Is "Consciousness" Used Here?

Although it is true to say that in the ultimate analysis the function of consciousness is cognitive, this statement describes its nature only in a very general way; for in this function consciousness seems to be only a reflection, or rather a mirroring, of what happens in man and of his acting, of what he does and how he does it. (The distinction between what *happens* in man and what he *does* is of great importance in all our future discussion of action and will be fully examined in the next chapter.) Consciousness is also the reflection, or rather the mirroring, of everything that man meets with in an external relation by means of any and all of his doings – also cognitive – and all the things happening in him. This is all mirrored in consciousness. "Contained" in it, so to speak, there is the whole man, as well as the whole world accessible to this concrete man – the man who is me, that is, myself. How is all this "contained" in consciousness? The question is important and the answer is that whatever consciousness "contains" is held by it in its own specific manner. We shall now seek to define that "specific manner."

It lies in the essence of cognitive acts performed by man to investigate a thing, to objectivize it intentionally, and in this way to comprehend it. In this sense cognitive acts have an intentional character, since they are directed toward the cognitive object; for they find in it the reason for their existence as acts of comprehension and knowledge. The same does not seem to apply to consciousness. In opposition to the classic phenomenological view, we propose that the cognitive reason for the existence of consciousness and of the acts proper to it does not consist in the penetrative apprehension of the constitutive elements of the object, in its objectivation leading to the constitution of the object.[16] Hence the intentionality that is characteristic for cognitive acts – to which we owe the formation, and an understanding, of the objective reality on any of its levels – does not seem to be derived from acts of consciousness. These are not essentially intentional by nature, even though all that is the object of our cognition, comprehension, and knowledge is also the object of our consciousness. But while comprehension and knowledge contribute in an intentional way to the formation of the object – it is in this that consists the inherent dynamism of cognizing – consciousness as such is restricted to mirroring what has already been cognized. Consciousness is, so to speak, the understanding of what has been constituted and comprehended. The purport of the preceding remarks is that the *intrinsic cognitive dynamism*, the *very operation of cognition, does not belong to consciousness*. If acts of cognition consist in constituting in a specific way the meanings referring to cognitive objects, then it is not consciousness that constitutes them, even if they are indubitably constituted also in consciousness.

It seems, therefore, impossible to deny the cognitive properties or even the cognitive function of consciousness, though the nature of the properties and the function is specific. What we may perhaps call the "consciousness trait" is peculiar to the particular acts of consciousness as well as to their current totality, which may be viewed as the sum or the "resultant" of those acts and which we usually simply refer to as consciousness. As "consciousness" we understand then "reflecting consciousness" – that is, consciousness in its mirroring function. If we see it as if it were the derivative of the whole actively cognitive process and of the cognitive attitude to the external reality, like the last "reflection" of the process in the cognizant subject, it means that we recognize this reflecting or mirroring as possible insofar as we attribute to consciousness the specific quality of penetrating and illuminating whatever becomes in any way man's cognitive possession. (But such penetrative illumination is not tantamount to the active understanding of objects and, subsequently, to the constituting of their meanings.) If we are to keep to this description, the penetrative illumination is rather like keeping objects and their cognitive meanings "in the light," or "in the actual field of consciousness."

Consciousness Is not an Autonomous Subject

Obviously the aim of our present discussion is not to elaborate a complete and finished theory of consciousness. To deny the intentional nature of the acts of consciousness seems to be contrary to most contemporary opinions on that issue. Looking at consciousness, however, we see it not as a separate and self-contained reality but as the subjective content of the being and acting that is conscious, the being and acting proper to man. Disclosing consciousness in the totality of human dynamisms and showing it as the constitutive property of action we strive to understand it, but always in its relation to the action, to the dynamism and efficacy of the person. This manner of seeing and interpreting consciousness – consciousness in what we call the substantival and subjective sense – protects us from conceiving it as an independent, self-contained subject. Indeed, to recognize that consciousness is an independent subject could pave the way to a conception of it in absolute terms and consequently would lead to idealism, if it were taken as the sole subject of all the contents – which would then be nothing but an expression of its own doing (thus, $esse = percipi$). This line of reasoning, however, lies beyond the scope of the present considerations. Our concern here is solely with consciousness considered from the point of view of the person and his existential efficacy; it is this consciousness that we are striving to describe when we speak of the mirroring and illuminating function peculiar to both the particular acts of consciousness and to the resultant of those acts.

It is necessary nevertheless to note that the sum or resultant of the acts of consciousness determines the actual state of consciousness. The subject of this state, however, is not consciousness itself but the *human being*, of whom we rightly may say that he is or is not "conscious," that he has full or limited consciousness, and so on. Consciousness itself does not exist as the "substantive" subject of the acts of consciousness; it exists neither as an independent factor nor as a faculty. A full discussion of the arguments in support of this thesis is the task of philosophical psychology or anthropology and lies beyond the scope of the present enquiry. Nevertheless, from what was already said of the nature of the consciousness it is clear that it is entirely dissolved in its own acts and in their specific character of "being aware"; and though this specific character is connected with the mirroring function it is a different thing from cognitive objectivation. Indeed, it is not only cognitively that man enters into the world of other men and objects and even discovers himself there as one of them: he has also as his possession all this world in the image mirrored by consciousness, which is a factor in his innermost, most personal life. For consciousness not only reflects but also *interiorizes* in its own specific manner what it mirrors, thus encapsulating or capturing it in the person's ego. Here, however, we come to another and supposedly a deeper function of consciousness, which we shall have to discuss separately. We shall then have to answer the question how this interiorization may be accomplished by the mirroring and illuminating functions of consciousness, which we have identified in the preceding analysis. At any rate, our investigation brought us closer to the conscious aspect of action and at the same time of the conscious aspect of the person. We have found that consciousness of action differs from an action conceived as consisting in *acting* consciously. The consciousness of an action is a reflection, one of the many mirrorings, which make up the consciousness of the person. This reflection belongs by its very nature to consciousness and does not consist in the objectivation of either the action or the person, even though it carries within itself a faithful image of the action as well as of the person.

3. CONSCIOUSNESS AND SELF-KNOWLEDGE

Consciousness Conditioned by Its Reflecting Function

From what we have said so far we gather that consciousness mirrors human actions in its own peculiar manner – the reflection intrinsically belongs to it – but does not cognitively objectivize either the actions or the person who performs them, or even the whole "universe of the person," which in one way or another is connected with man's being and acting. Nevertheless, the acts of consciousness as well as their resultant are obviously related to everything that lies beyond them, and especially to the actions performed by the personal ego. This relation is established by means of the consciousness, which is constituted by the meanings of the particular items of reality and of their interrelationships. When we speak of the aspect of consciousness that refers to meanings, and at the same time state that consciousness as such has no power of cognitive objectivation, we come to the conclusion that the whole of human cognition – the power and the efficacy of active comprehension – closely cooperates with consciousness. Consciousness itself is thus conditioned by this power and efficacy – it is conditioned, so to speak, by the cognitive potentiality, which conformably with the whole Western philosophical tradition appears as a fundamental property of the human person.

The power and the efficacy of active understanding allows us to ascertain the meaning of particular things and to intellectually incorporate them, as well as the relations between them, "into" our consciousness. For to "understand" means the same as to "grasp" the meaning of things and their interrelations. Insofar as all this is alien to consciousness the whole process of active comprehending neither proceeds in it nor is owing to it. The meanings of things and of their relations are given to consciousness, as it were, from outside as the product of knowledge, which in turn results from the active constitution and comprehension of the objective reality and is accumulated by man and possessed by him by various means and to different degrees. Hence the various degrees of knowledge determine the different levels of consciousness.

All the forms and kinds of knowledge which man acquires and possesses and which shape his consciousness with respect to its content, that is from the side of objective meanings, have to be distinguished from what we call "self-knowledge." There is no need to explain that self-knowledge consists in the understanding of one's own self and is concerned with a kind of cognitive insight into the object that I am for myself. We may add that such an insight introduces a specific continuity to the diverse moments or states in the being of the ego,[17] because it reaches what constitutes their primary unity, which comes from their being rooted in the ego. Hence it is not surprising that self-knowledge more than any other form of knowledge must be consistent with consciousness; for its subject matter is the ego, with which – as will be fully demonstrated in the course of further analysis – consciousness remains in an intimate subjective union. At this point self-knowledge and consciousness come closest together, but, at the same time, they deviate from each other, since consciousness, for all the intimacy of its subjective union with the ego, does not objectivize the ego or anything else with regard to its existence and its acting. This function is performed by acts of self-knowledge themselves. It is to them that every man owes the objectivizing contact with himself and with his actions. Because of self-knowledge consciousness can mirror actions and their relations to the ego. Without it consciousness would be deprived of its immanent meanings so far as man's self is concerned – when it presents itself as the object – and would then exist as if it were suspended in the void. This situation is postulated by the idealists, because it is only then that consciousness may be viewed as the subject producing its own subject matter regardless of any factors outside of it. Had we pursued this line of thought we might be led to ask whether consciousness should not be regarded as a real subject or even whether it, so to speak, does create itself. As already noted, however, such questions are of only peripheral interest in the present study.

Consciousness Opened to the Ego by Self-Knowledge

Owing to self-knowledge the acting subject's ego is cognitively grasped as an object. In this way the person and his action have an objective significance in consciousness. The reflection or mirroring by consciousness, which is not only subjective but also constitutes the basis for subjectivation (about which more will be said later), does not abolish the objective meaningful constituents of the ego or of its actions; rather, it derives them continuously from self-knowledge.

The coherence of self-knowledge and consciousness has to be recognized as the basic factor of the equilibrium in the inner life of a person, especially so far as the intellectual structure of the person is concerned. The "subject" man is also the "object"; he is the object for the subject, and he does not lose his objective significance when mirrored by consciousness. In this respect self-knowledge seems prior to consciousness, and cognitively relates it to the ego and its actions, even if consciousness in itself were not intentionally directed toward them. At the same time, self-knowledge sets, so to speak, a limit to consciousness, the limit beyond which the process of subjectivation cannot proceed.

What is more, the objectivizing turn of self-knowledge toward the ego and toward the actions related to the ego is also a turn to consciousness as such, so far as consciousness also becomes the object of self-knowledge. This explains why, when man is conscious of his acting, he also knows he is acting; indeed, he knows he is *acting consciously*. He is aware of being conscious and of acting consciously. Self-knowledge has as its object not only the person and the action, but also the person as being *aware* of himself and *aware* of his action. This awareness is objectivized by self-knowledge. Thus the objective meaning in what consciousness reflects appertains not to any being or any acting of the person who is my own self, but solely to the being and the acting that involves consciousness and of which I am aware. Man has the self-knowledge of his being conscious and because of it he is aware of the consciousness of his being and acting. But the process does not extend indefinitely; the limit to the reflecting of consciousness is set by self-knowledge. If, on the one hand, it provides the basis for this mirroring – because it forms the content of consciousness – then on the other hand, it marks out the boundary circumscribing its own sphere owing to which consciousness is established in the existence of man, and ascertains itself as immanent in the being instead of spiralling away in an unending sequence of "self-subjectivations."

Earlier in this discussion we emphasized the point that consciousness itself was to be seen neither as an individual subject nor as an independent faculty. The subsequent analysis has shown even more clearly that what we understand by "consciousness" has at its roots the same cognitive potentiality as that to which man owes all the processes of comprehension and objectivizing functions. It springs from the common stock of this potentiality, emerging, as it were, from the background of the processes of comprehension and objectivizing cognition; but at the same time, it appears to be seated more deeply inside the personal subject. It is precisely the reason why, as it seems, all interiorization and subjectivation is the work of consciousness – of which more will be said later.

Self-Knowledge as the Basis of Self-Consciousness

That man can be aware not only of his own self and of the actions related to it but also of the consciousness of his actions in relation to the ego appears as the work of self-knowledge. In such phrases as "It is how I became conscious of my action" or "I became conscious of ... this or that," we speak of an actualization of a conscious process, though in fact we mean an actualization of a self-knowing process; for consciousness itself cannot make us aware of anything, because this can be achieved only intentionally, that is, by an act of cognition. Nevertheless, since consciousness is intimately united with cognition, we have expressed ourselves correctly.

It is highly symptomatic and not without reason that we have these two terms in our vocabulary. They bring order into many problems of a noetic as well as of an ontological nature and clarify, on the one hand, the objective aspect of the subject and, on the other, that composite and complex structure of the subject's nucleus which is the ego. It is this subjectiveness of the object that we shall now have to analyze. But before we begin we must stress once again that what is meant when speaking of "being conscious of an action" is not just the reflection itself in consciousness of a conscious act but intentional self-knowledge. By this phrase we mean that by an act of self-knowledge I objectivize my action in relation to my person. I objectivize the given essential constituent of my action in the actual *acting* of my person and not of what would only *happen* in my person; furthermore, my acting is a conscious event (thus indirectly equivalent to the exercise of the free will), and thus, by being performed according to the will, may have a moral value, positive or negative, and so is either good or evil. All this which is constitutive of the action and objectivized by an act of self-knowledge becomes the "content" of consciousness. This objectivation allows us to see the objective sense of consciousness, that is, the relation of consciousness to the "objective" world. We may thus speak of consciousness from an "objective point of view" by virtue of the meanings of the different objects through which it manifests itself. But we may speak of consciousness from the objective point of view also in a more specific manner with respect to the meaningful structure appertaining in consciousness to the ego, to its mode of being and operations spreading through a radius of interconnectedness. This sense, or more strictly speaking, this set of senses, consciousness owes to self-knowledge. Because of its various senses consciousness appears also in a special modality of "self-consciousness." It is self-knowledge that contributes to the formation of self-consciousness.

The Specific Position of Self-Knowledge in the Totality of Human Cognition

Having outlined the interrelation existing between consciousness and self-knowledge we shall now – before carrying on our analysis of consciousness and in particular of self-consciousness – briefly consider self-knowledge as such. In our approach to the problem we will for the moment ignore the functions of consciousness, as if the concrete ego were nothing else but the object of its own cognition, that is, of self-knowledge.

The preceding analysis has shown that every man's ego constitutes, in a way, a meeting point where all the intentional acts of self-knowledge concentrate. This is the knowledge that at the very point constituted by the objectified ego meets everything in any way connected with or in any way referring to the ego. Hence we have, for instance, moral self-knowledge, which precedes fundamentally the science of morals, not to mention ethics; we have also religious self-knowledge prior to anything we know of religion and theology; or again, there is the social self-knowledge independent from what we know about society, and so on. Self-knowledge is concentrated on the ego as its own proper object and accompanies it to all the domains to which the ego itself extends. Nevertheless, self-knowledge never objectivizes any component of these domains for its own sake but solely and exclusively because of and in relation to the ego.

From the preceding remarks we now see more or less clearly that the function of self-knowledge is opposed to any "egotistic" approach to consciousness, to any approach that would tend to present consciousness (even if only vicariously) in the guise of the "pure ego" – the subject. Nor has self-knowledge anything in common with an objectivizing cognition that would be concerned with an abstracted and generalized ego, with any sort of egology. To self-knowledge the object is the concrete ego itself, the self as such. Indeed, there may be even some question whether "knowledge," which strictly speaking has a general object, is the right term in relation to self-knowledge;[18] for self-knowledge not only has as its object the unique, individual ego, the self, but is also permanently and inextricably entangled in the details referring to the ego. In our analysis we have in focus "self-cognition" rather than "self-knowledge." It consists in the acts of objectivizing penetration of the ego with all its concreteness and its concomitant detailedness, which yields to no generalization whatever. But even so, it is still the real knowledge of oneself as an integral whole; for it is not restricted only to the recording of details that have a bearing upon the ego but continuously strives after generalizations. Such generalizations are, for instance, all the opinions one has of oneself or judgments of oneself, which belong to self-knowledge, and it alone can form them. It is to be noted, however, that these opinions – any overall view of the ego – are mirrored in conscious-ness; thus, not only are the singular data which have a bearing upon the ego mirrored in consciousness but, in addition, the continuously developing overall complex that the ego keeps on unfolding. In the opinions about this complex there is never just one self-knowing theory of one's own ego, for they also have an axiological character, which varies with respect to different moral points of view, the aspect of value being of no less importance for self-knowledge.

Self-knowledge is not just a specific instance of the knowledge of the human being in general, even though the ego, which it strives to objectivize as comprehensively as possible, is, both from the ontolo-gical and intentional points of view – as the object of self-knowledge – a human being. Nevertheless, all the cognitive work it performs proceeds solely from self-experience to self-understanding but does not go as far as to include any generalizations about man as such. There is in our cognition a subtle but precisely marked out boundary between the knowledge of man in general and self-knowledge, the knowledge of the ego. The knowledge of the ego, however, might in its concreteness come prior to the knowledge of man. Yet it draws upon it, because self-knowledge of my very self makes use of all I know about man in general, that is to say, of different opinions about the human being I might hold or only know about, as well as of the cognition of concrete men, in order to gain a better understanding of my own ego and the ego as such. But it does not resort to the knowledge of its own self for a better understanding of other men or of the human being in general. The knowledge of man, in general, turns to the resources of self-knowledge to obtain a deeper insight into its own object. Self-knowledge, on the contrary, as we have mentioned takes the knowledge of man into consideration, but in its direct orientation stops at the ego and keeps to its singular specific cognitive intention; for it is in the ego that man always finds fresh material for cognizing himself. The old adage says, *individuum est ineffabile.*

4. THE TWOFOLD FUNCTION OF CONSCIOUSNESS AND THE EXPERIENCE OF SUBJECTIVENESS

Mirroring and Experience

The analysis of self-knowledge gives us a better understanding of that function of consciousness which we have assigned to it previously, namely, the function of mirroring; in this respect consciousness is not restricted to a simple mirroring of everything that constitutes the object of cognition and knowledge – and specially the object of self-understanding and self-knowledge – but it also in its own peculiar manner permeates and illuminates all it mirrors. We do not mean by that to deprive consciousness of its specifically characteristic cognitive vitality.[19] In point of fact, all that has been said here about self-knowledge may lead to the false impression that the reflecting or mirroring function of consciousness may appear lost in self-knowledge, in the objectivizing processes of self-comprehension, which concentrates on the ego as the object. The question may then well be asked whether in view of the prominent role assigned to self-knowledge there are any reasons for the distinctive existence of consciousness at all. This question leads to another, of a methodological nature: how has the conception of consciousness here outlined been reached, and, particularly, how did we come to the conception of the relation of consciousness to self-knowledge? Obviously, these questions are of paramount significance in view of both the foregoing remarks and the forthcoming analyses.

To answer them it is necessary to recall that in this study the approach to consciousness is founded on experience, which allows for the objectivation of the full human dynamism, in particular the dynamism already referred to in the title of *The Acting Person*. Thus the interpretation of consciousness in its relation to self-knowledge already assumes, albeit antecedently, the total, overall conception of the man-person, which we intend to develop in the course of this study. In that approach the decisive factor for unraveling the problem of the consciousness–self-knowledge relation seems to be the question of the objectiveness and the simultaneous subjectiveness of man. Consciousness is the "ground" on which the ego manifests itself in all its peculiar objectiveness (being the object of self-knowledge) and at the same time fully experiences its own subjectiveness. We thus have emerging into view the other function of consciousness, as if another trait of it, which in the living structure of the person complements the permeative and illuminative function of mirroring, and in a way endows consciousness with the ultimate reason for its presence in the specific structure of the acting person.

Attention was already drawn on more than one occasion to the fact that the tasks of consciousness do not end with its illuminative and reflecting function. In some respects this function might appear primary but not unique. In fact, the essential function of consciousness is to form man's experience and thus to allow him to experience in a special way his own subjectiveness. This is precisely why, if we are also to understand the "acting person" and the "action" issuing from the person *so far as this constitutes an experience* – hence in the experiential dimension of the person's subjectiveness – we cannot restrict our analysis of consciousness solely to its mirroring. The task of consciousness does not end with the reflecting of an action in its relation to the ego – this takes place as if on the outside but proceeds into the inner dimension. The mirror of consciousness gives us a yet deeper insight into the interior of actions and of their relation to the ego, and it is only there that the role of consciousness comes into full view. Consciousness allows us not only to have an inner view of our actions (immanent perception) and of their dynamic dependence on the ego, but also to *experience these actions as actions and as our own.*

It is in this sense that we say man owes to consciousness the subjectivation of the objective. Subjectivation is to some extent identifiable with experiencing; at least, it is in experience that we become aware of it. While constituting a definite reality which as the object of self-knowledge reveals itself in its own peculiar objectiveness, the acting person, owing to his consciousness, also becomes "subjectified" to the extent to which consciousness conditions his experience of the action being performed by him as the person, and thereby secures the experience had of the person in its dynamically efficacious relation to action. But then, everything that constitutes the intentional, objective "world" of the person also becomes subjectified in the same way. This "world," with its objective content, may be analyzed also in its image mirrored in consciousness. But it is then, if it becomes the material of experience, definitely incorporated into the sphere of the individual subjectiveness of every human ego. Thus, for instance, a mountain landscape cognitively reflected in my consciousness and the same landscape in my experience based on this reflection become superimposed on each other, albeit they also subtly differ from each other.

Experience of the Ego Conditioned by the Reflexive Function of Consciousness

In connection with all that has been said so far we have now to mention a new trait of consciousness, one with a new, distinctly separate function, which differs from the illuminative, reflecting function already described, and thus having a constitutive significance. We call it *reflexive* and assume it appertains to consciousness itself as well as to what the so-called actual state of consciousness is composed of, to that specific resultant of acts of consciousness. This state of consciousness points not only to the mirroring and all that is reflected or mirrored at any given moment, but also to experience, in which the subjectiveness of man, as the subject having the experience, gains a special (because experiential) prominence. It is in this sense that the *reflexive trait* or *reflexiveness* of consciousness denotes that consciousness, so to speak, turns back naturally upon the subject, if thereby the subjectiveness of the subject is brought into prominence in experience.

The reflexiveness of consciousness has to be distinguished from reflection proper to the human mind in its cognitive acts. Reflection presupposes the intentionality of these acts, their cognitive direction upon the object. If we consider the activity of the mind at the level of abstract "thinking," then we might say that "thought" becomes reflective when we turn toward a previously performed act in order to grasp more fully its objective content and possibly also its character, course, or structure. Thus reflective "thought" becomes an important element in the development of all understanding, of all knowledge, including the knowledge of the ego. Hence reflection accompanies and serves consciousness. But reflection and reflectiveness are of themselves insufficient when it comes to constituting an experience. This necessitates a special turning back upon the subject, and it is to this turn that we owe, along with experience, the emphasized subjectiveness of the experiencing ego. It is this particular mode of the constitutive function as proper to consciousness that we define as "reflexive," whereby we mean that it directs everything back upon the subject. In this perspective we speak of the *reflexiveness* and not the reflectiveness of consciousness.

The function of consciousness, in which it turns back upon the subject, differs from the mirroring and reflecting when the self-knowledge of man, who is the subject and the ego, is present as the object. The consequence of the reflexive turn of consciousness is that this object – just because it is from the ontological point of view, the subject – while having the experience of his own ego also has the experience of himself as the subject. In this interpretation we also understand by "reflexiveness" an essential as well as very specific moment of consciousness. It is, however, necessary to add at once that this specific moment becomes apparent only when we observe and trace consciousness in its intrinsic, organic relation to the human being, in particular, the *human being in action.* We then discern clearly that it is one thing to *be* the subject, another to *be cognized* (that is, objectivized) as the subject, and a still different thing to *experience* one's self as the subject of one's own acts and experiences. (The last distinction we owe to the reflexive function of consciousness.) This discrimination is of tremendous import for all our further analyses, which we shall have to make in our efforts to grasp the whole dynamic reality of the acting person and to account for the subjectiveness that is given us in experience.

Indubitably, man is more than just the subject of his being and his acting; he is the subject insofar as he is a being of determinate nature, which leads to consequences particularly in the acting. Man approached as a type of being, that is, from the ontological point of view, appears – in contradistinction to processes, events, and ideas – as an autonomous, self-centered individual being. In this fundamental notion, abstraction is made from that aspect of consciousness owing to which the concrete man – the object being the subject – experiences himself as the distinctive subject. It is this experience that allows him to designate himself by means of the pronoun *I*. We know *I* to be a personal pronoun, always designating a concrete person. However, the denotation of this personal pronoun, thus also of the *ego*, appears more comprehensive than that of the autonomous individual being, because the first combines the moment of experienced subjectiveness with that of ontic subjectiveness, while the second speaks only of the latter, of the individual being as the ground of existence and action.[20] Obviously, the present interpretation of the ego relies upon the conception of consciousness being unfolded here, as does its relation to man as the real subject. We may even say that it implies the reflexiveness of consciousness; for if we detach that experience of our subjectiveness, which is the ground for my saying, "I am the ego," from the real subject that this particular ego is, then this experiential ego would represent nothing but a content of consciousness. Hence the fundamental significance of the reflexive turn of consciousness upon the real subject, whereby consciousness co-constitutes it in its own dimension. It is thus that the ego is the real subject having the experience of its subjectiveness or, in other words, constituting itself in consciousness.

The Ego Constituted as the Subject

What has been said so far clearly shows that conformably with the epistemological assumptions made in the introduction it is impossible to detach the experiential ego from its ontological foundations. The present analysis of consciousness ought even to have grounded the ego on a more secure ontic basis of its own. Every human being is given in a total or simple experience as an autonomous, individual real being, as existing and acting. But every man is also given to himself as the concrete ego, and this is achieved by means of both self-consciousness and self-knowledge. Self-knowledge ascertains that the being, who objectively is I, subjectively constitutes my ego, if it is in it that I have the experience of my subjectiveness. Hence not only am I conscious of my ego (on the ground of self-knowledge) but owing to my consciousness in its reflexive function I also experience my ego, I have the experience of myself as the concrete subject of the ego's very subjectiveness. Consciousness is not just an aspect but also an essential dimension or an actual moment of the reality of the being that I am, since it constitutes its subjectiveness in the experiential sense. This being, which in its ontic structure is basically a real individual object, would never without consciousness constitute itself as the ego. It seems that this is how we have to interpret the manner in which consciousness is incorporated into the ontological structure of the being that is man if we are to bring out in the correct proportions his subjectiveness, that is, the subjectiveness that makes of every concrete human being the unique, individual ego.

It is perhaps worth considering still another aspect of the way that our discussion of consciousness leads from its mirroring function to experience, and not inversely, as is current in present-day philosophy. Consciousness, as we view it here, is a specific dimension of that unique real being which is the concrete man. That being is neither overshadowed by nor absorbed in consciousness, albeit this would be the case according to the fundamental tenet of idealistic thought that *esse* equals *percipi*; for idealists maintain that "to be" is the same as to be constituted by consciousness, and do not recognize any mode of being apart from consciousness and consciousness alone.[21] Our approach to the matter however is the opposite: consciousness in intimate union with the ontologically founded being and acting of the concrete man-person does not absorb in itself or overshadow this being, its dynamic reality, but, on the contrary, discloses it "inwardly" and thereby reveals it in its specific distinctness and unique concreteness. *This disclosing is precisely what the reflexive function of consciousness consists in.* We may even say that owing to the reflexive function of consciousness man's being is directed, as it were, "inward," but still maintains the full dimensions of his rational essence. Being directed "inward" is accompanied by experiencing, and is, to some extent, identical with experience. In this interpretation an experience is seen as manifesting more than a reflex that appears as though on the surface of man's being and acting. Indeed, experience is that specific form of the actualization of the human subject which man owes to consciousness. Because of it the actual "energies" which we discover through action in man as a type of being – the energies, which, when taken together, constitute the multifarious and differentiated wealth of his virtualities – are actualized according to the pattern of subjectiveness proper to man as a person (more will be said of this in further chapters). Moreover, while so actualized they receive in experience their final, so to say, subjective shape.[22] Later we shall see that this is not equally true of all human energies.

The Experiential Manifestation of Human Spirituality

Consciousness, as long as it only mirrors and is but a reflected image, remains objectively aloof from the ego; when, however, it becomes the basis of experience, when experience is constituted by its reflexiveness, the objective aloofness disappears and consciousness penetrates the subject shaping it experientially every time an experience occurs. Naturally, the mirroring and the shaping of the subject are accomplished in different ways: to mirror consciousness one retains the objective meaning of the subject – its so to speak objective status – but one shapes the ego in the pure subjectiveness of experience. This is very important. On the one hand, the functional duality in consciousness allows us to remain within the limits of our subjectiveness without losing the actual objectiveness in the awareness of our being. On the other hand, the fact that our experience is formed because of consciousness, that without consciousness there is no human experience – though there may be different manifestations of life, different actualizations of human virtualities – is in its own way explained by the attribute *rationale* from the Aristotelian conception and definition of man, or by the Boethian conception and definition of man as *rationalis naturae individua substantia*. Furthermore, consciousness opens the way to the emergence of the spiritual enactment of the human being and gives us an insight into it. The spiritual aspect of man's acts and action manifests itself in consciousness, which allows us to undergo the experiential innerness of our being and acting. Although it seems that the foundations, or rather the roots of human spirituality, lie beyond the direct scope of experience – we only reach them by inference – spirituality itself has its distinctive experiential expression shaping itself through the complete sequence of its manifestations. This is brought to light in the intimate and in a way constitutive relation between experience proper to man and the reflexive function of consciousness. Indeed, man's experience of himself and of everything making him up, of all his "world," is necessarily occurring in a rational framework of reference, for such is the nature of consciousness, and *it* determines the nature of experience as well as man as an experiencing being.

Consciousness and the Experience of Action in the Dimension of Moral Values

How does man have the experience of himself in action? We already know he is conscious of himself as the one who acts, as the subjective agent of action. A separate question concerns how we are to understand the mirroring of the action in consciousness when it extends beyond the subjective sphere of man and is, so to speak, enacted in the external world. But even then man has the experience of his actions within the limits of his own subjectiveness and this experience, like any other, he owes to the reflexive function of consciousness. He experiences an action as acting, as doing, of which he is the subjective agent and which is also a profound image and manifestation of what his ego is composed of, what it actually is. He draws a strict distinction between his acting and everything that only takes place or *happens* in his ego. Here the difference between *actio* and *passio* has its first experiential basis. The distinction itself cannot be but the deed of self-knowledge; it belongs to the significative aspect of the mirroring function of consciousness. But it is also present in experience: the human being experiences his acting as something thoroughly different from anything that only happens, anything only occurring in him.

It is also only in connection with his acting (that is, action) that man experiences as his own the moral value of good and bad (or as is sometimes wrongly said, of the moral and immoral). He experiences them in the attitude he assumes toward them, an attitude that is at once emotional and appreciative. At any rate, he is not only conscious of the morality of his actions but he actually experiences it, often very deeply.

Objectively, both action and moral values belong to a real subject, that is, to man as their agent, from a point of view equally formal as existential; simply, they exhibit in their being the derivative type of reality that is in a specific manner related to and dependent on the subject. Simultaneously, both the action and its corresponding moral value – goodness or badness – function, if we may say so, in a thoroughly subjective manner in experience – which consciousness conditions by its reflexive function rather than only mirroring it because of self-knowledge, for this would still give but an objectified awareness of the action and its moral value.[23] As is to be seen, both functions of consciousness participate in this remarkable drama of human innerness, the drama of good and evil enacted on the inner stage of the human person by and among his actions. Thus consciousness, owing to its mirroring function closely related to self-knowledge, allows us, on the one hand, to gain an objective awareness of the good or evil that we are the agents of in any particular action – while, on the other hand, it enables us to experience the good or evil in which its reflexiveness is manifested. As already noted, this experience is by no means merely an added or superficial reflexing of an action or of its moral qualification as good or evil. On the contrary, what we are considering here has a reflexively inward direction that makes of the action itself as well as of the moral good or bad the fully subjective reality of man. In the human subjectiveness they get their, so to speak, finishing touches. It is then that man has the experience of good or evil simply in himself, in his ego; he thereby experiences himself as the one who is either good or evil. So we come to see the full dimension of morality in the subjective and personal reality.

How Does the Ego Help in Understanding Man?

The "full dimension" is also the dimension of that experience in which the good and the evil, as the moral values of a person, as well as the acting person himself become the object of comprehension or exfoliation; indeed, this exfoliation is always becoming more and more profound, a point already asserted in the introductory remarks to this study. Mention was there made that the experience of the human being and of morality served as the ground for an unraveling of the nature of both one and the other. This experience and this exfoliation was unquestionably broader than either the self-experience or the simultaneously developing self-comprehending contained in experiencing one's ego. The question we then asked was whether this self-experience (that is, experiencing of one's self) and the self-comprehending that developed with it (that is, the awareness of the self based on self-knowledge) were at all transferable to that ever expanding sphere of man's experience of things external to the ego. This of course is a significant question. We took it up again in our discussion of self-knowledge, and now we have to consider it once more. For there is no denying that the sphere of self-experience and self-comprehending serves as a privileged vantage point, a point specially productive of meanings in experience and in the understanding of man. That is why, while retaining all the specific uniqueness of self-knowledge (see the preceding section) as well as of the experience had of the ego, we strive in one way or another to draw our knowledge of man from the source of self-experience and self-knowledge. This happens presumably because from the very start we take, as it were, a double stance: beginning "inside" ourselves we go out of our ego toward "man" and at the same time we proceed from "man" back to the ego. Thus our knowledge of man proceeds as if in cycles. This course of the cognitive process is obviously valid, if the object of our cognition is not to be our ego alone but also the human being – all the more so if the human being is among others "myself," when he is also my ego.

5. THE EMOTIONALIZATION OF CONSCIOUSNESS

The Element of Consciousness and the Emotive Element in Man

We now have to consider a particular problem, which should be preceded by a brief reference to its broader context. But as the full presentation is deferred to a later chapter, here, as in the rest of the present analysis of consciousness, some account is necessary of things discussed later in greater detail. The problem we will now examine is that special area of human vitality which has its origin in the emotive element of his psychic processes. We know that man's conscious actings, his actions, are on the one side dependent in different ways on the functioning of the emotive element of man's psychic life, and on the other side generate it and are themselves constituted by it to some degree. The free exercise of the will, which has an essential significance for actions, is variously modified by this side of the human psyche. These modifications are of great import for our investigation into the person and his actions. First, however, we

have to look at them as an aspect, or perhaps a dimension, of consciousness – of consciousness such as we have shown it here, as if it
were isolated and brought to the forefront of our argument.

Consciousness reflects man's ego as well as his actions; but, at the
same time, it allows him to have the experience of the ego, to have
the experience of himself and of his acting. His body is somehow
engaged in the one just as in the other. Man is conscious of his body,
and he also experiences it; he has the experience of his corporality
just as he has of his sensuality and emotionality. These experiences
are linked with the mirroring function of consciousness and hence are
also guided by self-knowledge, whose participation is easily noticeable in a certain abstractness of what becomes the content of consciousness and is subsequently experienced. After all, to have the
experience of one's body is not the same thing as to have the
experience of one's corporality. The difference lies in the degree of
the mental abstraction which pertains to the process of comprehension and, in relation to the ego, to the process of self-knowledge.
Self-knowledge builds that significative aspect of the image we have
of ourselves in our consciousness which is transferred in the operation of the reflexive function of consciousness to experience and
which determines its content. In the acts of self-knowledge man, with
the support of self-experience, gains an understanding of his ego both
in details and as a whole. As to the comprehension of the body,
self-knowledge – and with it consciousness – relies to a great extent
on the particular bodily sensations. We know that neither the
organism, with all its composite inner structure, nor the particular
vegetative processes going on in it are – generally speaking – the
object of self-knowledge or consciousness. Self-knowledge, and with
it consciousness, reaches only as far, or rather as deep, into the
organism and its life as sensations allow it to reach. Very often, for
instance, owing to disease, which activates the corresponding bodily
sensations, man becomes aware of one of his organs or of a vegetative process within himself. Generally, the human body and everything associated with it becomes the object of sensations first and
only subsequently of self-knowledge and consciousness. "First" and
"subsequently" do not necessarily indicate an actual time sequence;
they are used in the sense of the natural adequacy of the object and
of the subjective acts. The experience of the body has as its counterparts
acts of sensation rather than acts of comprehension, of which in a way

consciousness is built up. Nevertheless, man not only feels his body, but he is also aware of it.

The world of sensations and feelings in man, who is a feeling and not only a thinking creature, has an objective wealth of its own. To some extent this wealth corresponds to the structure of the human being as well as of the external world. The differentiation of feelings is not merely quantitative but also qualitative, and in this respect they come in a hierarchical order. Feelings of qualitatively "higher rank" participate in man's spiritual life. In a further chapter we shall deal separately with the analysis of emotions as a specific component of the human psychic life. It is common knowledge that the emotional life of man exerts a tremendous influence in the formation of his actions. It is also well known and corroborated by numerous treatises on ethics that emotions may in some respects enhance our actions, but in others they have a restraining or even crippling effect on what in acting is essential, namely, the exercise of the free will. The participation of the free will in acting is restricted to action insofar as it is seen as conscious. Indeed, in this chapter we are concerned with conscious acting – hence also with the exercise of the free will – in the aspect of its being conscious.

What Does the Emotionalization of Consciousness Consist in?

It is only in this aspect that we shall attempt an analysis of the influence exerted by the emotive element. Our discussion is thus limited to one aspect only without aspiring to anything like a total view. We are concerned with what we have agreed to call the "emotionalization of consciousness," that is to say, the specific influence of the emotive element on the consciousness of acting. (Obviously, this influence cannot be without significance for the whole dynamism of the human person, for his conscious acting, for action.)[24]

The essence of the problem consists in this, that emotions – the different forms in which emotive facts occur in man as the subject – are not only reflected in consciousness but also affect in their own specific way the image that is formed in consciousness of various objects, including, of course, man's ego and his actions. Diverse feelings emotionalize consciousness, that is to say, they blend with its two functions – mirroring and reflexiveness – thereby modifying in one way or another their character. This is first manifested in the image formed in consciousness, which, so to speak, loses its aloofness with regard to emotion and the objects that emotion is attached to. As was demonstrated in previous analyses, this aloofness of consciousness is due to self-knowledge, which to some extent possesses the power to objectify emotions and feelings. In this way the meaning of the emotive facts taking place in the subject becomes accessible to consciousness, and thus it can maintain its objectivizing aloofness from them and from the objects they refer to. While emotions themselves occur or happen in man, he is aware of them, and owing to this awareness he can in a way control them. The control of emotions by consciousness has a tremendous significance for the inner integration of man. Obviously, the sway consciousness exerts over emotion is not achieved outside the sphere of the will and without its cooperation. Hence it is only against the background of such control that we can form moral values. We are thus faced with the fact of interpenetration of consciousness and the will; the control of consciousness over the spontaneous emotive dynamism conditioning the exercise of the free will – the proper function of the will – is simultaneously conditioned by the will.

The emotionalization of consciousness begins when the image of the meanings of the particular emotive instances and of objects they are related to fades in consciousness, so that feelings may outgrow their current understanding by man. This is practically tantamount to a breakdown of self-knowledge; for consciousness, without ceasing to mirror the emotive distances just as they come, loses its controlling, that is to say, its objective, attitude toward them. We know that in this case objectivation is a function appertaining to self-knowledge. The objective attitude of consciousness toward feelings and emotions occurring in man and toward objects they are attached to collapses when self-knowledge stops, as it were, to objectivize. It no longer establishes the meanings and so does not hold emotions in intellectual subjection.

What are the reasons? They may be different. The one most often suggested mentions the strength or intensity of emotions, their changeability, and the rapidity with which they follow one after another. But this explains only one side of the problem. On the other side we have to consider also the higher or lower efficiency of self-knowledge; like any other knowledge it has to comply with the laws of efficiency, so that its ability to cope with its proper object may vary. (The reference here is to objective material, which for self-knowledge consists of all the facts related to the ego, and such are of course emotive facts.) Let us stress once again that we are not speaking of the effective "control" of emotions as such, which is the task of the will (and of the relevant moral virtues of the Aristotelian conception) but only of that specific control of feelings which is the task of self-knowledge and consciousness. (An attempt at explaining the relationship between feelings and emotions is deferred to a later chapter, which deals with problems of emotiveness.)

The task of self-knowledge in this respect is essential, and that is why its efficiency is so important. It seems that consciousness itself is not subject to the laws of efficiency. We do not see it as being either less or more efficient, though it may be less developed and mature, or more so. The efficiency side of consciousness seems to be wholly taken over by self-knowledge. Indeed, the task of self-knowledge is to prevent the emotionalization of consciousness from going too far, to protect consciousness from being deprived of its objectivizing rela-tion to the totality of emotive occurrences. Feelings in the subject that is man come as if in waves. Sometimes they swell – they come in whole sequences, or, what is more important, are enhanced. But every man has in him as an objective psychical component a specifically emotive dynamism, which expresses itself in the intensity of the particular feelings, of sets of feelings, or of their resultants. (We may perhaps also speak of resultants of various emotional experiences in man.)

Emotionalization and the Twofold Function of Consciousness: Mirroring and Experience

The normal, indeed, the correct functioning of consciousness requires emotions at a certain level of intensity, albeit when this level – like a threshold – is exceeded, and the over-emotionalization of conscious-ness begins. If feelings are either too many or too strong, or if the efficiency of self-knowledge is too low, then self-knowledge is in-capable of objectifying, that is to say, of intellectually identifying them. In this way the significative aspect of occurrences having an emotive character is, as it were, lost. At first consciousness still mirrors them as "something that happens in me," but when their intensity is further enhanced or self-knowledge becomes for the time less effective, consciousness still mirrors the occurrences as "something that happens," though now it is as if they had lost their relation to the ego. The core itself of consciousness – the ego – is then rushed to the background while the enhanced feelings behave as if they are up-rooted from the soil in which their unity as well as the multiplicity and separate identity of their meanings develop. For it is self-knowledge that in the normal course of events objectivizes both this unity within the ego and the separate identity of the meanings of the particular emotions. Nevertheless, when over-emotionalization, es-pecially in its extreme forms, gains ascendency, emotions are taking over directly the field of actual consciousness, which still continues to mirror them; but now their reflection is devoid of the element of objectivation or comprehension, because this is no longer provided by self-knowledge. Man is then aware of his emotions, but he does not control them any more.

Emotionalization in the sphere of the mirroring function of con-sciousness is accompanied by an emotionalization of experience. The assertion here made is that consciousness does not cease to mirror even in a state of the utmost intensity of emotions and feelings, and even then we still can discern its mirroring; now, however, this function no longer has its proper significance for the formation of experiences had in the emotional sphere of the whole inner life of man. Thus the reflexive function of consciousness, which is respon-sible for the formation of experience, loses its decisive role. It is remarkable that emotions and passions are not experienced by the human being when too strong; they are then only "undergone" by him or, strictly speaking, allowed to grow in him and prevail upon him in some primitive and, as it were, impersonal fashion; for "personal" signifies only that experience in which also the experienced sub-jectiveness of the ego is to be discerned. This being so, emotive instances in the form of passions, though they have their own primitive subjectivity, do not help to experience subjectiveness in a way that brings into prominence the personal ego as the source of experiences, as the center governing emotions. All this, however, is connected with the reflexive influence of consciousness. This in-fluence is often hindered by impulsions of invading feelings, in the face of which the reflexive function of consciousness is, so to say, inhibited. Man then only experiences his emotions and allows them to dwell in him according to their own primitive forms of subjectivity, but does not experience them subjectively in a way that would bring out the personal ego as the true pivot of experience.

We now see the full complexity of the emotionalization of consciousness which presents throughout a particular and thus unique problem. Sometimes even the most powerful emotions may fail to over-emotionalize consciousness in the sense here considered, so that emotions remain under the control of consciousness. Sometimes, on the contrary, emotionalization of consciousness is stimulated by emotions that are (objectively considered) still relatively weak. But we do not intend to analyze these things here; what we are now interested in is – as we tried to show in the preceding section – the essence itself of the problem, especially from the point of view of consciousness, and that co-constituting of the personal subjectiveness of the human ego in which consciousness takes part. The emotional threshold mentioned earlier seems to be the necessary condition in the truly human, personal experiencing of emotions and, in this sense, also emotional experiences. As long as the intensity of feelings remains at a certain level, consciousness performs normally its mirroring and reflexive functions. It is only then that the genuine emotional experiences, with all their subjective completeness, are formed – instead of the primitive emotive occurrences, which, though they indubitably proceed from the subject, cannot be endued by consciousness with the subjective profile appertaining to the personal ego. This is so because the emotionalization of consciousness obstructs or even prevents its proper actualization.

In all that was said above no final pronouncements about the value of feelings and emotions for the inner life of man and for morality should be seen. The discussion of these questions is deferred to another chapter.

6. SUBJECTIVITY AND SUBJECTIVISM

Subjectivity Inherent in the Reality of the Acting Person

The preceding analyses have brought us to the point when it becomes possible, and even in a way necessary, to discriminate clearly between man's "subjectivity" – which we are here considering together with the analysis of consciousness – and "subjectivism" as a mental attitude. To have shown the subjectivity of the human person is fundamental for the realistic position of this study. Indeed, man has appeared in our analysis as the subject, and it is he as the subject that is experiencing himself. That is the ground on which the dynamic relation, or rather interrelation, between the person and the action is actualized. The failure to recognize man's subjectivity would deprive us of the level on which can be grasped all the aspects of this interrelation. The aspect of consciousness has an essential signi- ficance for asserting man's subjectivity, because it is conscious- ness that allows man to experience himself as the subject. He experiences himself as such and therefore he "is" the subject in the strictly experiential sense. Here the understanding springs directly from the experience without any intermediate steps, without any recourse to arguments. He also experiences his actions as acts of which he himself is the agent. This efficacy, which we shall discuss fully in the next chapter, is made evident by experience and is seen by us from the aspect of consciousness. Thus, in order to grasp efficacy as a fully experiential datum, it is necessary to come close to experience as well as to man's subjectivity, which is the proper ground of experience. Viewing subjectivity solely from the metaphy- sical standpoint, and stating that man as a type of being constitutes the true subject of existing and acting, autonomous individual being, we abstract, to a large extent from what is the source of our visualizations, the source of experience. It is far better, therefore, to try to coordinate and join together the two aspects, the aspect of being (man, person) with the aspect of consciousness; the aspect of acts (acting and action) with the aspect of experience.

This is important not only for methodological reasons, which were already discussed in the introduction, but also for the sake of our subject matter. We made this point a moment ago when asserting that without outlining a possibly complete explanation of man's sub- jectivity it would be impossible to grasp the full depth of the dynamic interrelation of person and action. For the interrelation is not only mirrored in consciousness, as if it were reflected in an inner mirror of man's being and acting; in addition, it is owing to consciousness that it obtains in its own way its final, subjective form. The form is that of experience, the experience of action, the experience had of the efficacious interrelation of person and action, and of the moral value that germinates in this dynamic system. All these are objective data, but data that hold their objectivity and reality status only and exclusively in the subjectivity of man. Without completely revealing this subjectivity it is also impossible to reach and bring to light the whole, objectively multifarious composition of those factual data. It is important to stress, however, that the bias of subjectivism may also develop in connection with a narrow and one-sided bias of objectivism.

The Difference between Subjectivity and Subjectivism

Subjectivism, as here considered, seems to consist first, in a complete separation of experience from action and second, in reducing to the mere status of consciousness and moral values that, as we have figuratively put it, germinate in this action as well as in the person. What we are speaking of now was previously seen as the "absolutization" of a single aspect. The reduction which operates such absolutization of the experiential aspect is characteristic of the specific mental attitude inherent in subjectivism and, in a more distant perspective, in idealism. Indubitably, consciousness is that aspect of man which lends itself to being absolutized: but then it ceases being merely an aspect of the human functioning. As long as consciousness is maintained as merely an aspect – and throughout this chapter we have tried to treat it as such – it serves only to gain a better understanding of the subjectivity of man, in particular of his inner relation to his own actions. However, when consciousness is absolutized, it at once ceases to account for the subjectivity of man, that is to say, his being the subject, or for his actions; and it becomes a substitute for the subject. Subjectivism conceives consciousness itself as a total and exclusive subject – the subject of experiences and values, so far as the domain of moral experience is concerned. Unfortunately, with this approach, experiences and values lose their status of reality; they cease being anything real and remain only as the moment of consciousness: *esse = percipi.*[25] Ultimately consciousness itself ceases being anything real: it becomes but the subject of a meaningful network. The path of subjectivism ends in idealism.

We may even say that this trend has some support in the purely conscious character of the "acts of consciousness." It was asserted earlier that acts of consciousness as such and consciousness as wholly contained in them are neutral or indifferent to external real things and beings, as well as to the ego conceived as a nucleus of man seen as a real being. They do not establish anything – in the sense of positing its actual existence; rather, they only mirror things. They contain only subject matter which owes its objectiveness and its status of reality to self-knowledge. The boundary of objectivism and realism in the conception of man – in our case this applies to the person–action totality – is marked out by the assertion of self-knowledge. In spite of its specifically conscious character, consciousness integrated by self-knowledge into the whole of a real person retains its objective significance and thus also the objective status in the subjective structure of man. In this perspective and due to this status consciousness appears but the key to the subjectivity of man, and so it in no way can serve as the basis for subjectivism. It owes its role in human subjectivity to its being the condition of experience, in which the human ego reveals itself (experientially) as the object.

Conclusions Leading to the Analysis of Human Efficacy

Now that we have examined the aspects of consciousness in the acting person we are ready for the next step, and we can embark upon an analysis of efficacy. We must retain, however, all the significant conclusions reached so far as a contribution to our further investigations into the dynamism proper to the human person. This dynamism, and in particular the efficacy, which forms an essential moment in the dynamic emergence of action from the person, is not only realized in the field of consciousness but is, as we have tried to show here, also thoroughly pervaded by consciousness. Even if in the course of our discussion we placed the aspect of consciousness somewhat apart and in isolation – like the mathematician who puts an expression outside the brackets – the effect aimed at was to show up more sharply the presence of consciousness in the person's action. Moreover, we could see better the specific function performed by consciousness in the formation of the characteristic subjectivity of the person – the subjectivity from which, because of its virtual efficacy, the action issues.

The features of human efficacy differ from those of consciousness, though obviously the specificity of the former cannot be grasped in isolation from the latter. Each of them in its own specific manner determines both person and action.

CHAPTER TWO

AN ANALYSIS OF EFFICACY IN THE LIGHT
OF HUMAN DYNAMISM

1. THE BASIC CONCEPTIONS AND DIFFERENTIATIONS
OF HUMAN DYNAMISM

Introductory Remarks on the Relation of Dynamism to Consciousness

We now abandon the aspect of consciousness in order that we may understand better its functions through an analysis of the fact that man acts. The fact is given us first in the experience of "I act." Because of the experience we ourselves are placed, as it were, right inside this fact. Similarly, the fullness of an experience is inherent in our process of experiencing, and thus by analogy and generalization it is the basis for the formation of the human act. For every ego is a human being and every human being is this, that, or any other ego. Hence, when it is "you," "he," or "anybody else" who acts, their acting can be understood on the ground of experiencing our own acting, in "I act." The experience of acting is subjective in the sense that it keeps us within the limits of the concrete subjectivity of the acting human ego, without however obscuring the intersubjectivity that is needed for the understanding and interpretation of human acting.

The objectivation of the fact of "man-acts" requires an equally objective presentation of integral human dynamism.[26] For this experiential fact occurs not in isolation but in the context of the entire human dynamism and in organic relation to it. The dynamism in question is the total dynamism that is present in the complete experience of man. Not everything belonging to the human dynamism is reflected in consciousness. For instance, practically nothing of the vegetative dynamism of the human body is mirrored in consciousness. Similarly, not all the factors of the human dynamism may be consciously experienced by him. We already had the opportunity to mention briefly the disproportion between the totality of man's life and the scope or range of his experiences, and we shall return to the question to expound and complement it. At any rate, it is the conditions themselves of experience that seem to dictate in the analysis of the human dynamism the need to put aside at present the aspect of consciousness and the questions bearing only upon experiencing. It is not by accident that in the Introduction we discriminated the total experience of man from its various aspects, of which its inner aspect was even then seen as being closely connected with consciousness.

All the same, it is not only the dynamism proper to man that receives its basic reflection in consciousness; the human being is aware as well of the main trends in his dynamism, this awareness being connected also with his experiencing them. Indeed, he experiences acting and doing as something essentially different from the mere happening, that is to say, from what only takes place or goes on in him and in what he as man takes no active part. Having the experience of the two, objectively different structures – of the "man-acts" and the "something-happens-in-him" – together with their differentiation in the field of experience, provides the evidence, on the one hand, of the essential contiguity of man's consciousness with his being; on the other hand, the differentiation of experience gives each of these structures that innerness and subjectiveness which in general we owe to consciousness. At present, however, we are not interested in experiencing as such but in those structures which to be objectively differentiated require that we rely upon the total experience of man and not merely on the evidence which might be supplied by our consciousness. The immanent experience itself is insufficient with respect to all the processes, operations, events and states of the human body, all that pertains to the life of the organism. We always have to reach to other sources than the merely spontaneous and instantaneous evidence of consciousness itself and the experiences associated with it; we have to supplement it continuously from the outside in order to make our knowledge of man in this dimension as complete as possible.

The Juxtaposition of "To Act" and "To Happen" as the Experiential Basis of Activeness and Passiveness

The two objective structures, "man-acts" and "something-happens-in-man," determine the two fundamental lines of the dynamism proper to man. Their directions are mutually opposite, so far as man's "activeness," that is to say, his acting, is visualized – and actualized – in one, while his certain passiveness, and passivity, are in the other. In each of these elemental lines of the dynamism proper to man the phenomenon or the content of visualization corresponds to the actual structure, and, conversely, each structure manifests itself as the phenomenon. The activeness and the passiveness visualized in either line are the constituents of the structures and the objective ground for their differentiation. The "activeness" in the "man-acts" structure is something different from the "passiveness" of the "something-happens-in-man" structure, the two being mutually opposite. In this opposition the whole structure, the one and the other, takes part.[27]

Just as we may consider "activeness" and "passiveness" to be not only mutually opposed but also conditioned and determined by each other, so we can draw a line separating what we do from what happens in us, though the things on either side of the line not only differ but also mutually account for themselves. This has the greatest importance for understanding the "man-acts" structure and subsequently for its possibly complete interpretation. We may say that man's actions and all that happens in him are not only mutually opposed but also distinctly correlated in the sense of a certain parity of both facts or both structures. For speaking of acting we say "man acts," and of what takes place in him we say it "happens in man," so that in either statement man stands as the dynamic subject. Man's actions just as much as the things that happen in him provide – all in their own way – the realization of the dynamism proper to the human being. Both have their source in man; and thus if in another aspect we speak of activeness and passiveness as of two different directions in the same dynamism, we thereby assert that the direction "from within" is common to both – the more so as it forms part of the essence of all dynamism. Though activeness and passiveness differentiate the dynamism they do not deprive it of the unity issuing out of the same dynamic subject; this, however, in no way alters the fact that action differs from the rest of the dynamic manifestations of the man-subject, the manifestations that are included in the category of passiveness.

It also seems necessary to call attention to two different forms of passiveness that are expressed in the propositions, "Something happens in man" and "Something happens with man." In ordinary speech these propositions may sometimes be used indiscriminately; often, in speaking of something happening *with* a person, we actually think of what takes place *in* him. Actually, when speaking of what happens with a person we refer to what the person undergoes from outside. This is an entirely different kind of passiveness. Rather than the dynamic subject, and the source of what occurs, man is then merely an object that only undergoes what another subject or even another force is doing with him. Undergoing as such refers to the passiveness of man, the subject, but says nothing, at least not directly, of the subject's inner dynamism, in particular nothing of the dynamism referred to in the proposition "Something happens in man."

The Potency and Act Conjugate as Conceptual Homologue of Dynamism

In the traditional approach to the person and to action the dynamism proper to man is interpreted by analogy to the dynamism of all beings. The dynamism of being is the subject of traditional metaphysics, and to metaphysics – in particular to its great founder, Aristotle – we owe the conception in which the dynamic nature of being is expressed in philosophical terms. This is not limited to the concept of "act" alone but includes the conjugate conceptual whole formed by the pair, potency and act. The dialectic – as we would say nowadays – conjugation of the pair makes them so essentially referring to each other that when pointing to one we at the same time indicate the other; for to grasp the correlated meaning of either, the understanding of the other is indispensable. It is for this reason that act cannot be understood apart from potency and vice versa.[28] The terms potency and act need little explanation. Potency, the Latin *potentia*, may be defined as a potentiality, as something that already is but also is not yet: as something that is in preparation, is available, and even ready at hand but is not actually fulfilled. The act, the Latin *actus*, is the actualization of potentiality, its fulfillment.

As is to be seen, the meanings of both concepts are strictly correlated and inhere in the conjugate they form rather than in each of them separately. Their conjugation reveals not only the differentiated, though mutually coincident states of existence, but also the transitions from one to the other. It is these transitions that objectivize the structure of all dynamism inherent in being, in being as such, which constitutes the proper subject of metaphysics, and at the same time in every and any being, regardless of the branch of human knowledge whose specific concern it constitutes. We may with justice say that at this point metaphysics appears as the intellectual soil wherein all the domains of knowledge have their roots. Indeed, we do not seem to have as yet any other conceptions and any other language which would adequately render the dynamic essence of change – of all change whatever occurring in any being – apart from those that we have been endowed with by the philosophy of potency and act. By means of this conception we can grasp and describe precisely any dynamism that occurs in any being. It is to them we also have to revert when discussing the dynamism proper to man.

The concept of the "act" – we may call it so, for short, once we keep in mind the correlate it implies – has primarily an existential significance. The two different states of being, to which correspond two different forms of existence, are not indicated solely by the two terms (potency and act) essential to this conception. In addition, the transition from potency to act, termed *actualization*, is a transition in the order of existence; it indicates some sort of becoming, not in the absolute sense – this is possible only when something comes into being out of nonexistence – but in the relative sense, that is to say, becoming based on an already existing being and from within its inner structure. The dynamism of being is intrinsically connected with its very existence and is also the basis for, and the source of, all the structures that may be distinguished in it. Every actualization contains in itself both the possibility and the act, which is the real fulfillment of the possibility; hence it contains them not as two entities but as two interrelated forms of existence. Actualization always implies the following pattern of existences: what exists as a possibility may, because it thus exists, come into existence in an act; and conversely, what came into existence in the act did so because of its previous existence as potentiality. In actualization possibility and act constitute, as it were, the two moments or the two phases of concrete existence joined together in a dynamic unity. Moreover, the act does not signify solely that the state of fulfilled potentiality has ended; it also signifies the transition itself from potentiality to fulfillment, the very fulfillment. It now becomes evident that there is need of a factor that would allow this transition or fulfillment to be accomplished; this problem, however, we will not discuss at present.

The Ambiguity of the Concept of "Act" and Differentiation of the Experiences of Acting and Happening

Applying the conception of the act to the dynamism that is proper to man and constitutes the vital core of the dynamic conjugate of action and person, we have to assert at this stage of the discussion that it fits both essential forms of the human dynamism known from and by experience. The structure of "man-acts" as well as the structure of "something-happens-in-man" constitute the concrete manifestation of the dynamism proper to man. Some of their equivalence consists in man being present in either as its dynamic subject. The equivalence exists from the point of view of the human dynamism itself. From this viewpoint, having assumed the analogy of being, we may regard man's acting as well as what happens in him to be the fulfillment of a potentiality. The one and the other is an actualization, the dynamic unity of potentiality and act. This way of grasping the problem is justified by the general dynamism of man. It also enables us to search for and determine those potentialities which are inherent in man at the beginning of his various actings and of what we may perhaps call the various happenings, the different things that happen in him.

The difference of the activeness–passiveness type that occurs between the acting of man and the happening in man, the difference between dynamic acting and certain dynamic passiveness, cannot obscure or annul the human dynamism, which is inherent in one as well as in the other form. It does not obscure in the sense of the phenomenological experience and does not annul in the sense of the need of a realistic interpretation. Essentially, the human dynamism is interpreted by the concept of the "act." In this sense the term "act" adequately denotes the dynamic content of both structures: "man-acts" and "something-happens-in-man." The question remains whether it is equally adequate to show the specific nature of action. To put the problem precisely we have to ask whether the word "act," while designating the dynamism of all being, as well as every human dynamism – activeness as well as passiveness – has also the capability of revealing the whole specific nature of action.

2. THE DEFINITION OF EFFICACY

The Experience of Efficacy and the Differentiation of the Experiences of Acting and Happening

A distinction may be drawn between *human act* and *act of man*. In this way action is distinguished from all the other actualizations taking place in man (*act of man*) by means of the attributive *human*. It seems, however, that this distinction has a merely verbal significance and serves to accentuate rather than to explain the difference. For *human act*, or, equivalently, "human acting," is also an *act of man*. Hence, it is first necessary to demonstrate why and when the act of man is not human acting; for only then will it be possible to understand why human acting alone is the acting proper to man, that it alone corresponds to what actually is contained in the structure of "man-acts." We shall now endeavor to find such an explanation while adhering to our initial position as defined above.

Thus, the starting point in our argument will be the experiential difference that is discernible in the totality of man's dynamism between man's acting and what happens in man. An examination of the facts discloses that it is the moment of efficacy that determines this fundamental difference. In this case the moment of efficacy is to be understood as the having of the experience of "being the actor." This experience discriminates man's acting from everything that merely happens in him. It also explains the dynamic contraposition of facts and structures, in which activeness and passiveness are distinctly manifest. When acting I have the experience of myself as the agent responsible for this particular form of the dynamization of myself as the subject. When there is something happening in me, then the dynamism is imparted without the efficacious participation of my ego. This is precisely the reason why we speak of the facts of the latter kind as of something that happens in man, indicating thereby that then the dynamism is not accompanied by efficacy, by the efficacious participation of man. It is thus that in the dynamism of man there appears the essential difference arising from having the experience of efficacy. On the one hand, there is that form of the human dynamism in which man himself is the agent, that is to say, he is the conscious cause of his own causation; this form we grasp by the expression, "*man acts*." On the other hand, there is that form of human dynamism in which man is not aware of his efficacy and does not experience it; this we express by "something happens in man."

The contraposition of acting and happening, of activeness and passiveness, brings forth still another contraposition that arises from having, or not having, the experience of efficacy. Objective efficacy is the correlate of the experience of efficacy, for having this experience opens to our insight the structure of the efficacious ego. But not having the experience of efficacy – when the ego does not efficaciously participate in all that only happens in man – is by no means equivalent to the absence of objective causation. When something happens, when an inner change takes place in man, it must have a cause. Experience, in particular the inner experience, only supplies the evidence that the ego is not the cause in the manner that it is in an action, in acting.

The Experience of Efficacy and the Causal Relation of Person and Action

We now see that the moment of efficacy, which is present in acting and absent in happening, does not at once explain what efficacy is, but only points to the specifically dynamic structure of human acting as well as of the one who acts. Having the experience of himself as the agent the actor discovers himself to be at the origin of his acting. It is upon him that the existence of acting as such depends: in him it has its origin, and he sustains its existence. To be the cause means to produce an effect and to sustain its existence, its becoming and its being. Man is thus in a wholly experiential way the cause of his acting. There is between person and action a sensibly experiential, causal relation, which brings the person, that is to say, every concrete human ego, to recognize his action to be the result of his efficacy; in this sense he must accept his actions as his own property and also, primarily because of their moral nature, as the domain of his responsibility. Both the responsibility and the sense of property invest with a special quality the causation itself and the efficacy itself of the acting person. The students of the problems of causality, on the one hand, and psychologists, on the other, often note that human acting is in fact the only complete experience of what has been called by Aristotle "efficient causation." Without going into the details of this thesis, we have at any rate to accept that part of it which asserts the special self-evidence of man's efficient causation in acting, the efficient causation of the acting person.

The Experience of Efficacy and Man's Transcendence of His Acting

Efficacy itself as the relation of cause and effect leads us to the objective order of being and existence and is thus of an existential nature. In this case efficacy is simultaneously an experience. There lies the source of the specific empirical significance of human efficacy related with acting. For, as already mentioned, the efficacy of man draws him, on the one hand, into that form of his dynamism which consists in acting and, on the other, it allows him to remain above this dynamism and this acting. In the structure of "man-acts" we also have what may be defined as the immanence of man in his own acting and at the same time what has to be regarded as his transcendence relatively to this acting. The moment of efficacy, the experience of efficacy, brings forth first of all the transcendence of man relatively to his own acting. But then the transcendence proper to the experience had in being the agent of acting passes into the immanence of the experience of acting itself: when I act, I am wholly engaged in my acting, in that dynamization of the ego to which my own efficacy has contributed. The one could not be accomplished without the other. The "efficacious ego" and the "acting ego" each time form a dynamic synthesis and a dynamic unity in any particular action. It is the synthesis and unity of person and action.

This unity, however, neither obscures nor abolishes the differences. It is here that we come to the distinguishing trait in the structure of "man-acts," the trait that sets it off essentially from the structure of "something-happens-in-man." Being the agent, man is definitely the subject in his acting. When something happens, it is not man but the "something" that stands out as the agent while man remains as the passive subject. He experiences passively his own dynamism. What takes place in him cannot be, on the evidence of experience, defined as acting, even though it is still some sort of actualization of his own potentiality. The term "act" is not as strictly exfoliated phenomenologically as is *acting* or even *action*. Its reference is not to any actualization, to any dynamization of the subject that is man, but only to that actualization or dynamism in which man is active as the ego: the man who is the ego has the experience of himself, as the agent. According to the evidence of the integral experience it is then, and only then, that man performs an action.

The Experience of Efficacy and the Differentiation of Action out of Various Activations

Every dynamization of man in which he is not active as the concrete ego – that is to say, he as the ego, does not have the experience of his efficacy – we shall call *activation*. There is activation whenever something happens only in man and the something that happens is derived from the inner dynamism of man himself. But now the mode of the inner derivation is different from that which man does, in what is his action. The term *activation* seems to combine most adequately the moment of certain passiveness with the moment of activity, of certain activeness or, at any rate, actualization. The word is much used in natural science, but does not seem to have been applied in the study of the human being, in spite of its apparent adequacy for defining, and in a way even for explaining, the difference existing between the fact that man acts and the fact that something happens in him. Moreover, being rooted in everyday speech it expresses well the semantic difference and even contraposition between it and action.

By now the dynamism proper to man seems to have been sufficiently explained in the first approach. This first approach has dealt with the experiential differentiation of the human dynamism by the facts of acting and the facts of happening, which take place in the human being. In addition, in the first experiential approach we have already been able to discern within the structure of "man-acts" all the specificity of the conjugate of person and action. It has been brought into view by the moment of efficacy, which is simultaneously the moment of the transcendence of the person with regard to his acting. As the person–action conjugate occurs owing to this moment of transcendence we shall now consider it separately for a thorough analysis.

Man "Creates" Himself in Action: the Roots of Human Ethos

Efficacy and transcendence bring with them a special dependence of acting upon the person. Man is not only the agent of his acting, he is also the creator of it. It lies in the essence of efficacy that it produces and maintains the existence of an effect. On the other hand, the essence of creativeness is to shape the created work. In a sense, acting is also a work created by man. This characteristic trait of acting is specifically evidenced by morality as one of its properties (and which we have frequently referred to in this study). Morality and acting differ essentially, but at the same time they are so strictly united with each other that morality has no real existence apart from human acting, apart from actions. Their essential separateness does not obscure their existential relationship. The one and the other are most strictly related with the efficacy of the person, indeed, with the phenomenon of the experience had of efficacy. (At this point phenomenology seems to infringe boldly upon metaphysics, and it is here that its reliance upon metaphysics is most needed; for phenomena themselves can visualize a thing clearly enough, but they are incapable of a sufficient explanation of themselves.)

If it is in acting that man forms his own moral value – wherein is contained an element of the specifically human creativity – then this additionally confirms that man, the actor, himself shapes his acting and his actions.[29] The old Aristotelian problem, whether actions are the products of the acting man or the product is solely the outward effect of his acting – for instance, whether the product is the sheet of paper covered with writing or the strategic plan worked out by the mind – supplies sufficient evidence that human efficacy is also creative. Its creativeness uses man himself as its raw material. In the first plan, the human being forms himself by his acting. In the contraposition of man as "creator" and man as the "raw material" we again discover a form, or rather an aspect, of the contrast between activeness and passiveness, which we have been tracing here from the start. Indeed, it is a new aspect rather than a new form; for we cannot simply and definitely identify man as the "creator" with human acting, and man as the "raw material" with what happens in the human subject. On the other hand, there can be no doubt that action always consists in overcoming human passiveness in one way or another.

The moment of creativeness, which closely accompanies the moment of efficacy, the experience of efficacy that sets up the objective structure of "man-acts," brings out even more vividly the dominant role of efficacy in the integral dynamism of the human being. Efficacy itself is dynamic: indeed it constitutes, as it were, the culmination of the dynamism of the human being. But, at the same time, it distinctly differs from this dynamism as a whole. The difference between them has to be adequately emphasized by their interpretation.

3. THE SYNTHESIS OF EFFICACY AND SUBJECTIVENESS. THE PERSON AS A BASIC ONTOLOGICAL STRUCTURE

The Differentiation between Acting and Happening Contrasts Efficacy with Subjectiveness in Man

An analysis of the dynamic entity "man-acts" must account for both "man" and "acting" as the two constitutive elements of a whole. What is the man who acts, and what is he when he acts? That is the question which we must now consider. Man is the subject of his actions – this assertion is often made and as a rule is accepted without reservations. But what does "subject" really mean?

Following the line of our argument we reach the conclusion that within the integral experience of man, especially with reference to its inner aspect, we can trace a differentiation and even something like a contrast of subjectiveness and efficacy. Man has the experience of himself as the subject when something is happening in him; when, on the other hand, he is acting, he has the experience of himself as the "actor," this difference having been already emphasized in our discussion. To the experiences thus had corresponds a fully experiential reality. Subjectiveness is seen as structurally related to what happens in man, and efficacy as structurally related to his acting. When I act, the ego is the cause that dynamizes the subject. It is the attitude of the ego that is then dominant, whereas subjectiveness seems to be indicating something opposite – it shows the ego as if it were subjacent in the fact of its own dynamization. Such is the case when something happens within the ego. Efficacy and subjectiveness seem to split the field of human experiences into two mutually irreducible factors. Experiences are associated with structures. The structure of "man-acts" and the structure of "something-happens-in-man" seem to divide the human being as if they were two separate levels. The two levels will turn up on various occasions in the course of our further analyses.

For all the sharpness and distinctness – especially in the inner aspects of experience – of the differentiation and the contrast, it is impossible to deny that he who acts is simultaneously the one in whom something or other happens. Similarly, it is impossible to question the unity and the identity of man at the roots of acting and happening. Neither is it possible to question his unity and identity at the roots of the efficacy and the subjectiveness structurally contained in the acting and the happening that occur in man. For the human being is, as already stated, a dynamic unity, so much so that in our earlier analyses we called him outright the dynamic subject. This designation is here regarded as valid. Man's acting and that human efficacy which constitutes it experientially, as well as all that happens in him, combine together as if they issued from a common root. For it is the human being, as the dynamic subject, who is their origin. Speaking of the subject we simultaneously refer to subjectiveness. Subjectiveness has here a different sense from the subjectiveness we discovered in the experience of something happening in man when we contrasted the experience (and its corresponding structure) with acting and the efficacy contained in it. On that plane subjectiveness and efficacy appeared to be mutually irreducible, while now they can both be comprised by subjectiveness in its distinctive aspects. For, as is shown time and again by experience, they both spring from it.

How the Subject is an Ontological Basis of Action

However we analyze the structure, conditions, and source of action we cannot bypass its ultimate ontological foundation. The subjectiveness present both in man's acting and in what happens in him, implies or refers to an ontologically subsequent factor as its necessary condition. Of course, in principle, man "underlies" all his actions and everything that happens in him insofar as they are but his manifestations. And yet we still need to differentiate in man a structural ontological nucleus that would account for the fact itself of man being the subject or the fact that the subject is a being. It is in the subject as a being that every dynamic structure is rooted, every acting and happening. It is given as a real, actually existing, being, the man-being that actually exists and hence also "really" acts. There is, indeed, between existence and acting a strict relationship. This relationship seems to be the basic datum of man's cognition upon which evidence his most elementary vital existence relies. Philosophically we may interpret this state of affairs by an assessment that "for something to act, it must first exist." However, let us not forget that action is an enactment of existence or actual being. And yet it seems that in the perspective of our investigations existence lies at the origin itself of acting just as it lies at the origin itself of everything that happens in man – it lies at the origin of all the dynamism proper to man.

Existence (or actual being) has to be differentiated, however, from its structural (ontological) foundation. It is only its derived constitutive aspect, and yet it is of immense importance. For if the "something" did not exist, then it could not be the origin and the subject of the dynamism which proceeds from its being, of the acting and the happening. If man were not to exist, then he would not actually act nor would anything actually happen in him. Considered as such a fundamental condition of the actual existence of every existing being, it may be said that this structural/ontological basis is itself a being insofar as it is the subject of existing and acting. Coming into existence may, indeed, be seen as the first act of every being, that is, the first and fundamental factor establishing its dynamism.[30] The entire dynamism of man's functioning which consists in the acting of, and happening in, the dynamic subject simultaneously proceeds from (but also enacts) the initial dynamism due to which a being exists at all.

Man's Ontological Foundation of Action

In the first and fundamental approach the man-person has to be somewhat identified with its basic ontological structure. The person is a concrete man, the *individua substantia* of the classical Boethian definition. The concrete is in a way tantamount to the unique, or at any rate, to the individualized. The concept of the "person" is broader and more comprehensive than the concept of the "individual," just as the person is more than individualized nature. The person would be an individual whose nature is rational – according to Boethius' full definition *persona est rationalis naturae individua substantia*.[31] Nevertheless, in our perspective it seems clear that neither the concept of the "rational nature" nor that of its individualization seems to express fully the specific completeness expressed by the concept of the person. The completeness we are speaking of here seems to be something that is unique in a very special sense rather than concrete. In everyday use we may substitute for a person the straightforward "somebody." It serves as a perfect semantic epitome because of the immediate connotations it brings to mind – and with them the juxtaposition and contrast to "something." If the person were identified with its basic ontological structure, then it would at once become necessary to take account of the difference that distinguishes "somebody" and "something."

The person as such possesses, however, its own ontological structure, though one very different from all the others that surround the human being in the visible world. This difference, the proportion or rather the disproportion that is indicated in the words "somebody" and "something," reaches to the very roots of the being that is the subject. The fundamental dynamization of the being by existence and consequently also all the subsequent dynamizations, which are reflected by acting, operating, and the happening, also manifest the same difference, the same proportion with its inherent disproportion. The person, the human being as the person – seen in its ontological basic structure – is the subject of both existence and acting, though it is important to note that the existence proper to him is *personal* and not merely individual – unlike that of an ontologically founded merely individual type of being. Consequently, the action – whereby is meant all the dynamism of man including his acting as well as what happens in him – is also personal. The person is identifiable with an ontological basic structure in which a provision is to be made: the ontological structure of "somebody" manifests not only its similarities to but also its differences and detachment from the ontological structure of "something."

Differences between Efficacy and Subjectiveness and Their Synthesis

Once we reach the insight into the man-person as the ontological basis for existence, we can see in him a synthesis of those experiences and those dynamic structures which we have distinguished in this chapter. The two structures, that in which man acts and that in which something happens in man, cut across the phenomenological field of experience, but they join and unite together in the metaphysical field. Their synthesis is the man-person, and we discover the ultimate subject of the synthesis in its ontological groundwork. Not only does this groundwork underlie the whole dynamism of the man-person, but it itself is also the dynamic source of the dynamism. The dynamism derived from the actual existence has as its consequence the dynamism pertaining to activity.

The synthesis of acting and happening, which takes place on the ground of the human basic structure, is indirectly also a synthesis of the efficacy proper to acting with the subjectiveness pertaining to all that takes place in man. Ultimately, the synthesis not only has its foundation but also occurs actually through the mechanism of the basic ontological structure, that is to say, in the ontic subject. This is the reason why the human being, even while he is the agent in acting, still remains its subject. He is both the actor and the subject, and he has the experience of himself both as actor and as subject, though the experience had of his efficacy is overshadowed by the experience of his subjectiveness. On the other hand, if something only happens in man, then we have the experience of subjectiveness alone; in this case efficacy is not experienced, for then the human being as the person is not the agent.

The difference in these experiences and structures is in no way diminished by the fact of the synthesis of efficacy with subjectiveness, which reduces them to the structural support alone. Indeed, the dynamism proper to man cannot be adequately interpreted and fully understood without this difference, and thus it will have to turn up time and again in the course of our considerations. The structural nucleus functions as the subject, which means that it is simultaneously both the basis and the source of the two different forms of dynamism. It is in this that is rooted and from this that springs forth not only the dynamism of what happens in man, but also the total dynamism of acting with that conscious efficacy which is constitutive of it. The unity of the human structural nucleus can in no way obscure the deep differences that make the actual wealth of the human dynamism.

4. THE PERSON AND NATURE: THEIR OPPOSITION
OR INTEGRATION?

The Significance of the Problem

The discussion of the ontological basis of man-person has brought us definitely to the analysis of the subject of acting. We shall now have to proceed with this analysis even further, in order to uncover, so to speak, the most deeply hidden roots of the dynamism of man, and more particularly the roots of efficacy, for it is efficacy that is the key for the understanding of the person–action relation. Man as the subject of acting and the acting of the subject are the two correlated limbs in our discussion, and each has to be cognized and cognitively deepened by means of the other. It may seem that when we identify the person with its structural nucleus – evidently, by applying the analogy of proportion – we regard as already definitely settled the place that in our analysis of the subject of acting we intend to assign to nature. However, the person and with it its ontological foundation have here been conceived not only as the metaphysical subject of the existence and the dynamism of the human being, but also as, in a way, a phenomenological synthesis of efficacy and subjectiveness. Thus *nature* has to assume to some extent a double sense, a point which we now intend to examine.

Nature Defines the Subjective Basis of Acting

Etymologically the term "nature" is, as we know, derived from the Latin verb *nascor* ("to be born"), hence *natus* ("born") and *naturus* ("about to be born"). Thus "nature" denotes literally everything that is going to be born or is contained in the fact itself of birth as its possible consequence. Accordingly, the corresponding adjectives of the natural are *inborn*, an Anglo-Saxon word, and *innate*, a word of Latin etymology. *Nature* in its substantive use has many senses: it may refer to the material world with all its phenomena, whether animate or inanimate, though in the latter case it goes beyond its etymological source, which relates it to birth; as this is possible only in living creatures inanimate nature is in a way a contradiction in terms; it may also be used with an attributive limiting its meaning when we speak, for instance, of human nature, of animal or vegetative nature, and even of the nature of a concrete person, who may be good or bad natured. In all these uses the noun *nature* seems to point to some property of a specific subject, to something we may also call its essence. Occasionally, the two words are used almost interchangeably – for instance, we may speak of the nature or the essence of a thing – though their meanings never exactly overlap. Speaking of essence we refer to a different thing than when speaking of nature.

Nature does not denote a real and actual subject of existing and acting; it is not to be identified with the ontological foundation of a being. It can only apply to an abstract subject. For instance, in speaking of human nature we refer to something which has the status of real existence as the ontological structure of man only in an actual human being, but which has no real existence apart from him. Nevertheless, if we, so to speak, prescind from the nature of every human being, in whom it actually exists, then we may conceive it as an abstract being, which stands in relation to all men. In this way human nature directly points to what is the specific trait common to all human beings by the very fact of their being humans, and indirectly also to those to whom it belongs, that is, to the human beings themselves. It is at this point that, semantically speaking, nature comes nearest to essence, for it is here that it refers to what is specific to man as such, that is, points to what is essentially human, what makes man to be nothing or nobody but man.

Nature Determines the Manner of Acting

Taken semantically, nature, conformably with its etymology, also reaches in another direction. It is not confined to the domain of the subject of acting, which to some extent we have already explored, but also signifies the manner of acting open to it. Without going into the problem of the manner of acting specific to nature as such we have first to look closer at the orientation itself of nature in the direction of acting or, more broadly, in the direction of dynamism. Nature, because of its etymology and the close resemblance to the Latin participle that it is derived from, tells of what is about to be born and what is contained in the fact of birth itself as its possible consequence. The fact of birth is in itself something dynamic; but it also marks the beginning of the dynamism proper to the subject that is

being born. Birth is also the beginning of existence – it contains the
initial and basic dynamization caused by existence, from which will
issue all the subsequent dynamism of functioning. Hence, in the case
of man the consequence of birth would be the whole synthesis of
acting and happening which we have been tracing in this chapter. Is it
nature that lies at the basis of this synthesis? If so, it would have to
be either identical or very closely integrated with the human ontological nucleus. Or is it that nature only points to a certain domain of
the human dynamism, to a definite form of actualization? Then it
would be possible to attribute to it and deduce from it only a certain
mode of acting rather than all human acting.

Why the Antagonistic Conception of Nature and Person?

It is the latter understanding of nature that seems to result from the
phenomenological reduction. By phenomenological reduction we
mean the moment of the fullest and simultaneously the most essence-
centered visualization of a given object. Assuming man to be a
specific dynamic whole we may rightly regard as the moment of the
complete and the most essential manifestation of nature the moment
when something happens in man rather than that of his acting; the
moment of what we have called activation rather than that of action;
the moment of subjectiveness rather than that of efficacy. Why so?
Because the concept of nature includes that dynamism which is
directly and solely the consequence of birth itself; the dynamism that
is exclusively inborn or innate, exclusively immanent in the given
subject of acting, as if it was determined in advance by its properties.
Nature reveals the dynamism of the subject, that is, it reveals that
activeness which is wholly and entirely contained in the subject's
dynamic readiness; as if this activeness was from the start an attribute of the subject and was entirely prepared in its subjective
dynamic structure. This activeness does not rely on efficacy in the
sense that efficacy occurs in every action or in the structure of
"man-acts" where it takes the form of a certain predominance or
transcendence of the acting subject in relation to the dynamization
itself of the subject.

When so conceived nature presents itself as a strictly defined
moment of the dynamism proper to man rather than as the basis of all
this dynamism. It is manifested solely in the activation of the man-

subject, while actions show him to be a person. While contained in actions efficacy brings into view a concrete ego as the self-conscious cause of action. It is this that is the person. So conceived, the person would differ from the nature in man and would even be in a way its opposite. As can be seen, this differentiation and this opposition comes after the first experiential differentiation; that is, the differentiation and the opposition between, on the one hand, the experiences and structures of man's acting and, on the other, those referring to what happens in man. This separation of experiences and structures would divide the human being, as it were, into two worlds: the world of the person and the world of nature. Emphasizing some moments in experience we may miss and disregard the transition between man's nature and his person, and we may fail to grasp their integrity. Let us note, however, that person and nature would then denote practically nothing more than a certain mode of acting and hence also a certain form of the dynamism proper to man, but would not in any significant way denote the subject of this dynamism and acting; indeed, they would almost completely disregard it.

Why the Integrated Conception of Nature in Person?

There seems to be in that approach a kind of transposition that puts the aspects of experience above its total significance. The total experience, which gives both a simple and fundamental perception of the human being – whether it be in the pre- and even nonscientific approach, or in the domains of learning, especially philosophy – supplies the evidence for the unity and the identity of the man-subject. This is accompanied by the synthesis, on the ground of the one and the same ontological support, of acting and happening that takes place in man, the synthesis of actions and activations, of efficacy and subjectiveness. There is, therefore, no valid reason for the mutual opposition in man of person and nature; on the contrary, we now see the need of their integration. From the particular moments or aspects of experience we have to pass to the whole and from the particular moments or aspects of man as the subject of experience to the total conception of man. (In the course of an actual cognitive process there is no such passing from one to the other and no such lines of cognizing: all the moments and aspects are firmly embedded in the cognitive whole. Nevertheless, we may here consider both the passage itself and the lines followed in it, in order to base our knowledge on firmer grounds. Another important aim is to show how phenomenology and metaphysics both scrutinize the same object, and that phenomenological and metaphysical reductions are not mutually contradictory.)

5. NATURE AS THE BASIS FOR THE DYNAMIC COHESION OF THE PERSON

Efficacy of the Person and Causality of Nature

How is the integration of nature in the person accomplished? The answer was already indicated in the analysis of the mutual relation of the internally differentiated human dynamism to its ontological basis. When viewed from the standpoint of the ontological nucleus of the human structure the difference and the opposition between acting and happening, between the efficacy proper to acting and the subjective-ness proper to happening, to what takes place in man, must yield to the obvious unity and identity of the human being. For it is man who acts. And though, even if he – who is the personal "somebody" – does not act when there is something happening in him, the whole dynamism of activations belongs to him just as much as does the dynamism of actions. It is in man, the personal "somebody," that the activations that happen in him have their origin just as much as it is from him that spring the actions he as the actor performs.

Man's experience culminates in the experience of his ego. It is the ego that is the agent of actions. When man acts, the ego has the experience of its own efficacy in action. When, on the other hand, there is something happening in man, then the ego does not experience its own efficacy and is not the actor, but it does have the experience of the inner identity of itself with what is happening and, at the same time, of the exclusive dependence of what is happening upon itself. What takes place in myself in the form of various activations is the property of my ego and, what is more, it issues from my ego, which is its only appropriate substratum and cause, though then I have no experience of my causality, of my efficacious participation, as I have in actions. Any attempt, however, to attribute what is happen-ing in myself – to attribute this activation – to any other cause but myself would be immediately contradicted by experience. The human experience had at the crucial point where man experiences his own ego leads us directly and definitely to the conclusion that everything taking place in the human being appertains to the ego as the dynamic subject. This appurtenance includes also the causal relation, which though different in activations than in actions is still experiential and real. To put in doubt this appurtenance or this causal relation is tantamount to contradicting the evidence of the experience we have of our own self, of the experience had of the unity of the ego and its dynamic identity not only with all that man does but also with everything that happens in him.

These considerations have already brought us on the road leading to integration, regardless of whether or not we keep to the basic distinction between nature and person. Even if *nature* is to be identified only with the moment of activation, as opposed to the moment of action, which reveals the person in the human being, then the former moment at any rate is not external to the unity and identity of the ego. The experience of the unity and identity of the ego is objectively precedent to and also more fundamental than the experiential separation of acting from happening, of the efficacy from the nonefficacy of the self. The experience of unity and identity extends into the other experience constituting thereby the experiential basis for the integration of nature in the person, in the structural center of its ontological foundation. In this way nature still denotes that form of dynamism as its derivative, which is different from that of the person. The integration does not abolish the differences in the manner the very structural core of a being is dynamized, but simply prevents any tendency to treat person and nature as two separate and independent subjects of acting. In this way nature, conceived as that unique type of support of being which is man and hence the person, still indicates its different causations. Are these causations non-personal? The personal causation is contained in having the experience of efficacy of the concrete ego – but only when man is acting. On the other hand, when there is something happening in man, efficacy is not experienced and consequently there is no causation that would be proper to the person. Nevertheless, for the causes underlying this form of the dynamization of the subjective ego we have also to look within the ego and not to the outside of it; for then nature itself would appear as the cause of the dynamism. Nature integrated in the unity of the specific structural nucleus, which is man, would then refer to and indicate a different causal basis of the subject than the person.

In this approach we attempt to distinguish nature from the person as clearly as this is possible.

The Meaning of the "Priority" of Existence over Action

The metaphysical reduction, on the other hand, leads to the full integration of nature in the person. Paying no heed to nature as a specific moment in the dynamization of the subject it considers nature, as a basic property of the acting subject, which in our case is the man-subject. In the metaphysical approach nature is identical with essence, and thus nature in man is the same as the whole of his *humanness*, though humanness that is dynamic rather than static – because conceived as the basis of all the dynamism proper to man. It is at this point that we touch upon the essential difference between the metaphysical and the previous, more or less phenomenological, conception of nature. Nature in the metaphysical sense is equivalent to the essence of any being, where essence is regarded as the basis for the dynamism of this being.

The first elementary understanding of the relation existing between action and an acting being is expressed above in the priority attributed to existence over action. We must now take a closer look at the meaning of this assertion. In the first place we note its existential significance, for it states that in order to act it is first necessary to exist. It also states that acting as such is different from existence as such; merely to act does not mean to be contributing or perpetuating the process of existence; it is not just its homogenetic continuation or extension. There is a real difference between the two manifestations of man, "man as existing" and "man acting," even though it is the same man who exists and who acts. When man acts, his acting also has a kind of derivative existence of its own. The existence of the acting depends indeed on the existence of man, and it is here that there lies the proper moment of their existential causality. The existence of acting flows from and is subsequent to the existence of man; it is its consequence or effect.

The existential relation between action and being with which we are here concerned allows us to clarify and grasp these relations not only in the order of existence. It also brings to light the relation between the acting process and the acting subject – in this case the man-subject – in their essential status. The statement that action is subsequent or follows existence is meant to indicate a specific cohesion of the acting process and the acting agent. This cohesion is impossible to express otherwise than by resorting to the conception of nature. For nature is none other than the basis of the essential cohesion of the one who acts (though the acting agent need not be human) with his acting. To put it more generally and more precisely, we may say nature provides the basis for the essential cohesion of the subject of dynamism with all the dynamism of the subject. The attributive *all* is important, because it allows us to reject once and for all that meaning of nature which exhibits it as only a moment and only one mode of the dynamization of the subject.

Personal Existence as the Basis of the Dynamic Cohesion of Man

The cohesion considered here is confirmed in experience. When man is considered as the subject of dynamism the cohesion applies to both his acting and what is happening in him, to every one of his actions and to every one of his activations. It includes the efficacy experienced in action by a concrete ego and the subjectiveness itself of the ego in the case of activations when efficacy is not experienced. There is cohesion whenever an *action* is operated by, or proceeds from, the human being as its agent. It is based on human nature, that is, on the humanness pervading all the human dynamism and shaping it so that it becomes really human.

The experience of man's coherence with all his dynamism, with his acting as well as with what happens in him, allows us to understand how nature is integrated in the person. The integration could not consist solely in the individualization of nature by the person. The person is not merely an "individualized humanness"; it actually consists rather in the mode of individual being that pertains (from among all the types of existing beings) to mankind alone. This mode of being stems from the fact that the peculiar type of being proper to mankind is personal. The first and foremost dynamization of any being appears as being derived from its existence, from its actual being.

Dynamization by the personal being must lie at the roots of the integration of humanness by the person. At any rate, considering the experiential cohesion of the whole human functioning with his existence, we are led to accept that it is human nature that constitutes the appropriate basis for the cohesion of the man-subject – whatever kind of inner dynamism it has – with any of its dynamizations. Of course, nature as the basis of this dynamic cohesion really inheres in the subject, while the subject itself having personal existence is a person. Hence, every form of dynamization of the subject, every operation – whether it consists in acting or in happening, that is, in activation – if really related to humanness, to nature, must also be really personal. The integration of human nature, of humanness, in and by the person has as its consequence the integration of all the dynamism proper to man in the human person.[32]

Person as the Real Existence of Human Nature

At the same time it is important to stress that because of man's nature, because of his humanness, such integration is possible only in man. Humanness or human nature is equipped with the properties that enable a concrete human being to be a person: to be and to act as a person. Moreover, it prevents him from being and acting otherwise. As these properties will be discussed more fully below, they need be only briefly mentioned here. Even so we see clearly enough that the integration of nature by the person in the human being not only presupposes nature, presupposes humanness, but also derives from it its real constitution. Hence, no other nature has any real (that is, individual) existence as a person – for this pertains to man alone.

The element of nature, of humanness, introduced into the preceding analysis has enriched our knowledge and our understanding of the person as the existential ontological support and also as a living, always expanding, synthesis of the dynamism proper to man, the synthesis of actions with activations and thus of efficacy with subjectiveness. With this element the whole interpretation of the person–action relation confirms its human import. Acting and happening are both human insofar as they derive within the person from nature, from the humanness of man. It is the person itself that is human and so are its actions. The efficacy of the human ego pertaining to action reveals the transcendence of the person, without, however, separating the person from nature. It only indicates the special properties of nature; it indicates the forces that constitute the being and the acting of man at the level of the person.

6. POTENTIALITY AND ITS RELATION TO CONSCIOUSNESS

The Nature–Person Relation in the Potentiality of the Man-Subject

The integration of nature in the person achieved by way of the metaphysical reduction brings to light the unity and the identity of man as a subjective being. The integration of humanness by the person, which is equally the integration of the person by humanness, does not however abolish in any way that difference between the person and nature which is manifest in the total experience of man, especially in its inner aspect. The fact of the unity and identity of the human being as the subject of the dynamism proper to him does not abolish in any way the fact of the difference between man's acting and all the things only happening in him, between action and the various activations. Neither does the integration of nature in the person abolish or in any way obscure the fact that man's personality is ascertained from his actions, that is to say, from his conscious acting, while everything else is contained in the person because of the identity and the unity of that subject which acts consciously and performs actions. "Personality" as here used means that man is a person. Man's being a person and the fact that this is manifested or visualized in his conscious acting as well as in his consciousness was discussed in the preceding chapter. We owe to consciousness and especially to its reflexive function, that man – the subjective autonomous being – has the experience of himself as the subject, which makes his being fully "subjective."

The difference between person and nature within the frame of the same ontological structure of man is obvious, even when we consider their metaphysical integration: if there were no distinctiveness, there would be no need to integrate. Humanness and personality (the fact of being a person) are two different things. In this study, where we are striving to arrive at the deepest possible understanding of the structure of man's acting, nature as humanness may be but another step in our analysis and comes in only as if it was its background. In the foreground there is nature as the ground of causation for the human ontological basis, and following it comes a certain form of dynamization of that ontological basis. In other words, we are interested in the relation of nature to the person from the viewpoint of the potentiality of the man-subject. We may even say that hitherto our whole analysis was indirectly an analysis of his potentiality.

Potentiality Indicates the Source of the Inner Dynamization of the Subject

The reason for this last conclusion lies in the fact that we take note of the potentiality of the man-subject by ascertaining its dynamism. Either form of this dynamism – man's acting or action, and all that happens in him and that we have called "his activation" – issues from within and has its origin in the subject, which in our account we have rightly defined as dynamic. The dynamism of the subject is derived from his potentiality; for potentiality consists in having at one's disposal certain powers inherent in the subject. At this point, however, we have to define some of our terms. *Dynamism*, etymologically derived from the Greek *dynamis*, means force or power, while *potentiality*, derived from the Latin *potentia*, here denotes power or faculty. We thus see that etymologically the two terms are very closely related. But their application in the present discussion also shows the clearly marked differences between them. Thus *dynamism*, as we could see, refers primarily to that actual dynamization of the man-subject which issues from within and may have the form either of acting or of happening. *Potentiality*, on the other hand, denotes the source itself of this dynamization of the subject, the source that is inherent and that ceaselessly pulsates in the subject, and which comes to the surface in one or the other form of the subject's dynamization. In the traditional conception of man based on metaphysical premises this source is called "faculty"; a faculty is equivalent to the point where a force is focused, the center where power resides and is wielded.

We ascertain the potentiality of the man-subject while ascertaining his dynamism. Accordingly, our knowledge of it is in fact experiential: contained in either form of dynamism – whether acting or happening – there is also potentiality as the basis and as the source of the then existing dynamization. This basis is not, however, as apparent in experience as is the dynamization itself of the subject and the actual form of the dynamism. Our interpretation of it, that is, of the dynamic source of either form of the actual dynamism, rests on a reasoning that is strictly connected with the overall object of experience; far from being detached from the object, our reasoning goes deeper into the heart of the matter than when the dynamism in any of its forms is merely taken note of. When man acts and when anything happens in him, it is first of all this concrete form of the dynamization of the man-subject that is given us experientially, whereas its basis and its source are given us only indirectly, as if they came at secondhand; for experience clearly shows that this form of dynamism issues from within. But, while revealing the innerness of the source, experience must also show what is the source of the dynamization within the subject; it must point not just to the subject as a whole but to the particular, clearly defined dynamic source for one or other form of the dynamization of the subject. Without these well defined but varied sources it would be difficult to explain why the subject is dynamized in such different ways.

The Different Basis of Activity and Passivity in the Potentiality of Man

The most striking difference is that which occurs between the dynamization of the subject when man acts and when there is something happening in him. Underlying this difference in the dynamism of man there must be a different potentiality of the human ontological nucleus with its regulative organization. To grasp and define the specific nature in the structure of man's acting from the point of view of the subject's potentiality is one of the chief aims in this study. We advance toward this objective step by step, by analyzing the separate contents of both structures. The structure of something happening in man indicates a different basis for the potentiality of the man-subject than for the structure of man's acting. However we may venture to guess that if the difference in the forms of the dynamism itself is so striking, then there has to be a corresponding difference in the potentialities, which means that different faculties must lie at the dynamic roots of acting and happening, of action and activation.[33] The problem was fully investigated by traditional philosophical anthropology (psychology), and as we are here striving to focus our attention on the person with all his specific dynamism, we will not follow the traditional path of discriminating between man's particular faculties as such. The road of tradition being well trodden and fully explored we must abandon it at this point. We shall instead follow the basic intuition of the person as it manifests itself in actions. Accordingly, in approaching the end of the analysis of this dynamism, which has already brought out the specific role of the efficacy of the personal ego in every action, we have now to turn again to our earlier discussion of consciousness. In doing so our aim is to develop a more precise conception of the relation of consciousness to potentiality in man.

The Relation of Consciousness to Psychoemotive Potentiality

With this purpose in view we are going to consider two very different kinds of both dynamism and potentiality, which may also be spoken of as two structural levels of the dynamic man-subject. They also constitute two levels of the subjectiveness of every concrete ego, because at these levels the ego has the experience of itself only as the subject and not as the actor, which it would have when acting consciously, that is, in actions. The two levels in the dynamism as well as in the potentiality of man are the psychoemotive and the somato-vegetative.

It is worth noting that we are always concerned with the relation of dynamism to potentiality, so far as the relation is visualized in the experience of man (and especially with reference to his inner aspect). It is in this aspect that, because of the different relation to consciousness, the vegetative dynamism and indirectly the vegetative potentiality differs in man from the emotive dynamism and also indirectly from the emotive potentiality. Consciousness in its mirroring function, and the reflexive consciousness that follows, is the condition of having a subjective experience, in this case of having the experience of what is happening in man. Thus we are not at present concerned with the objective difference between those acts and faculties as such which pertain to the somato-vegetative and the psychoemotive levels, but with what we may call their position in the reflecting of consciousness and in experience, and with the range of consciousness in these areas of man's potentiality. All this is not without significance for the complete image, in which we consider the man-person not only as an objective being who is the subject, but also in connection with the experience he has of the subjectiveness of his being and acting. These conditions are not without significance in the effort to understand the vegetative and emotive forms themselves of both the dynamism and the potentiality.

The difference between the two forms of the dynamism as well as between the two levels of man's potentiality manifests itself among others in our awareness of one but not of the other. This refers first of all to the character of the dynamism itself, that is to say, of the corresponding actualizations. The acts of the emotive sphere – or, in other words, that form of dynamism which in the subject is based on and springs from the psychoemotive potentiality – are clearly mirrored in consciousness. They have, if one may say so, their place in the field of consciousness, and they proceed in the subject as more or less distinct experiences. We may even say that not only are we aware of them, but that they are inherently accessible to consciousness, which means that consciousness must necessarily reflect them and include them as experiences in the inner profile of man's subjectiveness.

The Relation of Consciousness to Somato-Vegetative Potentiality

The acts of the vegetative sphere – that sphere or form of the human dynamism which in the subject is based on and springs from the somato-vegetative potentiality – do not on the whole attain man's awareness, and they even seem to be inaccessible to consciousness. It is to be stressed that the somato-vegetative dynamism and its corresponding potentiality in the man-subject are connected with the human body so far as it constitutes the organism. The term "vegetative" is used here in a wider sense than when we speak, for instance, of the vegetative system in medicine. Its meaning corresponds approximately to the old Aristotelian idea of the vegetative soul. The somato-vegetative dynamism is that form of the dynamism proper to man which is vital to the human body as an actual organism and, moreover, so far as the organism conditions the various psychical functions.

The whole of this dynamism and consequently also its corresponding potentiality seems to have an entirely different margin in the field of consciousness, one that is much more restricted and indirect than that of the psychoemotive dynamism. Man is aware of his body but as something that has its specific life. Having the awareness of the body leads indirectly to having the awareness of the organism. But the human being has no direct and detailed consciousness of his organism; he is not conscious of the particular dynamic instances of acts which compose the whole of the vegetative dynamism. These factual instances, these forms of the dynamism of the human subject, remain inaccessible to consciousness. They occur and develop spontaneously without the accompaniment of their being mirrored in consciousness. The dynamic facts, the acts of the somato-vegetative nature, are not included as experiences in the inner profile of the human subjectiveness. It is only by means of sensations that we can have the experience of anything that happens at this structural level of the human subject, a fact already mentioned in the preceding chapter. Accordingly, when we have, for instance, the experience of physical pain or physical well-being and fitness, then the nature of the experience is basically psychical and not vegetative, though its objective roots are on the somato-vegetative level, in the potentiality of this level.

The total experience of the body and the consciousness of the body seem to rely extensively on the sphere of sensations, the so-called bodily sensations. Since the significance of somato-vegetative and psychoemotive factors in the study of the acting person is indubitable, and since these questions deserve a fully detailed and comprehensive analysis, their discussion is deferred to a separate chapter.

7. THE RELATION OF POTENTIALITY TO CONSCIOUSNESS EXPRESSED BY SUBCONSCIOUSNESS

Potentiality Comes before Consciousness

Man who is the actor, who performs actions, is also the dynamic subject of everything that happens in him, whether the occurrences are at the emotive or the vegetative level and whether they are or are not accessible to consciousness.[34] The subject is always one and the same; it is the subject that is all a person, a "somebody," and does not cease to be a person in the whole sphere of the causations of nature which, as already noted, differs from the causation of the person. The fact of the man-subject being a person is not altered by the activations that fashion the dynamism pertaining to the emotive sphere of man's integral existence. The unity and identity of the being who is the subject bear witness to the reality of the potential unity, and hence also to the dynamic unity of this subject. Its unity is not abolished by those structural differences which, for instance, are manifest in the relation of potentiality to consciousness and vice versa. We have already seen that consciousness does not reflect to the same degree the whole potentiality of the human being with its consequent dynamizations. The vegetative potentiality and dynamism of the human being both remain essentially inaccessible to consciousness; they are not registered in consciousness though they form part of the structure of the dynamic subject who is a person. Undeniably, vegetative potentiality constitutes a factor in countless instances of conscious human acting, in countless actions, which of course does not mean that vegetative potentiality itself is their source.

We now see that it is not owing to consciousness that the dynamic unity of the man-subject is achieved at the vegetative level. The unity is attained apart from and in a way outside of consciousness, which in its reflecting function is not instrumental in this respect; for, as we saw, dynamic unity is antecedent and primary to consciousness in both its mirroring and reflexive functions. In the man-subject it consists – at least at the somatic level – primarily in the unity of life and only secondarily and, as it were, accidentally in the unity of experience. This assertion supports the priority of potentiality with regard to consciousness. An analysis of the human being, of the acting person, if it were to be grounded on consciousness alone, would from the first be doomed to inadequacy.

Consciousness and the Delimitation of the Psychical and the Somatic

The priority of potentiality with regard to consciousness has to be taken into account also at the emotive level, even though the role of consciousness at this level of the human dynamism is very distinct and very effective. All elements composing the emotive sphere of the human dynamism – the various sensations or emotions – are not only spontaneously recorded in consciousness but are also vividly experienced by man. The dividing line between these experiences and the great wealth and variety of data that belong to the somato-vegetative life and are not had in experience coincides to some extent with the line dividing the psychical from the somatic. Although the latter delimitation, which refers only to objective structures, is established according to different criteria, they are to some extent adopted from the criteria of the former division. This is basically permissible as long as the adoption is carried out on the right plane, which is important because otherwise confusion may result among the different aspects of experience, and consequently in the understanding of man – a confusion we must avoid. If the human being is a specific field of experiences and understandings then consciousness and experience, which help in obtaining a comprehensive grasp of this field primarily in the inner experience, cannot be interchanged with what determines the relations among the objective structures themselves. It is to such objective structures that the division of the psychical from the somatic, not to mention the soul and the body in man, seems to refer. Every one of these divisions has a different significance and issues from different premises, even though we may say they all have a common root where they meet.

Introducing Subconsciousness into the Analysis

So far our analysis has allowed us to distinguish in the totality of the human dynamism a sphere accessible to consciousness and another that remains inaccessible to it. Thereby the way is opened to introduce the factor of "subconsciousness." With reference to the same man-subject, who is a person, the dynamism accessible to consciousness is distinguishable from the dynamism inaccessible to it. We may even say that in a way they are opposed to each other, if the relation of the dynamism to consciousness is taken as the dividing criterion. But in the concept of subconsciousness there is more than just the inaccessibility to consciousness of the dynamic facts, of the activations that occur in the man-subject, especially at the somato-vegetative level. The subconscious, as we know it from researches in psychoanalysis, designates a different source of the content of human experience than the source that feeds consciousness. Such is the case, for instance, with sexual objects in the treatment by Freud of the subconscious, and with other objects in the approach of Adler or Jung. Genetically, this content of human experience is connected with instincts, such as the sexual instinct or the ego instinct.

At a later stage of our discussion we shall deal with the problems of instinct and impulses in the whole structure of human dynamism. It is obvious, however, that these problems are of great significance in the present context, insofar as we are tempted to seek in the sub-conscious the potentiality of the human subject. Moreover, this tendency might lead us to attribute specific priority of potentiality with respect to conscious functions. We mean by that a priority concerning the structuring operations of the human mind and con-sequently priority in the terms of interpretation and hence of under-standing: in point of fact, it seems that it would be impossible to understand and explain the human being, his dynamism as well as his conscious acting and actions, if we were to base our considerations on consciousness alone. In this respect, as it seems, potentiality of the subconscious comes first; it is primary and more indispensable than consciousness for the interpretation of human dynamism as well as for the interpretation of conscious acting. Consciousness stresses the subjective aspect of conscious acting and to some extent also of what happens in man, but it does not constitute the inner structure of the human dynamism itself.

The Relation of Subconsciousness to the Dynamism and Potentiality of Man

All that has just been said is confirmed by subconsciousness in a specific manner, specific so far as the subconscious itself is primarily related to the inner aspect of human experience. Speaking of the subconscious we refer to, as it were, an inner space, to which some objects are expelled or withheld and prevented from reaching the threshold of consciousness. Both one and the other – the expulsion and the holding back – show that subconsciousness is also controlled by laws of a specific dynamism. This is evidenced by the threshold over which some elements must force their way before they can reach consciousness and enter into the process of experience; while remaining in subconsciousness they are beyond the flux of experience or, to put it more accurately, they remain in a state of *subexperience.* What is it that keeps guard at the threshold of consciousness? Is it the task of consciousness itself or of still another factor ranking higher in man, namely, the will? The threshold of consciousness does not seem to be always closely guarded, and it is not always that the control or censorship by that dominant factor in man is exercised. The ordinary emergence into consciousness, the coming to awareness, takes place spontaneously and in an uncontrolled manner: for instance, when we feel pain in a bodily organ we become aware of its existence and of its malfunction. But in this case there is only transition from the nonconscious to the conscious. Psychoanalysts have, however, designated subconsciousness solely for the elements whose reaching the threshold of consciousness is associated with the exercise of the factor dominant in man, with the special vigilance of this factor.

Then, however, the consideration of subconsciousness allows us to see all the more clearly the dynamism and the potentiality in man; for it is indicative, on the one hand, of that dominant dynamism – and with it of that underlying dominant potentiality which keeps watch at the threshold of consciousness – and on the other, of that potentiality which in the man-subject stays below the level of consciousness or, at any rate, below the current threshold of consciousness. Indeed, the elements that have been expelled from consciousness – sometimes they are even called repressed – or prevented from reaching it, do not float in the void but obviously remain with the subject. They are, moreover, maintained in a dynamic condition, waiting to be carried over the threshold of consciousness. Psychoanalytical researches tell us that they are always waiting for a suitable opportunity to emerge: for instance, when consciousness is weakened or inhibited by over-work or in sleep. Should we not conclude that these lower levels of human potentiality – that is, the vegetative and in a way also the emotive – assist, as it were, with their own dynamism rather than shelter the objects shut off from consciousness? But while the dynamism of the vegetative level remains almost entirely inaccessible to consciousness, the emotive dynamism, which will be more fully discussed below, seems very helpful in the psychical reproduction and vividness of various objects as well as of those that have been rejected by consciousness and the will.

Subconsciousness Shows Consciousness as the Sphere of Man's Self-realization

The remarks referring to subconsciousness are of special significance at this stage of our discussion when we are considering primarily the human being as the subject of acting and more generally as the subject of dynamism.

First, they clearly show the potentiality of the subject in the inner aspect itself.

Second, they help us to see at least to some extent, the inner continuity and cohesion of the subject; because it is seemingly subconsciousness that brings into view the transitions between, on the one hand, what only happens in man owing to the natural vegetative, and possibly also emotive activations and, on the other, what man consciously experiences and what he considers to be his actions. The continuity and cohesion exist within the frame of the subconscious, but they also span the gap between subconsciousness and consciousness. The threshold of consciousness not only divides the one from the other but it also connects them with each other.[35]

Third, subconsciousness, with its continuous relation to consciousness, allows us to see the human being as internally subjected to time and thus having his own internal history. This history is determined and formed to a great extent by factors in man's dynamic structure itself. Consciousness has often been compared with a stream of contents flowing continuously in the man-subject; by allowing us to better comprehend how this stream is related to the potentiality of the subject, subconsciousness shows indirectly where the springs to the histories of individual human beings are to be sought.[36]

Finally, in what is but a comment to the preceding point, we may say that subconsciousness brings out vividly the hierarchy of human potentialities. There is something highly significant in the constant drive toward the light of consciousness, in the constant urge emanating from the subconscious to attain the level of consciousness and to be consciously experienced. Hence both the existence of subconsciousness and the functions it performs indubitably indicate that consciousness is the sphere where man most appropriately fulfills himself. The subconscious is to a high degree shaped by consciousness, but otherwise it is only a repository where what is contained in the man-subject is stored and awaits to emerge in awareness. For it is then that it will also assume a fully human significance.

Let us add that the transfer to the domain of consciousness of moments captured in subconsciousness, and especially those hindered from coming to a genuine objectivization, stand out as one of the chief tasks of morality and education. This, however, is a problem that goes far beyond our present concern and will not be considered in this work.

8. MAN IN BECOMING: THE MANIFESTATION OF FREEDOM
IN THE DYNAMISM OF THE MAN-SUBJECT

The Being–Acting–Becoming Relation

So far in the analysis of the dynamism proper to man we have tried
first to identify and define its manifest differences and then to indicate
what are the necessary relations between dynamism and potentiality
in the man-subject. There is still another problem that we have to
examine. Every form of the dynamism we find in man, whether it be
acting, that is, action, or happening in its manifold forms here called
activation, is also associated with a certain form of becoming of the
man-subject. By "becoming" we mean such an aspect of the human
dynamism – whether it is the aspect of man's acting or the aspect of
what happens in him – that does not only center on man himself, the
subject of this dynamism, insofar as it introduces or carries on a
process of change. In point of fact, in all dynamizations the subject
does not remain indifferent: not only does it participate in them, as
demonstrated to some extent above, but it is itself in one way or another
formed or transformed by them. (At this point we will touch upon the
inner structure of the life-process itself.)

Thus our analysis brings us down again to the innermost dimension,
the dimension we refer to when speaking of the concrete ontological
nucleus of man. It is not a passive substratum but, on the contrary,
the first and fundamental level for the dynamization of the being that
is the personal subject; it is a dynamization by the process of
existence itself – by the very fact of existence. It is to this that in the
ultimate analysis we have to refer all becoming, the entire becoming
process occurring in the already existing man-subject. Indeed, to
come into existence is as much as to become. The initial, original
dynamization of the individual being as such is simultaneously the
first instance of becoming of the human being, his coming into
existence. All subsequent dynamizations due to any form whatever of
the becoming process do play the role of maintaining in existence the
already originated being. Nevertheless, in each subsequent dynamization something begins to exist in the man-subject that already is. In metaphysical terms, such coming into existence is accidental relatively to that original coming into existence which constitutes the being itself. Having come substantially into existence,

man changes one way or another with all his actions and with all that happens in him: both these forms of the dynamism proper to him make *something* of him and at the same time they, so to speak, make *somebody* of him. An analysis of the human dynamism ought to exfoliate this becoming. In the metaphysical analysis it is this aspect that is first of all brought into prominence. It is only indirectly that the act as such tells us of man's acting or of what happens in him, but it very adequately indicates any definite instance of change, trans-formation – that is, of becoming – of the man-subject himself or of his faculties.

The Subject's Differentiated Potentiality and the Corresponding Spheres of Man's Becoming and Development

In the present analysis the question of the becoming of man comes to the fore, the becoming that is referring to the whole human dynamism. As it may be easily seen, every form of the dynamism is in some way more or less directly connected with a different form of becoming; the becoming of man is internally differentiated and depends on the form of the dynamism that contributes to the whole process of becoming as well as on the potentiality on which the dynamism is grounded. At an earlier stage of the discussion a line was drawn dividing the somato-vegetative from the psychoemotive dynamism and at the same time separating the two levels of the potentiality proper to the human subject. Now we may add that the becoming takes place, as it were, on two different levels, which correspond to the two levels of potentiality and the related dynamisms. First, there is the becoming of man at the somato-vegetative level. During all life the human organism undergoes change: first there is growth and development, then come exhaustion and gradual dying away. These changes are visible with the naked eye. But our knowledge of the human organism allows a much more precise definition of its becoming when connected with the poten-tiality and the dynamism at the somato-vegetative level. We know, for instance, that the physicochemical composition of all tissue cells is completely exchanged every few years. The natural activities of the organism consist not only in self-sustenance but also in permanent reconstruction. We do not need, however, to go into such details here, this being the task of the particular sciences. Our main question is not how the organism is built, which in itself is highly interesting, but how it is integrated in the person and how the dynamism proper to it is integrated in the actions of a person, in the conscious acting of man.[37]

Let us now turn to the psychoemotive dynamism and the level of the human potentiality at which it develops in the man-subject. Also at this level there is a corresponding specific type of becoming, a becoming and psychical development of man. We may think of it and discuss it by analogy with the becoming of the human organism. An attempt to comprehend the psychoemotive type of becoming of man will be made later in a separate chapter. At present it suffices to say that both kinds of becoming – one connected with the vegetative potentiality and dynamism of the organism, and the other with the psychoemotive potentiality and its corresponding dynamism – depend on a certain passiveness in man. It is the kind of passiveness pertaining only to that which happens in man and to that which we see in the causation of nature itself and not to that conscious efficacy which involves the causation of the person. In this connection, however, we have to note at once that the manner in which the vegetative dynamism remains receptive and accessible to conscious influence differs entirely from that of emotive dynamism. The human organism determines almost entirely its own development, and only the conditions of the development are established by man. The situation is the opposite in the psychoemotive sphere, which itself establishes the conditions and, as it were, supplies the material for its own development; consequently, the formation of this sphere mainly depends on the human person.

Actions Make Man Good or Bad

The formation of the psychoemotive sphere brings us to that aspect of the type of becoming human which will next receive our attention. It is man's actions, his conscious acting, that make of him *what* and *who* he actually is. This form of the human becoming thus presupposes the efficacy or causation proper to man. It is morality that is the fruit, the homogenetic effect of the causation of the personal ego, but morality conceived not in the abstract but as a strictly existential reality pertaining to the person who is its own proper subject. It is man's actions, the way he consciously acts, that make of him a good or a bad man – good or bad in the moral sense. To be "morally good" means to be good as a man. To be "morally bad" means to be bad as a man. Whether a man, because of his actions, becomes morally better or morally worse depends on the nature and modalities of actions. The qualitative moments and virtualities of actions, inasmuch as they refer to the moral norm and ultimately to the dictates of the conscience, are imprinted upon man by his performing the action.

The becoming of man in his moral aspect that is strictly connected with the person is *the* decisive factor in determining the concrete realistic character of goodness and badness, of the moral values themselves as concretized in human acting. Without in any way constituting the content of consciousness itself they belong integrally to the personal, human becoming. Man not only concretizes them in action and experiences them but because of them he himself, as a being, actually becomes good or bad. Moral conduct partakes of the reality of human actions as expressing a specific type and line of becoming of the man-subject, the type of becoming that is most intrinsically related to his nature, that is, his humanness, and to the fact of his being a person.

Freedom Is the Root of Man's Goodness or Badness

When we search deep into the integral structure of moral conduct and becoming, into the integral structure of man's becoming morally good or morally bad, we find in it the proper moment of freedom. It is in the structure of man's becoming, through his actions, morally good or bad, that freedom manifests itself most appropriately. Here, however, freedom is not only a moment; it also forms a real and inherent component of the structure, indeed, a component that is decisive for the entire structure of moral becoming: freedom constitutes the root factor of man's becoming good or bad by his actions; it is the root factor of the becoming as such of human morality. It also takes place in efficacy and thus plays a decisive role in man's acting. By being interwoven with efficacy, freedom and efficacy together determine not only acting or action itself, which are performed by the personal ego, but their moral goodness or badness, that is to say, the becoming of man morally good or bad as man.

The Moment of Freedom Emerges from the Analysis of Human Dynamism. Freedom and Efficacy of the Person

It is by means of the moral value which man crystallizes through actions as enhancing his own being that these actions, or man's conscious acting, are brought down to the exercise of the moment of freedom. This freedom is best visualized by the human being in the experience aptly epitomized in the phrase, "I may but I need not." It is not so much a matter of the content of consciousness alone as of a manifestation and actualization of the dynamism proper to a man. This dynamism is in the line of acting, and it is along this line that it becomes part of the efficacy of the personal ego but remains distinct from all that only happens in man. The manifestation and actualization of the dynamism proper to man must have its correlate in the potentiality of the man-subject. We call the correlate the *will*. Between the "I may" on the one hand and, on the other, the "I need not," the human "I want" is formed, and it constitutes the dynamism proper to the will. The will is what in man allows him to want.

The identification of freedom as the decisive moment of the experience of efficacy and at the same time as the factor that, on the one hand, actually constitutes the structure of "man-acts" and, on the other, distinguishes it structurally from all that only happens in man (from the structure of "something-happens-in-man") brings to a conclusion the present stage of our investigations into the dynamism of the human person. For it is the person that is the real subject of the dynamism – and so far as acting is concerned not just the subject but also the actor. The discovery of freedom at the root of the efficacy of the person allows us to reach an even more fundamental understanding of man as the dynamic subject. Conformably with our basic experience the totality of the dynamism proper to man is divisible into acting and happening (actions and activations). This distinction rests on the difference between the real participation of the will, as in conscious acting or actions, and the absence of the will. What happens only in man has no dynamic source; it lacks the element of freedom and the experience of "I may but I need not." In the perspective of the person and of his proper dynamism, that is, as dynamized by action, everything that happens in man is seen to be dynamized out of inner necessity without the participation of the moral becoming of man free from constraints, in this dynamism;

the moment of the dynamic transcendence is lacking however; the moment of freedom is immanent to the conditions of man's moral becoming and connected with the causation by nature. Action proper, on the other hand, exhibits – owing to the causation by the person – the transcending feature that passes into the immanence of the acting process itself: for acting also consists in the dynamization of the subject. The dynamic transcendence of the person is itself based on freedom, which is lacking in the causation of nature.

PART TWO

THE TRANSCENDENCE OF THE PERSON IN THE ACTION

THE PERSONAL STRUCTURE OF
SELF-DETERMINATION

1. THE FUNDAMENTALS OF THE PERSONAL STRUCTURE
OF SELF-DETERMINATION

In Self-Determination the Will Is Seen as an Essential of the Person

A complete description of the will cannot refer simply to the moment of "willing" alone, neither to the exercise nor to the experience of "I will," in which is contained the moment of freedom identifiable with the experience of "I may but I need not." Although these experiences are an essential element of the action – as well as of morality – the will and the inner freedom of man have still another experiential dimension. In it the will manifests itself as an essential of the person, whose ability to perform actions derives directly from the possession of this essential rather than from some inherent feature of the action performed by the person. It is even possible to reverse this relation and to say it is the person who manifests himself in the will and not that the will is manifested in or by the person. Every action confirms and at the same time makes more concrete the relation, in which the will manifests itself as a feature of the person and the person manifests himself as a reality with regard to his dynamism that is properly constituted by the will. It is this relation that we call "self-determination."

Self-determination is related to the becoming mentioned in the last section of the preceding chapter. It is that becoming of the person which both has its own specific nature which may be disclosed in a phenomenological way, and indicates its own, separate ontic identity, while in morality it stands out as an existential fact characteristic of man. This is why in the conclusion to the preceding chapter attention was drawn to morality. Self-determination, which is the proper dynamic basis for the development of the person, presupposes a special complexity in the structure of the person. Only the one who has possession of himself and is simultaneously his own sole and exclusive possession can be a person. (In a different order of things, the person as a creature may be seen as "belonging to God," but this relation does not eliminate or overshadow that inner relation of self-possession or self-ownership which is essential for the person. It is not without reason then that medieval philosophers expressed this relationship in the phrase, *persona est sui iuris.*)

Self-Determination Shows the Structure of Self-Governance and Self-Possession as Essential to the Person

Owing to the will, self-possession finds its manifestation and its confirmation in action. The simple experience of "I will" can never be correctly interpreted in the dynamic, complex whole without reference to man's specific complexity, which is introduced by self-possession and is proper only to the person. Self-determination is possible only on the ground of self-possession. Every authentically human "I will" is an act of self-determination; it is so not in abstraction and isolation from the dynamic personal structure but, on the contrary, as the deep-rooted content of this structural whole. Because "I will" is an act of self-determination at a particular moment it presupposes structural self-possession. For only the things that are man's actual possessions can be determined by him; they can be determined only by the one who actually possesses them. Being in the possession of himself man can determine himself. At the same time the will, every genuine "I will," reveals, confirms, and realizes the self-possession that is appropriate solely to the person – the fact that the person is his own judge.

Self-possession has as its consequence still another relation that occurs in the very structure of man as a person and is most strictly connected with the will. It is the relation of self-governance, which is indispensable for the understanding and the interpretation of self-determination. Self-governance may also be expressed in terms of a specific complex whole: the person is, on the one hand, the one who governs himself and, on the other, the one who is governed. "Self-governance" is here used in a different sense than the "self-control" of colloquial speech; self-control is the power to control oneself and applies only to one of the functions of the dynamism appropriate to man, to one of his powers or virtues, or to a set of these. Self-governance, on the other hand, is something far more fundamental and far more strictly related to the inner personal structure of man who differs from all other structures and all other existents in that he is capable of governing himself. Thus self-governance is man's power to govern himself and not only to control himself.

Self-Possession Is Presupposed in Self-Governance

Since man's power to govern himself is his distinctive property it presupposes self-possession and is in a way one of its aspects or its more concrete manifestations. The self-governance that is found in the person is possible only when there is self-possession that is proper to the person. Self-determination is conditioned by one as well as by the other. Both are realized in an act of self-determination, which is constituted by every real human "I will." Because of self-determination every man actually governs himself; he actually exercises that specific power over himself which nobody else can exercise or execute. In virtue of this self-determinating agency man is encapsulated, closed within his own "reasons." This network of exclusively his own "reasons" for life decisions makes him incommunicable to his fellowman. The actual meaning of the expression "incommunicable" has an even richer content than that with which we are here concerned, though this is also included in it. Man owes his structural "inalienability" (incommunicability) to the will to the extent to which self-governance is realized by the will, and in acting this is expressed and manifested as self-determination. If this structural trait of the whole person were to be left out of our discussion, it would be impossible to understand the will correctly and to interpret it adequately.

Indeed, it is impossible to understand or interpret the will except within the personal structure. It is only in this structure that it operates and can manifest its true nature. In nonpersonal beings, whose dynamism is achieved solely at the level of nature, there are no reasons for the existence of the will. Self-determination, on the other hand, is specific to the person; it is self-determination that at the level of the person binds together and integrates the different manifestations of the human dynamism. It also constantly constitutes, defines, and brings into view this level as such. Because of it, in experience – primarily in self-experience – man is given as the person. In self-determination the will is present first of all as the essential of the person and only then as a power.[38] When we consider this difference more fully below, its meaning will explain itself. Then also the relation between person and nature – as revealed by the experience of freedom that is contained in self-determination – will be seen more clearly.

2. AN ATTEMPT TO INTERPRET THE INTEGRAL DYNAMISM OF THE WILL

The Reference to the Ego as Object Is Essential to Self-Determination

Self-determination, that is, the will as an essential of the person rooted in self-governance and self-possession, reveals in the dynamic order the objectiveness of the person or, in other words, of every concrete, consciously acting ego. We are not concerned here solely with ontological objectiveness, with the fact a person is objectively and really a being, somebody actually existing, for this was the object of our account in the preceding chapter. What we are now concerned with is that in this action the person is, owing to self-determination, an object for himself, in a peculiar way being the immanent target upon which man's exercise of all his powers concentrates, insofar as it is he whose determination is at stake. He is in this sense, the primary object or the nearest object of his action.

Every actual act of self-determination makes real the subjectiveness of self-governance and self-possession; in each of these interpersonal structural relations there is given to the person as the subject – as he who governs and possesses – the person as the object – as he who is governed and possessed. This objectiveness is, as may be seen, the correlate of the person's subjectiveness and, moreover, seems to bring out in a specific manner subjectiveness itself. At the same time, this objectiveness constitutes an essential correlate of that complexity which, together with the structure of self-governance and self-possession, manifests itself in man, in the human person.

The objectiveness we are now considering is realized by and also manifested in self-determination. In this sense we may speak of an "objectification" that is introduced together with self-determination into the specific dynamism of the person. This objectification means that in every actual act of self-determination – in every "I will" – the self is the object, indeed the primary and nearest object. This is contained in the concept itself, and the term expressing it – "self-determination" – means that one is determined by oneself. The concept as well as the word expressing it contain simultaneously and correlatively both the subject and the object. The one as well as the other is the ego.

Nevertheless, the objectification of the subject does not have an intentional character in the sense in which intentionality is to be found in every human willing. When I will, I always desire something. Willing indicates a turn toward an object, and this turn determines its intentional nature. In order to turn intentionally to an object we put the object, as it were, in front of us (or we accept its presence). Obviously it is possible to put in this position our own ego as the object and then to turn to it by a similar volitional act, the act of willing. But this kind of intentionality does not properly appertain to self-determination. For in self-determination we do not turn to the ego as the object, we only impart actuality to the, so to speak, ready-made objectiveness of the ego which is contained in the intra-personal relation of self-governance and self-possession. This imparting of actuality is of fundamental significance in morality, that specific dimension of the human, personal existence which is simultaneously both subjective and objective. It is there that the whole reality of morals, of moral values, has its roots.

Objectification Is More Fundamental than the Intentionality of Volitions

The objectification that is essential for self-determination takes place together with the intentionality of the particular acts of the will. When I will anything, then I am also determined by myself. Though the ego is not an intentional object of willing its objective being is contained in the nature of acts of willing. It is only thus that willing becomes self-determination. Self-determination does not mean merely proceeding from the ego, as the source and initial point of willing and choice; it means also the specific returning to that same ego which is its primary and basic object and with regard to which all intentional objects – everything and anything one wills or wants – are in a way more remote, transitory and just as external. The most direct and innermost is the objectiveness of the ego, that is, of the ego's own subject. This subject is formed by man in one way or another when he desires an object, a value of some kind. At this point we touch upon the innermost personal reality of the action: by *forming his ego in one way or another man becomes someone or someone else.* This shows how deeply rooted is the objectification referred to here, that is to say, the objectiveness of self-determination:[39] the objectiveness of the ego in self-determination.

The tendency toward this objectification is contained as a function of self-determination in the dynamism of the will, but its foundations reach down to the structure itself of the person to self-governance and self-possession. Mention was already made of the impossibility of understanding and interpreting correctly the will without a clear idea of the way in which it proceeds from the structure of the person, in the specifically personal structure of the human being. It would be impossible to present the peculiar dynamism of the will if we were to refer only to the intentionality of the particular volitions. Willing as an intentional act, that is to say, an experience directed toward its proper object, which may be defined both as an end and as a value, differs from the experience of "I will" in its full content. For the experience of "I will" contains also self-determination and not only intentionality. The turning to any external object that is seen as an end or a value implies a simultaneous fundamental turn toward the ego as the object.

Self-Determination and the Distinction between the Experiences of "I will" and "I am willing"

Volition as an intentional act is embedded in the dynamism of the will only to the extent self-determination is contained in it. Introspection informs us of various types of volition that arise in man's interior life and are authentic intentional acts but which are not embedded in the proper dynamism of the will. We may then say that some kind of volition is "happening" in the subject even when man does not will – it does not emerge with the experience "I will." An important point to note in this connection is that it lies in the nature of the experience of "I will," in the nature of the will itself, that it never consists in something that only happens in man; on the contrary, it always occurs as an instance of "acting," indeed, is the very core of every acting. It is the person as such that is then "active." All the same, volitions, including those that are not within the frame of self-determination, are – according to the phenomenological conception – intentional acts. We see them directed toward a value which they adopt as their end; their directing toward it may sometimes be very acutely experienced and, for instance, their "appetitive" character then becomes specially evident. Even such acuteness is, however, insufficient to ascertain the will. This situation becomes clearer when we compare the experience of "I will" with that of "I want." In either case we deal with a type of volition, but only the former contains in it the true dynamism of the will.

The Experience of "I will" Reveals the Transcendence of the Person in the Action

The dynamism of the will cannot be reduced to volition with its specific intentionality. An essential trait of this dynamism is that it involves the person in its own specific structure of self-governance and self-possession. It is thus that every genuine "I will" reveals the person's transcendence in the action. The significance of this transcendence, noted in the preceding chapter, will here be submitted to a more comprehensive analysis. At any rate, it is connected with self-determination and the objectification peculiar to self-determination and not solely with the human ego's "subjectiveness" or the intentionality of volitions that arise within the ego and are directed outward to various values as their goal.

The term "objectification" is here used to bring to attention the objectiveness of the ego itself, the objectiveness that manifests itself every time man says "I will." In philosophical and psychological tradition the tendency seems to have prevailed to consider the human willing somewhat one-sidedly, mainly from the point of view of the outside object, emphasis being laid on the "willing of something," rather than from that of the inner objectiveness, of the simple willing itself. From the latter point of view human willing has special significance first for the philosophy of the person – in our considerations the acting person – and then in a more distant perspective for personalistic ethics. Occasionally one should be attentive not to confound in the consideration of action as human action, the acting person with the action of the person. This is by no means a mere play on words but a meaningful distinction relevant to the interpretation of the action. The problem lies in defining how the human act, the action, is the real act of the person; for in it not only is an individual rational nature actualized, but also an act is performed – as evidenced in experience – by the unique individual person. The performing of an action is at once the fulfillment of the person. Here "fulfillment" may be regarded as having a correlative meaning with "actualization" and thus with the metaphysical meaning of the term "act." Nevertheless, experience, intuition, and the phenomenological analysis connected with it allow us to take a new look at the person–action relation, and this may play an important and fruitful role in the interpretation of the action as the act of the person.

In Self-Determination the Reference to the Ego as Object Is Influenced by Consciousness

From the metaphysical point of view the person is both the object and the subject. He is an objective being or somebody – a being existing as "somebody" in contrast with all other beings existing as "something" – at the same time he is his own ontological foundation, which means he exists as the subject of his own structures and dynamisms. Already in the discussion of the preceding chapter, in which we dealt with the person and the action in relation to the general dynamism of man, we noted that in the person we had to consider a kind of synthesis of efficacy and subjectiveness. Since we are now considering the integral dynamism of the will we have first to gain a deeper insight into the problem of efficacy. This will bring us to view, as it were, a new dimension of the synthesis of efficacy and subjectiveness; for we shall now see the objectiveness appropriate to efficacy, the dynamic core of which consists in self-determination identifiable with the experience of "I will." Self-determination puts the ego, that is to say, the subject, in the place of the object. Thus simultaneously it effects the objectiveness of the ego in subjectiveness.

The objectification of the ego that is derived from self-determination has as its correlate in the integral dynamism of the will, and also in the specific structure of the person himself, the subjectification that consciousness reveals in the personal structure. The person, so far as he is a specific existent possessing consciousness, lives in his own peculiar fashion (to "live" is here understood in the sense of the vital existence of living beings); he lives – or exists – not only in his own reflection, the mirrored image the person has of himself, but also in that specific self-experience which is conditioned by the reflexive function of consciousness. Owing to this function the man-person has the experience of himself as the subject, as the subjective ego. The experience of his own subjectiveness is, as it were, superimposed on the "metaphysical subjectiveness" of the human ontological foundation.

Although objectification is brought about by the will as self-determination, this takes place within the frame or, we may perhaps say, in the current of the simultaneous, actual subjectification by consciousness. After all, man has the experience of each of his willings, of every act of self-determination, and this makes of it a thoroughly subjective fact. We then see the subject as if it were ceaselessly disclosed in its innermost objectiveness; we witness the disclosing, so to speak, of the objective constructing of the ego's own subject. When consciousness brings all this into the orbit of experience, then the inner objectiveness of the action, the objectification proper to self-determination, stands out sharply in the profile of the full subjectiveness of the person who experiences himself as the acting ego. Then the person, the acting ego, also experiences the awareness that *he is the one who is determined by himself* and that *his decisions make him become somebody*, who may be good or bad – which includes at its basis the awareness of the very fact of his being somebody.

The Will Is Governed by the Objectifying Function of Cognition

While it is true that the experiencing of self-determination is conditioned by consciousness, there are no grounds to suppose that it is also guided by consciousness. In point of fact, the guidance of the cognitive function, which is indispensable in self-determination, in the dynamization of the will (as confirmed by experience and supported by philosophical tradition as well as empirical psychology), should on no account be confused either with the mirroring or the reflexive function of consciousness. The last of these functions plays an important role in objectification, which has an essential significance for man. The guidance of the cognitive function, on the other hand, has an objectifying character. Thus, if self-determination and the whole dynamism of the will are to be guided by anything (this applies first of all to the intentionality of the will, to its orientation toward values or aims in general), then this can only be self-knowledge together with man's whole knowledge of the existing reality, in particular, his knowledge of values as possible ends and also as the basis of the norms that he refers to in his acting.

The objectiveness of self-determination and volition can only be correlated with the objectiveness of cognition. It is only by its objectifying function that cognition guides the will: nothing may be the object of will unless it is known. In its subjectifying function of consciousness, on the other hand, it accompanies the will and supplements it within the framework of the specific structure presented by the person, but it does not guide or control the will. Failure to recognize this fundamental difference leads inevitably to solipsism, subjectivism, and idealism, that is, to a situation in which the subject seems lost in its own specific reality or objectiveness. This assertion also has a vital significance for the interpretation of the action. When speaking of conscious acting we stress primarily and basically the guiding function of cognition in acting and not only the awareness or the aspect of consciousness that accompany it.

The Dialectics of Objectification and Subjectification Appropriate to the Integral Dynamism of Will

This is how the acting person – the person acting consciously – reveals himself as a specific synthesis of objectiveness with subjectiveness. Looking at the two – as representing the "inner" and "outer" aspect of the integral human experience – and taking into account the experience of morality, we come to the conclusion that objectification and subjectification mutually supplement and in a way balance each other out. In this sense consciousness supplements and is the counterpoise of self-determination and vice versa. While consciousness, as was already asserted in Chapter 2, brings with it subjectification as well as a certain measure of inwardness; self-determination introduces also some outwardness.

The Immanent Act Is Also an External Manifestation of the Person

Every action is an external manifestation of the person, even when it is wholly performed internally. But an action confined strictly in its process as well as manifestations to the performing subject alone may be called an "immanent act." Such action does not even involve anything of what in man makes his acting externally manifested and discernible. An act that carries the features of a manifestation external to the performing subject has been termed by some contemporary philosophers "transcendent." But the external discernibility is not the only, and even less the best, test of that outwardness with regard to the person which we assert in the action. For the person is not only objectified in every one of his actions but also manifests himself externally even if its actions have, from the point of view of the criterion of discernibility, all the traits of immanence. On the other hand, parallel to the subjectification due to consciousness every action, however external it may appear, also remains to a certain degree immanent to the subject who performs it. We now see that the synthesis of objectiveness with subjectiveness is thus projected in the dynamic image of the person as the synthesis of externality with immanence.

3. FREE WILL AS THE BASIS OF THE TRANSCENDENCE OF THE ACTING PERSON

Self-Determination Reveals Freedom as a Uniquely Personal Factor

The preceding discussion allows us to grasp the fundamental significance of the free will. We may now identify freedom with self-determination, with the self-determination we discover in the will as a constitutive element of the personal structure of man. Freedom thus manifests itself as connected with the will, with the concrete "I will," which includes, as noted, the experience of "I may but I need not." In the analysis of self-determination we reach right down to the very roots of the experience of "I will" as well as of "I may but I need not." The freedom appropriate to the human being, the person's freedom resulting from the will, exhibits itself as identical with self-determination, with that experiential, most complete, and fundamental organ of man's autonomous being.

We are thus considering freedom as real, the freedom that constitutes the real and privileged position of man in the world and also the main condition of his will. This premise is of essential significance, inasmuch as any discussion concerning the free will, if it starts with the concept of freedom as such instead of the reality that is man risks deviating into an unwarranted idealism.[40] The fact of self-determination and all that self-determination relies upon in the structure itself of the person, namely, self-governance and self-possession, provides the key to the reality of the person we are attempting to reach. Indeed, self-determination manifests itself as the force holding together the human dynamism and integrating it at the level of the person. We may now distinguish between the dynamism at the level of the person and the dynamism at the level of nature. The latter does not seem to contain the necessary factors for self-determination, and we may thus conclude that neither does it contain any acting in the sense we have established in the preceding chapter.

The Difference between the Dynamisms of Self-Determination and Instinct

Let us reaffirm that at the level of the dynamism of nature itself there is no acting, there are no actions, but only what, strictly speaking, we may call "activations"; at this level there is in every particular instance a specific sum total of all that is taking place in the subject and that forms the distinct whole of its life and of its dynamism. The formation of this whole is oriented in a certain direction or along a kind of bioexistential axis, which depends on the natural endowment of every individual being or on its potentiality. Thus nature may to some extent be identified with the potentiality that lies at the origin of activations themselves. The significance of "nature," however, is broader than the sphere of activations alone and extends also, or even primarily, to the direction of, or the general trend in, the integration of these activations. Thus all that happens in an individual being bears the mark of some purpose, which depends on this direction. The subjective basis for both the integration and the purpose at the level of nature is called – especially in animals – "instinct." Instinct is not to be confused, in spite of close similarity of meaning, with drive, which will be considered in some detail later.

It is by instinct that in an individual animal everything that, strictly speaking, only happens in it receives direction and is brought together into a whole, which may give the impression of acting even though it is – however splendid in its own way it may appear – but a coordination of activations. Acting – the action in the strict sense, that is, in the sense that finds justification solely in the total experience of the human being – can be spoken of only in the case of self-determination. When, however, instinct is the guiding force we only have a certain external analogy with acting; the operating dynamism has the semblance of acting but does not satisfy the essential conditions of acting, of the action.

The reasoning just presented in order to introduce some necessary comparisons leads us further afield than the experience of man alone, it brings us, as explicitly stated, to the world of animals. The problem in itself has many, obviously interesting, aspects but this is not the place to consider them in detail. The point to be made here in connection with these comparisons is that the dynamism at the level of nature is in opposition to the dynamism at the level of the person, and that the cause of this opposition is the fact of self-determination. In the dynamism at the level of nature there is no self-determination to serve as the basis from which acting itself as well as its direction and purpose are derived. The dynamism at the level of nature lacks that special dependence on the ego which is the characteristic mark of the specific dynamism of the person.

Free Will Reflects the Self-Dependence of the Person

It is the dependence of acting on the ego that serves as the basis of freedom, while the absence of this dependence places the whole dynamism of any individual being (say an animal being) beyond the sphere of freedom. "Necessity" is the conceptual equivalent of the lack of freedom. Necessity as the opposite of freedom – which owing to self-determination is exclusively "personal" – is thus attributed to the dynamism at the level of nature alone, the dynamism that has instinct as its integrating factor. The person is dynamized in his own manner only when in the dynamization he depends on his ego. This is precisely what is contained in the experiential essence of self-determination and what conditions the experiencing of efficacy. In this case efficacy derives from freedom.

Special note should be taken of the fact that the fundamental significance of man's freedom and of his free will, elucidated in its concrete exercise and experience, brings to the forefront the relational network establishing the exercise of its dynamism in its essential dependence on the ego. It is at this point that the realism of experience belies the idealism of pure abstraction: for taken in abstraction from the concrete notions among the elements of the person, freedom may be seen as epitomized by "independence" from all possible factors. Actually, however, the reverse is true. The lack of the relational concatenations of numerous factors within and with reference to the structure of the man-person in its dependence on the ego in the dynamization of the subject precludes the freedom of human action; this latter has then no proper groundwork to emerge from by its own proper mechanism. It is here that there runs the intuitive, best evidenced line dividing within a primitive type of experience the person from nature, the world of persons from the world of individuals (e.g., animal individuals), whose whole dynamism is limited to the level of nature. In this last case the distinctive trait is the lack in their dynamization of a necessary connection with the ego. In point of fact, the structure of mere individuals differs from that of the person. We do not find in it the structural-dynamical complexes which we have earlier identified as "self-governance" and "self-possession" and which form the structural condition of self-determination. At the level of nature, the dynamism of the individual flows in and is absorbed by the potentiality of its own subject, which consequently establishes the direction of dynamization (e.g., instinct is a manifestation of nature's directing the functioning of an individual as well as of the actualization of this supremacy).

Such a structural connectedness is possible chiefly due to the absence of the ego. In fact, within natural species as such there are only individuals but no constituted egos. The necessary factor in constituting the ego, that is, the person in his strictly experiential profile and content, is the presence of consciousness and self-determination. It is through self-determination that the transcendence of the person in the action is justified, whereas the action itself is constituted as the *act* of the *person* (which we have clearly differentiated from the *acting person*). Action so understood reveals the experiential moment of the relation and dependence upon the ego, in which consists, first, the very foundation of personal freedom. With freedom it accounts, second, for the *person's transcendence in the action*.

The Contextual Meaning of the Transcendence of the Person

At this stage it seems necessary to examine the idea of "transcendence" more closely – in particular, the sense in which the term is used in this study. Etymologically "transcendence" means to go over and beyond a threshold or a boundary (*trans-scendere*). This may refer to the subject's stepping out of his limits toward an object, as is in different ways the case in what is known as intentional acts of external ("transcendent") perception. The manner in which the subject transgresses his limits in this type of cognitive act differs from his outgoing in acts of willing, whose character is conative. Later in our study we will consider in more detail the characteristic features of the particular intentional acts. Transgressing the subject's limits in the direction of an object – and this is intentionality in the "external" perception or volition of external objects – may be defined as "horizontal transcendence." But it is not the kind of transcendence we are concerned with when speaking of the transcendence of the person in the action (though, as we shall see later, the other is also involved). The transcendence we are now considering is the fruit of self-determination; the person transcends his structural boundaries through the capacity to exercise freedom; of being free in the process of *acting*, and not only in the intentional direction of willings toward an external object.[41] This kind of transcendence we shall call "vertical transcendence," in contrast to the other kind of transcendence that we have called horizontal.

Thus conceived, transcendence as an essential of the person can be best characterized by comparing the dynamism of the person with the dynamism of nature. First, concerning the person, self-determination accounts for the dominant position of the ego. This dominance serves as a kind of guide line. In contrast, there is no such domination in an individual who is but the subject of activations coordinated by instinct. On the one hand, by analogy with the expression "the acting person," we should use the expression "the acting individual." On the other hand, the adequate and fundamental formulation of the action finds its expression in "human action" which only by analogy can be tentatively transposed to nonpersonal individuals as "individual action," though in fact there is nothing to justify this definition. Acting, the action, in the strict sense cannot occur where there are no means to make one's dynamization depend on the ego.

The Rolè of the Objectification of the Ego in the Structure of Freedom

The fundamental significance of man's freedom, of the exercise of his "free will," forces us to see in freedom first of all that special self-reliance which goes together with self-determination. To say that man "is free" means *that he depends chiefly on himself for the dynamization of his own subject.* Hence the fundamental significance of freedom presupposes the objectification which we discussed earlier. The precondition of freedom is the concrete ego, which while it is the subject is also the object determined by the acts of will. The dynamism at the level of nature alone, to which we refer as an illustrative comparison, does not manifest that objectiveness of the subject. This deficiency was already asserted on the occasion of the analyses in the preceding chapter, where the distinction was drawn between subjectiveness and efficacy. We noted then that the ontological foundation when there is something only happening in it, manifests subjectiveness alone; but when it acts it manifests its subjectiveness together with efficacy. As the efficacy is based on self-determination and as the subject efficaciously determines itself, it is then also its own object. This is how objectification enters into the fundamental significance of freedom: it conditions the self-reliance.

4. THE SIGNIFICANCE OF THE WILL AS THE PERSON'S POWER OF SELF-DETERMINATION

Autodeterminism Conditions Independence in Relation to Intentional Objects of Volition

Having indicated the fundamental significance of freedom we may now consider it in greater detail. Indeed, we discover the structure of freedom in volitions as intentional acts directed toward a value as their end. This structure is not confined solely to the willing itself in the act "I will" but comprises the whole sequence "I will something." It is here that we come upon a specific independence of the act of will from its object. For if we just want one thing or another – an X or a Y – then we experience an intentional directing toward the object as the freedom from compulsion or necessity: thus I may, but I need not, desire the object of my willing. But on the contrary, once our willing is set on object X or Y that has been presented to it, then obviously we are already, so to speak, past the threshold of choice and decision. Our willing now has a *definite* object – it has its value-end – and has thus been determined; if it were not, it would be but *hesitant*. Nevertheless, even in this determination the experience of "I may, but I need not" is somehow continued; the definition of value as the end or aim of conation does not abolish altogether my intrinsic independence from the object of volition.

Before we examine further the significance of freedom, we have to emphasize that this inner independence of the ego in relation to the intentional objects of volition (i.e., the value-end) is justified by self-reliance. Thus any interpretation of the free will, if it is to conform to reality, must rely on man's *autodeterminism* instead of floating in the air by stressing merely *indeterminism*. It is clearly visible in the structure of experience that in the interpretation of the functional aspect of freedom indeterminism assumes a secondary role while autodeterminism has primary and fundamental significance. This approach is strictly related to the main current of our entire discussion, in which the will has been shown as manifesting itself first of all in self-determination; the will is indeed a mode of functioning of the person and is firmly rooted in the structure of self-governance and self-possession.

The Dynamism of Self-Determination Consists in Man's Use of the Will

Experience discloses that will is not only a property of the person but is also a power.[42] The will then appears like another experiential aspect of the same reality. For we call "will" not only what reveals and actualizes the structure of self-governance and self-possession but also what man resorts to, and even in a way makes use of, in order to achieve his aims. From this point of view, the will is subordinate in relation to the person, and does not determine or govern the person. The experience of the subordination of the factor of will to the complete set up of the person is also important for understanding the problem of freedom. The expression "free" will does not mean some kind of independence of will from the person. If we agree that the freedom of will manifests itself in experiencing that "I may but I need not," then it expresses the person who *may* but need not use his freedom as a power. This is precisely the reason why the first stage in the crystallization of the free will within the personal functioning is the primary and elementary fact that flows from the person, or from the person's power of self-determination. Thereby the elementary manifestation of free will simultaneously brings to light the person's exclusive power to control the will. Independence appears there as reliance of man upon external conditions constituted and formed through his immanent structure of self-reliance and the indeterministic feature of will through man's intrinsic structure of his autodetermination. It is because of the person's exclusive power over the will that *will is the person's power to be free.*

The interpretation of the will as a power, as proceeding from as well as serving the person to achieve self-determination, which is simultaneously a striving toward a value-end, brings us back to the discussion of the preceding chapter on the interrelation of dynamism and potentiality. It is to the will that the person owes his specifically human form of dynamism, the dynamism of self-determination, and the dynamism of the human action. This dynamism must have as its correlate an appropriate potentiality. When in the terms of traditional philosophical anthropology we say will is a power, it is this poten- tiality that we have in mind. Such potentiality is contained – according to the same traditional terms – in the rational nature of man. But "rational nature" has real existence solely and exclusively as a person. The will is dynamized in a way in which only a person could accomplish it – in a way in which nature alone could not. To conclude then, we can assert that freedom is the specific factor through which the person is dynamized, while the dynamization of nature we have attributed solely to the instinct.

The Meaning of the Instinct of Freedom

Within the dynamism appropriate to the person and his acting we may also detect the "instinct of freedom." But the phrase may be used only in a metaphorical sense. It then denotes that, for the person, self-determination is something absolutely proper and innate, even something "natural" – after all, we do speak of the nature of the person. On the one hand, when a person is acting, he is "dynamized" within the functional system of self-determination and will; they manifest themselves in their specific way spontaneously and so to speak, "instinctively" in his acting. On the other hand, the person as such repudiates a merely instinctive acting, since his dynamism, as we have attempted to show, is neither directed nor integrated by instinct.

The Meaning of the Phrase "Man's Instinctive Acting"

Probably not even when man himself refers to his acting as instinctive can we regard his dynamism as functioning solely at the level of nature. For instance, he *instinctively* turns away from danger or pain and he instinctively reaches for food when hungry. It would be difficult to interpret this kind of instinctive acting without an analysis of the notion of "drive" in the sense in which it occurs in man. First, we have to assert that man not only acts but is also the subject of all that happens in him. Much light is shed on this problem by the drive aspect connected with bodily potentiality and also with the natural emotivity of man (these will be more fully discussed below). At any rate, neither potentiality nor impulsions are to be identified with instinct as the factor integrating the dynamism of an individual and determining its direction. It seems therefore that very often when speaking of man's instinctive acting we actually refer to an enhanced spontaneity or even a greater intensity of acting with a simultaneous decline in the clarity of self-determination. Self-determination is identifiable with deliberate choice and decision; "spontaneity" or even "impulsive acting" may, on the contrary, be interpreted as an orientation of the drive itself insofar as it is connected with the bodily potentiality (or even some tendency to emotiveness).[43] It is through the predominance of this orientation that conscious decisions are limited and may be sometimes blocked out.

The potentiality of the will is set off and enhanced in conscious choice and decision; it *is* the power of conscious choice and decision. This is the point of view we take in the discussion that follows. But marginally to what has been said about man's instinctive acting, we have first to note that, although self-determination is appropriate and even natural to the person, there is in man a certain tension between, on the one hand, his will as the power of self-determination – the power of deliberate choice and decision – and, on the other, his bodily potentiality, emotiveness, and impulsions. Experience tells us that it is in this tension rather than the simple and pure self-determination that consists the lot of man. Only in the perspective of this tension can we see the complex nature of the dynamism of the human person.

5. DECISION IS THE FOCUS OF THE ACTIVITIES OF FREE WILL

Transcendence versus Appetite

The remainder of this chapter will be almost entirely concerned with the extended significance of freedom, and we shall thereby continue to constructively complete our image of the person. This image emerges more completely alongside the increasing prominence given to the transcendence in the action which, owing to freedom, that is, self-determination, is the privilege of the person. Because of the fact itself of being free – the fact of self-determination and its related ascendancy over the human dynamism – we call this transcendence "vertical." The experience of this ascendancy is not impeded by the spontaneity of freedom, though the ascendancy is perhaps better marked when there is more reflectiveness in self-determination, in the rational maturation of decisions. At any rate, now that we are equipped with a more or less clearly defined notion of "vertical transcendence," we can embark upon a deeper analysis of the will. The consecutive steps of this analysis will, so to speak, unveil deeper and deeper levels of that transcendence of the acting person in which the person's structure, in its existential status of reality, is manifested experientially. The outer, overlying layers of this reality, those we can uncover and objectify first, are conditioned by the inner ones, and as we proceed in depth each will tell us more about the person, about his specific structure. They will allow us to define more and more fully the person's specificity and his spiritual nature.

This procedure for the analysis of will and, at the same time, the in-depth study of the person's inner structure, seems to differ in some respects from the traditional approach, in which the will seems to be viewed rather in the dimension of "horizontal" transcendence. Some philosophers and psychologists in their discussions and analyses have treated it as if it were an "appetite." Their stand brought into prominence, not without reason, the will's characteristic urge toward good as its object and end. Thus the most important part of the analysis of the will was that which dealt with its intentionality, with the intentional acts or volitions whereby it was manifested and actualized. It seems, however, that an analysis of volitions themselves with all their variety of tone and all their modifications fails to bring us right down to the roots of the will. For these grow out – as we have been trying to demonstrate – from the structure of the person; and apart from this structure the will finds no justification. As to the intentionality of willings, the turn they manifest toward a value-end is insufficient to constitute or determine the will fully and comprehensively or to allow a sufficiently clear insight into the dynamism and potentiality appropriate to it.

Appetition, Intendedness, and Intentionality

Special note ought to be taken of the term "appetite," especially when used in conjunction with the attributive "rational." Its content with all its connotations has to be closely examined and properly grasped. There is in it the element of striving, and as striving is necessarily directed toward an end, appetite is intrinsically incident to an end. But there is also in appetite an element of desire, which, insofar as will is concerned, adds to the term a certain semantic convergence as well as a divergence. For desire, with its connotations, seems to point only in the direction of what is *happening* in man, to what lies beyond the range of his conscious decision. Thus from this point of view, to speak of "rational appetite" seems somewhat strange, almost a contradiction in terms, though at the same time the element of conation makes "appetite" more neutral and seems to offset the contradiction.

From the semantic point of view appetite can hardly be attributed to the will, at any rate, to the extent to which it retains any connotation of sensual passivity and as such originates and unfolds on its own, spontaneously, outside of conscious choice and decision. In this context questions of language and terminology are by no means futile; our purpose is to find a definition that would be in all respects adequate for every human willing or, more broadly speaking, for every "I will something," regardless of whether the desired object be *X* or *Y*. We are considering will as endowed with some features of "intentionality" that are appropriate to it but also with others diametrically different from the intentionality of cognition, of cognitive acts. We differentiate in fact between what could be termed "intention" and "intent."[44]

An intentional act of man's experience consists in being oriented or directed outward toward an object. Its "intention" is a special kind of going out toward an object, a motion in which the limits of the subject are overstepped. This takes place in acts of volition as well as in acts of cognition, of thinking. Being intentional the acts of thinking and volition resemble each other in that they are directed toward their object and thereby overstep the limits of the subject; but they differ in their whole specific nature. Beyond that, the act of will crystallizes into a peculiar "intent." In this respect "to know" or "to understand" and "to will" are dissimilar. It is the distinction between "tending toward something," on the one hand, and "being intent upon something," on the other. In either case the experience the subject has of being directed toward an object has entirely different consequences for the subject and for the object. In this study we view thinking as an "intentional act" *par excellence*, distinguishing it clearly from an "intended" act as expressing foremostly the manifestation of will. Having introduced these explanations we can proceed to examine the act of volition.

Decision as the Crucial Constitutive Moment in the Experience of "I will"

The first point to make is that the moment of decision always forms part of volition envisaged as an intentional act, that is to say, in the specific way in which the will is directed toward its appropriate object. This moment is an essential part of volition and is crucial for both the inner structure and the dynamic distinctness of volition. It is contained in what psychologists, such as Ach or Michotte, call a "simple volitive act" as well as in what is sometimes referred to as a "compound" or "expanded" act.[45] We shall later attempt an explanation of this distinction by examining the two kinds of volitive acts separately. At present it suffices to note that volition is present in our willing as its essential and constitutive moment, regardless of whether we simply want something or we choose something – that is to say, we want it at the conclusion of a process of motivation. Choice and decision define the intrinsic essence of volition (of "I will"), especially in what concerns its intentional attribution to an object ("I will either X or Y").

In true willing the subject is never passively directed to an object. The object – which may be a good or a value, though the meaning of these conceptions would require a separate differential analysis – never leads the subject back upon itself; it never forces the subject into its own reality thereby determining it from without; that kind of subject–object relation would in fact amount to determinism; it would mean that the subject was in a way absorbed by the object and also that innerness was absorbed by outerness. The moment of decision in the human will rules out any such pattern of relation. Thus when I will something, I myself am moving outward toward the object, toward whatever I will. We already saw that it is not the directing toward a value as such but the *being* directed that is appropriate to volition. The passive voice of "being directed" brings out very well the distinctness that results from the active engagement of the subject. It is here that we touch upon the root itself of the experiential difference between man's acting and the happening of what only occurs in man. The will is the factor of acting, of the action. The remarkable thing is that this is due to the mechanism of decision to which the will is essentially related. This relationship brings into full view the person in his efficacy as well as in his transcendence and, what is more important, it shows the person as a person.

Readiness to Strive toward Good Underlies All Volitive Decisions

Choice and decision are obviously no substitute for the drive toward good that is appropriate to will and constitutive of the multifarious dynamism of the human person. The greater the good the greater becomes its power to attract the will and thus also the person. The crucial factor in determining the maturity and the perfection of the person is his *consent* to be attracted by positive, authentic values, his unreserved consent to be drawn in and absorbed by them. But this makes it all the more necessary to stress that all the forms and degrees of such absorption or engagement of the will are made personal by the moment of decision.[46] Decision may be viewed as an instance of threshold that the person as a person has to pass on his way toward the good. Moreover, this personal outgoing has to continue throughout his absorption by the good, even when it may rightly appear that the human being will be literally engulfed by the good, by the glorified end of his striving. Indeed, the more he becomes engulfed, the more fundamental is his decision and vice versa. We may

also look upon this interpretation from another side: the consequences of the initial decision augment as the good is approached,
in the intercourse and union with it. But these consequences would
never be possible without the person's going beyond the threshold of
his own structural borderlines, transgressing his own limitations.

The will's ability to decide in no way condemns it to an attitude of
cool aloofness either toward its object or toward values. Indeed, there
are no grounds to assume that there is a neutral attitude to all values,
a kind of indifference to their attractiveness and to their visible
hierarchy in the world, lurking somewhere deep at the bottom of the
person, at the origin of all the dynamizations that are proper to the
will. On the contrary, it lies in the nature of every "I will" – which is
always object oriented and consists in an "I want something" – that it
is constantly prepared to come out towards a good. In a sense this
readiness is more primitive and more fundamental for the dynamic
essence of the will than the ability to make decisions; for the ability
presupposes a dynamic readiness to strive toward good. If however
we were to conceive of the will, of man's "I will," solely or even
primarily in terms of this readiness, then we would miss what in the
dynamism of the will is most essentially personal, what most strictly
binds the dynamism of will with the structure of the person and
through this structure allows us to exfoliate and interpret the nature
of the person.

6. RESPONSIBILITY IN THE ACTS OF WILL – MOTIVATION AND RESPONSE

What Is Motivation?

We have to continue, or rather take up again from the beginning, our
analysis of choice and decision, for it seems that so far we have only
outlined the significance of the problem without going into its structure. Thus we have now to consider the structure of human decisions.
But first we will examine in some detail the problem of motivation.
By motivation we mean the effect motives have on the will, and this
strictly corresponds to the intentionality of the will. When I want
something, I approach the object that is presented, or rather that
presents itself to my attention as a good and thus shows its value.

Presentation is an essential element of motivation, its correlate on the side of man being a specific kind of cognition. It is broadly speaking the cognition of values. But as is evidenced by the term "motive" itself, which etymologically is derived from the Latin *movere* ("to move"), more than this is contained in the notion of motive. We owe to motivation the impulsion, the movement of the will toward the object that is being presented – not just a turn toward it but an outright movement. To will means to strive after a value that thereby becomes an end. When Aristotle identified good with aim he only followed consistently in his reasoning the evidence available in elementary experience.

The subjective complexity of man requires precision and forces us to draw a sharp distinction between the impulsion of the will, which we owe to motivation, and emotions. This brings us to a very subtle boundary that runs within man and which may easily be overlooked if our in-depth vision is not sharp enough. We shall consider this boundary again when we come to the discussion of man's emotional life, of emotivity. Essentially, motives only stimulate the will but do not arouse emotions: they stimulate the will, which means that they stimulate man to will something, either X or Y. When I want something, I thereby simply will – even though our earlier considerations revealed a subtle difference between the one and the other. It is easy to establish that "I will" is something primary – like the foundation of the will – and durable in man, while the willing takes place in his intentionally directing himself toward different objects, this directing being secondary and variable. Motivation meets the variable intentionality of man's willing, it meets the possibility of attaching his willing to different objects that present themselves as values.

The Motivation of Simple Willing and the Motivation of Choice

When psychologists discriminate between the simple act of will and the compounded or expanded one, they do so essentially because in either case the motivations have a different form, and this entails two different forms of decisions appropriate to the will. A simple act of will corresponds to motivation of the kind in which the will is presented with only one object, only one motivating value. Then, because of the value presented in the object, man simply desires it, he experiences no internal split or doubts, he does not have to make a choice, which always entails a momentary suspension of the process of willing. We may then speak of an unequivocal motive and an unequivocal decision; for while choice is unnecessary there is still a decision to be made. The simple "I will something" or "I will X" is an authentic decision.

Far better than in a simple act of willing, the nature of decision is expressed and visualized when the choice is preceded by a more complex and developed process of motivation. Such is the case when the will is presented with more than one object as the end of possible striving, when it can choose from a number of values, which perhaps compete against each other or may even be mutually contradictory. Each of them in its own way seems to vie with the others in attracting the will and in trying to win the human "I will." Unequivocal decisions are then impossible, at least not before a separate process, which precedes and conditions the decision and is sometimes defined as the deliberation of motives. The process deserves a detailed analysis of its own, which we cannot give here, though we shall have to consider some of its most important elements. Such an analysis would have to include, on the one hand, the object of motives, that is to say the domain of values, which can be seen clearly only against the background of the deliberation of motives. On the other hand, it is necessary to examine the willing itself with all its specific complexity and potentiality; for there are many potential willings that appear to be taking part in the deliberation of motives, so that the will may address itself, or rather is ready to address itself, to any of the values that are presented. This indirectly confirms that the versatile and multifarious readiness of striving toward good is primary and fundamental in the dynamic essence of the will.

The Ability to Decide Is Seen in Choosing

In the deliberation of motives there is, besides the readiness, something akin to a momentary suspension of the process of willing. Not till the moment of decision, which in this case coincides with choice, can any one of the potential willings be actualized. In a simple decision there is no choice, because an unequivocal motive eliminates the need to choose. When motivation is complex each decision must become a choice. Man, then, not only has to decide to dynamize his own subject and thereby turn to an object, to some X or Y, but, in addition, has to decide to what object he is going to turn. It is this decision about the object of willing that we call "choice." And choice always entails the renunciation of a spectrum of objects, of possible values, for the sake of one single object or value. It also necessitates putting off some potential willings for the actual one. This one willing together with the chosen value forms a whole, in which the dynamic essence or nature of the will – and indirectly also the person in his transcendence – is visualized in a special way.

The one is interlinked with the other, and here again we find a confirmation of the view, which we have been emphasizing throughout this chapter, that the will is deeply rooted in the specific structure of the human person. In view of the whole process involved in an act of will, the deliberation of motives, and the suspension of willing, we come to the conclusion that what we call the "will" is not primarily connected with horizontal transcendence, with the subject's ability to go out toward the objects, which are the different values as objects of volition. What we call the "will" is primarily connected with the ability of decision, in which also the power to momentarily suspend willing in order to make a choice is contained. Thus the will is definitely included in the vertical transcendence, which is associated with self-governance and self-possession as the specific properties in the structure of the person. Indeed, it also determines and forms this transcendence. The ability to decide is more fully manifested in choice than in simple willing, though any "I choose" is also a definite "I will." We have thus a confirmation of the homogeneity of the will, notwithstanding the fact of the multiformity of the objectives of willing and also of the evolution in the forms that willing itself assumes according to whether motivation is simple or compound.

Considering the component itself of decision, which occurs in every act of will, whether simple or compound, we may say, on the one hand, that choice is willing expanded and enriched by the wealth of motivations and, on the other, that every simple willing is a choice reduced and simplified by the unambiguous plainness of motivation. For every time I make a decision, it has to be preceded by some sort of choice.

Free Will Manifests Itself in an Independent Determination of Objects

This brings us again to the question of freedom, which continues to be the object of our analyses in this chapter. It seems that in more than anything else, freedom is present and manifests itself in the ability to choose; for this ability confirms the independence of the will in the intentional order of willing. In choosing, the will is not cramped by the object, by the value as its end; it is the will and only the will that determines the object. This is how indeterminism enters into the formula of *autodeterminism*. Independence of the object, of the values as the end of willing, confirms for its part self-determination, which, so far as the grasping of the will is concerned, seems to be the most elemental experience of all. If, however, there was in man – within his whole accessible sphere of experience – anything that would allow his being determined in advance by the object in the intentional order, then self-determination would be impossible. Such determination would unavoidably abolish within the domain of the person the experience of efficacy and self-determination, the experience of decision or simply of willing. It would also mean the suppression of the person, insofar as in all these experiences he reveals himself and evidences his own existence. The person's existence is identical with the existence of a concrete central factor of freedom.

This freedom – the specific independence from objects in the intentional order, the ability to choose among them, to decide about them – does not, however, abolish the fact that man is conditioned in the broadest sense by the world of objects, in particular, by the domain of values. For his is not the freedom *from* objects or values, but, on the contrary, the freedom of, or rather *for* objects or values. We discover this meaning of freedom not only in the essence itself of the human "I will" but also in each of its forms. Willing is striving, and as such it carries in itself a form of dependence on objects, which does not however in any way abolish or destroy the independence that we find expressed in every simple willing and even more so in every choice – the independence that in either case is due to the fact of decision.

The Original Dynamism of Acts of Will Disproves Moral Determinism

There are those who, without due attention to the experiential nature of choice and decision, and on the grounds of the dependence on the world of objects alone, assert the existence of moral determinism; thus they reject freedom and indirectly also the person, indeed, the whole reality, that we have here defined as "the acting person." Determinism assumes its materialistic form when a certain pre-conception of matter tends to intervene into the interpretation of the experience of the person rather than to allow experience to present all its evidence to the end. This passing remark obviously cannot replace a full-scale discussion of the different materialistic treatments of determinism and this is not the place for it, the more so as our prime concern in this study is *to allow experience to speak for itself as best it can and right to the end.* As to the critical discussion of materialistic determinism, it suffices to consult any suitable handbook or treatise.

Besides the materialistic form of determinism there is also the view that associates determinism, which denies the freedom of the person, with what we have here accepted as the foundation of freedom or, to put it more concretely, as the condition of the decision present in every authentic "I will." Thus there is the line of thought that sees the irrevocable source of determinism in motivation, that is to say, in the presentation of the objects of will. According to this conception the will is restricted not by the object itself but by its presentation; inasmuch as man cannot desire an object without it being presented to him, his so-called choice in fact complies with the presentation; he chooses what is presented to him and how it is presented to him. For instance, if, as often happens, he chooses a lesser and passes by a greater good, this cannot be taken as evidence of free will, that is to say, an independence on objects, because interposed between the object and the will there is the presentation or motivation that definitely determines the direction of willing. Thus when as in our example man chooses a "lesser" good, he does so because *hic et nunc* it is presented to him as the "greater."

It seems, however, that hidden in this deterministic approach there is a far-reaching simplification, that it reduces the experience of the person to the point where the essentials are omitted or even sacrificed to a schematic pattern of thinking. In this connection much valuable service can be rendered by the phenomenological method with its suitability to exploit adroitly the available experiential data. The dynamic specificity appertaining to decision – whether in simple willing or in the more complex choosing – is essential in the will and is of the kind that makes impossible any determination. All determinism, not only by intentional objects (values) but also by the presentation of objects, is contrary to the original dynamism of decision. This is so because decision involves and reveals that relation to intentional objects as values which is proper solely to the will. The relation is to the object itself while presentation only establishes it and thereby enables and conditions decision. The deterministic thesis, that this relation is wholly constituted by presentation alone, fails to draw the distinction between the actual cause and a condition.

The Act of Will as the Person's Response to the Appeal of Values

Decision is connected with the dynamic structure of the "impulsion" that is essential in the will. The real cause of the impulsion is the good or value of the object, but the object has first to be presented. Presentation, however, does not in itself stimulate the impulsion of the will; it is, therefore, but a condition and can never be an essential factor either in determining or even in directing the impulsion. On the other hand, decision refers to objects themselves, to the presented values. It comprises not only a passive acceptance or assimilation of a presented value but also an authentic response to the value. Every instance of "I will" constitutes such an individual and unique response, which is specially apparent in every instance of choosing.

When the analysis of the will is conducted in the abstract, that is, when it is conducted so that will is viewed as if it were an independent reality – an entity in itself – this remarkable trait of its dynamism may easily be lost. But if we place the analysis of the will within the framework of the whole dynamic structure that is constituted by the person and based on self-governance and self-possession, then the will is exhibited as self-determination while its relation to intentional objects is clearly seen as an active response. The ability to respond to presented values is will's characteristic trait. In making a decision man always responds to values. In his responding there is that independence with regard to objects which does not abolish all the bonds and thus leaves a certain measure of dependence on objects. Nevertheless, it is not the objects and values that have a grip of man; on the contrary, in his relation to them he governs himself: he is his own master. The reflexive pronoun shows best the essential active element of will. The specific response to the values presented in motivation seems to be indicative of the proper active demand of the will and at the same time also of what constitutes the acting of the person, what distinguishes acting from any submission to action, which is the term we have been using from the beginning to define all that only takes place, only *happens* in the person.

7. THE MOMENT OF "TRUTH ABOUT GOOD" AS THE BASIS FOR THE ACTING PERSON'S PERCEPTION AND TRANSCENDENCE

Dynamic Structure of the Object Common to Cognition and Will

Our analyses seek to uncover deeper and deeper layers of the reality that is the action, while we continue to trace the primitive experience that allows us to distinguish between acting and happening in man. By asserting that the ability to respond to presented values is the characteristic trait of the will, which shapes the form of the process of acting, we uncover a new layer of our inquiry. It allows us to investigate the nature and conditions of the person which allow him to respond to the will. For in fact this responsiveness flows from the promptings of the intellectual sphere of the human person; it is in speech, implying thought, that we may see the first symptom of man's ability to respond either to values on the one hand or to the promptings of will on the other. The assertion that the active, dynamic ability to respond to values is a characteristic of the will, however, refers not only to a certain analogy between will and thought but also to the nature itself of the will. In traditional philosophy, from the great thinkers of the Middle Ages up to and including Leibniz, this nature of the will was conceived as the *appetitus rationalis*. This conception, which because of its conciseness and precision has become almost classical, allows us indeed to grasp that relation between will and cognition which has never ceased to be one of the most fascinating questions of philosophy and psychology.

It is expressed in the traditional view that nothing may become the object of will unless it is already known. The question still remains as to what is the common dynamic structure of the object as already known and as again object of the will.[47] We will attempt to disclose this common dynamic structure on our own account in order to see how much a clarification of the relation between cognition and will contributes to the overall vision of man, of the person, and at the same time how deeply it is itself rooted in this vision. In attempting to elucidate this relation we find all those traces of interpretative integration and disintegration which ultimately must lead us to experience as the prime source of our knowledge of man. This is the reason why in our study we had first to conceive of experience as the source of cognition and knowledge and only then to consider the way of exploiting it for explanatory purposes. For experience and understanding together constitute a whole, and interpretation is interchangeable with comprehending.

The Will's Reference to Truth as the Inner Principle of Decision

The remarkable feature in the interpretation of acting, of the action, that we are presenting in this study is that the person is already presumed in it; to unveil step by step the reality of action we have simultaneously to uncover the deeper layers of the person. The person's dynamic activation is, on the one hand, the primordial experiential fact and, on the other, the final theme and objective of interpretation, which we are gradually approaching. Can this theme be fully explored, and is this final objective attainable? Or is our investigation only a series of successive approximations leading progressively to a better, more complete unfolding of our object, which is the acting person, and at the same time confirming the assertion that the person as such in his complete nature is rationally ungraspable, inexpressible? This last assertion paraphrases the classical definition, *individuum est ineffabile*; but as the person is an individual, though also more than an individual, the paraphrase seems permissible. At any rate, the assertion will be confirmed by our analysis, even though in our study we are considering the person as such and not just some concrete individual, a person-individual, hoping to bring to light this approach as self-justified.

Having made these general remarks, which have reference to the introductory considerations and principles already outlined in Chapter 1, we have to go back to our analysis at the point where we left it.

The assertion of the specific nature of the will connected with the ability to decide and to choose allows us in turn to disclose another significant trait in the dynamism of the will: the reference to "truth." The reference to truth forms an intrinsic part of the very nature of a decision and is in a special manner manifest in choice. The essential condition of choice and of the ability to make a choice as such, seems to lie in the specific reference of will to truth, the reference that permeates the intentionality of willing and constitutes what is somehow the inner principle of volition. To "choose" does not mean to turn toward one value and away from others (this would be a purely "material" notion of choice). It does mean to make a decision, according to the principle of truth, upon selecting between possible objects that have been presented to the will. It would be impossible to understand choice without referring the dynamism proper to the will to truth as the principle of willing. This principle is, as we will see, intrinsic to the will itself, and at the same time constitutes the essence of choice. It is, also, by the same token, the essence of decision, and this includes also decisions with univocal motivations when only the so-called simple act of will is involved.

If striving for intentional objects according to the principle of the recognition of their validity as cognized were not to form part of the dynamic essence of the will, then it would be impossible to understand either choice or decision with all their dynamic originality. The hypothesis that the reference to truth has an entirely external origin, that it derives merely either from cognition – from a knowledge of the objects of choice – or simply from volition, is insufficient for the satisfactory interpretation of the relation between knowledge of the object of will and the act of will. Since it is owing to the knowledge of objects that the reference to truth is actualized, their knowledge is a necessary condition of choice and decision making; but the reference to truth, with all the originality proper to choice and decision making, is itself derived from the will and belongs to the will's own dynamism. The dynamism of will is not in itself cognitive; "to will" never means "to cognize" or "to know." It refers in a specific manner, however, and is internally dependent on, the recognition of truth. This is precisely the reason why it is accessible to cognition and specifically consistent with cognition. This in turn also explains the fact that in choosing and deciding, the will – and thus of course the person – *responds* to motives instead of being in one way or another only determined by them. The ability to respond is manifested by the "free will" conceived in the broad sense. From the above it seems evident that this response presupposes a reference to *truth* and not only a reference to the *objects* which elicit it.

The Will's Dependence on Truth and Independence of Objects

We have mentioned in our argument the will's "reference to truth" and also its accommodation to truth. These expressions adequately render the state of affairs that we are considering: for in the inner dynamism of will we discover a relation to truth that goes deeper and is different from the relation to the objects of volition. The relation to truth is not restricted to the structure of volition as an intentional act; nevertheless, it plays a decisive role in this act as proceeding from its anchorage in the person. In its element of choice and decision, every volition manifests its specific dependence on the person from whom it flows, a dependence that may be called the "surrender to truth." The exact meaning of this expression has to be fully explained. At any rate, it is the essential surrender of will to truth that seems finally to account for the person's transcendence in action, ultimately for his ascendancy to his own dynamism.

We said earlier that it is the transcendence that we owe to self-determination, that is, in the final analysis to the free will. The person "transcends" his actions because he is free and only so far as he is free. Freedom in its fundamental sense is equivalent to self-reliance. Freedom in the expanded sense is the acting person's intentional flexibility and partial independence with respect to the possible objects of volition, insofar as man is determined neither by the objects themselves nor by their presentation. His independence in the intentional sphere is to be explained by this inner reference to truth and dependence on truth inherent in the will. It is this dependence that makes will independent of objects and their presentation, and grants the person that ascendancy over his own dynamism which we have here described as the transcendence in action (as vertical transcendence). The person becomes independent of the objects of his own acting through the moment of truth, which is contained in every authentic choice of decision making.[48]

The Moment of Truth and the Moral Value of Actions

Let us stress once again the need to examine more precisely the "moment of truth." But first it is perhaps worth noting that this moment, which belongs to the will, is to be distinguished from the truthfulness of the *particular choices and decisions* that may be actually made. At the beginning of this study we mentioned the integral experience of man, in particular, his moral experience, and this point brings us back to it again. First, there is the painfully evident fact that not all of the particular choices or decisions of the human will are correct. Too often man seeks and chooses what is not good for him. Such a choice or decision is not just an error, because errors stem from the mind and not from the will. Choices and decisions, which take as their object what is not a "real good" – especially when contrary to what has been recognized as a real good – lead to the experience of "guilt," or "sin." But it is the reality of guilt – of sin or moral evil – known from the moral experience that brings to light explicitly the fact that the reference to truth and the inner dependence on truth is rooted in the human will.[49]

If choice and decision were to be without their inherent moment of truth, if they were to be performed apart from that specific reference to truth, moral conduct most characteristic for the man-person would become incomprehensible. For it refers essentially to the opposition between what is morally good to what is morally bad. This opposition not only presupposes the will's specific relation to truth – insofar as will's intentionality is concerned – but also raises this relation to the role of *the* principle of decision, choice, and action. Briefly speaking, in the opposition between the good and the bad which direct moral conduct there is presupposed that in human acting the willing of any object occurs according to the principle of the truth about the good represented by these objects.

8. THE COGNITIVE EXPERIENCE OF VALUES AS THE CONDITION OF CHOICE AND DECISION

Motivation Leads the Will Out of Initial Indetermination

The foregoing discussion seems to have thrown much light on the manner in which the object of will and the cognition of the corresponding object together form the dynamic schema of man's specific functioning. The will's own relation to truth – the relation that is decisive for the dynamic originality of every choice and decision making – has allowed us to argue away the form of determinism which has its source in the erroneous assumption that it is the object as cognitively presented that elicits the act of will. If such were the case, then motivation would amount to determination, and this would foil all the originality of choosing and decision making, and indirectly also of self-determination. Nevertheless, though the will's proper relation to the truth in action does not derive solely from the cognitive presentation of objects, it is distinctly influenced by it. Without being presented with objects the will would not be in a position to deliberate and select, and by a single fixating upon "simple decision" it could not develop its own relation to it. Motivation is not to be identified with determination, but it is the condition of autodetermination.

By "autodetermination" we mean the moment of freedom not only in the fundamental sense of the self-reliance of the person but also in the broader sense when it refers to the possible objects of willing. At the origin of this relation there is a certain indetermination, which, however, in no way implies an indifference to objects and to values; it rather means the readiness to direct our intention of will to any one out of the complete range available without any prejudical preference. Motivation serves to urge the will out of its initial, still undetermined state, though this is achieved not by its being a determining factor but by being the condition enabling autodetermination. It is this distinct trait of autodetermination in choice and decision that establishes their personal originality. As self-determination is both manifested in and made concrete by choice and decision, they reach right to the structures of self-governance and self-possession of the person. On these same structures also relies the transcendence that distinguishes the acting person from a mere individual.

The Special Nature of Cognition as Condition of an Act of Will

Knowledge appears then as the condition not only enabling but also influencing choice, decision making, and more generally the exercise (and mechanism) of self-determination; it is the one condition of the person's transcendence in the action. We have already seen how this transcendence springs from the relation to truth. Now, if this mode of transcendence is in its own way the essential moment of the will that manifests itself in every choice or decision making, then within the human person's dynamism as a whole this moment is in a specific way knit together with the relation to truth as the constituent of the cognitive structure. We see thus how cognition plays the role of one of the conditions of will. But at the same time we have to note the reciprocity of this exercise of the will. For the exercise of will, because of its own relation to the truth of all the objects to which it turns by means of its intentionality, or in other words, the intentionality of volition, also influences cognition. This influence does not amount to freedom to change "at will" the nature of the cognized or the processes of cognition and thinking; the will acknowledges objects as cognized but proposes to, and imposes specific tasks on, cognition and thought; the recognition and preference of these tasks are given in the deliberating moment of will to the truth about good. "To will," in virtue of its essential structure of recognizing truth with respect to its objects, comports essential structural extension in its foundational connectedness with the structures of "to cognize" and "to know," so that we are tempted at first to conclude that this dependence is one-sided without giving due attention to its effect, namely, that cognition is specifically influenced by the will's demand on it.

The Moment of Truth about Good is Essential in the Experiencing of Values

This is how we may in the most general terms explain the basis in man for that branch of cognizing and knowing that we call "axiology," the knowledge of values.[50] For in the experience of value the moment of truth also seems to play an essential role. It is the truth about this or that object which crystallizes this or that moment of good. When for instance we experience the nutritive value of a food, we at once come to know what is the good of the object, which serves us as food. When we have the experience of the positive educative value of a book, we realize at the same time that the book as an object crystallizes a definite good. In either case our knowledge need not be provoked by, or serve, any concrete willing (though this would be the case if we were testing the value of a food in order to eat it, or inquiring about the educative value of a book in order to make use of it). The cognitive experience of value, that is to say, the apprehension of the good of this or that object, is not directly dependent on a concrete willing, though in principle it is very closely related to it. For the relation to truth then evolved in cognition is of such a kind that it may become the principle of willing when a choice or a decision is made. It is because of a definite value that we decide on an object of willing or choose among possible objects of willing. The cognitive experience of value is always an underlying factor in motivation.

The knowledge of values and its relation to the will can be, and usually is, considered as a separate problem in itself. The reason is the wealth of its various aspects. (In this chapter we still have to examine the emotional component in the experience of value.) In our study, however, there seems to be no place for its separate discussion, and indeed it would be fallacious to isolate the investigation of values from that of will. Perhaps another study will provide a better opportunity to go into it more fully.

At this point of our discussion the cognitive experience of value is of paramount importance for the understanding of the person, of his specific dynamism in action, and the transcendence that is strictly related to the moment of truth in acting. Summarizing the results of our discussion we might say that included in the experience of value there is the knowledge of the truth about the objects that the will turns to by the power of its specific intentionality. It is the intentionality of volition, this intentional willing, that because of the experience of value – that is to say, through the moment of the truth about the good that the willed objects constitute – assumes the form of deliberation, choice or decision making. The characteristic trait of the will is not the intentionality itself of willing (that is, its turning toward objects that are recognized as valuable) but the directing itself of the intention of the act of will, through deliberation, choice or decision toward its objective. This turning may be done exclusively by the person.

The Axiological Truth and the So-called "Practical Truth"

The moment of truth contained in the essence itself of choice or decision thus determines the dynamism of the person as such. It is the dynamism conductive toward the action. The moment of truth

liberates the acting of the person and, in the deepest sense, determines the boundary between the acting and the submission to action
or between the acting and the happening, in which the person may in
different ways be the subject. Again, it is this moment that stays
under the jurisdiction of the cognitive experience of value. Choice as
well as decision making – each in its own way – is performed in
reference to the truth of the object recognized as a positive good.
Thus in both there is presupposed the *cognitive experience of truth*;
for the cognitive experience to which the deliberation of the will takes
recourse is not merely constitutive of objects of cognition but is first
and foremost evaluating them with respect to that "truth" about the
object which shows it as a positive or negative good. That is, we
speak here about the axiological (or moral) truth, which is differentiated from the ontological and logical "truth." In grasping it we
assert the value of an object rather than what the object itself or as
cognized actually is. The "axiological truth" – or rather truth in the
axiological sense – which is disclosed by our investigation is not,
however, the same as the so-called "practical truth" and does not
belong directly to so-called "practical knowledge." It is an essential
element in the vision one has of human reality. It is also the factor
that plays the most essential role in the structure of our acting to the
degree that we may say that "to know" passes into "to will."

9. THE CREATIVE ROLE OF INTUITION IS UNDIMINISHED BY THE JUDGMENT OF VALUES

Thought and the Efficacy of the Subject

So far in our analysis of knowledge as a condition of the person's
transcendence in action we have concentrated on the content of
cognition. But human cognition is a highly diversified and very
complex function of the person and needs to be analyzed also from
the side of the person in order to elucidate its share in the action and
in the person's transcendence in connection with acting. The whole of
human cognition is also contained within the limits of the experience,
which in this study we are trying to interpret through the dynamism
of man. As we have already pointed out, the characteristic mark of
this dynamism is the distinction between acting and submitting to an

impact. This distinction is also applicable, though in a specific manner, to cognition as a function of the person. Cognition is given us in experience essentially in the form of acting. Its proper moment consists in the fact that to cognize and also to think proceeds in sequences of acts; that is, it amounts to "act." Thinking, however, is a different function from cognizing. But alongside the active experience of cognition we also have the experience of thinking, which though of a more active nature has a cognitive significance. But if we consider the thinking process, at its already accomplished and thus passive stage, as the kind of experience in which thoughts just pass or flow "through" the field of actual consciousness – in such an experience it is the cognitive import accomplished already that belongs to the content of the flux; and the attitude of the human ego to it is that of the *passive* subject and not of the active agent. An experience of this kind is in a way analogous to the experience of "I want," when the psychical form of volition is by no means inherent in the personally efficacious "I will." This is the reason why we have asserted more than once that the intentionality of volition is in itself insufficient to constitute the dynamism of the will.

The difference between thinking and willing in general lies, broadly speaking, in their different directions: willing implies a certain outgoing toward an object and entering upon it as remaining external to the willing subject (the essence of willing being "to strive"), while thinking consists in first tending toward an object and then constituting it by introducing it within the immanence of the subject. Thus, for instance, the introduction of an object to the subject may be achieved by presentation in intuition of its noematic fragments in the object's "bodily selfhood" – or by means of imagination. But it may also be achieved by comprehension and interpretation. In each case the object is in a different way cognitively introduced to the cognizing subject; in the case of noematic self-presentation and imagination it is by means of direct intuition and in comprehension by means of the intellect.

In Judgment Man Has the Experience of Himself as the Agent of Thought

The direction simultaneously toward the object and backward to cognition (especially to the so-called "external perception") is also implied in experiences of the type when "thoughts" just pass through the mind. Nevertheless, even the experience of "immanent perception" of our cognitive acts, e.g., in the perception "I am thinking," exhibits the cross currents of passiveness and the proper activeness of the personal ego. For on the one hand, we may consider that in certain of its processes thinking "happens" in man, but, on the other hand, in its other modalities it is – as Husserl has emphasized – active *par excellence*. It seems, however, that even "happening" itself is already a manifestation of the cognitive dynamism of man; thus there is also presupposed in it man's cognitive potentiality with all its complex implications. The passive mode of thinking seems to be radically differentiated from the active, however, on account of the role of judgment. Only with emergence within the schema of man's cognitive function of the instance of judgment has man the experience of being the agent of cognition and of thought. The action of judging seems to constitute the crucial and decisive factor of human cognitive activity. There is presupposed in it a still more elementary function of the mind, namely, that of ideation – an aspect strongly emphasized by contemporary thinkers. But experientially this function is inherent in the function of judging, and it is by judgment that in consciousness it manifests itself as the action, in which the ego is not merely the subject but also the agent.

The function of judgment has an "outer" structure on account of the objects that are its raw material. This structure becomes apparent in sentences expressed in speech or writing. For instance, in the sentence "The wall is white" the function of judging consists in attributing to a thing (the wall) a property that it actually has (whiteness); this is expressed in the "outer" structure that appertains not only to speech but also to thought; for we speak in sentences because we think in judgments. But there is more in judgment than the outer structure; a judgment grasps a truth about the object that is its raw material. Thus in "the wall is white," in addition to the outer structure assumed by the function of judging on account of its object, there is also present the inherent, "inner" structure of this function expressing the grasping as such. That is, the function of judging establishes also the correctness of the way in which the "raw material" (or subject of the judging) is conceived by the predicate which is attributed to it in the judgment. It means that the judgment grasps this correctness of attribution as the "truth" of the object. To grasp the truth is the same as to introduce an object to the person-subject through one of his inherent properties. This property, which not only belongs to the subject as his self-transcendent, but also his experienced relation to truth, reveals at once the spiritual nature of the personal subject. Indeed, as we shall see in our subsequent analysis, truth is not only essential for the possibility of human knowledge, but it is simultaneously *the basis for the person's transcendence in the action.* For the moment of truth in this respect, or the truth about the moral good, makes of the action what it actually is; it is this moment that gives to the action the authentic form of the "act of the person."

Correspondence of Judgment and Decision

There is a distinct correspondence or correlation between judgment and deliberation, choice or decision making in the process of the will. It is the correspondence of the already known to what becomes the object of willing. To apprehend properly this correspondence or correlation it is necessary, however, to approach and envisage the person in his transcendence. Through judgments the person attains his proper cognitive transcendence with respect to objects. But beyond the recognition of the correctness with which the attributes express the nature of objects, there is also a type of judgment in which the value is attributed to the subject, and the correctness of this attribution, grasped in the judgment itself (its *apodictic* aspect), constitutes "axiological" or "moral truth." The cognitive transcendence toward the object as known is the condition of the transcendence of the will in the action with respect to the object of the will. The judgment of values is presupposed in deliberation, in choice and decision, because it is not only preconstituted in and by itself through the truth about objects (the so-called "apodicticity" which we see as essential to judgment) but it also makes possible and lays a foundation for that proper relation of the will to objects. Whenever the person chooses or decides, he has had first to make a judgment of values.

It may be worth noting that every decision – and every choice seems to entail essentially a decision – comes as the nearest analogue of judgment, so much so that a judgment is often identified with decision. But the essence of *judging is cognitive and thus belongs to the sphere of knowing* while *the essence of decision is strictly con-*

nected with willing. "To will" means not only to strive toward an end but also *to strive while deciding.* It is for this reason that the will is so deeply inherent in the structure of the person, and every authentic, wholehearted "I will" actualizes the proper self-governance and self-possession of the person.

The Creative Role of Intuition in the Discursive Perception of Values

The prominence given here to the significance of judgment in the interplay of the object of cognition and that of will is not intended to belittle in any way the creative role of cognitive intuition, especially in what concerns the experience of values. We have pointed already to the cross currents of a certain passiveness and the proper activeness of the personal ego, which are apparent within the sphere of human thought. When judging, when formulating judgments, the ego has the experience of himself as the agent – the one who acts – of the act itself of cognizing. But we may also cognitively experience directly the value of the object of cognition. The subject – the ego – then remains as if absorbing this value, "contemplating" it and passive rather than active. It remains then in the passive role of the subject more than in that of the agent. These occasions are of extreme importance: they are creative and rich in consequences for cognition of human reality.

Although intuition seems at first sight only to happen in man we are not to belittle the active moment in its operation. First, it seems that the intuitive experience of objects is always accompanied by judgment; inasmuch as values are the object of intuition, it is a judgment of values, a judgment positing a given value. The character of this kind of judgment is not then discursive; the value is not reached in the course of a process of reasoning; instead, we find it in our knowledge as if it were ready-made rather than formed by reason. It is to this extent that we can speak of a kind of "cognitive experience." This experience is very often the outcome of earlier cognitive ventures, of those often countless intentional endeavors at grasping a value which, however, at the time failed in attaining its perception. When here and now we grasp a value intuitively, we have reason to suppose that this is an indirect result also of earlier repetitive efforts making up instances of a sequence.

Intuition and discourse are both involved, though in different ways, in the processes of cognition as a whole; sometimes it is intuition that lies at the origin of discursive thinking and sometimes it marks the end and is the indirect outcome of mental processes. From the point of view of the transcendence of the person the question, whether the cognitive process proceeds more intuitively or more discursively, has no major significance. The important thing is the moment of truth, for it is the relation to truth that explains all choice and decision. The intuition lying at the origin of a discursive process seems to indicate that the intuitive truth needs to be further exfoliated. Intuition that comes as the fruition of discursive processes, on the other hand, is like a retrieval of truth and somehow like abiding in truth. The person's transcendence in the action seems much more connected with the praxis – that is, the truth of the objective reality, in which man continuously strives to make right choices and decisions – than with the intellectual function of judging.

CHAPTER FOUR

SELF-DETERMINATION AND FULFILLMENT

1. PERFORMING AN ACTION BRINGS PERSONAL FULFILLMENT

The Crucial Significance of Fulfillment in an Action

When we assert that the performance of an action brings fulfillment and then look at the content of this assertion, we can glimpse the wealth of meanings it carries and also notice the bearing it has on our previous discussion of the person's transcendence in the doing of an action. It is this fulfillment in performing an action, the performer's fulfillment of himself, that we must now consider.

All the essential problems considered in this study seem to be focused and condensed in the simple assertion of fulfillment in an action. Indeed, we are here concerned with the person and the action not as two separate and self-sufficient entities but – and we have emphasized this from the start – as a single, deeply cohesive reality. Insofar as this cohesion has real existence, it must be reflected in comprehension or interpretation. If so, then undoubtedly the existential and essential cohesion of the person and the action is best and most adequately expressed by the fulfillment resulting from performance of an action. This is the reason why it is necessary to include this fact in the philosophical interpretation of the acting person. We shall consider it here as a continuation of our earlier analysis of the personal structure of self-determination, and supplement it with an analysis of this structure from the point of view of the fulfillment that in the action corresponds to self-determination, which we already know to be deeply rooted in the dynamic structure of the person.

The Inner and Intransitive Effects of an Action

The fact that every performance of an action means fulfillment makes "to fulfill" almost synonymous with "to perform." This is why fulfillment seems to be the best homologue of the term "act," indicat-

149

ing the fullness which corresponds to a definite possibility or potentiality. In our approach we are looking for what could be an adequate
manner of expressing the person as the subject and the agent of an
action and at the same time of expressing an action as the authentic
act of a person. When we speak of "performing an action" we see the
person as the subject and the agent while the action itself appears as a
consequence of the efficacy of the agent. This consequence is external with regard to the person, but it is also internal to, or immanent in,
the person. Moreover, it is both transitive and intransitive with regard
to the person.[51] In either case it is most strictly connected with the
will, which we already saw in the preceding chapter to consist in both
self-determination and intentionality. Self-determination is something
more basic for the will, and it is to it that the fundamental significance
of freedom is related. Intentionality, on the other hand, is in a way
secondary to and integrated by self-determination. It is this intentionality that reveals the expanded significance of freedom.

Self-Fulfillment in Action Is Presupposed in Morality

It seems necessary to stress at this stage in our discussion that we are
here primarily, if not exclusively, concerned with action as the *inner
and intransitive consequence of a person's efficacy*. In taking this
standpoint we intend to analyze the whole dynamism of the
fulfillment which comes from performing an action, beginning with
the personal structure of self-determination. What was said previously about the dynamism of the will explains why actions which
are the effect of the person's efficacy, namely those actions "proceeding" from actual existing, have simultaneously the traits of
outerness and innerness, of transitiveness and intransitiveness; for
every action contains within itself an intentional orientation; each
action is directed toward definite objects or sets of objects, and is
aimed outward and beyond itself. On the other hand, because of
self-determination, an action reaches and penetrates into the subject,
into the ego, which is its primary and principal object. Parallel with
this there comes the transitiveness and intransitiveness of the human
action.

Every action has in some respects the existential status of a
transitory reality, which has a beginning and an end in either of its
dimensions, the external and the internal. The latter of these dimen-

sions is of special interest for us inasmuch as we are primarily concerned with the relation itself between the action and the person rather than with the effect man's activities have on the outer world. In the inner dimension of the person, human action is at once both transitory and relatively lasting, inasmuch as its effects, which are to be viewed in relation to efficacy and self-determination, that is to say, to the person's engagement in freedom, last longer than the action itself. The engagement in freedom is objectified – because of its lastingly repetitive effects, and conformably to the structure of self-determination – in the person and not only in the action, which is the transitive effect. It is in the modality of morality that this objectification becomes clearly apparent, when through an action that is either morally good or morally bad, man, as the person, himself becomes either morally good or morally evil.

In this way we begin to glimpse the proper meaning of the assertion that "to perform the action brings fulfillment." Neither performing nor fulfillment is identifiable with efficacy. The performing of an action, through the fulfillment it brings, is coordinate with self-determination. It runs parallel to self-determination but as if it were directed in the opposite sense; for being the performer of an action man also fulfills himself in it. To fulfill oneself means to actualize, and in a way to bring to the proper fullness, that structure in man which is characteristic for him because of his personality and also because of his being somebody and not merely something; it is the structure of *self-governance* and *self-possession.* Implied in the intentionality of willing and acting, in man's reacting outside of himself toward objects that he is presented with as different goods – and thus values – there is his simultaneous moving back into his ego, the closest and the most essential object of self-determination. This structure serves as the basis of morality – or of moral value as an existential reality – and it is owing to it that morality as a modality of conduct participates in the innerness of man and achieves a measure of durability in him. It is connected with the intransitiveness of actions but it also in a special manner itself constitutes the intransitiveness. Human actions once performed do not vanish without trace: they leave their moral value, which constitutes an objective reality intrinsically cohesive with the person, and thus a reality also profoundly subjective. Being a person man is "somebody" and being somebody he may be either *good* or *bad.*

Morality as the modality of conduct is to a certain extent extricable from the interwoven existential whole that it forms together with the person. In a way this distinction becomes unavoidable because the whole is too intricate to admit of an evenly balanced interpretation simultaneously of the person–action structure and of morality, not to mention the whole normative sphere that includes the problems belonging to ethics. This is why the usual method of ethics is to treat the existential moral reality more or less separately, that is, to bracket it. Nevertheless, as an existential reality morality is always strictly connected with man as a person. Its vital roots grow out of the person. Indeed, it has no existence apart from man's performance of actions and his fulfillment through actions. This fulfillment is equivalent to the implementation of self-governance and self-possession as the result of self-determination. It is only in such a dynamic cycle that morality can be concretized in the actual performance of action, as, so to speak, into an "actual reality." In its axiological nature morality means the division between, or even the contraposition of, good and evil – a specific differentiation of moral values – with respect to man; from this point of view it is studied by philosophy and presupposed in ethics. But it shows also an ontological status, namely, an existential reality, *the reality of fulfillment in an action*, that is appropriate solely to the person. In its axiological nature morality is anchored and rooted in the ontological reality – but at the same time it inversely unfolds its ontological reality and helps to understand it. This is precisely the reason why the experience of moral features of action and of the person are so strongly emphasized in this study.

2. THE RELIANCE OF SELF-FULFILLMENT ON THE CONSCIENCE

The Moral Dimension of the Person's Fulfillment in an Action

We may see at present how action – as well as the fulfillment it brings about – is connected not only with the outer and transitive effect of acting but also with its inner intransitive effect, and has a fundamental significance for the interpretation of the person. It also simultaneously opens an approach to an interpretation of the conscience, which again only seems possible on the assumption that to act stays in a necessary dynamic relation to the fulfillment of the person in the action. There seems to be no other possible road to an understanding of that specific progress expressing the vitality of the conscience, of its purely personalistic sense. Obviously it does not consist in a more or less abstract dialectic of the moral values of good and evil but reaches with its roots to the ontological status of the personal fulfillment of the ego in the action. Man fulfills himself as the person, as "somebody," and as such he may become either good or bad, which means that he may or may not achieve self-fulfillment.

With this contraposition we come to view morality as an "axiological reality"; for in this perspective existentially every action is some kind of fulfillment of the person. Axiologically, however, this fulfillment is reached only through the good, while moral evil leads or amounts to, so to speak, nonfulfillment. This approach appears somewhat convergent with the view that all evil, including moral evil, is a defect. The defect occurs in the moral order and thus in the axiological order from which it is instilled into the existential-ontological order; for the significance of moral values for the person is such that the true fulfillment of the person is accomplished by the positive moral virtuality of the action and not by the mere performance of the action itself. Morally evil virtualities of action, on the other hand, lead to nonfulfillment even though the person is acting. When performing an action the person fulfills himself also from the ontological point of view. Thus we come to the conclusion that the deepest significance with respect to the real existence of morality can be grasped as man's fulfillment, whereas his allegiance to evil means in fact nonfulfillment.

The Contingency of the Human Person as Revealed by Self-Fulfillment

In the ontological perspective man's fulfillment of himself – which is achieved every time he acts and concretizes positive moral virtualities – shows us the human person to be a potential and not a fully actual being. If the human person were to be seen as a "pure consciousness" constituted of a stream of acts, then there would be no possibility whatever of his actualization. It seems obvious, however, that the person, the action, and their dynamic union are more than merely an enactment of consciousness; indeed, they are a reality that exists also apart from consciousness. Since the person acts and fulfills himself in and through action, morality evidences a specific ontological transitoriness or contingency of the individual real being: man is a contingent being. Every being that must strive to attain its own fullness, and that is subjected to actualization, appears indeed to be contingent. This seems to be evidenced also, in a different way, by the modality of action as seen in its axiological status; the possibility of being good or being bad, that is to say, of fulfilling oneself through goodness or of nonfulfilling oneself, shows a special feature of the contingency of the person. The fact that the person can "be" either good or bad is of course the consequence of his freedom, and at the same time it reveals and establishes the existence of this freedom. It reveals, moreover, that the way this freedom is used may be right but may also be wrong. Indeed, man is not unconditionally led to concretize the positive values of the moral good in his action; neither does human action as such contain positive moral virtualities. Thus he cannot be sure of his freedom. It is precisely in this conditionality and this uncertainty that the ethical aspect in the contingency of the person consists, and on it rests the significance of the conscience.

Action's Dependence on the Recognition of Moral Goodness as Revealed by the Conscience

It is also the conscience that reveals the dependence on a specific mode of "truth," as we express it in a colloquial way, inherent in the freedom of man. The dependence is, as we asserted earlier, the basis for the self-dependence of the person, that is to say, for freedom in the fundamental sense of autodetermination. Simultaneously this dependence serves as the basis for the person's transcendence in the action. The transcendence of the person in the action does not consist solely either in the ontological autonomy, or self-centered dependence on the ego. It includes also the indispensable and essential moment of reference to "truth," and it is this moment that ultimately determines freedom. For human freedom is not accomplished nor exercised in bypassing truth but, on the contrary, by the person's realization and surrender to truth. The dependence upon truth marks out the borderlines of the autonomy appropriate to the human person.

But, in addition, the human person has the "right" to freedom, not in the sense of unconditioned existential independence, but insofar as freedom is the core of a person's self-reliance that essentially relates to the surrender to "truth." It is this moral freedom that more than anything else *constitutes the spiritual dynamism of the person.* Simultaneously it also shows us the fulfilling as well as the nonfulfilling dynamism of the person. The criterion of division and contraposition is simply the truth that the person, as somebody equipped with spiritual dynamism, fulfills himself through reference to, and by concretization within himself of, a real good and not otherwise. The dividing line, the line of separation and contraposition between good as a positive moral value and evil as a negative moral "countervalue," is marked out by "truth," the unique type of truthfulness of the good of which man has the experience in his conscience. It is the dependence on this truth that constitutes the person in his transcendence with respect to the reality of his own existential conditions; thus the transcendence of freedom with respect to the various existential conditions passes into such a transcendence of morality itself.

The Person's Transcendence and its Relation to Truth, Good, Beauty

The notion of the "transcendence of the person" may be broadened and examined in relation to all the traditionally distinguished absolute exponents of values: "truth," "good," and "beauty." Man has access to them through knowledge, and in the wake of knowledge, of the mind, through the will and through action. In this approach the action serves to approach and crystallize the experience of truth, good, and beauty. It is in this perspective that action was often examined in traditional metaphysics. The approach to the problem by Platonic metaphysics is somewhat different from the Aristotelian approach; but for all the differences, some themes remain the common property of the different metaphysics and of the anthropologies constructed on their basis. The vision of the transcendence of the man-person that is formed through his relation to these absolute points of reference does not, however, lose anything of its significance, when reference is made to experience – in particular, to the experience of morality. For the transcendence of the person understood metaphysically is no abstract notion; the evidence of experience tells us that the spiritual life of man essentially refers to, and in its strivings vibrates with, the reverberations with the experientially innermost attempts to reach truth, goodness, and beauty. We may thus safely speak of the role of these absolute modes of values that accompany the experience of the personal transcendence.

The Conscience as the Person's Inner Normative Reality

In this study reference is primarily made to only one dimension and one significance of the person's transcendence in the action, namely, the transcendence of freedom that also finds its realization in the ethical modality of action and person. When man acts, he at once fulfills himself in the action, for as a human being, as a person, he becomes either good or evil. His fulfillment is based on *self-determination*, that is to say, on freedom. Freedom, on the other hand, carries within itself the surrender to truth, and this fact is most vividly brought into prominence in man's conscience. The function of the conscience consists in distinguishing the element of moral good in the action and in releasing and forming a sense of duty with respect to this good. The *sense of duty is the experiential form of the reference to (or dependence on) the moral truth*, to which the freedom of the person is subordinate.

The function of the conscience is essentially more than cognitive; it does not consist solely in informing one that "X is good, X is the real good" or that "Y is evil, Y is not the real good." The appropriate and complete function of the conscience consists in relating the actions to the recognition of the truth that has been made known. In this relating by awakening appropriate virtualities in the action, the surrender to the recognition of the moral good means a simultaneous self-determination and surrender of the will to the recognized moral good.

We thus see that this surrender to the good in truth forms in a way a new moral reality within the person. This new reality has also the normative factor and manifests itself in the formulation of norms and in their role in human actions.[52] These norms play a specific role in the performance of actions and the simultaneous fulfillment of the person in the action. The study of the normative factor in the moral reality of the person belongs to the sphere of moral philosophy and ethics, but it also extends to other domains. Here it suffices to mention that alongside the norms appertaining to the moral modality of action, which may be defined as the norms of ethics, we find in the integral experience of man the norms of logic, of aesthetics, and, perhaps, of still others. Some are connected with the domain of theoretical knowledge and theoretical truth, others with the domain of beauty and art. We thus see in outline a kind of affiliation of the normative order with, on the one hand, the world of absolute types of values and, on the other, the diversified activities of man.

The Conscience as the Source of Norms of Actions Conditions the Fulfillment of the Person

The norms of ethics, however, differ from the norms of logic and aesthetics, and this difference has always been stressed by traditional philosophy. Only the norms of ethics, which correspond to morality, bear upon man's actions and upon man as a person. It is through them that man himself as a person becomes morally good or evil, with "through" construed as the relation based on a compliance or a noncompliance with norms. The norms of logic as well as those of aesthetics never have such a strong effect on man, for they are not, as Aristotle rightly observed, the norms of acting, of the action, but only of knowing or producing. Within their scope they do not refer to man as the person but to man's products, to his works. These may also be considered from the point of view of the properties of truth or beauty, and they will then prove either true or false (wrong), either beautiful or ugly. All the same, to qualify in this way a work or a product, even if behind the qualification stands the world of norms, is quite a different thing than to qualify – or disqualify – the person himself.

At any rate, it is only in the person that the fulfillment, which ontologically corresponds to the structure itself of the person, can be achieved. The person finds fulfillment in performing the action and thus in attaining his appropriate plenitude or completeness, which in its structure conforms essentially the structural condition of self-governance and self-possession. In the action the person achieves his own accomplishment by becoming "somebody" and the being "somebody" is his manifestation of himself. Together with this in-dividual fulfillment – stress is to be laid on "together" – or indeed in a direct union with it, comes the fulfillment of the self in the axiological and ethical sense, the fulfillment through crystallization of moral value. This fulfillment or nonfulfillment depends directly on the conscience, on the judgment formed in the conscience. The function of the conscience is thus determined by the basic ontological structure of the person and the action – in particular, by that dependence of freedom upon truth which appertains to the person alone; this is the focus in which the person's transcendence in the action and the spirituality of man converge.

3. CONSCIENCE DEPENDS ON TRUTHFULNESS

Why Is the Normative Power of Truth Rooted in the Mind?

The foregoing analysis leads to the conclusion that fulfillment is connected with the inner and intransitive effect of the action. This effect causes the acting of man to be arrested and preserved in the person and is achieved by means of self-reliance, which is the basis for the structure of man's free will and contains in itself the manifest power to subordinate man, his will and his actions to the recognized truth. As manifested in man's conscience, the capacity to surrender to truth shows how deeply the relation to truth is rooted in the potentiality of the personal being of man. It is this capacity, with its persuasive and prompting power, that we have in mind when we speak of the "rational nature" of man, or when we attribute to his mind the ability to know the moral truth and to distinguish it from moral falsehood. The mind is commonly regarded as the organ of thought: the function of thinking itself and also of comprehending is usually connected with the intellect. In fact, the mind is first of all merely a faculty of the man-person. Thinking and comprehending are the manifestations of its intellectual function, but besides its shaping of means and projecting their relations, its practical function consists in the evaluating and distinguishing of what is true and what is not. As one of man's faculties and powers, the mind in these two functions allows man to keep alive the widest possible contacts with reality. Every being can become the object of the mind's concern, and it is not merely cognition but recognition of moral truthfulness that is the primordial element in the mind's concern with this being.

Because of its ability to grasp the truth and to distinguish it from fallacy, the mind provides the basis for man's peculiar ascendancy over reality, over the objects of cognition. This ascendancy forms part of the integral experience of the person's transcendence – in particular, of the person's transcendence in action, which is the main theme of our present inquiry. This is clearly seen in and confirmed by the analyses of Chapter 2. Man's consciousness has indubitably a mental character, but even so its proper function does not consist solely in searching for truth and distinguishing it from fallacy, because this belongs to judgments. Consciousness in its mirroring function draws its significative contents from the active intellectual and practical processes that are directed toward truth. In this way the state of truthfulness also becomes their share and thus consciousness in its reflexive function conditions the experience of truthfulness. But as we already asserted in Chapter 2, neither the knowledge nor the active evaluation and understanding of truth constitute the proper function of consciousness. This must have a bearing upon the interpretation of the person's transcendence in the action, in particular, in what concerns the function of the conscience, on which in our approach the transcendence depends.

It is the activity of the mind, the whole effort directed toward moral truth and not consciousness alone that seems to supply the basis for the transcendence of the person. When we speak here of truthfulness, we have in mind this effort and man's intellectual activity at its crucial point. The grasping of truth is connected with a special striving in which truth as a value is the end that is sought. Man strives for truth and in his mind the ability to grasp it as a value – by distinguishing it from nontruth – is combined with the urge to search and inquire. Already in the striving we see his necessary dynamical need for truth as a value. It is the surrendering of the mind with regard to truth that conditions the transcendence of the person. Far from being but a passive mirror that only reflects objects, man acquires through truth as a value a specific ascendancy over them. This "superiority," which is inscribed into the spiritual nature of the person,[53] is connected with a certain distance or aloofness toward mere objects of cognition. This is precisely why the use of reason, or of the mind as the distinctive trait of the person, is so rightly stressed in the Boethian definition quoted above.

The Person's Transcendence and Fulfillment Depend on the Truthfulness of the Conscience

Earlier in this study mention was made of the structural trait of the person manifesting itself in self-governance and self-possession.

These structures are fundamental for the interpretation of the action in its intrinsic relation to the person and in its simultaneous transitiveness and intransitiveness. The persistence of an action in the person, because of its moral value, derives from and depends on the conscience. On the other hand, man's conscience is connected with the mind not only by consciousness but also by moral truthfulness. It has often been stressed that the function of the conscience is to judge of the moral value of an action, of the good or the evil contained in the action. This interpretation though correct does not seem to be fully satisfactory. It seems impossible to grasp the specific totality of the conscience without first outlining the structure of the person, the structure of self-governance and self-possession. Against the background of these structures we can perceive and interpret the dynamism of self-determination with its parallel dynamism of fulfillment – and it is there that conscience is rooted. Now, the conscience is the necessary condition of man's fulfillment of himself in the action. The man-person, as we already noted, fulfills himself in both the ontological and the axiological or ethical sense. In the latter case fulfillment follows the surrender to the recognition of the moral goodness while nonfulfillment is the result of missing it – and this directly depends on the conscience.

The role of conscience is to experience not only truthfulness but also duty, which will now be analyzed. Moral truthfulness, on which the sense of duty relies, thus comes to the forefront. When we say judgment is a function of the conscience we are referring to what is in a sense the last stage of this function and very often its purely formal aspect (this in many cases is connected with an intellectualized interpretation of the conscience). Actually, the conscience, when considered as a distinctive system, consists in a very specific effort of the person aimed at grasping the truth in the sphere of values, first of all in the sphere of moral values. At first it is a search for and an inquiry into the truth before certitude is reached and becomes a judgment. After all, we know all too well that the conscience may falter and often be at fault, that it may be in disaccord with the reality of the good. But all this is only additional evidence that the conscience has to be closely related to truthfulness and not only to consciousness – even though in the light of the earlier and the present analyses it seems evident that it is consciousness that supplies the judgments of the conscience with the subjective experience of truthfulness. Similarly it brings into these judgments the experience of certitude. In other situations it will bring the experience of incertitude, of a faltering conscience and, at worst, of bad faith or of a "false conscience."

The effort of the conscience itself, so far as it is the task of the mind striving for truth in the sphere of values, does not consist in theoretical inquiry. On the other hand, it is very closely connected with the special structure of the will as self-determination and also with the structure of the person. It issues from, and in its own specific manner is aimed at, the person. The will, as we know, always has an intentional direction; it is always a willing directed to an object that is seen as a value. Such willing is consequently not merely a detached intentional act; on the contrary, it has an intransitive significance in the person. When willing something even beyond myself I thereby also in one way or another bring back the discretion of the will upon myself. Since willing is an intentional act, it can never pass unheeding by the ego, which in some respects is the ultimate object of the will. Freedom conceived of as based in self-reliance is presupposed in the freedom that consists in independence from the possible objects of willing. It is with this reality of the human will and of human liberty that the effort of the conscience is most closely related. When it is an effort of the intellect striving for truth in the sphere of values, then its aim is to grasp not only any detached values as such of the objects of willing but also – together with the intransitiveness of the action – the *basic value of the person as the subject of the will and thus also the agent of actions.*

Normative Power as the Union of Truth and Duty

The question then arises how to be good and not bad;[54] how through action to become good and how not to become bad. In so stating the substance of the problem we touch upon those normative roots of truthfulness which spring from the conscience. Indirectly we also touch upon the essence of man's fulfillment of himself, of the fulfillment of the person that in the dynamism appropriate to the person runs, so to speak, parallel to self-determination. Due to the role of conscience, it is the normative function of the evaluated and recognized truth to condition not only the performance of an action by the person but also his fulfillment of himself in the action. It is in such fulfillment that the structure of self-governance and self-possession peculiarly appropriate to the person is confirmed and at the same time acquires the status of reality and may be actually functioning. Truthfulness, seen as the normative rule of truth put to exercise by the conscience, is like the keystone of the whole structure. Without truthfulness (or while out of touch with it) the conscience or, more broadly speaking, the whole specific system of the moral function and order cannot be properly grasped and correctly interpreted. This refers essentially to the norms of morality, inasmuch as it is they that serve the performance of the action and the fulfillment of the personal ego through the action, while the norms involved only in cognitive and thinking operations apply – as we asserted earlier – solely to man's products or works. This is the reason why in the present study we are primarily concerned with that normative power of truth which appertains to conscience.

More recently, the students of these problems with an interest in far-reaching abstraction have taken as the theme of their analyses only the truthfulness or the falsity of normative propositions. Moreover, they have often held that no logical value can be assigned to such propositions, inasmuch as truth or untruth can be asserted only of propositions with the word "be" in the copula but not of sentences with "should" as their syntactic functor.[55] This view in no way changes or belittles the statement that conscience is that basic experiential reality in which the person manifests (or perhaps even reveals) himself most fully to himself and to others. The fact of the conscience, for all its subjectiveness, still retains a measure of inter-subjectivity; it is in the conscience that there is achieved the peculiar union of moral truthfulness and duty that manifests itself as the normative power of truth. In each of his actions the human person is eyewitness of the transition from the "is" to the "should" – the transition from "X is truly good" to "I should do X." Faced by this reality the person never remains unsupported by ethics seen either as a philosophical clarification of conduct or wisdom, which is both a knowledge and a method of seeking the exact truth. Thus ethics is in the right when it sees its main task in justifying the norms of morality so as to contribute thereby to the establishment of the truthfulness of the human conscience.

It seems it is now the most appropriate moment to introduce ethics into the analysis of the reality constituted by the person and his acting.

4. THE OBLIGATION TO SEEK SELF-FULFILLMENT

Duty and the Person's Fulfillment in Actions

The explanation of the normative power of truth is to be sought in its reference to the sense of duty, while it also explains the sense of duty because of the reference to values. The fact that the assertion "X is truly good" activates the conscience and thus sets off what is like an inner obligation or command to perform the action that leads to the realization of X is most strictly related with the specific dynamism of the fulfillment of the personal ego in and through the action. It is from this point of view that duty is discussed here, albeit it may also be considered from different angles. Duty may be viewed as in a way the consequence of a ready-made and preexistent moral or legal principle. This principle we may call a "norm" because of its content, which is not only declarative – it cannot be expressed by the copula "be" – but obligatory because to be expressed it requires the semantic functor "should" or "would." In this approach a duty – regardless of whether it is a moral or legal obligation – may appear to be something derived from without the subject-person. It then expresses the individual's social obligations toward other people and toward the whole society to which he belongs. The *person's duties* with regard to other people present themselves differently; they occur in virtue of an interpersonal *nexus* of "participation" that manifests itself in the personal intertwinings of the coexistence and collaboration of people, and will be considered separately in a subsequent chapter.

The Truthfulness of Moral Norms as Such

Inherent in all the obligations man has toward other people and which are the foundations for the codes of moral and legal norms is the presupposition that a duty is a specific interpersonal reality. It is a dynamic reality that forms an integral part of acting whereby the person – as we have more than once insisted – also finds the fulfillment of himself as a person. The state of affairs that in the performance of an action man simultaneously fulfills himself through the truth of the action is visualized in the conscience. There is a correlation between the conscience as the interpersonal source of duties and the objective order of moral or legal norms, the order that in its significance and application extends far beyond an individual person and his concrete innerness. Nevertheless, the operative role of these norms to determine duties derives from the fact that in the social sphere as well as in the partly interpersonal and partly suprapersonal dimensions they emphasize objectively the good, as relevant to the person which thus takes for him the form of an obligation. The fundamental value of norms lies in the truthfulness of the good they objectify and not in the generation itself of duties; this is so even though the normative formulas used in actual practice accentuate their mandatory aspect by such expressions as "necessary," "duty," "must," and so on. Nevertheless, the sense of the moral or legal normative sentences lies essentially in the truth of the good that they objectify. It is owing to their truthfulness that they become related to the conscience, which then, so to speak, transforms their value of truth into the concrete and real obligation. Such is the case even when the conscience responds as if its acceptance of an obligation was based solely on an objective moral or legal norm. We have to remember, however, that the truthfulness of the good contained in norms may be directly evident, and this then determines the direct acceptance of their normative contents by the conscience and furnishes them with their own normative power. At other times, when the merits of the case are not as evident, the conscience very definitely checks and in its own manner verifies the norms by testing, as it were, their truthfulness within its own limits.

This is due to the fact that truthfulness and duty are strictly concomitant; for the real issue is not just an abstractly conceived objective truthfulness of norms but experiencing their truthfulness, the kind of experiencing that expresses itself in the conviction or subjective certitude that such-and-such a norm corresponds to a good. The deeper the certitude the stronger becomes the sense of obligation. Experience of obligation is intimately united with experience of truthfulness. Often, or indeed almost as a rule, we then speak not of *truthfulness* but of *rightness*. Theoretical judgments may be true or may be false, but norms are right or wrong. The right norm is a source of obligations for the conscience, which, conformably with the etymology of "obligation" and "to oblige," means to bind the conscience and bring it to act in compliance with the precepts of the norm. A right norm is thus one that it is proper for the conscience to obey; a wrong norm, on the contrary, one that is not to be followed.

The Creative Role of the Conscience

For all the fitness and adequacy of the attributes *right* and *wrong* with reference to norms, it seems that they tend to leave in the shadow the moment of truthfulness, of the experience of truth as value, and (as associated with this experience) the transcendence of the person in an act of conscience. There is no question of assigning to the conscience, as Kant argued, the power to make its own laws – followed by an identification of this power with the notion of autonomy and thus in a way with an unrestricted freedom of the person. The conscience is no lawmaker; it does not itself create norms; rather it discovers them, as it were, in the objective order of morality or law. The opinion that man's individual conscience could itself establish this order distorts the correct proportions in the relations between the person and the society or community and – on a different level – between the human creature and the Creator. Such views are the source of arbitrary individualism and threaten to destroy the ontic and ethical balance of the person; in addition, the rejection of natural law in ethics leads to similar consequences. At the same time, we have to recognize that from the point of view of the integral experience of man as a person the function of the conscience cannot be reduced to a mechanical deduction or application of norms whose truthfulness inheres in abstract formulas, formulas that in the case of established legal systems may be codified.

The conscience plays a creative role in what concerns the truthfulness of norms, that is to say, of those principles of acting and behavior which form the objective core of morality or law. Its creativity goes beyond simple recognition of the norm or injunction that generates the sense of obligation resulting in passive obedience. The experience of rightness is preceded and integrated by the experience of truthfulness. The latter inheres in the acceptance of a norm which occurs upon the *strength of the subjective conviction*. The creative role of the conscience coincides with the dimension of the person; it is wholly internal and applies to the acting, as well as to the moment of the person's fulfillment of himself. Indeed the creative role of the conscience consists in the fact that *it shapes the norms into that unique and unparalleled form they acquire within the experience and fulfillment of the person*. The sense of conviction and certitude, whereby the truthfulness of a norm is molded within the personal dimension, are followed by the sense of duty. Its mandatory power, the normative power of truth within the functioning of the person, is intimately related to the conscience and evidences the freedom the person has in acting. Far from abolishing freedom, truth liberates it. The tension arising between the objective order of norms and the inner freedom of the subject-person is relieved by truth, by the conviction of the truthfulness of good. But it is, on the contrary, intensified and not relieved by external pressures, by the power of injunction or compulsion. This is best formulated in St. Paul, in his demand of *rationabile obsequium*, which is the personalistic synonym of obligation.[56] The use of compulsory measures overshadows the transcendence of the person or reflects an immaturity in the person. Even if it is impossible to deny that such immaturity may happen, it would be inhuman to equate obligation with external pressures.

The Transition from Value to Obligation

There is ample evidence to show that the transcendence of the person through freedom is realized in the quest after the value of truth or truthfulness. Insofar as truth is the ultimate point of reference for the transcendence of the person, the traditional definition of the person is right in stressing that this transcendence, especially the transcendence of a person in action, has its source in the mind. It seems, however, that – as we already noted – the metaphysical reduction implicit in this definition emphasizes the intellectual nature (i.e., rational nature) rather than transcendence of the person through the relation to the value of moral truth. It is this transcendence as the constitutive feature of the person that we are trying to disclose in this study. Obligation evidences once again what has already been explained in the preceding chapter, namely, that the will and the freedom of the person in their own dynamic way surrender to truth, that they have their own dynamic relation to truth. This relation determines the specific originality of every choice and decision and in a special manner the individual originality of the varied instances of duty or obligation. For obligation is in a way a special stage in the dynamization of the will in its specific reference to truth.

We are not speaking here – as already stressed – of truth in the theoretico-logical sense and not even of that axiological truth which is connected with the cognitive experience of value. The cognitive experience of values does not necessarily initiate the willing of values, not to mention the experience of obligation. If a value is to give birth to obligation it needs first to intercept in a special manner, and as a specific appeal, the path of the person's acting.

The passage from value to obligation presents a separate problem, which we shall outline here but not analyze in detail. It very often has the form of an obligation to abstain from doing something in recognition of a value; many of the moral norms are presented in the form of prohibitions, as for instance most of the commandments in the Decalogue. This form, however, in no way excludes or obliterates their value, but, on the contrary, underscores it. Thus, the commandment, "Thou shalt not bear false witness," accentuates all the more strongly the value of veracity, while the commandment, "Thou shalt not commit adultery," brings into light the whole system of values connected with marriage, the person, the rearing of children, and family life in general. The passage from value to obligation in what seems to be the negative way characteristic of morality and legislation, is neither the only way nor the most important. The positive way seems to have a greater importance. The best and the most comprehensive example of obligation initiated by value in the positive sense is now and will always remain the evangelical commandment, "Thou shalt love." Obligation is then directly released by value with all its intrinsic content and all its attractive power. But the content and the attractiveness of a value are, so to speak, checked at the threshold of the person's innerness, the threshold erected by the conscience, which tests the truthfulness of the good presented in the value; it is with this test that obligation begins.

The Calling to Self-Fulfillment in Action

An obligation arising in a positive way because of the attractiveness and acceptance of values, which are spontaneously or reflectively recognized as true, may become a vital manifestation of the person's "calling." In recent moral philosophy there seems to be a clear tendency to distinguish between or even to oppose the roads leading to obligation: the negative, commonly identified (though without sufficient justification) with a system of norms conceived primarily as prohibitions, and the positive, identified with the attractiveness and the acceptance of values. The latter is usually understood as consisting in the "calling" of the person. The issue of a calling or vocation deserves in itself a separate investigation, as does the problem of the relation of values and norms. But here this issue is approached only from the viewpoint of the performance of an action and thus in terms of man's fulfillment of himself through action. For it is difficult to deny the objective closeness or perhaps even partial overlapping of this fulfillment and the person's calling. It seems, moreover, that any obligation, also that to which the passage from value is along the negative path, tells in one way or another about the calling of the person. For in every obligation there is an imperative: be good as man – do not be bad as man. It is in this imperative that the ontological and the axiological structures of man as *the* person come, so to speak, together. All other more detailed callings and vocations, or perhaps we may call them challenges by values, are ultimately reducible to this first, fundamental calling.

The Person's Transcendence Evidenced in the Drama of Values and Obligations

The intimate connection between values and obligations reveals the human person in his peculiar relation to a broadly conceived reality. This relation, as should be perfectly clear by now, is more than that purely cognitive one which like a lens focuses the reality in the microcosmos of man. The whole cognitive process merely interiorizes, as it were, the extrapersonal reality in the subject-person (this reality together with the subject himself is in a special manner interiorized by consciousness). Whereas, obligation goes in the other direction: it introduces the person through his actions into that characteristic drama enacted in the context of reality of which it makes of him the subject (*dramatis persona*). On the side of the man-person it is the drama of values and obligations. Outside of the drama man cannot fulfill himself as a person. Indeed, the fulfillment appears to be the more mature, the more profound and radical is the drama of values and obligations in man. Obligation – both as an element in the total calling of man and as the concrete content of a particular action – appears capable of telling much about the transcendence of the person. It brings into view, on the one hand, the reality of this transcendence and, on the other, its equally real limits, the limits of the reality within which man is to fulfill himself. Being a specific structure of self-governance and self-possession the person realizes himself most adequately in his obligations. He realizes himself neither by the intentionality of volitions nor through self-determination but through *his sense of obligation as the peculiar modification of self-determination and intentionality.*

At the same time, through obligation the person opens himself to values while still retaining toward them the measure set out by the transcendence that conditions the action and also allows us to distinguish acting from what only happens in the man-subject.

5. RESPONSIBILITY

Obligation Relates Responsibility to Efficacy

The analyses so far provide a sufficient ground for grasping and interpreting the relation that in man's action exists between efficacy and responsibility, in particular for interpreting the notion of "responsibility" itself. The relation between the efficacy and the responsibility of the person may serve as the framework for establishing the elementary facts on which rests the whole moral and legal order in its full interhuman and social dimensions. Nevertheless, this relation, like obligation, is in the first place an inner reality of the person, a reality that exists within the person. It is only owing to this interpersonal reality that we in turn can speak of the social significance of responsibility and lay down for it some principles in social life. Already the first look at the notion of "responsibility" shows that if we want to bring out in full relief its social and interhuman implications, we have first to make man himself with his personal structure and his transcendence in acting the object of our analysis.

The very fact that we relate responsibility directly to efficacy and can say that "man as the doer of X is responsible for X" reveals how complex as well as cohesive and condensed are the elements constituting the simple whole contained in the phrase "man performs an action." From our previous discussion we see how numerous are the elements which the reality of performing an action is composed of on the side of self-determination and parallel to it also on the side of fulfillment, the fulfillment that says more of the performing person than of the performed action itself. Similarly, responsibility informs us primarily about the person performing an action and fulfilling himself in the action. Although we have related responsibility directly to efficacy, its source is in obligation rather than in the efficacy itself of the person. Man can be responsible for X only when he should have done X or, conversely, should not have done X. The one is contained in the other inasmuch as the way the passage from value to obligation is achieved may be either positive or negative. For instance, a man being untrue to others or telling lies is responsible for misleading others, and this he should not do because of his obligation to truthfulness. The relationship of responsibility with efficacy implies obligation.

Responsiveness to and Responsibility for Values

The relationship of responsibility and efficacy also indicates that there is included in obligation an opening out of the person to values. Responsibility, as an intrapersonal fact that man has the experience of in an intimate relation with his conscience, seems to presuppose the specific dynamism of the will noted in the preceding chapter. The analysis of choice and decision with their own originality then led us to the conclusion that the will consisted in the ability to respond independently to a value rather than in the ability to strive for an object because of its value. The ability to respond to values integrates in its own special manner man's acting and impresses it with the mark of personal transcendence. Following it comes responsibility, which is most intimately connected with the action, because it is action that carries in it the response to values that is characteristic of the will. Thus we see outlined the response–responsibility relation. When man agrees to be responsible for his own actions, he does so because he has the experience of responsibility and because he has the ability to respond with his will to values.

This relation presupposes moral truthfulness; it presupposes that relation to truth in which obligation is rooted as the normative power of truth. And obligation constitutes that mature form of responding to values which is most intimately related to responsibility. Responsibility bears within itself the element of obligatory reference to values. Thus whenever the sense of obligation, an "I should," leads to a response, we have in outline the obligation–responsibility relation. Because of obligation the response to values characteristic for the

will assumes in the person and in his actions the form of responsibility for values. Owing to the intentionality proper to the will,
human actions are, as we know, directed toward various objects,
which present such-and-such a good or, in other words, such-and-
such a value. The important thing in human striving is its
truthfulness – the striving must correspond to the true value of its
object. For instance, when a person's action has as its object another
person, the directing to the object must correspond to the value of the
person. We have here the obligation to refer to the object in ac-
cordance with its true value; parallel to it we see the responsibility for
the object in connection with its value or, briefly stated, the responsibility for values. This responsibility is somehow inherent in the
formation itself of the obligation and itself has its source in this
formation. Responsibility is conditioned by obligation and, simultaneously, participates in the constituting of an obligation.

The Subject's Responsibility for His Own Moral
Value Is Based on Self-Determination

The responsibility for the value that is appropriate to the object of
acting is strictly connected with the responsibility for the subject
himself, namely, for the value that in the course of acting is formed in
the subject, in the concrete ego. For the first and the most important
feature of the will is its reference to the ego, the objectification of
the ego in acting, and not only the intentionality in the reference to
objects external to the ego. Together with the responsibility for the
value of intentional objects, the first and fundamental responsibility
that arises in acting on the basis of self-determination and self-
dependence is the responsibility for the subject, for the moral worth
of the ego who is the agent performing the action. This integrated
structure of "responsibility for" constitutes a whole, which approximately corresponds to what is usually called moral responsibility. It is at this point that, through the analysis of responsibility,
we can probably see most vividly why morality cannot be reduced to
some heterogeneous dimensions external to the person but achieves
its adequate dimension within the person himself, within his ontology
and axiology. The transcendence of morality as an objective order with
respect to transient life conditions, which, so to speak, outgrows the
person, is simultaneously strictly correlated with the transcendence of

the person. The responsibility for the intentional object of acting – and more so for the subject and agent of this acting – manifests an intimate relationship with the fulfillment of the self, with the autorealization of the personal ego in every action.

The Relation of Responsibility to Personal Authority

The whole of the reality constituted by responsibility has still another aspect, which we shall here designate as "responsibility to," and which presupposes "responsibility for." This other aspect, which is undoubtedly inherent in the very essence of responsibility, tells us a great deal about the surrender of man to the world of persons. For it lies in the nature of responsibility that we are always responsible to somebody and thus to a person. The world of persons has its interhuman structure as well as its social structure. Within this structure the need to be responsible to somebody is obviously one of the sources of power, in particular, of judicial power. The world of persons has also its religious structure very distinctly apparent, especially extensively articulate in the religion of the Old and New Testaments; within this structure the responsibility to somebody assumes the religious meaning of being responsible to God. It is a responsibility both in the eschatological and in the temporal sense. In the latter sense man's conscience – in performing its judicial rather than its directive function, both being appropriate to it – assumes a special authority. It is this authority that allows us to conceive and to speak of conscience as the "voice of God." In the philosophy of religion and also in theology (moral theology) this circumstance occupies a key position.

In our present discussion the fact of responsibility – of being responsible to somebody – sheds a new light on the structure itself of the person in his relation to the action. Once again we find in this aspect a confirmation of the intransitiveness of the action, which means that on the basis of efficacy and obligation it is specifically vested in the person. Moral truthfulness – the person's proper relation to moral truth – stands guard not only when the action issues forth but also when it penetrates into the person. Through the conscience, truthfulness, so to speak, keeps a watch over the roads of the transitiveness as well as the intransitiveness of the action. It is this innermost and thus most fundamental relation of the person to truth, which we have often referred to as truthfulness, that lies at the origin of both obligation and responsibility. Responsibility to somebody, regardless of any other appropriate relations, develops and is expressed in relation to its own subject. I myself am also the "somebody" to whom I feel and am responsible. If this elementary form of responsibility were not inherent in the whole dynamism of fulfillment, it would be difficult to understand any responsibility whatever. The world of persons finds its experiential starting point and foundation in the experience of the ego as the person. At the ego-person begins the road which leads to other persons seen both in the community of mankind and in religious perspectives.

In His Conscience Man Is Responsible to Himself

The responsibility to somebody when integrated in the voice of the conscience places my own ego in the position of judge over myself. It would be difficult to doubt the actual presence of such a judicial function in the experience of the conscience. Responsibility to somebody in the sense of self-responsibility seems to correspond to the self-dependence and self-determination proper to man; it is in this correspondence that the will and the freedom of the person is expressed and embodied. As the structure of the person which we have described here is centered on self-governance and self-possession, these together form the basis of man's self-determination. If man as a person is the one who governs and possesses himself, then he can do so also because, on the one hand, he is responsible *for* himself and, on the other, he is in some respects responsible *to* himself. Such a structure of the person is, as previously noted, indicative of the specific complexity of the man-person. For he is at once the one *who governs* and the one *who is governed by himself*, the one *who possesses* and the one *who is his own possession*. He is also *the one responsible* as well as the one *for whom* and *to whom* he is responsible.

Thus the structure of responsibility is the characteristic structure of, and appropriate only to, the person.[57] A diminished responsibility is equivalent to a diminution of personality. The structure of responsibility is also intimately connected with man's acting, with the person's action, but not with what only happens in man, unless what only happens is a consequence of and thus depends on his acting or nonacting. Moreover, it is first appropriate to the person from within; and only because of the primordial intersubjective nexus of moral and social participation, coexistence, and collaboration within the human world does it become a responsibility *to* somebody. The great problem of the personalistic significance of responsibility to God ought to be considered separately in a comprehensive theological analysis, but such an enquiry does not fall within the scope of the present work.

6. HAPPINESS AND THE PERSON'S TRANSCENDENCE IN THE ACTION

Self-Fulfillment as a Synonym of Felicity

The analysis of fulfillment as the reality that in the dynamic whole of the person–action relation unrolls parallel to self-determination cannot be continued without at least touching upon happiness, that classical theme in the philosophy of man. "Happiness" and "felicity" are susceptible of subtle distinctions in meaning which do not reduce to differences in degrees of intensity. We can sense, however, that "felicity" fits better than "happiness" into the general line of our analysis. We may consider this problem here not only out of loyalty to a certain philosophical tradition but primarily because of its part in the general framework of our discussion. In the notion of "felicity" there is something akin to fulfillment, to the fulfillment of the self through action. To fulfill oneself is almost synonymous with felicity, with being happy. But to fulfill oneself is the same thing as to realize the good whereby man as the person becomes and is good himself. We can now see clearly the lines joining felicity and the axiological system of the person. Their connection is in fulfillment, and it is there that it is realized.

Truth and Freedom as Sources of Felicity

The preceding remarks do not imply that action as the dynamism proper to the man-person is *eo ipso* making man happy, *the* source of man's happiness. We already know that to assert the performance of an action implies a twofold effect of the person's efficacy and self-determination, namely, the external and the internal, the transitive and the intransitive; the sphere of felicity is to be sought in what is internal and intransitive in the action, in what is identifiable with the fulfillment of the ego as the person. We also know that such fulfillment of the ego is constituted by various aspects, which we have been trying to distinguish step by step in our analysis. Two of them are connected with each other; they are moral truthfulness and freedom. The fulfillment of the person in the action depends on the active and inwardly creative union of truth with freedom. Freedom alone, as expressed in the simple "I may but I need not," does not seem to be rendering man happy in itself. Within these terms freedom is but a condition of felicity, albeit to deprive man of his freedom is equivalent to endangering his felicity. Thus felicity has to be identified not with the availability of freedom as such but *with the fulfillment of freedom through truth.* To fulfill freedom in truthfulness – that is to say, according to the relation to truth – is equivalent to the fulfillment of the person. It is the fulfillment that plays the role of creating the state of felicity of the person.

Felicity Derived from the Relation to Others

Admittedly, it is not an easy matter to consider in isolation this most intimate dimension of the person in which he experiences happiness at his own unique scale; nor, indeed, to sort it out, first, from the whole network of interpersonal and social relations and, second, from the whole multilateral system of references to the "world," that is, to nature in the most general sense, which includes the many different kinds of beings less developed than, and yet necessary to, man. All these relations are in one way or another meaningful for the happiness of man, but man's relation to other persons plays a special and crucial role. Further on in this study we shall take a closer look at the problem of the interpersonal system of mutual participation in each person's strivings, modalities of existence and concerns that brings together and unites human persons on a specifically personal plane. Experience shows that this sort of mutual participation is the source of a special type of happiness. It is also on the level of personal participation that – though only by suitable analogy – we may interpret felicity in the religious sense, the felicity or beatitude that derives from the intercourse with God and the communion with Him. A profound understanding of the person is certainly of great significance for the understanding and the interpretation of the revealed Christian doctrine on the eternal beatitude consisting in the union with God.

The Intrapersonal Profile of Felicity

In our discussion we limit ourselves to drawing attention to what felicity seems to be in the inner and intransitive dimension of the acting person. We limit our account to this dimension in order to be able to better understand the other dimension just mentioned. In addition, when in his quest for happiness man reaches out beyond himself, the fact of the quest itself seems to indicate a special correlation between felicity and his own person. The correlation has a dynamic character and is established and realized by the action. But its foundations are to be looked for within the person, in the freedom and moral truthfulness that are the person's constitutive features, and, in that dynamic relation to cognitive truth and action which is rooted in the mind. We may perhaps go as far as to say that felicity displays a kind of special responsibility with regard to the person, to his structure of self-governance and self-possession. This responsibility is so distinct that we may speak of the "personal structure of felicity," that would have no meaning apart from or outside the person.

Felicity and Its Reverse Belong to Personal Structure

The personal foundation of felicity implies that it may be experienced only by beings who are also persons. It seems impossible to predicate felicity of nonpersonal beings even when, like animals, they possess a psyche. Indubitably animals feel natural satisfaction and pain, a kind of comfort or discomfort felt at the sense level. Felicity – like its extreme opposite, which may best be exemplified by "despair" – seems, however, to be the exclusive privilege of the person, with that special unique structure of the person which has no analogue in the world of nature. It is only in the structure of the person that the fulfillment of the ego is achieved through the action, but it cannot be extrapolated beyond the person.

Felicity Is Not Pleasure

The same reasoning may apparently be followed in establishing the principle that allows us to distinguish felicity from pleasure. The dividing line runs within the limits of the experiential distinction, which we have been referring to from the beginning. It is the distinction between the fact "man acts" and the fact "something happens in man." The former involves not only the performance of the action according to the principle of self-determination but also the person's fulfillment based on the same principle; for self-determination always consists in a concrete instance of actualized freedom. The actualization of freedom is *the* dynamic core of the fact "man acts." Man's acting – the action – as the actualization of freedom, however, may be in accord or disaccord with the conscience, that is to say, with truth in the normative sense, and this means that man as the person either fulfills himself or he does not. What is strictly related to this fulfillment we call felicity but not "pleasure"; thus we see that felicity is structurally conjugated with the experience of acting and with the transcendence of the person in the action. The argument applies similarly to the opposite of "felicity," to despair, which is a result of acting contrarily to the conscience and recognition of moral truth.

We would seek in vain for pleasure as the element of this integral structure. On the one hand, is it possible to speak of pleasure in having a "clear conscience" or in fulfilling an obligation? Indeed, in this case we rather speak of joy or satisfaction. The fact that the satisfaction may also be pleasurable is only secondary – as the vexation caused by remorse is also secondary. But neither pleasure nor vexation is in itself connected with the personal structure of the fulfillment of the ego through the action. On the other hand, pleasure as well as vexation *happens* in man. This circumstance appears to inhere in the essence of pleasure and to distinguish pleasure from the felicity that corresponds to the content of personal fulfillment. Felicity points to the *personal* structure while pleasure can be related to what may be viewed as the simply *natural* structure of the individual, with reference to some aspects of the comparison between the person and nature made earlier.

The Person and the Action Remain within the Sphere of Pleasure and Displeasure

We have thus established tentatively what may serve as the dividing line between felicity and pleasure. This distinction, however, is not easy to make; felicity and pleasure tend to overlap in human experience, so that they may be easily confused or mistaken for each other. Such confusions appear to be frequent, and we often find felicity being treated as but a form of pleasure, or pleasure as a constituent of felicity.[58] The difference between them is often treated solely as a matter of intensity or rather of depth; pleasure is then thought of as a more superficial or less profound experience than felicity. These distinctions are suggested primarily by the emotional side of experience of felicity and pleasure. Such, for instance, is the stand of Scheler. For others felicity is a spiritual instance while pleasure is only sensual or "material." All these views seem to oversimplify the problem.

Actually, the dividing line appears to run along the fundamental experience of "man acts" and "something happens in man" and to refer to the structures contained in these experiences. Felicity would then correspond to the structure of the person and to fulfillment. It would be wrong, however, to maintain that pleasure is connected only with what happens in man, for we know acting may be accompanied by pleasure or displeasure. We also know acting may have, and often has, as its aim to provide oneself or others with pleasure and to avoid displeasure; it is these premises that serve as the basis for all of the so-called utilitarian ethical systems, not to mention commonplace hedonism. In the integral experience of man there is nothing to warrant the supposition that the notions of "person" and "action" are to be separated from the sphere of pleasure and displeasure. This would be equally unwarranted as to separate man as the person from nature. The sense of the distinction drawn here does not lie in detaching the person and the action from the sphere of pleasure and displeasure; its purpose is to indicate that the performing of the action, or rather the personal fulfillment of the ego through the action, is correlated with felicity (or its reverse) as something so completely specific that it can never be resolved into the pleasure–displeasure elements or can in any way be reduced to these elements. It is that specificity and irreducibility of felicity which seems to be most strictly related to the transcendence of the person.

7. THE TRANSCENDENCE OF THE PERSON AND THE
SPIRITUALITY OF MAN

The Various Meanings of "Transcendence"

The concept of "transcendence" has been the leading motif in our discussion of the person and the action in this and the preceding chapter. When it was introduced in Chapter 3 an explanation was provided of the sense in which it would be used in this study. This seemed necessary because the term has various meanings. One of these meanings is associated with metaphysics, the philosophy of being, and expressed in the absolute status of such general notions as being, truth, good, and beauty. None of these notions can be contained in a definition indicating either its nearest genus or its specific differential traits; for each of them transcends in its substance all species or genera under which are subsumed and defined the objects of the known reality. Another meaning of "transcendence" is primarily connected with epistemology, or more broadly speaking, with the so-called philosophy of consciousness. In this sense "transcendence" means reaching out and beyond the subject, which is characteristic of certain human acts, or the directing of these acts out of the cognizing subject beyond the objectifiable realm. In the preceding chapter we called this "horizontal transcendence," distinguishing it from the "vertical transcendence" that characterizes the dynamic person–action conjugate.

"Transcendence" Expresses the Essence of the Experience of Acting

The concept of "vertical transcendence" allowed us to contain within a descriptive analytical whole the essence of the experience "man acts." In this experience man manifests himself as the person, that is to say, as the highly specific structure of self-governance and self-possession. It is in and through his acting, in and through the action, that we see him in this highly specific structure. Thus the person and the action constitute together an intimately cohesive, dynamic reality, in which the action is the manifestation and the explanation of the person and the action. This parallelism of manifestation and explanation is characteristic for the phenomenological method.[59] The concept of the "transcendence," in the sense it has in this study, is well fitted to the method; it serves our attempts to interpret the inherent essence of the experience "man acts," to objectify that which allows the acting person to manifest himself and be visualized as the person. Since manifestation comes together with explanation, the concept of "transcendence" not only expresses the essence of the phenomenological insight in what concerns the person but also explains the person in his dynamic cohesion with the action. The phenomenological method in nowise stops at the surface of this reality but, on the contrary, allows us to penetrate deep into its content. Not only does it allow intuition but it also leads to explanation.

Against the background of this method the concept of "transcendence" serves the understanding of the structure, which manifests itself in the whole of the experiential fact "man acts." This is *the* structure of the person. The one who acts *is* the person and asserts himself as "somebody"; and at the same time he even more vividly and more completely demonstrates in his acting, in the action, why he deserves to be regarded as "somebody." Indeed, he shows himself as having the special ability and power of self-governance which allows him to have the experience of himself as a free being. Freedom is expressed by efficacy and efficacy leads to responsibility, which in turn reveals the dependence of freedom on truth; but this relation of freedom to truth constitutes the real significance of the conscience as the decisive factor for the transcendence of the person in his actions. It is in this way that transcendence determines that special structural trait of man as the person which consists in his specific domination of himself and his dynamism. This superiority above his actual being that the person exhibits leads to self-governance and self-possession. In virtue of his self-governance and self-possession man deserves the designation of "somebody" regardless of whether he has this distinctive structure actually or only virtually. Thus man is somebody from the very moment of his coming into existence as also when and if something intervenes and prevents his fulfillment of himself in actions, that is to say, if his mature actualization of self-governance and self-possession was to be prevented. That the designation "somebody" is appropriate to man can be deduced also in an analysis of man's being and not only from the experience of the person's transcendence.

The Spirituality of Man and the Person's Transcendence in Action

Thus we come to the conclusion that the evidence of the spiritual nature of man stems in the first place from the experience of the person's transcendence in the action, which we have been trying to describe and analyze. The notion of "spirit" and "spirituality" is often, somewhat one-sidedly, identified with the denial of a purely material nature of man. By "spiritual" we mean indeed an immaterial factor which is inherently irreducible to matter. The interpretation of spirituality through the negation of materiality presupposes, however, also a positive view of spirituality itself, to be found in the idea of the transcendence of the person. In point of fact, we may easily observe that everything of which the person's transcendence in the action consists, and which constitutes this transcendence, is in this sense spiritual. Since this, as we saw, is within the reach of the phenomenological insight, the acceptance of the spiritual nature of man in its authentic manifestations is not a result of some abstraction but, if one may say so, has its intuitional shape; spirituality is open to intuition as well as to an unfolding analysis. This shape, the shape of transcendence, is in concrete that of human existence: it is the shape of human life itself. Man as the person both lives and fulfills himself within the perspective of his transcendence. Is it not freedom, obligation, and responsibility which allows us to see that not only truthfulness but also the person's surrender to truth in judging as well as in acting constitute the real and concrete fabric of the personal life of man? Indeed, it is on them that, as we have more than once endeavored to bring to light in our analyses, the entire phenomenological structure of self-governance and self-possession is based.

The Real Immanence of the Spiritual Element in Man

In tracing that expressive whole of the experience of man we cannot limit our quest solely to an acknowledgment of the manifestations of spirituality without seeking to reach its roots. In point of fact, it appears that all the manifestations of the spiritual nature of man lead by the thread of their genesis to showing the real immanence of the spirit and of the spiritual element in man. Man could not exhibit the spiritual element of his nature had he not in some way been a spirit himself. This point of view refers to the fundamental principles of understanding the whole of reality: the principle of noncontradiction and the principle of sufficient reason. Although assuming these cornerstones of the traditional categorical way of grasping the whole of reality and man, it seems however that we have gone much farther than traditional philosophy in its conception of man, inasmuch as in our analyses we have accumulated sufficient evidence of the spirituality of man in the descriptive phenomenological sense which also led, even if only indirectly, to the ontological level. In the course of gaining an insight into the transcendence of the person, we saw how the spirituality of the human being is manifested.

The Sequence of Comprehensions

Let us first emphasize that our cognition of the spirituality of the human being comes from the transcendence of the person. The sequence of our comprehensions in this respect is as follows: to start with, we recognize that man is the person; next, that his spiritual nature reveals itself as the transcendence of the person in his acting; and finally, that only then can we comprehend in what his spiritual being consists. In establishing this analytic sequence we have to keep in mind that for a spiritual being like man the person is the proper existential foundation; in the evidence of experience we can neither detach the person from the spiritual nature of man nor detach the spiritual nature from the person. Thus when we speak of "spiritual nature," we use the expression as indicating some ontologically grounded permanence of the spiritual being.

Without assuming this permanence of the spiritual element in man it would be entirely impossible to understand and explain the discreet and yet consistently interrelated manifestations of his spiritual nature. We have to keep in mind, however, that the mode itself of existence and acting that reveals and crystallizes this element or, to put it differently, that liberates this element in man is, as we have noted before, the mode of existence and acting not of nature as such but of the person.

The following general conclusions can now be drawn from our investigation. The person can only partly and only in a certain respect be identified with nature, namely, only in his "substantiality." As a whole and in his intrinsic essence he reaches beyond nature. For the personal freedom repudiates the necessity peculiar to nature. But we have to emphasize the necessary relation between, on the one hand, humanness or human nature and, on the other, personality (being a person) and freedom. We then judge that free will belongs necessarily to human nature. Freedom itself is, however, opposed to necessity. Thus if we are to speak of the nature of the person, we can do so only in terms expressing the need to act freely.

8. THE UNITY AND COMPLEXITY OF THE MAN-PERSON

Phenomenological Intuition and the Unity and Complexity of the Man-Person

The preceding remarks about the relation of the transcendence of the person to the spiritual nature of man impel us to look more closely into the problem and to discuss the complexity of man as a corporeal and spiritual being – "corporeal" as here used referring to matter and to the material though primarily in the metaphysical rather than in the physical sense. Experience – seen as accessible in phenomenological intuition – tells us in the first place that man is a unity. His unity is also manifested in his dynamism, though in this respect we note a striking disparity between acting (the experience "man acts") and happening (the experience "something happens in man"), which so far has not received a full interpretation and will therefore be considered again in later chapters. The disparity in the dynamism of acting and happening does not prevent the unity of man as the person but reflects a certain complexity, which was already noted in Chapter 3. The unity of the person is most completely manifested in the action, that is to say, through transcendence. But again the person's transcendence in the action also shows a certain complexity; the one who possesses himself is simultaneously the one who, according to the principle of self-determination, is possessed by himself; according to the same principle he both governs and is governed by himself. His superiority is correlated with his subordination. Each helps to compose the unity of the person.

This complexity is clearly revealed in the phenomenological approach, but the remarkable thing about it is its structure, which is manifested first of all as a specific organic unity and not as an unintegrated manifold. It is how the complexity manifests itself in the action. The fact that in the performance of the action man also fulfills himself shows that the action serves the unity of the person, that it not only reflects but also actually establishes this unity. In point of fact the analyses in this chapter are meant to show that it is owing to the spiritual nature of man that the person's unity in the action is manifested and actually established. When speaking of man's spiritual nature we are not referring to the set of symptoms that determine the person's transcendence in the action but to the real source of all these symptoms, to the spiritual element in the human being. The experience we rely upon and the analyses we carried out suggest the conclusion that it is this element that constitutes the unity of man. Thus the transcendence of the person in the action, understood in the phenomenological sense, seems to lead to an ontological conception of man in which the unity of his being is determined by the spirit.

The Spiritual Element Underlies the Spiritual Virtuality of Man

We hope that our considerations have shown with sufficient clarity that the specific dynamism of the person has its source in the spiritual element. The dynamism itself is manifested in efficacy and responsibility, in self-determination and conscience, in freedom and the reference to truth that impresses upon the actions of the person and his being itself a specific "measure of goodness." As the source of the specific dynamism of the person, the spiritual element must itself be dynamic. Dynamism is, as already demonstrated in Chapter 2, proportional to virtuality. We infer from this the presence of the spiritual virtuality in man, the powers of his spiritual nature. The correlates of these powers are the dynamic reference to moral truth in the cognitive function and freedom together with the dynamic dependence of freedom on truth in the function of self-determination. The former we equate with the notion of the intellect and the latter with that of the will. Hence the powers of the intellect and the will seem to be partaking of and exhibiting themselves as a spiritual element. They constitute the dynamic conjunction of the person with the action. Consequently, these powers contribute creatively to the profile of the person, and they themselves bear a distinctly personal stamp. They are not reducible to nature. Attributing "spiritual aspect" to the intellect and the will may indicate that their appropriate dynamism, their mode of dynamization, does not pertain to and remain at the level of nature alone.

Spirituality Determines the Personal Unity of the Corporeal Man

This notion of "spirituality" may serve as the key to the understanding of the complexity of man. For we now see man as the person, and we see him first of all in his acting, in the action. He then appears in the field of our integral experience as somebody material, as corporeal, but at the same time we know the personal unity of this material somebody to be determined by the spirit, by his spiritual nature and spiritual life. Indeed, the very fact that the personal – as well as the ontic – unity of the corporeal man is ultimately commanded by man's spiritual factor allows us to see in him the ontic composite of soul and body, of the spiritual and the material elements. The phenomenological insight does not reveal directly this complexity but only brings into prominence the unity of man as the person. We also know that it does not obscure the complexity, but on the contrary leads up to it. For once attention is focused on the person's transcendence in the action because of his spiritual nature, the need immediately arises to understand better not only the manifestations of this spirituality but also its ontic basis and roots. Other questions then refer to the relation between the spiritual and corporeal, all that is visible in man and accessible to sense; for the spiritual is invisible and inaccessible to sense, even when in its manifestations it contributes to the vividly expressive content of intellectual intuition. Neither efficacy nor obligation, responsibility, freedom, nor moral truthfulness are in any way accessible to sense and thus they are "immaterial," they are not "flesh," but even so they indubitably belong to the experience of man; they are objects of intuition as evident data, which the mind can grasp and whose understanding it may itself cultivate and develop suitably.[60]

The Experience of Personal Unity Helps to Understand Man's Ontic Complexity

Thus the experience of the unity of man as the person stimulates the need to understand the complexity of man as a being. Such understanding entails extensive knowledge of how to measure the limits or perhaps the depth of things. It belongs to metaphysics, in which throughout the ages thinkers have been unraveling the nature of man as a being consisting of soul and body, of spirit and flesh. It is possible, however, that while returning to those arguments and analyses already attempted in this study, those reserved for later chapters may shed on them some new light of their own. For there is no question but that the conception of man as the person – though it is accessible in the original intuition within the frame of phenomenological insight – has to be completed and supplemented by the *metaphysical analysis of the human being*. Thus while the experience of the personal unity of man shows us his complex nature, the attempt at a deepened understanding of this complexity allows us in turn to interpret human nature as the one and ontically unique person.

The Experience of the Soul

It is to metaphysical analysis that we owe the knowledge of the human soul as the principle underlying the unity of the being and the life of a concrete person. We infer the existence of the soul and its spiritual nature from effects that demand a sufficient reason, that is to say, a commensurate cause. In this perspective it is evident that there can be no such thing as a direct experience of the soul. Man has only the experience of the effects which he seeks to relate with an adequate cause in his being. Nevertheless, people often think and speak of the soul as something of which they have had an experience. But in fact the content of what is meant as the "experience of the soul" consists of everything that in our previous analyses was attributed to the person's transcendence in the action, namely, obligation, responsibility, truthfulness, self-determination, and consciousness. It is the innerness of all these moments, however, that is most vividly manifest in this experience; they make the vital fabric of the inner man, they inhere in his inner life, and as thus experienced they are identified with the experience of the soul. But the possible knowledge of the soul is not limited solely to these moments and their specific role; it encompasses in and through them man's entire, as it were, spiritual ego. Thus the possible knowledge of the soul as the spiritual ego of man seems in its own way to point out the direction of metaphysical analysis.

PART THREE

THE INTEGRATION OF THE PERSON
IN THE ACTION

CHAPTER FIVE

INTEGRATION AND THE SOMA

1. THE FUNDAMENTALS OF THE PERSON'S INTEGRATION IN ACTION

Integration as a Complementary Aspect of Transcendence

The preceding two chapters have exhibited the human person in a dynamic specificity that manifests itself in and through the action. The essential moment in the action is that of self-determination, a point that we have already thoroughly examined and analyzed. Further, the performance of the action depends, as we have seen, on self-determination. That analysis of self-determination as well as of the performing of an action and the fulfillment this brings confirms our view of the person as a highly specific structure, namely, the structure of self-governance and self-possession. This structure differentiates the person from a merely natural being, for the elements of self-determination, of freedom, and of the consciousness of it, are wholly alien to nature as is also the transcendence in action formed within the person by his freedom and his conscious efficacy. It is that efficacy which is derived from freedom as the essential factor in the dynamic reality of the person and revealed by the experience of "man acts." The experience of being the agent, of being the actor, makes of acting the *action of the person* and distinguishes it from the other, numerous manifestations of the human dynamism, in which the moment of a conscious efficacy of the personal ego is lacking. The dynamic specificity of the action, the specificity molded by conscious efficacy and freedom, is brought into even greater prominence in contrast with all that which only "happens" in man as the subject.

The notion of the "transcendence of the person in the action" does not, however, exhaust all the contents of the dynamic reality of the person; and though through transcendence we perceive the structure of self-governance and self-possession as something specific to the human person and to his actions, this structure manifests what seems a characteristic duality or bipolarity of aspects. To observe the duality it suffices to look attentively at the content of the concepts of "self-governance" and "self-possession," which expose the dynamic reality of the person through and together with the action. The concept of "self-possession" denotes the person both as the one who possesses himself and as the one who is *in* the possession of himself. Similarly, the concept of "self-governance" denotes the person both as the one who governs himself and as the one who is in a way subjected and subordinate to himself. Thus the structures which articulate and grasp the dynamic reality of the person, also point to something other than the transcendence alone. For we call "transcendence" the aspect that consists in one's governance and possession of oneself and these are connected with self-determination, that is, with will.

There still remains the other aspect or the other pole of the structure we are considering here. He who governs himself is at the same time subjected and subordinate to himself. He who possesses himself is simultaneously *in* the possession of himself; to be in the possession and to be subordinate are elements of the same structure, of the same dynamic reality that is determined by the person and the action. These elements though strictly cohesive and intrinsically cor-related with transcendence are not identical with it. It is because of them that the other aspect is exposed within the whole constituted by the dynamic structure of self-governance and self-possession and thus also within the structure of the human action. We define this aspect by the expression "the integration of the person in the action," which is complementary to the notion of the "transcendence of the person in the action." "Complementary" is to be understood here not only in the sense that integration complements transcendence and that they thus form a dynamic "person–action whole"; its meaning is still deeper in the sense that without integration transcendence remains, as it were, suspended in a kind of structural void. This becomes apparent in light of our analysis of self-governance and self-possession. For there is no governing of oneself without subjec-ting and subordinating oneself to this governance; neither is it pos-sible to have *active* possession of oneself without a *passive* response in the dynamic structure of the person.

Integration as a Complex Unity

The concept of "integration" has thus emerged in our considerations from that fundamental vision which pervades all our previous analyses; it is also indicated by the concept of "transcendence." If we go even further back, the idea of integration emerges also from considerations of the efficacy and the subjectiveness of the human ego in his acting. Man experiences himself as the agent of his action and is thus its subject. He also has the experience of himself as the subject, but the experience of subjectiveness differs from that of efficacy. Moreover, the human being also experiences all that only happens in him. While in the experience of subjectiveness there is a certain passivity, the experience of efficacy – being intrinsically active – determines the human action. Nevertheless, every action contains a synthesis of the efficacy and the subjectiveness of the human ego. Insofar as efficacy may be viewed as the domain where transcendence manifests itself, integration is manifested in subjectiveness.

In this first approach to the notion of the "person's integration in the action" we shall endeavor to relate it essentially to our previous analyses of that dynamic reality which is constituted by the person and the action. The term "integration" is derived from the Latin adjective *integer* which means whole, complete, unimpaired. Thus "integration" points to a whole or the wholeness of a thing. "To integrate" means to assemble component parts so as to make a whole; thus integration denotes a process and its result. But in psychology and philosophy the term "integration" is used to denote the realization and the manifestation of a whole and a unity emerging on the basis of some complexity rather than the assembling into a whole of what was previously disconnected.

Our considerations have shown that it is in the latter sense that we should envisage the person as integrated in the process of action. A certain complexity in the structure of self-governance and self-possession manifested in and through the action, or, strictly speaking, in self-determination, is a characteristic and noteworthy trait of the person. Transcendence of the person is but one aspect of personal dynamism; it exposes but one of its poles. When it is accompanied by the subjective unity and wholeness of the structure of self-governance and self-possession, then it manifests the integration about which we are speaking. In the analysis of the dynamism of man, transcendence of experience passes into the immanence of the experience of acting itself: when I act, I am wholly engaged in my acting, in that dynamization of the ego to which my own efficacy has contributed.

The fact that "I am wholly engaged in my acting" cannot be explained by transcendence alone but requires for its interpretation also the integration of the person in the action.

2. THE INTEGRATION IN THE ACTION MANIFESTED IN DISINTEGRATION

The Many Meanings of "Disintegration"

The first and most important meaning we have been giving to "integration" in the course of our considerations refers, as already noted, to the intuition of the structure of the person which the person manifests in his dynamic characteristic. We are of course referring to the structures of self-governance and self-possession. It bears also upon another concept, that of "disintegration," which in psychology and philosophy denotes a lack of cohesion, a deficiency or defect of integration. We shall have to consider both of them.

"Disintegration" is a term used in various contexts and presumably with different meanings in those fields of learning which have the human being as their object. This applies to the different social and cultural domains of human activities as well as to the human person. Disintegration is most often considered by those disciplines that are interested in the psychological aspect of the personality of man and identify disintegration with everything that in some way departs from or fails to attain to ordinary human standards. In this approach the integrated man is seen as simply the standard or "normal" man and the disintegrated man is sub- or abnormal. The question may well be asked what in these disciplines is regarded as "normal" or accepted as the standard of human normality. It seems that in most cases the standard is established intuitively; common sense discloses which man is normal and which one is not quite or not at all normal.

Using this intuitive standard the disciplines engaged in the study of human personalities have thoroughly examined and defined the different symptoms of disintegration each within its own peculiar dimensions. These dimensions are contained in the notion of "psychological personality," of which man's moral personality forms an intrinsic part. We know that the experience of morality is an indispensable component of the integral experience of man and that as such it plays a crucial role in understanding man as the person, especially in understanding the dynamic conception of man. In fact, the notion of "disintegration," as it is used in the human sciences, not excluding medicine or empirical psychiatry, very often relies upon facts that have an essentially ethical nature.

Disintegration as a Structural Defect of Self-Governance and Self-Possession

Apparently the most important implications of the psychic phenomenon of disintegration are to be found already in the current as well as scientific uses of the term. However, in any branch of science dealing with man, the meaning of "disintegration" is corollary to the meaning of "integration." Now, the fundamental significance of "integration" – it always in one way or another consists in the person's integration in the action – is strictly connected with the person's intrinsic structure of self-governance and self-possession. The structure is essential for the very being of the person as actualized in the action; it is its manifestation. What we call the "psychological" or the "moral (ethical)" personality is derivative, something secondary with respect to being a person as such; in a sense, it is but an aspect of "being a person." "Integration" in its principal sense – and this applies also to "disintegration" – has to be considered with respect to the fundamental structure and not only as concerning the derivative structures, even though both terms also apply to the derivative structures. Indeed, it is only insofar as they relate to the fundamental structure that they apply also to the particular manifestations in the psycho-ethical dimension or psychosomatic dimension of man.

"Disintegration" in its fundamental sense signifies what in the structure of self-governance and self-possession of the person appears as a defect or a failing. The lower limit of disintegration is set by all the symptoms that reflect what is in fact a total absence of self-governance and self-possession. In this condition the creature, that is, a man and hence ontologically a person, is, or at least appears to be,

completely destitute of the specifically "personal" structures manifested in and with the action; indeed, this condition consists in the
disintegration of the person in the action. Such states of deep or
complete disintegration, which are well known and have their particular scientific denotations, fall under various psycho-medical
classifications. Since our objective is to grasp the meaning of "disintegration" in its fundamental sense rather than to provide a description of phenomena, these facts are mentioned here only as an illus-
tration of our argument. Important here is the fundamental sense of
"disintegration" which is, as already noted, connected with the
dynamic structure of the person. Since the structure is essentially
formed by self-determination, disintegration refers to self-determination. While self-determination means that man can govern himself and possess himself, disintegration on the contrary, signifies a
more or less deep-seated inability to govern, or to possess, oneself.

The ability to govern, or to possess, oneself so strictly connected
with self-determination, establishes – as we know from our previous
discussion – the transcendent backbone of the human person. In some
respects and in some cases disintegration may be considered as a
collapse of this backbone, though even then it does not contradict or
destroy the transcendence itself of the person in the action. A
disintegrated person is incapable of governing, or of possessing,
himself to the extent that this inability prevents him from subordinating himself and thus from remaining in possession of himself.[61] He is
characterized, so to speak, by an insubordinative and unpossessible
ego and not by a straightforward abolition or limitation of the transcendent ego. The defects and defaults of integration become,
however, the defects and defaults of transcendence; a fact clearly
apparent when we keep in mind that transcendence and integration
are two complementary aspects of the same dynamic person–action
reality.

Disintegration Reveals the Significance of the Person's Integration in the Action

In disintegration there are more than a few peculiar symptoms and
forms, which are the task of the particular branches of science to
classify and qualify; disintegration also manifests different degrees of
intensity. These degrees or stages correspond to the dynamic vision

of man that has been developed by Aristotelian and Thomistic philosophy. In its perspective we may distinguish three stages of disintegration: the actual, the habitual, and the "potential" (understanding disintegration itself as referring to the capacity of man). There is obviously a difference between, for example, a separate instance of not associating somebody's face or appearance with his name and the frequent or regular failure to associate the one with the other. The latter may have different causes. If we assume, however, that the failure to associate a person's name with his appearance is a symptom of disintegration, then a single, actual instance of such a failure corresponds to a lesser degree of disintegration than when it occurs regularly, that is to say, habitually. Yet another difference occurs between the habitual failure to associate a name with a face and a total inability to make this association correctly, for in the latter case we are dealing with man's capacity itself, that is, we touch upon the defects of this capacity.

There are innumerable examples that would illustrate more vividly that essential trait of disintegration which consists in the "insubordinativeness" or "unpossessibility" of the subjective ego. But this trait is noticeable also in our example because the inability to make correct associations is an essential basic defect of cognition itself which has its consequences in acting. An incapacity to correctly associate does not allow one to make correct choices and decisions; also, the self-determination of the person will be defective in one way or another, and the more serious this defect is the more strongly will it affect the person himself and the harder will it bear on the person's structures of self-governance and self-possession. We know from the observation of mental cases the tragic consequences of an incapacity to make correct associations.

In this way the concept of "disintegration" allows us a better insight into the fundamental significance of integration, as the aspect of the person's dynamic reality.

3. THE PERSON'S INTEGRATION IN THE ACTION IS THE KEY TO THE UNDERSTANDING OF MAN'S PSYCHOSOMATIC UNITY

Psychosomatic Unity and the Integration of the Acting Person

The crucial problem for understanding man's dynamic reality is to establish the fundamental significance of the integration and disintegration of the acting person. Very often man is defined as a psycho-physical unity and it is then assumed that this notion is sufficient to define and express adequately his essence. But in fact the notion expresses only everything that is accessible to the particular empirical sciences; all that makes man to be a person and allows him to realize himself as the person in the action undergoes, in this approach, a specific reduction. It is precisely the reason why in this study, in which we are trying to trace step by step the experience of the dynamic reality of the acting person, we have to abandon this approach and change drastically our way of looking at the problem.

An interpretation of the fundamental significance of integration as well as of disintegration may serve as a key to our point of view. In the light of the total experience of man the view that he is a psycho-physical entity presupposes the concept of the "person" who manifests himself first of all in action. It thus presupposes a comprehensive interpretation of the experience of "man acts" in which transcendence and integration are considered as mutually complementary aspects. It is only within the framework of that dynamic unity which is constituted by the person in the action that man can be seen as a psycho-physical unity.

The Person–Action Unity Has Precedence over the Psychosomatic Complexity

Such is the case especially with integration. This is clearly indicated by the fundamental significance of the integration as well as of disintegration of the acting person. The subordination of the subjective ego to the transcendent ego – that is to say, the synthesis of efficacy and subjectiveness – in itself implies the complexity as well as the unity of man as a psycho-physical entity. It seems, however, for reasons which will be discussed later, that the term "psychosomatic" is here more appropriate than "psycho-physical."

The subordination of the subjective ego to the transcendent ego also includes both the psychosomatic complexity and unity of man. The same applies to the integration of elements and functions within the structure of self-possession. An analysis of integration imposes, on the one hand, the necessity of assuming the existence of these personal structures – this we have already done – but on the other hand, it also makes absolutely necessary an insight into the psychosomatic complexity of man. This complexity has here a special importance because ultimately man owes his psychosomatic unity to the integration as well as to the transcendence of the person in the action. This insight does not receive adequate or sufficient prominence in interpretations conducted solely along the lines of inductive thinking characteristic of empirical sciences.

The crucial fact in the total experience of man is that it is in action that the whole psychosomatic complexity develops into the specific person–action unity. This unity has precedence relatively to both that complexity and the psycho-physical unity, if the psychosomatic unity is understood as a kind of sum total of the somatic and the psychical as well as of their appropriate natural dynamisms. Action comprises the multiplicity and diversity of the dynamisms that belong to the soma and to the psyche. In relation to them action constitutes that superior dynamic unity. This is, in fact, what the integration of the person in the action – as the complementary aspect of transcendence – consists in; for the human action is more than a sum of those other dynamisms; it is *a new and superior type of dynamism*, from which the others receive a new meaning and a new quality that is properly *personal*. They do not possess this meaning and this quality on their own account and, insofar as they are but the natural dynamisms of the psyche and the soma, they attain these only in the *action of the person*.

Consequently we may say that only the person's integration in the action justifies an insight into the elements of that natural dynamic multiplicity constituting the psychosomatic totality of man. This insight allows us to construct an image of man as a psychosomatic unity. But as the image presupposes that more fundamental view of the person–action unity which is given in the experience of "man acts" it also draws from this experience its features and significance. The notion of the "person's integration in the action" supplies, in fact, the key to this significance.

There are indeed various dynamisms of man at both the psychical and the somatic levels that take part in human action.[62] In every action these dynamisms are "blended" together, but blending implies forming a whole from more or less homogeneous elements, and this is not the case with action. What does actually happen has more import; the dynamisms of the psyche and the soma take an active part in integration, not at their own levels but *at the level of the person*. By being the complementary aspect of transcendence, integration of the person in the action allows the realization of the person's structure of self-governance and self-possession. Thus also in this case integration means introduction to a higher level of unity than that indicated in the expression "psychosomatic unity" taken in its empirical sense.

Integration Introduces Psychosomatic Activations into the Dynamic Unity of Action

At this higher level of the person–action unity the dynamism belonging to man's psyche and soma seem to disappear. They fuse together. This does not mean, however, that they cease to be in some way distinct. On the contrary, they continue to exist in their own right and essentially co-create the dynamic reality of the person's action. In every particular case the manner of their participation is different depending on the individual character of the action. For instance, when an action involves a definite movement of the body as the visible element of its individual character, then the somatic dynamisms, without which the movement would be impossible, collaborate to produce the action. On the other hand, we know from experience that when the action is wholly internal and consists, let us say, in making the final decision on some important issue, then the different psychical dynamisms of an emotional nature play their role in the individual character of the action and determine its concrete form.

We saw in our earlier analyses that these dynamisms are not as such an "acting"; they are rather to be identified with the experience of "something-happens-in-man" and not with that of "man-acts." A close examination of the dynamic elements in man's psychosomatic complexity allows an analysis of the diverse "happenings" or of what we then called the various "activations," this term being used both by analogy and in opposition to the action, which alone corresponds to the experience of "man-acts." At the same time the person's integration in the action introduces the various activations of the psychosomatic structure of man into the action. In the action they reach a new and superior unity, in which they play an active part, but apart from action, when they are only the dynamisms of the soma or the psyche, they only "happen" in the man-subject. The function of integration consists in this overstepping of the dividing line between what only "happens" and "acting."

The integrating function is necessary to bring about, in and through the action, the personal structure of self-governance and self-determination. Without the integration function taking place in action only man's subjectivity would be realized in his ontic basis, but not his efficacy. We know from experience, however, that it is efficacy that dominates in the ontic structure of man. Efficacy and the freedom that we discover in this experience as the constitutive elements of the action draw all the psycho-physical dynamism into that unity in which the ego becomes for itself the first object of its acting. Owing to integration these dynamisms play an active role in self-determination, that is, in making the human person's freedom emerge.

4. THE INTEGRATION AND THE "INTEGRITY" OF MAN ON THE BASIS OF INTERACTING PSYCHOSOMATIC CONDITIONINGS

The Fundamentals of Man's Psychical and Somatic Dynamisms

The aspect of integration in the analysis of the person and the action is, as stated above, strictly connected with the need for a deeper insight into the psychosomatic complexity of man and into the complexity of the dynamisms of both his somatic and his psychical aspects. In this respect our investigations must come very close to the particular sciences that see man – his body and his psyche – as an independent epistemological object. The knowledge obtained by them serves various practical applications concerning man as a psycho-physical being. In particular, it is to be found in medicine with its many specialized fields. Our investigations into the integration of the person in the action come close to the specialized sciences but can never be identified with them; the reason is, of course, the previously mentioned difference in the specific way of looking at the object of study.

Thus the aim of our subsequent analyses is not to gain insight into the dynamisms of man's psychosomatic complexity of the type pursued by the particular sciences. First, because the particular sciences are very much concerned with details, which would lead us away from viewing our object, namely, the person–action relation as a whole. Second, they seem to be preoccupied in investigating the different psychical and somatic dynamisms as such and, as it were, for their own sake. In doing so they overlook that specific personal totality which is essential to our approach. Our investigation into the dynamisms appropriate to the psyche and the soma of the human being will in contrast deal mainly with the essentials of these dynamisms, and with the characteristic nature the dynamisms assume because of their integration in the person's action. Our description can neither depart from the data supplied by the particular sciences nor be in any way inconsistent with them, nor can it accept their reliance on minute details and the methods they employ. We thus see what is to be in principle our characteristic of the psychosomatic dynamism of man, to whom we attribute *reactivity* as well as *emotivity*, the former corresponding more to the soma and the latter to the psyche.

We must here emphasize that trait of the dynamism which determines its inner content and makes possible its unity (or integration). Man in his psychosomatic complexity constitutes a highly diversified manifold, the particular elements of which are strictly interrelated, in such a way that they mutually condition each other and depend on each other. The most important of these interrelations is the conditioning of the psychical by the somatic, the dependence of the dynamism appropriate to the psyche on the soma.

The Outerness and Innerness of the Human Body

When speaking of the somatic element we refer to the human body, first in the current prescientific sense and then in the sense the term has in its scientific usage. The body is material, it is a visible reality, which is accessible to sense; the access to it is first of all from the "outside." The outer shape of the human body determines in the first place what is visible in man, it decisively affects his individual appearance and the definite impression that he makes. So conceived, the human body is composed of different members, each of which has its place and performs its proper function. For the moment we are considering only the functions "outwardly" discernible. In this way the human body forms outwardly a whole that is membered in a specific manner appropriate to man alone. This applies not only to the special distribution of bodily members but also to their mutual coordination in the whole of man's outward form. The noun "shape" has its corresponding adjective "shapely," which qualifies man from the point of view of the arrangement and the coordinations of the members forming his body.

This outwardly discernible entirety, however, by no means accounts for all the reality constituting the human body, just as it does not in the case of the animal body or of plants. The body has, in fact, simultaneously its own particular inwardness; on account of this inwardness we speak of the human organism. While the complexity is outwardly reflected by the diversity and the mutual coordination of bodily members, its inward reflection is in the diversity and the mutual coordination of the bodily organs. The organs determine that vitality or dynamism of the body which has somatic virtuality as its counterpart. The term "somatic" refers to the body in the outer as well as the inner aspects of the system; thus when we speak of somatic dynamism we refer both to the outer reality of the body with its appropriate members and to its inner reality, that is, the organism: to the system and the joint functioning of all the bodily organs.

The Principle of Man's Psychosomatic Integrity

The somatic side of man and his psychical side are strictly interrelated, the relation between them consisting in the fact that the psychical functions are conditioned by the sum total of the somatic functions and especially by some particular somatic functions. The term "psyche" applies to the soul, though not immediately in the metaphysical sense; its first application is in a "physical," or phenomenal, sense. Thus "psyche" and "psychical" apply to the whole range of manifestations of the integral human life that are not in themselves bodily or material, but at the same time show some dependence on the body, some somatic conditioning. For instance eyesight, feelings, emotions are not in themselves corporeal, but they show a measure of dependence on and a connection with the body. The important sphere of psychical facts is not difficult to distinguish and isolate from the total dynamism of man; but when distinguishing the psychical from the somatic, from what in itself is corporeal, it is also impossible not to notice how strictly it is related to and conditioned by the soma, by the body as an organism. The recognition of the differences as well as of the interrelations dates as far back in the history of human knowledge as does anthropology itself. In this respect we have profited most from the philosophy of Aristotle and his realistic approach to the physical world, the approach that gave a different basis to the metaphysics and the anthropology of the Stagirite than did Plato's attitude toward the world.

The person's integration in the action rests on the conditioning of the psychical by the somatic; it is from this conditioning that man's integrity is derived. This integrity is not limited solely to the presence in him of all the elements from the somatic and the psychical sphere, but it also entails a system of their interrelations and *mutual conditioning* that allow the functioning of each sphere in the specifically human manner. Thus the integration of man is not static; on the contrary, its nature is dynamic. As to the direction of these conditionings we see that in a way they operate from the outside and are directed inward (in the case of psychical functions conditioned by the somatic ones), and from the inside outward (in the case of the somatic expression of psychical functions). Psychology, or rather the Aristotelian-Thomistic anthropology, distinguishes in the former of these directions two alternatives: the somatic conditioning of psychical functions may be either internal (as is the case with all sense functions) or solely external (as are conditioned somatically by man's spiritual functions). This is so because spiritual functions are seen as remaining internally independent from matter. The integrity of man is, in the empirical sense, verified dynamically by the correct operation of functions, and this depends on the conditionings in general of what is psychical by the somatic and – in the direction of expression – of what is somatic by the psychical. The person's integration in the action is based upon this *dynamic totality*, while any defects in this domain we characterize as *disintegration*.

5. THE PERSON AND THE BODY

Reminiscences of Hylomorphism

It seems that we have now satisfied all the necessary preliminary conditions for embarking upon the discussion of the person and the body; in a sense we have already begun our investigation. Moreover, there is apparently no danger of so isolating the body and its role in the dynamic whole of the acting person as to risk attributing an absolute significance to this one aspect. Obviously, we cannot discuss the human body apart from the *whole that is man, that is, without recognizing that he is a person.* Neither can we examine the dynamisms and potentialities proper to the human body without understanding the essentials of action and of its specifically personal character. In this connection it seems appropriate to recall the vision of the human reality advanced in the traditional philosophy of Aristotle and Aquinas, which from the likeness of man to the other beings of the visible world discovers in him alongside of the hylic or material element also the element of *morphe* or form; hence the theory of hylomorphism and the analysis of the human being carried out within its frame. To accept the general principles of this vision, however, does not imply that we intend to repeat once again the formulations of the hylomorphic doctrine. So far all our discussions have reflected clearly enough the effort to rethink anew the dynamic human reality in terms of the reality of the acting person.

The Somatic Constitution and the Person

To begin, the problem of the body in its strict relation to the human person may as well be considered in a somewhat static approach. Its relation to the human person is absolutely necessary, so much so that it is contained even in that often used definition which sees man as a rational animal; in this definition "animal" denotes the body as well as corporality. It is the body that gives man his concreteness (this fact is in a way reflected in the classic metaphysical doctrine of man's individualization by matter). At any rate, this is so in the external experience, which allows us to grasp what is visible in man; we may equate here the "visible" with the "external." Man manifests himself – even from the static point of view – through his body, its specific, strictly individual build. The term sometimes used in this connection is "constitution," but it does not coincide exactly with the externally visible build of the body and seems to extend also to the internal system of bodily organs, which accompanies and, indeed, determines the external somatic whole. The notion of "constitution" includes not only the external shape of the body but also the dynamic system of the internal organic and structural factors that contribute to this shape. Although apparent already in the static approach, the constitutive trait of man reaches also to his dynamic aspects; it is manifest in the mobility that is characteristic for all human beings. Mobility is externally manifest and even from observing it we may infer certain differences between people. These differences have from ancient times inspired anthropologists with the idea of constitutive resemblances, of certain, somatically distinguishable, human types. Moreover, in relation to what was said previously about the human psyche being conditioned by the soma, these resemblances and human types also apply to the psyche. Hence the whole problem of temperaments, which has persisted throughout the history of anthropology from Aristotle to our days.[63]

The Human Body as the Person's Means of Expression

We have thus passed from the static image of man formed by the body to his dynamism. The anthropological knowledge is in this respect extensive, detailed, and highly ramified. But when we want to define the relations between the body and the person, everybody – not excluding the materialists – seems to agree that the problem lies essentially in finding out what exactly are the links between man's visible outwardness and his invisible inwardness. We are not concerned here solely with what is "contained inside" the body itself, that is, with the organism as the somatic foundation of the constitution. It is generally recognized that the human body is in its visible dynamism the territory where, or in a way even the medium whereby, the person expresses himself. Strictly speaking, the personal structure of self-governance and self-possession may be thought of as "traversing" the body and being expressed by the body. We already know that this structure manifests itself in action and is realized through action. It is intimately connected with the person's specific power of self-determination exercised through choice and decision, which establishes the dynamic subordination to truth. In this way the dynamic transcendence of the person – spiritual by its very nature – finds in the human body the territory and the means of expression. This is confirmed time and again by the actions, visible or at least perceptible manifestations of self-determination – that is, of the person's efficacy – in and by the body. In this sense, the body is the territory and in a way the means for the performance of action and consequently for the fulfillment of the person.

This common manifestation of the person's integration in the action, that may be thought of as "traversing" the body and being expressed in it, provides perhaps the simplest demonstration of the way the body belongs and is subordinate to the person. The problem of the relation between "body and soul" has been the theme of countless speculations and theories beginning with Plato, who conceived of man as a spiritual substance endowed with a material body for his terrestrial existence, and Aristotle, whose position was that of the "substantial unity" of soul and body (that is, of form and matter) within the individual human being. In our present discussion the problem is for the time being envisaged only from the point of view of expression. It thus also becomes – conformably to what was said in the conclusion to the analysis of the person's transcendence in the action – the territory and the means for the manifestation of the soul, of the specific dynamism of its spiritual nature, and of freedom in its dynamic relation to truth. The integration of the person in the action, taking place in the body and expressed by it, reveals simultaneously the deepest sense of the integrity of man as a person. It is the soul, indeed the spiritual soul, that appears to be the ultimate principle of this integrity. The person is not to be identified solely with the body as such. It seems that even behaviorists never go so far as to posit such an identity, all the more so as in their psychology they are preoccupied only with the external "manifestations" of man and do not seek any "inner" understanding. Behaviorism may serve as a descriptive approach to action but not as a method of interpreting man's acting.

The Man-Person Has and Uses His Body When Acting

The fact of the externalization of the person in and by the body, which takes place first of all in the action, has as its consequence the moment of objectification already discussed in Chapter 3. The person becomes the object of his own acting. In this objectification the body participates in a special manner. Whenever the person externalizes himself by means of the body he becomes simultaneously the object of his acting. The objectification of the body then becomes an integral element in the objectification of the whole personal subject, to whom the body "belongs" and of whose subjectivity it forms a structural part. The body is not a member of the subjective ego in the way of being identical with the ego; man *is not* the body, he only *has* it.[64] To "have" his own body leads to its objectification in actions and at the same time it is in this objectification that it expresses itself. Man has his body in a special way and also in a special way he is aware of his "possession," when in his acting he employs *his* body as a compliant tool to express his self-determination.

Such a compliance of the body also serves to attain the integration of the person in the action. The ability to objectify the body and to employ it in acting is an important factor of the personal freedom of man. It is through this somatic moment – and also somatic factor – in the personal subjectification that the specific structure of self-governance and self-possession of the human person is accomplished and manifested. Man as the person "possesses himself" in the experience of his embodiment precisely because it entails the feeling of possessing his body, and he governs himself because he controls his body. It is to this extent that the relation of the person to the body becomes "externally" apparent in the action of the person. This has various important implications in the psychology of acting and in ethics.

6. THE SELF-DETERMINATION OF THE PERSON AND THE REACTIVITY OF THE BODY

The Dynamism of the Body and the Total Dynamism of Man

The external experience does not, however, account fully for the relation that exists between the body and the person, in particular insofar as his acting, or the action, is concerned. The experience has to take us, so to speak, to the interior of the body, so as to allow us to feel its own inwardness. It is only then that the relation is seen more completely and its image becomes more mature. Our earlier analyses have prepared us to make a clear distinction between an insight into the person, who is man, and an insight into the interior of the human body; for the body, as we have already noted, has its own, purely somatic inwardness. But it is not this inwardness that we have in mind when we refer to the human body (and also that of animals) as an organism. The human body in its inwardness has a purely somatic dynamism of its own, on which the external dynamism of the body, its purely natural mobility depends; the two dynamisms in nowise prevent the human body from serving as means for the person's expressing himself in his actions. Now we have only to look into the purely somatic inner dynamism in order to grasp and understand more precisely the integration of the person in the action. This integration depends in the first place on the somatic organization of man, in which the somatic dynamism is an important if not the decisive element; we may say that it is the dynamism of the body as such.

Is it at all possible to distinguish this dynamism? It seems that in view of the generally accepted distinction between the body and the soul, or even more so between the somatic and the psychical, such a distinction is possible. But the discrimination of the somatic dynamism in the whole of the human dynamism presents a task that demands a high level of cognitive precision. These high standards are required from those who investigate the body itself as well as from those who with the methods of the particular sciences study the human psyche or at still another level of abstraction endeavor to define more accurately the nature of the soul and of its proper relation to the body. Our investigations into the human person cannot avoid dealing with this last problem, which has always been one of the most difficult in the history of human thought. Admittedly, it is not the aim of this study to involve itself in questions concerning the nature of the soul and its relation to the body; but in the course of an analysis of the acting person these questions arise and have to be considered.

The Reactivity of the Somatic Dynamism

At this stage of our considerations we are not concerned with that kind of knowledge of the human body which is the subject of investigation of the particular sciences but with certain characteristic aspects of the body. The starting point in this approach is the assertion that, because of his body, the man-person genuinely belongs to nature. This implies, on the one hand, his similarity to the rest of nature and, on the other, his partaking in the whole of the external conditions of existence that we also refer to as "nature." Man's position in nature comes closest to animals, in particular the so-called higher animals. The previously mentioned classic definition of man as rational animal contains a fundamental assertion about human nature, it is constantly being confirmed in the field of natural sciences and lies at the origin of the well-known evolutionary theory of the origin of man. These questions, however, have but a secondary bearing on our argument and there is no need to examine them here.

However, the close connection existing between the human organism and nature, so far as nature constitutes the set of conditions of existence and life, helps us to define the somatic dynamism of man. It seems that this dynamism may be contained and expressed in the concept of "reactivity" and also by the attribute *reactive*. "Reactivity" would refer to the human body as such. The purely somatic dynamism of man can be viewed as being "reactive," and we may also speak of the potentiality lying at its roots as reactive.

Why Can the Somatic Dynamism Be Called Reactive?

The human body has the ability to react like other bodies in nature. The notion of "reaction" is often used with reference to the whole pattern of human behavior; it is what we have in mind when we say someone reacted in such-and-such a manner to a piece of news, though in so saying we are not referring to the somatic reaction but to the psychical reaction that expresses itself in a definite emotion and is thus an "emotive reaction." But the colloquial "to react" often implies something more than just an emotive response; it may often denote a choice or decision and hence a definite response of the will to a presented value. There is no doubt that the term "reaction" can be adequately applied to various obviously differentiated components of human behavior and modes of acting. This indicates that the somato-reactive element is very deeply rooted in all human acting.

The reason why we are here restricting the use of the term "reactivity" to the soma, that is, to the dynamism of the body alone, lies in the direct connections of the body itself with nature; the psychical and emotive factors are only indirectly connected with nature by means of the soma and its somatic dynamism. In the notion of "reaction" there is of course presupposed the notion of some action or acting that has its source and its cause in nature viewed as the set of factors conditioning the existence and the activity (i.e., reactivity) of the human body. The ability to react is apparent already in inanimate bodies (e.g., the ability to expand under the influence of heat or contract in the cold). A comparable ability is observed in animate creatures, but their reactivity is manifested at the level of life. While the study of the reactivity at the level of inanimate beings is the task of physics or chemistry, at the level of animate creatures it belongs to biology. We find that reactivity is at that level a manifestation of life and to some extent even its principle, that is to say, the principle of formation, subsistence, and development. It is also the distinctive feature expressing man's somatic virtualities and consequently his bodily vitality. Hence, within its frame we have to attempt to trace the manifestations of the somatic dynamism, that is, the reactions of the body that constitute the body's own vitality.

The Relation between Reactivity and Vitality of the Human Body

The vitality of the human body is of an essentially vegetative nature; the life of the body itself is vegetative. In fact, the vegetation of a human being begins with conception and ends with death. The external conditions of the body's vegetation are similar to those of the vegetation of other bodies; they are determined by the natural environment – the climate, the atmosphere – and the food and drink as the means of vegetative process and regeneration. The body as an organism is by nature, that is to say, by the power of its innate endowment, adapted to vegetation and reproduction. Reproduction is made possible by the sexual differentiation of the human body, by those of its organs which physically enable the conception of man, his development until the moment of his entrance into the world, and finally his birth to a biologically autonomous life. The dynamic fabric of all the vegetative vitality of the human body consists of a sequence of purely instinctive reactions, that is, reactions that follow the way of nature itself. These reactions take place, that is to say, they happen, in the person without any special influence of the will, without participation in the person's self-determination. Consequently, they happen in the person but they are not the acting of the person, they do not constitute his action. The body activates itself according to the inner design and purpose of vegetation and reproduction; the character of this activation of the human body is reactive.

In this case "reactivity" denotes an instinctive and dynamic relation to nature conceived as a definite biological "environment," as a system conditioning both vegetation and reproduction. The relation is purposeful inasmuch as the particular, instinctive somatic reactions have as their object either vegetation or reproduction.

At this point we are already entering upon the question of the so-called instincts, which we consider below. The ability to react to stimuli is a particular feature of man's somatic system. This ability deserves special attention inasmuch as it imparts a specifically active character to the reactivity of the human body. The active nature of the body's reactivity in response to stimuli is clearly apparent when contrasted with the passive submissiveness of the body to the influence of external conditions insofar as its physico-chemical functioning is concerned. In the human organism the ability to react to stimuli is directly related to the nervous system, which serves the whole body and determines the particular directions of its reactive dynamism as well as of the somatic virtualities lying at its roots.

7. ACTION AND MOTION

The Meaning of the Body's Subjectivity

As we have indicated, the dynamism of the human body as such does not depend on the self-determination of the person. It is instinctive and spontaneous. The body as an organism constitutes its dynamic source, that is, its effective cause; the will is not its cause, for the dynamism of the body does not proceed from the person's self-determination. This is why we do not disclose it directly and immediately in the experience "man-acts," which reveals the efficacy of the person, but it is to be found in the experience "something-happens-in-man," where the efficacy of the person is absent. In reaction and reactivity the person's efficacy does not enter; we may then only speak of some kind of efficacy of the body and pertaining to the person only on behalf of the ontic unity of man. Moreover, the fact that the body's efficacy differs experientially from the efficacy of the person brings sharply into evidence the ontic complexity of man. We shall see presently that this complexity cannot be wholly comprised in the conception of a psycho-physical or psychosomatic being.

It is because of the autonomy of the body with its instinctive dynamism with respect to the self-determination of the person that in the totality of the personal structure of man his body is in a way a basis, an underlayer, or a substructure for what determines the structure of the person; of course the substructure itself forms part of the unity of the human being and thus of the unity of the person. What is more, in view of internal bonds and mutual conditionings the body seems to determine the integrity of this complex being. The unity and the integrity are not hampered by the fact that the reactive dynamism and the vegetative vitality appropriate to the body happen within the person independently of his self-determination and without any active participation of the will. They occur in spite of the fact that the normal course of the whole vegetative vitality and somatic reactivity of man seems to lie beyond the reach of his consciousness. This circumstance, let us reemphasize, by no means contradicts man's personal unity; on the contrary, in its own way it is a characteristic of this unity; we thus see that there is, intrinsically built into the personal structure of man's unity, a structure that exists and is dynamized according to nature – in a different way than the way of the person. Obviously, the human body does not constitute a separate subject standing apart from the subject that is the man-person. The unity of the body with the ontic subjectivity of man – with the human factor – cannot be doubted. The experience of oneself as the subjective ego, the experience of one's own subjectivity, is, however, related to the reflexive function of consciousness, which tends to include only the specific aspects of the body and its mobility; this seems to be sufficient for man to have experience of his own subjectivity.

We already noted that to have this experience man needs to be aware neither of the internal reactions of his organism nor of his whole, vegetative vitality. Neither does he need to be the active agent, the actor. (We know that the ascetic practices of the Yogis have as their aim the conscious control also of the internal reactions of the organism, but to control is not the same thing as to engender, which is always a matter of the efficacy of the body itself.)

The Synthesis of Action and Motion

From the preceding remarks we can see that within the frame of the integral subjectivity of the person – the subjectivity that is also reflected in consciousness – the body seems to have a somewhat separate "subjectivity" of its own – without, however, affecting in any way the ontic unity of man. Its subjectivity thus exists only in the sense that the body as such is the subject solely of reactions; hence its subjectivity is reactive, vegetative, and external to consciousness. The integrity of the man-person consists therefore in the normal, indeed, in the possibly perfect matching of "somatic subjectivity" with the efficacious and transcendent subjectivity of the person. Such integrity is *the* condition of the person's integrity in the action. Any defects in this respect are a threat to man's unity and may lead to his disintegration; that which is like the body's own subjectivity, the reactive and vegetative subjectivity of the body, is then out of tune with the person as the efficacious subject. We may say that it breaks out from the control of the person and gains a disadvantageous "independence." We then observe a kind of abnormality, something that seems contrary to nature; for it appears natural for the reactive and vegetative subjectivity of the body to be in tune with the person, the efficacious subject who is conscious of himself – at least in the sense in which such harmony corresponds to the human nature of the person.

To speak meaningfully of the body as if it were on its own is possible only because of the specific autonomy with respect to the person's self-determination – its conscious efficacy – of the somatic dynamism and the related vegetative vitality of man. It is against the background of this specific autonomy, which can be seen as the instinctive spontaneity of the somatic dynamism, that we can see more clearly how the realization of every action, which in a visible (i.e., "external" or a purely "internal") manner incorporates this spontaneous bodily dynamism, rests on a specific integration. Integration of the person in the action presupposes the integrity of the body. We may say that at the moment of self-determination man puts into operation the reactive dynamism of the body and in this way makes use of it, or, putting it differently, that at the moment of self-determination he consciously uses it by taking part in its operation.

This becomes apparent when we observe the dynamic synthesis of an action with a motion. Since external actions, that is, actions concretely and visibly manifested by the motions of the body, are very numerous, the synthesis is of frequent, indeed commonplace occurrence. A bodily motion is in itself something somatic and strictly related to the reactive potentiality of the body, to its ability to react to stimuli. This ability reaches deep into the inner system of the human body and is displayed as a distinctive power or skill, the *vis motrix* or motor power. Coming as a reaction to some definite stimulus a motion may be wholly spontaneous, instinctive, and is then called an "impulse." The occurrence of impulses in man seems to be an external indication of a certain measure of independence of the body from the will as well as of its potential ability and dynamic specificity. In a normal individual the synthesis of the action and motion takes place ceaselessly; while impulses may be viewed as activations of the body alone that lack the moment of personal efficacy, this moment is always present in the synthesis of the action with motion. In such a synthesis a given motion being dictated by the will may itself constitute the action or it may form part of an action that consists of a broader dynamic whole (for instance, the action of going to school includes many motions, in particular those of walking). The human body, as already noted, is for the person the territory and the means of his expression.

The Moment of Skill in the Action–Motion Synthesis

The element of skill or proficiency is a very important trait in the dynamic action–motion synthesis. The term "skill," as the equivalent of the Latin *habitus*, seems highly adequate here inasmuch as *habitus* denotes both a skill and a virtue; of these the latter refers to the *habitus* of spiritual life and the former, conformably with everyday use, to the body. Man may have a skilled or unskilled body and this is always reflected in his motions. The mobility of the body is innate in man and strictly connected with his somatic reactivity, which in turn may be converted in the appropriate nerve centers into definite motor impulses. The conversion itself is also instinctive and spontaneous. Bodily motions are the territory in which man develops his first skills, the earliest motor habits being formed in connection with instinctive reactions and impulses. At an early stage of motor development this process begins to be influenced by the will, which is the source of motor impulses coming from the interior of the person, of impulses that bear the mark of self-determination. When this happens we have that synthesis of the action with motion which functions as the frame wherein various skills continue to develop.

The presence of skill makes the whole motor dynamism, the whole of human mobility so spontaneous and fluent that in most cases we never notice the causative effect of the will in the synthesis of actions and motions. Our awareness is aroused only in the rare instances of motions that are exceptionally difficult or important and significant, for example, in mountain climbing, during a surgical operation, or for quite other reasons while performing liturgical functions. In such special circumstances nearly all our attention concentrates on making the necessary motions, and then we have a more or less clear experience of conscious efficacy. In ordinary and customary motions the element of proficiency or skill reduces the role of attention and thus weakens the experience of conscious efficacy. Habitual motions are made as if the will did not enter into play. It is a different question whether they can be treated as mere impulses, whether the efficacious engagement of the will played its part in developing the necessary habit or motor skill.

The Somatic Constitution and Human Mobility

There is still another point worth noting in connection with the question of motions and the mobility of man, namely, that in every individual case his mobility constitutes a specific, in a way phenomenological whole with the structure of the body, that is, with his entire constitution. This dynamic whole manifests itself outwardly but its origin has to be sought within the human body, in its reactivity, with the specific ability of the individual to transform stimulations into motor impulses. Mobility as the manifestation of the somatic reactivity, which is partly innate and partly acquired through early developed skills, corresponds to and derives from the specific traits of the organism. This presumption seems to have lain and still to lie at the origin of all the attempts to classify people according to their temperaments, though of course besides the somatic elements these classifications also account for the psychical aspects. Indeed, the definitions of the various temperaments are primarily concerned with the psychical rather than the somatic dispositions of man, albeit they also clearly attempt to establish a relation between the one and the other.

Finally, as a conclusion to these remarks on the dynamic action–motion synthesis, we should note that in this domain we sometimes observe various forms of disintegration that may be defined as purely somatic. Such disintegration may take the form of the absence of a certain organ or member of the human body resulting in the disability to make certain motions, or it may be due to an absence of some, purely somatic reactions or skills leading to impediments or disorders of human acting. These defects are to some extent outwardly observable, but their source always lies inside the human body. It is perhaps necessary to stress that the purely somatic obstacles as such have but a physical and in nowise a moral significance. A man who has lost an arm or has had a lung removed is subject to very definite limitations or difficulties in his acting, but these are external in the sense that they do not in themselves distort his consciousness or prevent his self-determination. On the contrary, very often a human being with a high degree of somatic disintegration may represent a personality of great value.

8. INSTINCT AND THE PERSON'S INTEGRATION IN THE ACTION

The Complex Nature of Instinct

Before we end our discussion of the person's integration in the action viewed from the somatic and reactive point of view, we have still to consider the question of instincts. The term "instinct" in the current usage stresses the drive aspect of impulse; it is in this sense that the term has been used in this study. Indeed, while we may perhaps speak of "instinctive reactivity" with reference to the human body or "instinctive movements" (reflexes), it would be difficult to associate them with the drive aspect or the urge inherent in instincts. Hence instinctive reactions are indicative of a dynamization that is appropriate to nature itself, while instinct with its inherent drive tells of nature's dynamic orientation in a definite direction. This is what we mean when speaking of the instinct of, or urge for, self-preservation and of the sexual or reproductive instinct or drive. So conceived "instinct" does not refer to any particular reaction as a purposeful activation of the somatic subject, which is what we have in mind when in everyday speech we call such a reaction "instinctive": the term seems to refer to the resultant of several instinctive reactions of the body and thus to a trait of nature itself in its dynamic and clearly defined directing towards an end; obviously we are now speaking not of nature in the abstract but as a concrete existing reality, that reality existing in the person which we tried to describe earlier in this study. It is from the standpoint of this reality that man is equipped with his proper instincts.

Instinct with its inherent drive is a form of man's dynamism on account of nature and, so far as man forms part of nature, so far as he remains in intimate union with nature; but at the same time instinct does not consist solely of the somatic dynamism in man. This is why its interpretation in somatic terms alone can never be complete. In fact, instinct as a definite dynamic trait affects also the human psyche, and it is in the psyche that it finds its proper expression. This is certainly true in the case of the instinct of self-preservation and perhaps even more vividly in that of the sexual drive. The psychical aspect of instinct is expressed in the specifically emotive urge that assumes the specific type of orientation of the particular instinct and even to some extent generates this orientation. The experience itself of this urge, of an incitement or an objectively felt necessity, has a psycho-emotive character while the reaction of the organism only supplies it with the somatic ground. Since we are at present concentrating upon the somatic side of man and its share in the person's integration in the action our concern is mainly with the somatic aspect of human instincts, but we must remain aware that they are not simply and solely a somatic dynamism.

The Relation of Instincts to Somatic Reactivity

The basic conditionings of instincts are, nevertheless, to be looked for in the human body, in the body's specific reactivity. So far as the instinct of self-preservation is concerned it constitutes something akin to a resultant; it is also the common element of several vegetative reactions; for the instinctual end of these reactions is to preserve vegetative life and to maintain its proper development. The maintenance and development of vegetation entail the need for its preservation, hence also the need for self-protection and self-defense against anything that could impair or destroy it. The human organism is equipped with the necessary mechanisms of self-protection which functions automatically, that is to say, according to the rules of nature without engaging conscious awareness or the person's efficacy. In this respect the human body's own efficacy is self-sufficient; its contact with consciousness is maintained by means of the so-called "bodily sensations." In such common statements as "I'm fine" or "I'm sick" we refer precisely to these sensations. Such assertions may often inform us also about man's spiritual condition though usually they serve to describe his physical state. Sensations of health or illness, of strength or weakness have a self-protecting significance: through them not only the body but also the instinct of self-preservation, which is strictly connected with the body's vegetative vitality, manifests itself. The elementary sensation of hunger and thirst – as well as their satisfaction – springs from the instinct of self-preservation; in addition, the enormous progress in medical science and art may be related to this instinct. Clearly the instinct is not restricted to the somatic but constitutes a dynamic trait of the human being and existence as a whole.

The Instinct of Self-Preservation

The full significance of this dynamic trait is metaphysical and so the understanding of instinct must also account for it. At the origin of the instinct of self-preservation there is indeed a principle and a fundamental value: *existence itself* constitutes this principle, and this value, for the instinct of self-preservation expresses the compulsion to exist, that "subjective necessity" to exist which pervades the whole dynamic structure of man. All the somatic dynamisms preserving the vegetation of the individual are subservient to this compulsion as well as to the emotive urge felt whenever the vegetation and with it the whole physical existence of man (his material existence) is threatened. This feeling meets the intellectual affirmation of existence, the awareness that "it is good to exist and to live" while it would be "bad to lose one's existence and one's life"; the fundamental value of existence is reflected in this intellectual affirmation. Hence the instinct of self-preservation becomes a consciously adopted attitude, a primary concern of man and a fundamental value. In his mind, man, as we well know, may reject the value of his own existence and substitute negation in the place of affirmation, which shows that the instinct of self-preservation has no absolute control over the person. However, even in this respect the question emerges whether the intent of those who commit suicide is not to exist *at all* or perhaps only cease to exist in a way that seems to them unbearable.

The Instinct of Sex and Reproduction

Even a brief analysis of the instinct of self-preservation shows how difficult it would be to reduce it in man to its somatic aspects alone, how powerfully it is reflected in the psyche, and how great is the share of consciousness in the shaping of the processes that it generates. The same applies, perhaps even in a greater degree, to the sexual drive. The drive of sex, which relies on the momentous division of mankind into male and female individuals, stems from the somatic ground and also penetrates deeply into the psyche and its emotivity, thereby affecting even man's spiritual life. While the desire to maintain the existence of one's own being derives from the instinct of self-preservation, likewise the desire for sharing with another human being, the desire that springs both from close similarity and from the difference due to the separation of the sexes is based on the instinct of sex. The sexual drive in its integral dynamism and purposefulness becomes the source of the propagation of life; hence it is simultaneously the instinct of reproduction, to which man owes the preservation of his species in nature. This natural desire is the basis of marriage and through marital life becomes the foundation of the family.

The reproductive, procreative trait is most clearly manifested at the somatic level of the instinctual dynamism, the dynamism manifesting itself in strictly defined reactions of the body that to some extent automatically or spontaneously *happen* in man. In spite of all their specificity and automatism, however, these reactions remain sufficiently conscious to be controllable by man. Essentially, this control consists in the adaptation of the body's instinctual dynamism of sex to its proper end. Though possible, the control of the sexual drive may, and often does raise many difficult problems, especially for individuals whose sexual desire is unusually strong; this does not consist in somatic reactions alone but also in a special psychical urge of the emotive type. The point of view of ethics on the need for controlling the sexual drive was discussed more fully by the author in another book, the theme of which is human love and the ensuing responsibilities,[65] where also the purely somatic structures, whereby the instinct of sex manifests itself, are considered. The structures, whose roots reach deep into the human organism, determine the significant somatic differences between men and women.

The Correct Interpretation of Instincts

These considerations suggest that the problem of instincts, here limited to two examples, is not a purely somatic one, even though both the instincts of self-preservation and of sex are rooted deep within the human body and its natural reactivity. Does the significance of instincts in the person derive first of all from the subjective force of those somatic reactions as such which are liberated because of instincts, or is it rather the outcome of the objective value of the ends, to which man is urged and directed by instincts? It is a separate problem, which cannot be discussed here. It suffices to say that in view of the rational nature of the human person it seems more plausible to accept the latter alternative. Since in this chapter we have been dealing with the relation of the somatic to the integration of the person in the action the problem of instinct is considered mainly from the point of view of the subjective reactivity of the body, in which both the instinct of self-preservation and that of sex are very clearly apparent. In this approach the integration of instincts in the actions of the person is but an element of the more general problem, which is presented by the integration of the natural dynamism of the body in the action. We have seen, however, that this one particular element does not provide the full solution to the question of the integration of instincts, a question requiring a broader look at the psycho-emotive element.

CHAPTER SIX

PERSONAL INTEGRATION AND THE PSYCHE

1. THE PSYCHE AND THE SOMA

The Fundamentals of the Psychical Component

At the beginning of the preceding chapter we presented an interpretation of the fundamental significance of integration, which in the
analysis of the personal dynamism of man plays the complementary
aspect to transcendence. The person's transcendence in the action
manifests itself and is brought into prominence by self-determination
and efficacy. Both of them are in turn the distinguishing trait and the
consequence of the structure of self-possession and self-governance.
Considering the characteristic complexity of the structure, we have
been trying to bring into relief its second feature by introducing the
notion of the "person's integration in the action." This feature is
indispensable inasmuch as every human action is due not only to the
transcendence of the person acquired in self-determination and
efficacy but also to the control exercised over the dynamic subjective
ego by self-determination and efficacy. We understand here the
dynamism of both the human soma and the human psyche. They may
happen to be activated automatically; however, in action they surrender to the direction and control of the will. The person's integration in the action depends on this surrender to the will, and thus
by complementing transcendence it plays its own role in shaping the
structure of self-possession and self-governance.

When approached along these lines the analysis of human action
allows and even compels us to investigate the psychosomatic
dynamism of man. We saw in the preceding chapter that this
dynamism constituted a specific kind of unity, a complex manifold
unity. The psyche and the soma are distinctive with respect to each
other even though they form a mutually conditioned unity in man. It
is the notion of integration that provides the key to the interpretation
and the understanding of their unity, and our aim in the preceding
chapter was to demonstrate this with regard to the soma; for man's

220

complexity in this respect allows us to isolate to some extent the somatic element from the psychical and to define more precisely their respective dynamisms. They appear to have a crucial significance in revealing what integration actually is. For this reason we tried to demonstrate, in the preceding chapter, how reactivity, a characteristic trait of the human soma related to the external mobility of the body, is constituted from the specific raw material of the action. Our aim at present is to undertake a similar analysis with regard to the psyche. It is only natural that though our analysis relates to the research of particular sciences, which with their own methods study the body and the psyche of man, we proceed by our own method and approach. We restrict our present analysis, as already noted, to the general description of the relevant dynamism.

The Meaning of the Term "Psyche"

It seems necessary, however, to stop for a moment in order to consider first the notion of the "psyche," which is to be distinguished from the notion of the "soul." In every day use we contrast the notion of the "soul" with that of the "body." But in this juxtaposition the correct significance of these notions is metaphysical and requires a metaphysical analysis of human reality. Since this study tends to keep within the limits of metaphysical analysis we shall return to the notion of the "soul" at the end of this chapter. Even though the Greek term "psyche" means the soul, the two terms are not synonymous. "Psyche" refers to that which makes man an integral being, indeed, to that which determines the integrity of his components without itself being of a bodily or somatic nature. And yet, precisely for this reason, the notion of the "psyche" is correlated with the notion of the "soma."

Approached in its distinctive features, the concept of the "psyche" and the adjective "psychical" apply to those elements of the concrete human being that in the experience of man we discern as in a way cohesive or integrated with the body but that in themselves differ from it. Subsequent analyses will help us in defining more precisely these elements as well as their relation to the somatic. Our above differentiation indicates the experientially intuitive basis of our conception of the "psyche" and the adjective "psychical." It draws upon intuitive insights close to a phenomenological approach in which we may distinguish clearly, on the one hand, their separateness from what is usually called "somatic" and, on the other, their specific unity with it. The disclosure of what is distinctively psychical but simultaneously related to what is somatic in man provides the groundwork for conclusions to be drawn first, about the relation between soul and body and second, on a still more distant plane between spirit and matter. For the moment, we will consider in some detail man's psyche from the point of view of the integration of the person in the action; for the modalities of integration are the key to grasping and understanding the human psyche, just as the psyche itself was the key to grasping and understanding the human soma.

It has been already pointed out that integration presupposes a certain integrity of the somatic and makes use of it. The presentation of this fact was perhaps the most adequate in the analysis of the relation existing between action and motion: it is in this relation that the integrating will not only generates the motion but also utilizes the resources of the natural somatic dynamism, the natural reactivity and mobility of the body. Thus the integration of the body is a notion that includes not only the, so to speak, static total of the mutually coordinated limbs and organs but also the ability to react correctly, "normally," and, insofar as it is necessary, efficiently. All this is contained in the notion of somatic integration. As is to be seen this integration manifests that most obviously exteriorized element of the bodily constitution which we are inclined to associate with the whole statics and dynamics of the human body.

Man's Psychical Functioning and His Somatic Constitution

Man's entire psychical functioning is the basis of the integration of the person in the action; it does not, however, exteriorize itself in the same way as does somatic functioning. There is no such thing as the "psychical constitution" of man, at any rate not in a sense comparable to his somatic constitution. In this assertion we have at once the simplest confirmation of the established belief that the psyche is essentially different from the body. It has not the "external" attributes of the body, it is neither "matter" nor "material" in the sense the body is "material." Likewise the whole inwardness of the human body – what we call the "organism" – cannot be seen as interchangeable with the psyche. The functions of the psyche are "internal" and "immaterial" and while internally they are conditioned by the soma with its own proper functions, they can in no way be reduced to what is somatic. When we speak of the inwardness of man as of his "inner life," we have in mind not only his spirituality but also his psyche, the whole of his psychical functions. These functions as such are deprived of that external manifestation which together with the somatic constitution are the attributes of the body, though the body, as stated previously, serves in some measure indirectly to exteriorize them and to express them. This is why there is a justifiable tendency to deal with man's psychical function as a whole in its relation to the somatic constitution, a tendency that has for long been reflected in different treatments of the so-called "temperaments." It seems that the notion itself of "temperament" and the attempts to classify men from this point of view have had as their objective a more accurate definition of man's psychical integrity – indeed, his psychical integrity as the basis of the integration of the person in the action.

2. A CHARACTERISTIC OF THE PSYCHE – EMOTIVITY

Etymological Interpretation of Emotivity and Emotion

What we are actually looking for, however, is a more general and at the same time a more fundamental characteristic of the psychical dynamism than a study of temperaments would entail – a characteristic that would take into account *the relation between the psychical dynamism and the soma with its appropriate dynamism.* Such a characteristic of the psychical dynamism also allows us to grasp man's psychical capacities, which lie at the source of this dynamism. In the preceding chapter we adopted an analogous approach with regard to the soma when we submitted that its appropriate dynamism had a reactive nature, by which we meant the body's ability to have reactions, which within the limits of the human body determine inwardly its vegetative vitality as well as its outwardly visible mobility.

Let us examine emotivity as the most significant trait of this dynamism as well as of man's psychic resource. The term "emotive" is usually associated with the rather common noun "emotion," very much like reactivity is associated with reaction. The association is perfectly adequate, though "emotion" is usually used with reference to only a certain group of manifestations of psychical emotivity. It seems that an "emotional experience" has more or less the same meaning as an "affective experience."

Neither the term "emotivity" nor its corresponding adjective "emotive" refers to feelings alone: they do not apply only to the affective side in man. Their meaning is broader and is connected with the whole wealth of the differentiated domain of human emotions, feelings, and sensations as well as with the related behaviors and attitudes. It would be beside the point to quote the different kinds of feelings and the long list of words and expressions denoting them, but the abundance of expressions reflecting the inexhaustible wealth and differentiation of all that in man is related to his feelings provides a cue to a better and broader understanding of emotivity. We may also add that the different emotions or feelings are often defined by an attributive, for instance, we may speak of "artistic emotions" or "moral feelings." It is noteworthy, moreover, that "sense" may in some uses have almost the same meaning, for instance, when we say, "somebody has a sense of art" or "a moral sense."[66]

Etymologically the words "emotive" and "emotivity" point to a movement or motion (from the Latin *movere*, to move) whose external origin is indicated by the prefix *ex*. It may be argued that in the etymology of the term there is nothing that cannot be asserted of the purely somatic dynamism, which also involves some kind of "motion," a change that originates from "outside." When we want to visualize the essential difference between the somatic and the psychical dynamisms we may find it useful to compare *reaction* with *emotion* and *reactivity* with *emotivity*. While the somatic impulse taking place in the case of reaction and reactivity in no way exceeds the capacity of the body, in the case of emotion and emotivity that capacity is definitely transcended both in quality and essence. This seems to be indicated by the prefix *ex*, for though the psychical impulse depends to some extent on the body and is in various ways conditioned by the somatic, it does not belong to the body, and differs from it and its somatic dynamism. Thus even before we go into the detail of human emotivity, we have to stress the irreducible nature of emotions to reactions and of emotivity to reactivity. An emotion is not a somatic reaction but a psychical event that is distinctive in its nature and qualitatively different from the reaction itself of the body.

Emotivity and Reactivity

We have so far pointed out the intrinsic relation between the somatic and the psychical aspects in man. The psychical is conditioned by the somatic. Emotivity, which appears to be the characteristic trait of man's psychical dynamism, is conditioned by reactivity, which is a characteristic of his somatic dynamism. It seems that at this point we come across an important trail of the traditional as well as the more contemporary anthropological and psychological explorations. The connection between the psyche and the soma in their dynamic aspect is an important element in practically all discussions of temperaments. Moreover, since emotivity is so deeply rooted in and conditioned by reactivity we often speak of "psychical reactions"; not only do we frequently refer to such reaction but we speak of someone "reacting in such and such a way," by which we mean not only his somatic reaction but his comportment as a whole in an action that includes also his conscious response to a definite value. Indeed, even such a response that is a choice or a decision comprises some elements of somatic reactivity; man constitutes the complicated unity underlying that integration of the action in the person which in one way or another always contains in itself all the elements of the psychosomatic complexity. We are then perfectly justified when we say "someone reacted in such and such a way," though it may be that thereby we stress one aspect of this complex whole more than others.

Emotivity and the Conscious Response of Will

Any adequate image of the person's integration in the action has to include the principle of complementarity; integration complements the transcendence of the person, which is realized through self-determination and efficacy. In this dimension human action is a conscious response through choice or decision to a value. But also this response has always to make use in one way or another of somatic and psychical dynamisms. The integration of the person in the action indicates a very concrete and, each time, a unique and unrepeatable introduction of somatic reactivity and psychical emotivity into the unity of the action – into the unity with the transcendence of the person expressed by efficacious self-determination that is simultaneously a conscious response to values. But the inclusion of the conscious response to values in the human action takes place in a specific way, that is, through the integration of the whole psycho-emotivity of man which is, moreover, indicative of a specific sensibility to values. Man's sensitivity to values based on emotive grounds has a spontaneous character; in this respect it manifests the same traits as emotivity itself, which always reflects what in the person takes place in a "psychical way" – similarly as reactivity reflects what in the person takes place in a "somatic way." Because of this spontaneous sensitivity to values the emotive potentiality supplies the will with, so to speak, a special kind of raw material; for in choice and decision an act of will is always a cognitively defined, intellectual response to values. Against this background we can see more clearly the special need of the person's integration in the action as well as the special significance of this integration, a significance that in some respects is not to be compared to somatic integration. Thus, in order to reach an independent interpretation of psychical integration we have to embark upon a comprehensive analysis of human emotivity.

If we establish the significance of the person's integration in the action from the point of view of emotivity – and this is what we aim at in the successive analyses in this chapter – we ought to gain a better insight into the person's transcendence in the action; for it is in the transcendence and not in the integration of the human emotivity itself that the deepest meanings of the spirituality of the person are manifested, and it is there that we find the most adequate basis for asserting the spirituality of the human soul. The psychical is by contrast also emotive and sensuous.

3. FEELINGS AND CONSCIOUSNESS IN THE EXPERIENCE OF THE BODY

Emotive Dynamism as a Concentrator of Experiences

Psychology and anthropology usually discriminate between the corporality, the sensuousness, and the spirituality of man. Without disclaiming in any way the profound validity of this discrimination, indeed with direct reference to it, we intend to stress here the significance of emotivity, inasmuch as our chief objective is to draw an integrated image of human dynamism, insofar as it is possible. In this image emotivity defines both a specific form of and a specific current in a dynamism that in a special manner forms part of the personal dynamism of human actions. The psychical strand in emotivity may be seen as running between corporality and spirituality, but far from dividing them it interweaves with the one and the other, bringing them together. Apparently the function performed by the emotive dynamism consists in concentrating human experiences, a fact that will come out more clearly later in our discussion. In spite of the distinct difference between the emotive dynamism and the reactive dynamism of the body, they are closely interrelated and condition each other. All that determines and constitutes the spiritual transcendence of the person – his attitude toward truth, good, and beauty with the accompanying faculty of self-determination – stimulates a very deep emotive resonance in the human being. The resonance – its quality and intensity – is thoroughly individual and in its own way also determines the quality and intensity of the personal transcendence itself, or at any rate provides a special basis for the personal transcendence in man. Emotions are also the source of the expressiveness of man's actions. It follows, therefore, that an insight gained along these lines into the innermost recesses of specifically human nature can lead us very far on the way to an understanding of the person and the action; it would be impossible to reach a sound understanding of the person's integration in the action without an analysis of the emotivity.

The Affective and the Motor Stimulus

We may begin our analysis at the point where the somatic dynamism, so to speak, stops and where simultaneously emotivity comes closest to the reactivity of the body. Emotivity, like reactivity, is strictly connected with the operation of stimuli. We know that somatic reactivity consists in the ability to react to stimuli and in the preceding chapter we were primarily concerned with motor stimuli. Alongside this ability and very close to it there seems to be another one, namely, the *ability to feel*. This ability at the somatic level also consists in the reception of stimuli coming from material objects, from various bodies; but their effect is not somatic and does not consist in a reaction or a movement of the body; their effect is psychical and is expressed in feelings. Although conditioned by a reaction at the somatic level, it itself transcends through and through the somatic reaction.

Feeling Places Psychical above Somatic Subjectivity

Feeling or sensation stimuli differ essentially from the motor stimuli, though they very often come together (e.g., the hand is instinctively jerked away from a hot object). Feeling or sensation itself is not a somatic motion or impulse; its relation to the body is similar to that of the subject to an object and though in a feeling as such there is no awareness of this relation, the body – even one's own body – becomes in it an objective sense element that also penetrates into the field of consciousness. Thus feeling and sensation allow man to emerge from and above what in the preceding chapter we called the "subjectivity of the body." While such "subjectivity" is in itself closely related to the somatic reactivity and to a large extent remains unrecorded in consciousness, the psychical subjectivity, which emerges together with feeling on the basis of the body, is already included in consciousness.[67] For feeling as such constitutes a cognitive sensuous reflection of the body, which thus becomes accessible to consciousness – because of feeling the body becomes an objective content of consciousness and is reflected in it.

Feeling Underlies the Consciousness of the Body

Since the relation of feeling and sensation to consciousness is of fundamental significance for personal dynamism, we must examine it here as carefully as possible. First, there is the feeling of one's own body; the body, its different states and movements are the source of sensation stimuli which play a decisive role in enabling man to have an experience of his body. In this experience feeling is included in consciousness and combines with it to form a single common basis of the experience, though sensuous feeling differs from mental awareness. Attention has been drawn on various occasions to the fact that the range of consciousness of the body is, so to speak, currently determined by the field of feeling. For instance, the whole inner dynamism of the body, of the organism, which is connected with the body's vegetative vitality, remains, as long as nothing of it penetrates into the field of feeling, beyond, as it were, the reach of consciousness. The clause "as it were" is important, because in being conscious of the body man also has a kind of general awareness of its inwardness and its inner dynamism. This consciousness is substantiated by means of the corresponding sensations and feelings, for instance, the feeling of a bodily pain makes the inward workings of one's own body come within the scope of consciousness. Such a concretization of consciousness in feeling is entirely sufficient as a basis for experiencing one's own body.

Self-Feeling

In the habitual experience of one's body there are sensations and feelings and thus sensory stimuli expressing the body and its reactive-motor dynamisms. These sensations reveal to every man not a separate "subjectivity" of the body but the somatic structure of the whole subject that he is, of the whole ego. They reveal to what extent he is a body, to what extent his soma participates in his existence and his acting. We may even say that a bodily sensation – a direct reflex of the body, a reflex that in a way is being continually formed and shaped – has in this respect a fundamental significance in one's own bodily ego. This habitual experience results, as noted above, from many sensations or feelings and manifests itself as a general *self-feeling*. Physically and psychically we always feel more or less "well" or more or less "bad"; man always has present in him some kind of feeling or self-feeling, which forms a sort of psychic fabric or undercurrent of his existence of acting. The direct and proper object of self-feeling is the whole somatic ego, which is not isolated from the personal ego but is, on the contrary, intrinsically cohesive with it.

It is important to stress that man's self-feeling manifests a distinctly qualitative trait and value element; we all know that we may feel either well or unwell and that within the limits of these essential distinctions there are various grades and subtle differences of tone. It is this that we want to express when saying "I feel well" or "I do not feel well," or in many other similar expressions such as weary, exhausted, ill, fine, fresh, and so on. Man can also feel that he is efficient or inefficient in his doings and this, because of psychical reflection, brings into prominence the significance of efficiency in the motor-reactive dynamism of the body. Time and again we have opportunity to see how this dynamism as well as its efficiency conditions the so-called "higher psychical functions"; for instance, we know all too well that physical weariness adversely affects the mental processes of thinking and that a good rest "clears" the mind and brings precision to our thoughts. In this way we also realize how intrinsically cohesive is our somatic ego with the whole of the personal ego, how strict is their mutual union.

"Precedence" of Consciousness over Feelings in Personal Dynamism

The feeling of one's body is a necessary condition for experiencing the integral subjectivity of man. In this experience the body and consciousness are, as it were, bound together by feeling, which is the most elementary manifestation of the human psyche as well as the nearest reflection in it of what is somatic in man. This sensory reflection in the psyche differs essentially from the reflexive function of consciousness, whose fundamental significance in having the personal experience of a concrete human ego we discussed at the beginning of this study. The interpenetration in this experience of feeling with consciousness brings into prominence the general relation that in the domain of human cognition exists between senses and mind. The relation is bilateral because a feeling we have of our own body allows us to establish an objective contact with it and at the same time reveals the psychical subjectivity integrated with the somatic body-subject. Does not a feeling "happen" in a psychic way within the human ego and does not this "happening" reveal subjectivity? Subjectivity is thus, so to speak, revealed to consciousness, which – with the exception of extreme cases when emotions overcome consciousness – retains a sort of "precedence" over feelings. In fact, we have the awareness (among other things) also of our feelings, which means that in the normal course of events they are "subordinate" to consciousness. On the other hand, we cannot assert the opposite, namely, that we have a "feeling of consciousness," that we feel our consciousness. It is this precedence of consciousness, which brings with it a certain order and "subordination" of feelings, in particular the feeling of one's own body, that is the condition of self-determination and thus also of self-governance and self-possession; it is the condition of the realization of the action, of the really personal dynamism.

The feeling of one's own body reveals the psychosomatic subjectivity of man. Since this occurs in relation to consciousness, which
performs both the reflective and reflexive function, the awareness of
that subjectivity brings with it the "subjectification" and interiorization of the ego in consciousness which also extends to and
contains the body as *something belonging only to myself* and different
from all other bodies. To have a feeling of his body allows man as
much insight into his own soma as he needs for self-determination in
the action. In the same way the person's integration in the action is
established; the integration is equivalent to a normal experience of
one's body, an experience that is conditioned by feeling and consciousness. Any defects or insufficiency of feeling that would obstruct
it becomes a factor of disintegration.

4. SENSITIVITY AND TRUTHFULNESS

The Consciousness of Feelings and Man's Individual Sensitivity

Experience of one's body is not the only instance in which feelings
attain the status of consciousness, just as bodily sensations are not
the only form of feeling. Man not only feels his body but he also has a
more integral feeling of himself, he feels what determines his own ego
and his dynamism. Moreover, he has a feeling of the world as a
complex and differentiated set of beings, among which his own ego
exists and with which it has different relations. The attainment by
feelings and sensations of the conscious state shapes the experience
of his own ego as being-in-the-world and also forms in one way or
another his experience of the world. This of course refers primarily to
the sphere that remains within the range of sense but not to the whole
of reality, not to the universe as a whole which is encompassed by the
human mind in its own manner. Having its own specificity and being
an emotive occurrence, feeling is directly linked with what lies within
the reach of sense; it is not divided from higher mental activities and
their contents. Careful observation supplies ample evidence against
any simplified compartmentalization in man (e.g., against any tendency to identify emotivity with sensuality). If we ascertain in man
not only a feeling of his body or of bodies in general – to which he has
cognitive access through sense – but also some aesthetic, religious, or

moral feelings, then we also have evidence that the emotive element in him somehow corresponds to what is spiritual and not merely sensual.

At this point we touch upon some crucial problems of psychology, anthropology, and epistemology. The question of emotivity, and more directly the question of the cognitive function performed by feelings, comes into our considerations, however, only in general and insofar as it concerns the integration of the person in the action. The individual sensitivity of every human being is formed by the occurrence of feelings as well as by their intensity and their accessibility to conscious reflection.

Sensitivity and the Personal Experience of Values

When we mention sensitivity we are obviously not referring solely to the sensibility, to sense stimuli in the strict sense; we are not thinking of the acuity of vision and of hearing or of the sensibility of touch; we refer also to the different intentional directions of human feeling that are deeply rooted in man's spiritual life. But sensitivity itself does not suffice to reach the evidence of the transcendence of the person, of his self-determination and efficacy. It seems to be rather an indication only of what happens in the person as a subject endowed with emotive capacities and of what in this respect demands to be integrated. *Sensitivity* is indeed related to *sensation*. They have the same origin. Sensation refers in turn to sense-perception. Sensitivity also in a way is present in the exercise of the sensory faculties of man, though its character is primarily receptive rather than active, and this is precisely the reason why it demands integration.

Integration, however, is not limited only to that for which consciousness is responsible, that is, to the attainment by the particular feelings and the intentional content they carry with them of the level of consciousness leading to the emergence of an authentic experience of values. For it is to values that all feelings or sensations are intentionally directed, a circumstance already explained in the analysis of bodily sensations. Every feeling or sensation is directed to some fact within or without the subject to whom it belongs, but it always has that "bent for" a value, that qualitative trait which is so clearly marked in the feelings one has of one's own body. This is why a feeling or a sensation becomes in man, so to speak, the nucleus for the crystallization of an experience of value. Emotionalists – such as, for instance, M. Scheler – go so far as to maintain that feelings are the *only* source of man's cognitive relations to values and that apart from them there are no other authentic means of knowing values.[68]

We will not discuss these problems here. We may note, however, that experience of values based on the integration of feelings through consciousness is not in itself sufficient; in view of the person's transcendence in the action still another integration is necessary – namely, the integration through "truthfulness." Indeed, integration of the person in the action refers essentially to truth which makes possible an authentic freedom of self-determination. Therefore, experience of values, which is a function of man's sensitivity itself (and hence also a function of feelings) has within the dimension of the acting person to be subordinated to the reference to truth. *The fusion of sensitivity with truthfulness is the necessary condition of the experience of values.* It is only on the basis of such an experience that authentic choices and decisions can be formed. In this case authenticity is indicative of the fulfillment of freedom which depends on the certainty of truth, that is to say, on the reference to an authentic value and thus the validity of the judgment about the positive value of the object, concerning which a choice or a decision is being made.

Such an understanding of the notion of "authenticity" – based on truthfulness – may sometimes be contrary to its understanding based on sensitivity alone. The latter approach would make of sensitivity the ultimate criterion of values and the sole basis for experience of values; just as if integration in consciousness of feelings and values felt were to prevent integration by truthfulness as well as reflection or mental appreciation and judgment of values. But this is not so. Actually it is the latter integration, the integration by truthfulness, that has a decisive significance for the acting person and is also the measure of the authentic transcendence of the person in the action. The man who in his attitude to values would rely solely on the way his feelings develop is confined to the orbit of what only happens in him and becomes incapable of self-determination. Indeed, self-determination and the closely related self-governance often require that action be taken in the name of *bare truth* about good, in the name of values that are not felt. It even may require that action be taken against one's actual feelings.

Sensitivity as a Source of Enrichment of the Psyche

The immediately preceding remarks do not, however, depreciate in any way the significance of sensitivity. This latter is itself a valuable endowment that greatly enriches human nature. The ability to sense, the spontaneous ability to feel, values is the basis for many human talents. Emotionalists are right when they contend that this ability in man is unique and irreplaceable. No intellectual approval of values leading to their objectively correct appreciation will ever by itself result in so expressive an experience as when it is guided by feeling. Neither can the intellect impart to man that closeness to a value and concentration on it as feeling does. Whether he remains blind to values when deprived of the necessary feeling, as claimed by emotionalists, is a matter for discussion, but there seems to be no doubt that he would then be incapable of having the right, the properly dynamic experience of them. In this sense sensitivity is indubitably an especially valuable asset of the human psyche, but in order to appreciate its real worth we have to take into account the degree to which it is pervaded by truthfulness. The same standards apply also to the integration of the person: the more there is truthfulness in his awareness of all values and in the way the actual relations and order among them are reflected in the experience he has of them, the more complete is his self-governance and mature his self-possession.

5. DESIRE AND EXCITEMENT

Concupiscent Appetite and Irascible Appetite

In Aristotelian philosophy a very definite line is drawn between man's sensuousness and his rationality, but at the same time the strict relation between them is clearly established. This relation occurs in the field of cognition where the senses are meant to establish a direct contact with objective reality and at the same time supply, so to speak, the raw material for the mind; this conception is justified inasmuch as man cognizes the external world, the world accessible to sense, and simultaneously constitutes the objects of that world by means of intellectual structuration. It is why man's knowledge of what is "accessible" to sense is not the same as the manner in which it is presented by sense. Moreover, intellectual cognition extends far beyond the givenness received in sensory experience. The relation between sensuousness and rationality occurs also in the realm of what in classic thought has been conceived of as *appetite*. A sensory experience is the foundation of cognition, so the appetite of volition, sensitive appetite, supplies material or objectives for volition. In certain respects it may function as "rational appetite," though in other respects man's sensuousness is a source of specific difficulties for the rational exercise of his will. Let us recall that already in the discussion on self-determination we saw the term "appetite" covered such meanings as striving and concupiscence though it was broader than either of them.

Concerning the will itself, we may ask whether we can attribute to it a concupiscent character; certainly there seems to be no difficulty in this respect in the case of sense; sensuous desire is a fact well known from actual experience. In order to describe precisely this experiential reality St. Thomas discriminated between "concupiscence" or the "concupiscent appetite" and "irascibility" or the "irascible appetite," each representing a specific, one may even say a typical, version of the sensitive appetite.[69] This distinction allows us to see in it, though in germinal form, an outline of a sort of typology. It rests on an axiological rather than psychological basis inasmuch as the difference between the concupiscent and the irascible appetites lies primarily in the differences between the types of objective, that is, their end, in the value accessible to sense; in the former case this is but an object of desire and in the latter an objective to be attained only by overcoming obstacles or opposition. According to Thomas Aquinas the two forms of concupiscence are simultaneously the basis for the differentiation of human sentiments and passions. In this form we find in his writings an integrated interpretation of the human psyche and the psychical dynamism on the side of sense; we also find there, as already noted, elements for a sort of typology of the human individual. This typology seems even to be confirmed to some extent by actual observation, for we know concupiscence is a dominant trait in some people and irascibility in others.

Excitement as a Distinct Emotive Fact

The discussion in this study stresses and brings to the forefront the emotive nature of the human psyche. The point where our approach meets again the traditional anthropology is the stress we put upon a definite experience of an emotive nature which is the experience of excitement. Excitement "happens" in the subject and thereby reveals his psychical potentiality; it is an emotive instance that differs from feeling, to which we have rightly attributed a certain cognitive intentionality. No such cognitive tendency of the psyche is present in excitement, whose character is never cognitive. But does it not show a desirous nature? "Desiring" consists, however, in pointing toward an object whereas excitement is essentially self-sufficient; it consists in the exercise of its process with which it is totally absorbed. Thus it seems that its nature is primarily and essentially emotive though its emotivity may show differences in quality and tone. Excitements occurring in man may be of an irascible or a concupiscent type. That is, *indirectly* excitement has an appetitive bent but what we have in view and put stress *directly* upon is the essential nature of the excitement as such. It does also entail an intentional bent "toward" or "against" something. As such, it is a manifestation of emotivity, a typical emotive activation of the human psyche.

Such activation is usually very distinctly set in the framework of somatic reactivity. Excitement is always manifested in a definite reaction of the body, indeed in a whole complex chain of reactions of the organism (blood circulation, breathing, a quickened heartbeat, etc.), which are very distinctly felt. It is a specific sensation of the body contained in the feeling of excitement itself; we feel and have the experience of the emotive and the reactive moment as one dynamic fact, and this circumstance allows us in a way to call the fact a "reaction." The somatic element accompanying excitement may then be seen as an extension to the body of a dynamism that is itself psychical. We have, however, to distinguish here between it and the "excitement" of the body as such, which itself is but a reactive fact producing but an emotive resonance. This near and readily felt relation to the body leads to the conclusion that excitement is something sensuous, a dynamic manifestation of sensuousness. It is usually accompanied by sensations of special intensity, by a rich sensational reflex, which adds to the vividness of the experience of excitement.

The Difference between Excitement and Elation

Nevertheless, to reduce excitements to sensuousness alone would be an oversimplification. The source of excitement, the stimulus that provokes it, does not necessarily affect the senses. The stimulation may come from the experience of a value that is entirely inaccessible to sense or from wholehearted acceptance of ideals; then, however, we tend to speak of "elation" rather than of excitement. "Excitement" as such remains indicative of the sphere of sensuous stimuli or stimulations; elation, being spiritual in nature, may be accompanied in the subject by sensuous or even bodily excitement of greater or lesser intensity. It seems, moreover, that such excitement may to a certain point help the elation of the spirit but if too strong it becomes an obstacle. This assertion supplies additional evidence for the need for integration.

Excitability

In this case integration must comprise not only the particular excitements but the whole of human excitability, which is the term we apply to this particular emotive element of the psyche. "Excitability" is the capacity for excitement; its direction and its tone can differ as can the excitements themselves. It designates also a certain sphere of human capacities that seems to be rather closely correlated with man's sensitivity. Though the two are interrelated there is also a clear-cut difference between them; excitability relates to other emotive facts than does sensitivity, with which, however, they are usually associated; for excitability itself, as well as excitement, which is its dynamic catalyst and nucleus, constitutes in man what may be called the "explosive sphere" of emotions. It seems, however, that this refers also to the quality of these emotions and to their subjective intensity. We thus see that there are reasons to distinguish between excitability and emotionality, which will be discussed separately. Excitability, in fact, tends to refer to an awakening of emotions, and because this is often rather sudden we have characterized it as explosive. The source of emotions is then seen as irrational and their experience is in itself "blind" – these are the same features that, apart from emotive intensity, we attribute to passions. Excitement establishes certain forms of human emotions and feelings, but obviously it does not exhaust their enormous wealth of tone and variation.

Excitability as a Constituent of Instincts

Sensuous-emotive excitability appears to be particularly well rooted in the soil of human instincts. In the preceding chapter we uncovered the somato-reactive layer in the instincts of self-preservation and reproduction; we also noted that an instinct could not be reduced to the dynamism of this one layer alone. It also has its own appropriate psychosomatic center, which apparently inheres in a particular excitability, it may be the sexual excitability or any of the different forms of excitability associated with self-preservation. In either case this consists in a special capacity for stimuli or, in other words, the aptitude for excitement. Nevertheless, this aptitude is insufficient to exhaust the notion of "instinct," just as the notion cannot be fully accounted for by the more or less determined reactivity of the body, the body's definite sexual reactions, or the reactions associated with self-preservation. A much more convincing understanding seems to be that both reactivity and excitability remain at the disposal of the powerful forces of nature that steer them in the direction of the most elemental and fundamental value that is existence itself.

6. "STIRRING EMOTIONS" AND EMOTIVITY

"Stirring Emotions" Differ from Excitement

Our analysis of human emotivity brings us now to a sphere that demands separate treatment, because if the reductive method were to be applied to it, its distinctness could easily be lost. The sphere is that of the experience of deep, stirring emotion, which differs from excitement. Such stirring emotions represent an entirely different kind of experience, a different subjective event, than does excitement. Although in either case we are dealing with essentially emotive and psychical events, the nature of a stirring of emotions is distinctly separate. The specific character of the experience involved seems best described as a deep emotional stirring, which differs from other emotions and feelings not only in its intensity, but in "depth," in "moving" and bringing to the surface man's psychic dimension otherwise remaining unnoticed. An emotional stirring, like excitement, "happens" in the man-subject, but these two psychical states are easily distinguished from each other and from among the various *passions of the soul*. (It is worth recalling here that the term "passion" derives etymologically from the Latin word for "to happen.")

Excitement, far more than deep emotion, appears as we have pointed out to be closely related to the sensuousness of man. While both are accompanied by some kind of somatic reaction, excitement is seen as more embedded in this reaction than even very deep emotions. We experience emotions as manifestations of a pure emotivity, as that activation of the psyche itself in which somatic underlayers are less clearly pronounced. This is the reason why in the experience of several types of deep emotions bodily feelings may appear to give priority to spiritual feelings; moreover, the content of such emotions is strictly related to the spiritual life of man. We may for instance experience an aesthetic emotion generated by the perception of something beautiful, a cognitive emotion that arises from the discovery of a truth, or various kinds of deep emotions connected with the sphere of good, in particular, moral good or evil. The last of these experiences, which Scheler sees as the deepest manifestations of man's emotivity, develops in strict relation to the processes of the conscience; remorse at a committed wrong is not only a judgment of oneself, but this experience of truth entails, as we well know from actual life, an unusually stirring emotional component. The same applies to the processes of repentance, justification, or conversion, when man's actual departure from evil and acceptance of good, at any rate in the initial stage of his acceptance, are also accompanied by deeply felt emotions. The content of all these emotions, and with it also their emotive tone, differs diametrically; man passes from the gnawing remorse of his conscience and the sometimes deep distress almost bordering on despair arising from his sense of guilt to a state of mental peace and equally deep joy, to a state of spiritual bliss.

The "Stir of Emotion" as the Core of Human Affectivity

We have been speaking of different emotions and feelings, of different manifestations of man's affectivity. At their root there is always a *stirring of emotion*; this emotive core may be said to be radiating internally and thus to produce every time a different emotional experience. It is this experience that we call "emotion." Each emotional experience is different, unique, and irreproducible, even though among them there are those that in respect of their emotive content are similar or indeed almost identical; they often differ in some detail of tone or intensity but their essential content is nevertheless the same. The sameness of content always has its experiential origin in a stirring of emotion, which is simultaneously colored by this content and subsequently, because of its internal radiation, spreads it to the whole of man's psychical sphere.

In this way an emotion springs forth and develops in man and fades away. Occasionally it may be fixed in what we may call an "affective state." While every emotion, a transitory one, represents an emotional state of the man-subject, an "affective state" is spoken of most appropriately only when an emotion has become fixed, though to what extent an emotion once fixed still remains but a stirring is another matter. What we call an "affective state," however, seems very often to have already departed from its original emotive core, which was a definite stirring of emotion, and has since been taken over by the will. The question of the penetration of emotions to the realm of will and thus also of the transition from emotional states to *affective attitudes* is of great significance in any discussion on the integration of the psyche, which is precisely the theme of this chapter.

The Multifarious Richness of Emotions

We must here return to the specific nature of emotions. We have just seen that it is also the specific nature itself of that emotional stirring or movement which spreads and infuses the psyche. When we try to characterize emotions and call them by different names, we in fact distinguish between *the different ways emotions are stirred.* For instance, different emotional stirrings mark the feelings of sorrow and of joy, of anger and of tenderness, of love and of hatred. The world of human emotions is rich and diversified, in many respects like the colors, tones, and shades on the palette of a painter. Time and again psychologists and to some extent also moralists have attempted to describe and discriminate the principal emotions, according to which the great wealth of man's emotional life could then be classed. It cannot be denied that they have had some success in their efforts, though the domain of human emotions, somewhat like the painter's palette, manifests an infinite spectrum of individual colors, tones, and shades. Moreover, emotions, like colors, can be mixed, they overlap and interpenetrate, they also enhance or complete and destroy each other. They constitute a separate and powerful realm within man, a separate sphere of the human subjectivity. Since emotions *happen* "in" man, subjectivity is here understood in the particular sense that has been distinguished earlier in this study. Their happening in man comprises their emergence, their growth, and their passing away. Emotional dynamism is at least to a large extent independent of the efficacy of the person. Already the Greek philosophers noticed that emotions did not depend on the mind and in their essence were "irrational."

Some Criteria of Differentiation

This alleged "irrationality" of human affectivity has perhaps been the cause of the one-sided and oversimplified tendency to identify it with sensuousness. Our views on this matter were propounded earlier and here we only have to stress once again the specific difference between the stirring of emotion and excitement. On the one hand, the difference lies in their distinctive natures, and not just in the degree or intensity of experience. (Even the strongest stirring of emotion is not excitement.) The components of the accompanying somatic reactions of the two seem also to be different. On the other hand, excitement is presumably necessary to initiate an emotional experience when an emotional stirring alone is insufficient: but then it is not so much the question of the intensity itself of an emotion as of the level at which man's emotive capacity is operative. Apparently it is this difference of level that we have in mind when we speak of an "emotional stirring" as of something different from excitement and when we discriminate between man's excitability and his affectiveness. But if we can refer to different levels, it means that in the emotional life itself there are inherent possibilities of its transformation, that is, of a transition from one level to another, for instance, from the level of excitement to that of emotion;[70] in this respect, the functioning of the human being is capable of "sublimation." Psychologists commonly agree to the distinction between the "lower" and the "higher" emotions. They also take note of the different "depth" of emotions as well as of their more "peripheral" or more "central" positional features. These distinctions presuppose an innerness of the man-person, something like an immaterial space, where on the ground of the role of feelings we may differentiate between the "central" and the "peripheral," where it is also possible to establish different levels of "depth" (though these levels are not to be confused with the levels of emotions, which, as we saw, may be either "lower" or "higher"). From another point of view, the different "levels of depth" point to a certain integration in the man-subject of his emotional stirrings (with the ensuing emotions) and project on the efficacy of the person.

This seems to show that the dynamism of emotions is specifically interrelated with the whole system of sensations and feelings, which penetrate to consciousness to determine in every particular case the form and the actual character of an emotional experience.

7. THE EMOTIVITY OF THE SUBJECT AND THE EFFICACY OF THE PERSON

Emotions Differentiate According to Their Emotive Content

The preceding analyses do not exhaust the immense wealth of the reality that is the emotional life of man; they only give some insight and help to draw its characteristic outlines. Every emotion has its own emotive core in the form of an emotional stirring from which it radiates in its own specific manner; according to its proper stirring, every emotion establishes itself as an original and unique psychical event. If it is vested with a content – and we know both emotional stirrings and emotions are – then this takes place also in an emotive way. The content, let us stress, is neither cognitive nor appetitive but solely emotive. Moreover, every emotion is itself a content directly and simply present in man; anger, love, hatred, yearning, sorrow, or joy are all different contents and each can be authentically realized only as a stirring emotion. Each is also a manifestation and actualization of man's psychical capacities and each reveals in a special manner his subjectivity. It is in the sphere of emotions (within the confines of human emotivity) that a certain tension between the efficacy and the subjectivity of man is most clearly marked. Because of this tension the synthesis of efficacy with subjectivity as well as the concrete significance of the integration in this domain deserve an especially attentive analysis.

Spontaneity and Self-Determination

Emotional experiences – stirring emotions or excitements and in their wake also the particular emotions and even passions – only happen in man as subject. Their happening is spontaneous, and this means they are not a product of personal efficacy and self-determination. We have thus to assume that at the root of the emotive dynamism there must be a special psychical efficacy, as otherwise it would be impossible to explain all that in an emotive way happens in the man-subject. In a sense *emotivity* itself signifies that spontaneous efficacy of the human psyche. When we say "it is spontaneous," we want to stress thereby its dynamic independence from the *proper efficacy* of the person, that is, from his self-determination. While experiencing feelings or passions man has the most vivid awareness that it is not he who is acting but that something is happening in him, indeed that something is happening *with him*, just as if he lost control of himself, as if he could not bring himself under control. In this connection we see that, because man as the person has the power of self-governance and self-possession, situations of deeply stirring emotions and passion present a special task for him to cope with.

Affectivity is not the Source of Disintegration

The fact that with the emergence of an emotion or passion man is prompted to seek some sort of integration and this becomes a special task for him, does not signify in any way that they are in themselves a cause of disintegration. The view about their disintegrating role appeared in the philosophy of the Stoic school and in modern times was to some extent revived by Kant. If the position advocating in various ways a rejection of emotions so as to allow man to act solely according to reason (Kant's idea of the Categorical Imperative) were to be maintained, then it would be necessary to accept the whole emotive capacity as being itself a source of disintegration in the acting person. The broadly conceived experience of man, with due attention paid to morality, prevents us, however, from accepting this view – just as it was rejected, for instance, by Aristotle in his anthropology and ethics or in his critique of the Stoics, and in Scheler's critique of Kant. The view that conceived of human emotivity – and in particular human emotionality – as a source of disintegration is a manifestation of a special sort of ethical and anthropological apriorism, and the essence of any apriorism is to disregard the evidence of experience. When we treat man's emotivity and emotionality solely as a source of disintegration in the acting person, we assume to some extent that he is *a priori* and inevitably doomed to disintegration. In this respect the Stoic position has to be seen as pessimistic. The pessimism in this question is derived, especially in Kant, from a specific sort of idealism.

The Creative Role of Tensions between Emotivity and Efficacy

The realism that we are trying to adhere to in our argumentation demands that no emotion or even passion be regarded as in itself the source of disintegration in the acting person. It is impossible to deny, however, that emotions and passions present man with special problems that he has to cope with. Inasmuch as self-governance and self-possession are elements in the structure of the person, these problems consist in the need for integration in human emotivity and emotionality, a need fully justified by the person's self-determination; for there is a clearly marked tension between the spontaneous efficacy of the human psyche and the efficacy of the person. The tension, which has manifold aspects, represents in a way the crucial moment of human personality and morality. In traditional anthropology it is seen primarily as existing between the faculties of the human soul, between the rational appetite (will) and the sensitive appetite. In the context of this study, however, we shall attempt to examine it first of all as a tension existing between the subjectivity and the efficacy of the person. We already know that the synthesis of efficacy with subjectivity in the person's action cannot be realized without a specific kind of effort that may be seen as the most appropriate effort of man's inwardness. It is this effort, this toil, that allowed us to compare the efficacy of the person in the action to creativity. We have also been to some extent prepared to deal with the problem by the analysis in this chapter of the relation existing between sensitivity and truthfulness in cognition. We can thus assert that the tension between the emotivity of the human subject and the personal efficacy in actions is specifically creative.

Emotions Tend to Be Rooted in the Subjective Ego

The tension between self-determination, or the proper efficacy of the person, and emotivity, or the spontaneous efficacy of the human psyche, can of course be reduced to the relation between will and emotion. When this relation is seen as the tension between the subjectivity and the efficacy of man, then it is obviously with reference not to the subject as the ontic basis but to subjectivity as the experiential correlate of what only happens in man but is not his acting, in which efficacy plays a decisive role. On the other hand, we know emotions occur only in man. This emotive happening may be but transitory, like a light touch on the surface of the soul, though it also manifests a specific tendency to be rooted in the subjective ego. Then, if an emotion turns into a permanent psychical state, correlatively to it an inner attitude develops in man. For instance, a sudden momentary fit of anger is one thing, but a lasting resentment is quite another – the anger that has turned into an inner attitude. Likewise a short-lasting affection or hatred differs entirely from love or hatred that has become fixed as an inner attitude. Such attitudes become an intrinsic factor of human life and an especially important product of man's emotive capacity and dynamism. It is here that we come to the point where "what happens in man" is nearest to his self-determination.

As we know, emotional attitudes develop spontaneously. Their fixation and rooting in the subject arises from the same emotive dynamism that was at the origin of the initial emotional stirring or excitement. The fixation and the rooting of emotion in the subjective ego is an indication of the range of emotive energy and at the same time constitutes a specific accumulation of subjectivity and immanence. Efficacy and the related transcendence of the personal ego are, so to speak, drawn in and included in the subject. The influence of emotions on the will may be such that instead of determining man's attitudes, the will tends to adopt the attitude presented by emotion thus leading to what we call "the emotional attitude." Such attitudes are subjectivistic. We now see why emotion may be rightly regarded as a special source of subjectivism. Structurally subjectivism signifies that efficacy is dominated by subjectivity – to some extent it signifies the preponderance of the psychical immanence over personal transcendence in acting.

The Role of Emotion with Respect to the Will Stresses Personal Efficacy

All these considerations do not, however, justify the conclusion that emotion is leading to disintegration. In spite of the emotionalization of consciousness, which we have already discussed, and the generally recognized limitations of responsibility in actions performed under emotional strain, there are no sufficient reasons to attribute a disintegrating role to emotions. Emotivity may tend to diminish the distance between the subjective ego and efficacy and it may to some extent thrust upon the will its own system of values, but by any standards it is no more than an obstacle to the integration of the person in the action. Indeed, integration remains possible and then emotion adds special vividness to efficacy and with it to the whole personal structure of self-governance and self-possession.

8. THE EMOTIVITY OF THE SUBJECT AND THE EXPERIENCE OF VALUE

Emotivity and Conscious Efficacy

Since in our analysis not all the elements of the relation between the emotivity and efficacy of man have been sufficiently attended to we will now examine them in some detail. We know that emotivity in man is a source of spontaneous subjectifications and interiorizations different from the subjectification and interiorization performed by consciousness. In a way the emotionalization of consciousness is a limiting phenomenon when excessive emotion damages consciousness and the ability to have a normal experience. Man then lives engrossed in his emotion, his excitement, or his passion, and though the condition is undoubtedly subjective, his "subjectivity" brings only negative results so far as efficacy, self-determination, and the transcendence of the acting person are concerned. Thus the limiting case of spontaneous subjectification by emotion may be said to be the separation of human subjectivity from conscious efficacy. Such are the situations when man loses his ability to act consciously and hence also to be responsible, the situations when in his acting there is no real acting but only a special sort of happening – something happens in and with him, something that he neither determines nor fulfills. Neither can he be fully responsible for what is taking place, though we may well ask what is his responsibility for the development of the situation in which he can no longer have responsibilities.

Apart from these extreme cases, when emotivity may be said to have destroyed the efficacy of the person, there are still many situations in which efficacy is only partly limited. The degree of these limitations differs and depends on the intensity of the emotion involved. To speak of the "intensity of emotions" is a simplification that in itself appears permissible but does not express the whole complexity of the actual facts; if we say the degree of the limitation of conscious efficacy – also of responsibility – depends on the intensity of emotion, then we appear to be opposing emotivity to efficacy, as if they were but two contrary forces. The actual difference between them is, however, far more complex so that even the idea of psychical force cannot be understood in a way similar to a physical force; for the force of emotion mainly derives from the experience of value. Thus, it is in this domain that there are special opportunities and possibilities for creative integration.

The Expressiveness of Human Experience is Emotional

Asserting that the intensity of emotion "mainly derives from the experience of value" we touch on what appears to be the most remarkable in human emotivity and what distinguishes it from the purely somatic reactivity. Admittedly, the somatic ability to react to stimuli, in particular when they relate to human instincts, has from an objective point of view the traits of reference to values, but in this sphere there can be no actual experience of value; perhaps the reason is that somatic dynamisms as such are not directly connected with consciousness, while the link – and in its turn the experience of the body – is established by means of sensations. The same is not the case with emotions, which are intrinsically accessible to consciousness and indeed have a specific ability, as it were, to attract consciousness. Thus we not only become aware of our emotions but also our consciousness and in particular our experience derive from them a special vividness. The vividness of human experience seems to have an emotional rather than a conscious nature. We may even say it is to emotion in the normal course of experience – that is, apart from extreme or nearly extreme situations – that man owes that special "value" of his experiences which consists in their subjective vividness; this circumstance retains its significance also with regard to the cognitive aspects of these experiences.

The Content of Emotions Refers to Values

Our interest, however, is concentrated on the experience of value rather than on the value of experience. The present considerations have been prepared by earlier analyses, in particular the analysis of sensitivity. Both the emotional stirring and the emotions of the human being always relate to a value and are born out of this relation. This is true when we are angry and it is equally true when we love, mourn, rejoice, or hate. The reference in all these cases is to a value, and the whole emotion may be said to consist of this reference. Nevertheless, it is neither cognitive nor appetitive; the emotional stirring as well as emotions themselves point to values, but as such they have no cognition or desire of values. We may only say emotions are an indication – but only in the special experiential way – of values that exist apart from emotions, outside the subject having that emotional experience. If parallel to this indication or demonstration of values there is some cognition of them, then it results from sensations and feelings, which constitute what is like an "emotive condition" or "emotive reflex." The more thoroughly consciousness is penetrated by this reflex, the fuller and more complete becomes the experience of value. The emotionalization of consciousness, however, hinders this experience and sometimes may even prevent it. Furthermore, any emotion – also excitements and passions – directs its emotive content beyond itself to a definite value and thereby it provides an opportunity for the experience of value, and for the experiential cognition of value.[71]

The Source of the Spontaneous Experience of Value

An emotion, when stirred, spreads out and, becoming rooted in the subject, spontaneously sets off reference to value. The very spontaneity of this reference appears to be in its own way valuable; it represents a specific "psychical value" or something "valuable for the psyche," because the psyche on the basis of its own proper emotive dynamism manifests a natural inclination. Spontaneity – and also the spontaneous experience of value – are well suited to the needs of the human psyche, not so much perhaps because they would be easy to come by or the value would be, so to speak, given and ready-made, but because of the specific emotional fulfillment that is brought by such an experience. Emotional fulfillment is simultaneously a special kind of fulfillment of the subjectivity itself of the human ego; it generates a feeling of being entirely contained within oneself and at the same time in an intimate nearness to the object, that is, to the value with which the contact is spontaneously established.

Relieving of Tensions between Spontaneity and Self-Determination

A tension between emotivity and efficacy – mentioned previously – that engages two of man's forces or powers develops because of a twofold reference to value. Efficacy and with it also personal self-determination are formed through choice and decision, and these presuppose a dynamic relation to truth in the will itself. In this way, however, a new transcendent factor is introduced into the spontaneous experience of value and to the related experience of striving to attain the emotional fulfillment of one's own subjectivity. This factor directs the person toward his fulfillment in the action not through emotional spontaneity alone but by means of the transcendent relation to truth and the related obligation and responsibility. In the traditional approach this dynamic factor in personal life was defined as the intellect, a definition often reflected in everyday speech and opinions, which oppose emotion to reason, the latter being then used in a broader sense than to denote the ability of intellectual cognition.

The intellect has precedence over emotion, over the emotive spontaneity of the human being, and denotes the power and the ability to be guided in choice and decision by the truth itself about good. This ability is decisive for that authentic spiritual power which determines the guidelines of human acting. The power itself, even if among its properties there is a demand for a certain detachment – the distance that lends truth – from spontaneously experienced values, is never manifested by a denial of these values, by their rejection in the name of some sort of "pure transcendence," a rejection that was apparently postulated by the Stoics and by Kant. On the contrary, the authentic subordination to truth as the principle controlling the choices and decisions made by the free human will demands an intimate inter-relation between transcendence and integration in the domain of emotions. Indeed, we know from what was said before that transcendence and integration are two complementary aspects that explain the complexity of man's acting. Especially in what concerns the emotivity of the human being it seems that only such an inter-pretation of the existing complexity and not a simplifying reduction is important and may become relevant to theoretical and practical issues concerning the human being.

9. ACTION AND EMOTION – THE INTEGRATING FUNCTION OF SKILL

Attraction and Repulsion in the Spontaneous Reference to Values

It is at this point that we have to examine the integrating function of skill or proficiency. We referred to the notion of "skills" in the preceding chapter while examining the integration of the acting per-son on the basis of the somatic dynamism. We then saw how much every synthesis of action with motion owed to the skills acquired by man from earliest childhood long before his coming to the age of reason. Our analyses of the human psyche and emotivity have dis-closed with sufficient clarity the tension that exists between the spontaneous dynamism of emotions and the efficacy of the person. Finally, we explained in what sense the tension between emotion and the intellectual reference to truth developed in connection with their relation to values. The appropriate integration in this field thus presupposes some reliance on the intellect and that relation to the objects of acting which is based on the truth about the good presented in these objects.

The tension between the person's efficacy and emotivity results from the fact that emotional dynamism introduces a spontaneous turn toward certain values. The turn may have an attractive or a repulsive character; in the former case its direction is "toward" while in the latter it is directed "away." While the emotive turn "toward" indicates a positive value, the repulsion, the turn "away," indicates a countervalue, something negative. Thus the whole emotive dynamism brings with it a spontaneous orientation, it introduces man into the profoundly antagonistic system of positivity and negativity. The fact that man is emotionally dynamized or oriented to the good and against the evil is not so much a function of any emotional stir or of emotions but reaches to the deeper roots of his nature. In this respect emotions follow the orientation of nature, which, as we already noted, is expressed by instincts. At present it is not a question of the instincts of reproduction or self-preservation, which were considered in the preceding chapter (though undoubtedly also on the ground of these instincts a split between attraction and repulsion occurs in the emotions of the relevant spheres). For the moment, however, we are interested in the urge, appertaining to human nature, "toward" the positive and "against" the negative. In this connection it is important to note that attraction and repulsion, of which we have spoken in only the most general terms, are not at first defined as to their object. To define them in this respect is the task and the function of the person and thus of the intellect, which cognitively forms man's attitude to truth, in this case the truth about "good" and "evil."

Moral Decision and Spontaneous Attraction or Repulsion

Different emotions introduce into man's attitude to truth their own spontaneous reference of an emotional and emotive character. Emotion is accompanied by a sense of value or countervalue. It is thus that a more or less distinct and vivid psychical fact is formed, a fact whose distinctness and vividness comprises also the intensity of the experience had consciously. For instance, the orientation of love, joy, or desire is attractive and to a good, while that of fear, dislike, or – in a different situation – sorrow is repulsive. St. Thomas rightly calls attention to another specific trait of emotions, which manifests itself in the element of irascibility, the most typical of these emotions being that of anger, an emotion essentially repulsive though in a special sense. In a different way this trait also appears in the emotional experience of courage. Earlier we noted the twofold character of human emotions, which are dominated either by the appetitive or the irascible element. The distinction according to the predominance in an emotional experience of attraction or repulsion seems, however, to have a special significance for the spontaneous orientation of the psychical subjectivity of man to the good and against the evil. It is this orientation, rooted deep in the urge of nature itself, that is the ground on which the main tension between the spontaneous emotivity of nature and the efficacy or self-determination of the person comes into play.

At this point we see the integrating function of proficiency. The significance of this function was expounded by the great masters of classical philosophy, and especially of ethics, in their comprehensive teaching on virtues or moral proficiency. Throughout this study we have stressed that morality intrinsically determines the humanity and the personal nature of man. The experience of morality is thus an integral component in the experience of man. Without it no adequate theory of the acting person – of the person and the action – would indeed be possible. The integration of the person and the action on the basis of emotivity (emotionality and emotivity) of the human psyche is accomplished through proficiency, which from the point of view of ethics deserves to be called "virtues." An essential element in the idea of "virtue" is that of moral value and this entails a reference to a norm. But even when in our analysis we put aside this relation pertaining to morality (at the beginning of this book we called the procedure "placing outside brackets") by leaving its examination to students of ethics, we still have facing us the purely and strictly personalistic problem of integration, that is, the need for finding the best ways for effectively relieving the tension between spontaneous emotivity and personal efficacy or self-determination. It is quite correct to speak in this connection of the "problem of integration" inasmuch as it consists in the realization of the personal structure of self-governance and self-possession on the basis of that psychical subjectivity which is spontaneously molded by the numerous and multifarious emotive events with their appropriate spontaneity of attraction and repulsion.

The Function of Moral Proficiency or Virtue

The personal structure of self-governance and self-possession is realized by means of different proficiencies and skills. Indeed, it lies in the nature of proficiencies to aim at subordinating the spontaneous emotivity of the subjective ego to its self-determination. They thus tend to subordinate subjectivity to the transcendent efficacy of the person. Their way to achieve this end, however, is to make the best use of emotive energy and not to suppress it.[72] We may say that the will to some extent restrains the spontaneous explosion of emotive energy and even assimilates some of it. When properly assimilated this energy adds considerably to the energy of the will itself, and that is precisely the task of proficiency. But in the process there is still another purpose to be achieved gradually. The proficiencies or skills acquired in different domains allow the will to secure – and without any risk for itself to adopt as its own – the spontaneity of emotions and generally of emotivity. In a way spontaneity is also a trait of proficiency, though not in its primitive state but after transformation in the course of a steadfast process of character formation. So far as the reference to truth is concerned, the integrating process of developing and improving the psyche gradually produces the result that the will – guided by the light of reason – learns how by spontaneous reference to emotion, by a spontaneous move of attraction or repulsion, to choose and to adopt the real good; it also learns how to reject the real bad.

In this sphere the integration of the acting person is a task that lasts until the end of a man's life. In some respects, however, it begins at a somewhat later phase than the somato-reactive integration, which is on the whole already completed when the psycho-emotive integration begins. A human child learns quickly the necessary movements and acquires the skills pertaining to this domain before he develops the particular virtues. Thus we may to a certain degree identify the latter of the two integrations with the task of character formation or molding one's psycho-moral personality. In either there is the moment of "bringing together," though as we noted at the beginning of the discussion on integration, it is not a question of bringing together in the literal sense – that is, to join parts to form a whole – but rather of the realization, and simultaneously outward manifestation, of a unity based on the specific complexity of the personal subject.

10. CONDUCT AND BEHAVIOR

The Meaning of the Terms

When attentively observing other people and ourselves we can draw a subtle distinction between what we are going to call "conduct" and something that in the same man we are inclined to identify as his "behavior." There will be no digressing from the main theme of these considerations if we devote some remarks to this distinction, all the more so as it brings into focus many questions mentioned in our analysis of the integration of the acting person both in the psychical and the somatic spheres.

The word "conduct" seems to denote the acting of the human being so far as it is an outcome or a resultant of his efficacy. In a sense this significance is metaphorical. Etymologically its meaning is associated with leading or guiding together or jointly, indeed, it seems to suggest a certain continuity of the guidance. Guidance, moreover, implies a knowledge of the road to be followed and thus, metaphorically speaking, it also has a certain normative significance: so "conduct" may be understood as "to keep to the marked-out course." There is nothing passive in this keeping to a course, it is not a result of what happens in or with man, but, on the contrary, it is something thoroughly active, based on efficacy and self-determination. Thus "conduct" points essentially to the actions that the man-person performs and that he fulfills himself in.

On the other hand, on careful examination "behavior" is found to contain different meanings. We use "behavior" to describe that way of acting or comportment of a person which is easily noticeable to an observer. Behavior is only connected but not identical with acting and does not refer to the same reality, or at least not to the same aspects of reality we have in mind when speaking of somebody's conduct. One's behavior, one's special way of acting that accompanies one's conduct, is composed of a number of elements, which are not necessarily, or at least not entirely, controlled by man and of which he is not, or at least is not the sole agent. These elements define the outward expression or simply the "appearance" of acting; it is through that aspect of outward expression or appearance that they determine how a man acts. But the "how" is to be referred neither to the essence itself of the action nor to the essential conjugation of the action and the person. The stress is on how a man behaves in his acting and not on how he actually acts.

Conduct and Behavior in the Person's Integration in Action

It is not difficult to notice how differently various people behave when performing similar actions; this applies to what may be said to be the phenomenal quality determined by somato-constitutive as well as psycho-emotive factors. These factors give an action performed by someone tall and of spare frame a different "appearance" than a similar action by someone square-built and stocky. Similarly, the speech, the gesture, and the pose of a spirited and vivacious speaker sound and look different from those of one who is slow and phlegmatic. Even when they do the same thing each does it somewhat differently, and this precisely means that he *behaves* differently.

The difference between conduct and behavior may throw some additional light on the problem of the integration of the person in the action, the problem that we have been investigating in this and the preceding chapter.

11. THE PERSON'S INTEGRATION IN ACTION AND THE SOUL–BODY RELATION

Human Complexity Revealed in Transcendence and Integration

So far "integration" has been understood as the manifestation, and simultaneously the realization, of unity on the basis of the multifarious complexity of man. In this sense integration is a complementary aspect of the dynamism of the person, an aspect that, as we saw, is complementary to transcendence. It is on this assumption that we have considered primarily the question how the unity of different dynamisms is manifested in the actions of the person. This unity itself is differentiated and diversified, which was also shown, if only indirectly, in the attempts to characterize the dynamisms of the soma and the psyche of man. So far, however, we have not investigated thoroughly the problem of the complexity of man. We may even assume that the dynamic approach to the acting person leads us to seek his unity rather than to dwell upon his complexity.[73]

To conclude these considerations let us emphasize that man's complexity appears to be most clearly revealed by the reality of integration. Integration not only brings into view the unity of various dynamisms in the action of the person but also discloses the structures and layers of the complexity of the human being. The different layers of the psychosomatic complexity were mentioned on various occasions in the course of the analysis of integration, but obviously to show the psychosomatic complexity in man is by no means equivalent to disclosing also the proper relation of soul to body and inversely.

The Relation of Soul and Body to Integration and Transcendence

An insight into the relation between the soul and the body may be reached only through the total experience of man. The notion of the "integration," as of the "transcendence," of the "person in the action" serves to circumscribe – in various perspectives – the content of this experience. When speaking of the "integration of the acting person" we are scanning the complete territory of human experience in search of not merely a description but a thorough and deep understanding of it in the phenomenological sense, inasmuch as the sum total of the data from this experience is comprised by the notion of "integration," just as, from a different point of view, it is comprised by the notion of "transcendence." We have tried to show this in our previous analyses. We find a great wealth of various types of dynamisms at both the somatic and the psychical levels; and it is due to integration that these dynamisms become "personal" and related as well as subordinated to the transcendence of the person in the action. They thus find their place in the integral structure of the self-governance and self-possession of the person. Our analysis of the integration of the acting person on both the psychical and the somatic levels has, as we have already stated, revealed the complexity in man. We cannot pretend, however, that to assert the complexity is equivalent to an insight into the soul–body relation of the human being. Experience of transcendence and integration presumably corresponds approximately to what was often referred to as the "higher" and the "lower" man, an expression stressing the difference derived from the experience of man and his self-consciousness.[74]

Here we have to recall our earlier remarks about the "experience of the soul." We have, in fact, submitted that man had no direct experience of his soul. Experience of the transcendence of the person in the action together with all the elements and aspects of this experience is in no way equivalent to a direct experience of the soul. Similarly, we have to assert that experience of integration (in connection with the transcendence of the person in the action) cannot be identified with the experience – the direct discovering and experiencing – of the soul–body relation. Both the reality itself of the soul and that of the soul's relation to the body are in this sense transphenomenal and extraexperiential. Nevertheless, the total and comprehensive experience of man shows the soul as real and as staying in relation to the body. They have been both discovered and are continuously being discovered in the philosophical reflection resulting from human experience.

We may add that the soul–body relation is also intuitively given – in an implicit way – in the experience of man as a real being. In this respect the subordination of the system of integration of the human person to the transcendence of the person in the action is revelatory.

The Current and Hylomorphic Meaning of the Soul–Body Relation

Intuition indeed appears to pave the way for, and lead us near to, an understanding of the soul–body relation, but as we have mentioned, it does not allow us to grasp this relation. We may approach it solely in terms of metaphysical categories. All the more so as the full meaning of this relation appears as a philosophical issue once the notions of soul and body receive a metaphysical interpretation. However they also have a current sense. This current sense of the "soul" and its relation to the "body" is a fruit of commonsense experience. It is this relation to experience in which is firmly grounded the essentially metaphysical significance of the notions of "soul" and "body," and only in which they acquire their complete meaning for metaphysics. For us the important things are thus, first, that on the evidence of experience and intuition we may exfoliate the complexity of man, and second, that we are able to define its limits.

The Soul as the Principle of Transcendence and Integration

An understanding of the soul–body relation is obviously promoted by a knowledge of the character of somatic and psychosomatic dynamisms and also of certain limits thereby disclosed within the total dynamic system of the man-person. It then becomes manifest that the total and also adequate dynamism of the person – resulting in action – transcends them. None of those other particularized dynamisms are identical with the action, though every one of them is in different ways contained in it. While the somatic dynamism and indirectly the psycho-emotive dynamism have their source in the body-matter, this source is neither sufficient nor adequate for the action in its essential feature of transcendence. This was one of the final conclusions in the analysis of the transcendence of the person in the action, where the relation between the transcendence and the spirituality of man was stressed.

Now, before we close the analysis of the person's integration in the action, it is necessary to go still farther in our conclusions. While the body itself is the source of the reactive dynamism, specific for the human soma, and indirectly also for the emotive dynamism of the human psyche, the integration of these two dynamisms has to have a common origin with the person's transcendence. Can we infer that it is the soul that is the ultimate source or, to put it differently, the transcending principle and also the principle of the integration of the person in the action? At any rate, it seems that this line of reasoning has brought us much closer to approaching the soul.

Our analyses indicate something like a boundary in man, which sets a limit to the scope of the dynamism and thus also of the reach of the body, or of what is also called "matter." They also reveal a capacity of a spiritual nature that seems to lie at the root of the person's transcendence, but also indirectly of the integration of the person in the action. It would, however, be a gross simplification if we were to regard this intuitively drawn limit of the body (matter) capacity as equivalent to the boundary *between* the body and the soul. Indeed, the experience of integration intervenes with such an oversimplification. Integration – precisely because it is the complementary aspect of the transcendence of the person in the action – tells us that the soul–body relation cuts across all the boundaries we find in experience and that it goes deeper and is more fundamental than they are. We thus have confirmed, even if indirectly, our earlier assertion that the complete reality of the soul itself and of the soul's relation to the body needs a more comprehensive metaphysical expression.

PART FOUR

PARTICIPATION

CHAPTER SEVEN

INTERSUBJECTIVITY BY PARTICIPATION

1. INTRODUCTION TO THE CONCEPT OF PARTICIPATION[75]

We cannot conclude our investigation of the acting person without considering, even if only in a cursory way, the issue of intersubjectivity.

Man's Acting "Together with Others"

The starting point for our discussions was the conviction that action marks a special moment in the manifestation of the person; and in the course of our study we have unraveled the various aspects of the person's dynamism in the action. Action has been indeed the road which led us to an understanding of the person and has simultaneously allowed us to grasp its own nature; for action not only carries the means, and a special basis, of the intuition of the person, but it also discloses its own self with every step that brings us nearer the person. On this road we have relied throughout on a strict correlation of the disclosure of the person and that of action, within one and the same pattern of which the person and his action are two poles; each strictly corresponds to the other; each displays and explains the other from its point of view. This correlation envisaged in its dynamic unfolding gradually reveals the main lines for the interpretation of the acting person.

The present chapter, the last in this study, adds one more element to the previously constructed and outlined whole. This new element, though actually contained in all the previous ones, has not received the attention it deserves and must be examined more thoroughly. We will now investigate that aspect of the dynamic correlation of the action with the person which issues from the fact that actions can be performed by human individuals together with others. The expression "together with others" lacks the necessary precision and does not describe sufficiently the reality it refers to, but for the moment it seems the most appropriate inasmuch as it draws attention to the diverse communal or social relations in which, in most cases, human actions are involved. This of course is a direct and natural consequence of the fact that man lives "together with other men," and indeed we may even go so far as to say that he exists together with other men. The mark of the communal – or social – trait is essentially imprinted on human existence itself.

Understanding "Cooperation" Requires an Understanding of Human Acting

The fact that man lives and exists together with others, as well as the effect this has on his manifesting himself in acting, on the action as such, relates to that reality we usually refer to as "society" or "community." Nevertheless, our purpose here is not to investigate the nature of society; and we do not intend to insist upon the assertion that human actions have a social significance, because this would lead our discussion to a totally new level and away from the level on which both our subject matter and our methods have been situated so far. On the contrary, our intention is to keep to our initial approach and to confine ourselves to the acting person as the first aim and the pivot of our investigations. In this chapter we wish merely to consider that aspect in the dynamic correlation of the action with the person which comes as a consequence of the fact that man lives and acts together with other men. This fact could also be defined as "cooperation," and yet between the two expressions there is a clear semantic difference: "to cooperate" is not the same thing as "to act together with others." For the time being we may as well use the latter expression, which appears to be more amenable to further differentiations and any subsequent, more precise definitions that may prove to be necessary in this connection.

We know human actions are performed in various interhuman relations and also in various social relations. When we say they are performed "together with others," we have all these different relations in mind without going into the details of any particular one. Together they form part of that aspect of the action and of the dynamic correlation of action with the person which we have not yet considered. The omission was not due to the inner logic of the problem as a whole; it appears natural that only a thorough understanding of the nature of man's acting can lead to a correct interpretation of cooperation, and not the other way round. The dynamic correlation of the action with the person is in itself a fundamental human reality and it remains such also in any actions performed together with others. In point of fact, only on the basis of this fundamental relation can any fact of acting together with other people assume its appropriate *human significance.* Such is the basic sequence, which cannot be reversed or neglected, and it is this sequence we shall follow in our inquiries.

The Participatory Aspect in the Person's Acting "Together with Others"

It is only natural that the fact of acting together with other people and the many different relations and reference systems it involves will raise new problems in our discussion. We well know how extensive and how rich is the realm of, for instance, sociology, which by its investigations of the nature and types of societies and social life indirectly shows man as a member of various social groups or communities that in turn influence his acting. But let us stress once again that we are not interested at present in the problems of acting from the point of view of all its complex and extensive sociological implications; in particular we will not consider its specifically sociological significance. Since the acting person is the focal point of our study, it would require a shift in our argument to a totally new level. This is further justified by the fact that the dynamic correlation of the notion of "action" with that of "person" is also the basic and fundamental reality in all the multifarious actings that have a social, communal, or interhuman character. Actions, which man performs in all his different social involvements and as a member of different social groups or communities, are essentially the actions of the person. Their social or communal nature is rooted in the nature of the person and not vice versa. And yet, to grasp the personal nature of human actions it is absolutely necessary to consider the consequences of the fact that they may be performed "together with others." The question emerges: How does this fact affect the dynamic correlation itself of the action with the person? This question is the more pressing if we emphasize that acting "together with others" is not only frequent and usual, but indeed of universal occurrence.

The answer we are seeking will emerge gradually from the series of discussions in this chapter entitled "Intersubjectivity by Participation." As we have insisted upon above, participation seems to be one of the basic channels of the dynamic correlation of the action with the person whenever acting is performed "together with others." An explanation of this statement, however, has to be reached step by step.

2. THE PERSONALISTIC VALUE OF ACTION

The Performance of the Action Is a Value[76]

Before we continue our investigations we must look back at the whole of the previous analysis to see the strictly personal content of the action. We will then notice that the performance itself of an action by the person is a fundamental value, which we may call the *personalistic* – personalistic or personal – value of the action. Such a value differs from all moral values, which *belong* to the nature of the performed action and issue from their reference to a norm. The personalistic value, on the other hand, inheres in the performance itself of the action by the person, in the very fact that man acts in a manner appropriate to him, that self-determination thus authentically inheres in the nature of his acting and the transcendence of the person is realized through his acting. This, as we have shown, leads to integration in both the somatic and the psychical sphere of man. The personalistic value, which inheres essentially in the performance itself of the action by the person, comprises a number of values that belong to the profile either of "transcendence" or of "integration," because they all, in their own way, determine the performance of the action. Thus, for instance, every synthesis of action and motion introduces a specific value that differs from that constituted by the synthesis of action and emotion, though the one and the other inhere in the dynamic whole of the performance of the action. Each in its own way conditions and brings about man's self-determination.

The "personalistic" value of the human action – that is, the personal value – is a special and probably the most fundamental manifestation of the *worth* of the person himself. (Since this study is primarily concerned with the ontology of the person there is no place in it for considering axiology. Even this approach, however, may give some insight into the axiology of the person so far as a definition both of the value of the person as such and of the different values within the person and the hierarchy of their mutual relations is concerned.) Although being is prior to action, and thus the person and his value is prior to and more fundamental than the value of the action, it is in actions that the person manifests himself – a fact we have been stressing from the first. The "personalistic" value of an action, strictly related to the *performing* of the action by the person, is therefore a special source, and the basis of knowledge about the value of the person (as well as about the values inherent in the person), according to their appropriate hierarchy. Essentially the correlation of the action with the person is valid also in the sphere of axiology, similarly as in the sphere of the ontology of the person.

The "Personalistic" Value of the Action Conditions Its "Ethical" Value

The personalistic value of an action is essentially to be distinguished from the strictly "moral" values and those values of the performed action which spring from their reference to norms. The difference between them is clearly apparent; the "personalistic" value is prior to and conditions any ethical values. Obviously any moral value, whether good or bad, presupposes the performance of the action, indeed full-fledged performance. If action fails to be actually performed or if it betrays in some respects the authenticity of self-determination, then its moral value loses its foundations or at any rate partly loses them. Hence any judgment about moral values, about any merits or demerits attributed to man, have to begin by determining *efficacy*, *self-determination*, and *responsibility*; in other words, we have first to establish whether this particular man-person *did* or *did not* perform the action. It is this precondition that all the discussions and differentiations concerning the will and its functions referred to in the traditional approach.

And yet the performance of the action by the person should not be seen as having a purely ontological significance; on the contrary, we should attribute to it also an axiological significance, since, as we have proposed above, the performance itself of the action by the person is a value. If we call this value "personalistic" it is because the person performing the action *also fulfills himself in it*, that is, acquires a personal feature. In reverse, "moral evil" may be regarded as the opposite of fulfillment; indeed, it is a nonfulfillment of the self in acting. When the person actualizes himself in the action, his appropriate structure of self-governance and self-possession is manifested. It is in this actualization, which we have defined as the "performance of the action," that ethical value is rooted; it emerges and develops on the "substratum" of the personalistic value, which it permeates but as we have already noted, is not to be identified with it.

The Relation of "Communal Action" to the Personalistic Value of Action

We have been moving, so far, on the borderline of personalistic and ethical values, and from time to time we have even, though only indirectly, moved from the first to the second. Nevertheless, the proper terrain for our investigations remains the personalistic value alone. It cannot be emphasized enough that it is the role of this value to allow us, in fact, to estimate the full-fledged performance – or the defects of the performance – in human actions. In this connection it is perhaps worth recalling the traditional teaching on human actions (*de actibus humanis*), which drew a distinction between the "perfect" and "imperfect" volitions (the term "volition" referring to the will as the "power" that action depends upon). Here action and performance are related to the person, not denying the traditional approach but supplementing it in an attempt to rethink it to the end. For does not the will as a power spring forth from the person in his self-determination whereby the person manifests his appropriate nature? To reduce the content of volition to will seen as an autonomous power alone may to some extent impoverish the reality manifested in the action.

To disclose the dynamic correlation of action–person and to explain it will take us along the shortest and the most direct road to the personalistic value of the action. Limiting the analysis of human acting to the level of the will understood as a power reduces the significance of action with regard to both its ontology and its axiology; it does so also with regard to "ethical axiology"; in this approach action appears to have a merely instrumental significance relatively to the whole ethical order. Moreover, the personalistic notion of the action through its many different aspects supplies convincing evidence of the authenticity of the personalistic value. This value is not yet, as stated above, in itself "ethical," but, springing from the dynamic depth of the person, reveals and confirms ethical values. It thereby allows us to understand them better in their strict correspondence with the person and with the whole "world of persons."

This has a fundamental significance in connection with the fact mentioned at the beginning of this chapter, namely, that man acts together with other men. We there asked: What are the consequences of this fact for the dynamic correlation itself of the action with the person? We now have to ask another question that makes the first more precise: What is the significance of acting "together with others" for the personalistic value of the action?

3. A MORE DETAILED DEFINITION OF "PARTICIPATION"

The Person in the Philosophy of Man

How does man, we ask, fulfill himself when acting together with others in the different interhuman or social relations? How does his action then retain that fundamental unity with the person which we have defined as the "integration" or the "transcendence" of the person in the action? In what way do man's actions preserve within the context of acting "together with others" the hierarchy of values that issues from both "transcendence" and "integration"?

Such questions as "how" and "in what way" do not imply doubt or uncertainty; they only draw attention to the problems that arise when the fact of acting "together with others" is considered. There is no need, however, to dissimulate any doubts, at any rate not when their source has a methodic character. Indeed, doubt permeates through and through the thinking and the mind of contemporary man. In philosophical anthropology, on the one hand, the controversial positions taken probably result from the transition from the traditional to new points of view where attention is centered precisely on the person. The traditional philosophy of man, on the other hand – even in its conceptions of the person – tended to underline the role of nature: the nature of man is supposed to be rational and he is the person in virtue of the function of reason; but at the same time he has a "social" nature. In this respect the way of thinking about man has evolved not toward the rejection of the principle itself but rather in

search of a better understanding and more comprehensive interpretations. Nobody seems to doubt either that the nature of man is
"rational" or that he also has a "social nature." We have to ask,
however, what does this mean? Our questions thus refer to the
meaning of these assertions from the point of view of acting, that is,
of the dynamic correlation of the action with the person.

Our aim is to explicate more fully the social nature of man for the
sake of gaining more insights into the human person. With this in
mind we must return to the starting point. At the origin of the
assertion concerning the social nature of man there can be nothing
more fundamental than the experience that man exists, lives, and acts
together with other men – an experience that we also have to account
for in this study. The expression "social nature" seems to signify
primarily that reality of existing and acting "together with others"
which is attributed to every human being in, as it were, a consequential way; obviously this attribute is the consequence of human reality
itself and not inversely.

Participation as a Trait of Acting "Together with Others"

In this approach the questions we are discussing are by no means
secondary; on the contrary, they are of primary importance. We have
now reached a point at which we can provide a more precise
definition of "participation." The term is used in its current sense, the
one best known and most widely applied in everyday use, but it also
has a philosophical meaning. In current usage "participation" is more
or less equivalent to having a share or a part in something. We may
speak for instance of participating or taking part in a meeting; we
then state the fact in the most general and, so to speak, static way.
We do not reach the core of the phenomenon of participation. The
philosophical meaning of "participation" indicates, on the contrary, its
very essence. In this latter sense the term has a long and eventful
history as concerns both its philosophical and theological applications. We are here concerned not so much with a superficial
assertion of the fact that a concrete man takes part together with
other men in some kind of interacting, but rather in disclosing the
basis of his role and his share in this interacting. It is in the structure
of the person that it is to be sought.

The notion of "participation" as conceived in traditional philosophy seems to have been more connected with nature. It is the person's transcendence in the action when the action is being performed "together with others" – transcendence which manifests that the person has not become altogether absorbed by social interplay and thus "conditioned," but stands out as having retained his very own freedom of choice and direction – which is the basis as well as the condition of participation. It also corresponds to the situation we emphasize over again, namely, of the integration of the person in the action; as we know, the latter is a complementary aspect relative to the former. To be capable of participation thus indicates that man, when he acts together with other men, retains in this acting the personalistic value of his own action and at the same time shares in the realization and the results of communal acting. Owing to this share, man, when he acts together with others, retains everything that results from the communal acting and simultaneously brings about – *in this very manner* – the personalistic value of his own action.

Participation as a Trait of the Person Acting "Together with Others"

The stress laid on the words "in this very manner" emphasizes the real nature of this participation. First, the idea of "participation" is used here in order to reach to the very foundation of *acting together* with other persons, to those roots of such acting which stem from and are specific to the person himself. Second, everything that constitutes the personalistic value of the action – namely, the performance itself of an action and the realization of the transcendence and the integration of the person contained in it – is realized because of acting together with others.

Participation thus represents a feature of the person itself, that innermost and homogeneous feature which determines that the person existing and acting together with others does so as a person.[77] So far as acting itself is concerned, participation is responsible for the fact that the person acting together with others performs an action and fulfills himself in it. We see now that participation is the factor that determines the personalistic value of all cooperation. The sort of cooperation – or, more precisely, of acting together with others – in which the element of participation is missing, deprives the actions of the person of their personalistic value. On the other hand, we know from experience that in acting with other people situations may arise which in different ways limit self-determination and thus also the personal transcendence and the integration of acting. Indeed, the limitation of the personalistic value may sometimes go so far that we can hardly speak of "acting together with others" in the sense of the "authentic" actions of the person. Under certain conditions "acting" (as the synonym of the "action") may change to denoting something that only "happens" to a particular man under the influence of other human beings. An extreme example of this is so-called "mass psychology," when a large group of men may begin to act in an uncontrolled way and so affect the behavior of individuals.

Participation Renders Multiform Interpersonal Relations Possible

All this must be taken into consideration when defining the notion of "participation" in its proper sense. In the diverse relations of acting together with others, participation presents itself as an adaptation to these relations and hence as a multifarious reference of the person to other persons. In explaining, if only in outline, the form and the content of participation, we must examine communal acting in its objective as well as subjective aspect. In addition, we must undertake some other analyses, although even then we shall not exhaust the essential meaning and the substance of "participation"; as conceived of here it not only applies to the different forms of the reference of the person to "others," of the individual to the society, but it also denotes that very foundation of these forms which inheres in and corresponds to the person.

First, participation corresponds to the person's transcendence and integration in the action because, as we have already emphasized, it allows man, when he acts together with other men, to realize thereby and at once the *authentically personalistic value* – the performance of the action and the fulfillment of himself in the action. Acting "together with others" thus corresponds to the person's transcendence and integration in the action, when man chooses what is chosen by others or even *because* it is chosen by others – he then identifies the object of his choice with a value that he sees as in one way or another homogeneous and his own. This is connected with self-determination, for self-determination in the case of acting "together with others" contains and expresses participation.

When we say that "participation" is a distinct feature of the person we do not mean the person in the abstract but a concrete person in his dynamic correlation with the action.

In this correlation "participation" signifies, on the one hand, that ability of acting "together with others" which allows the realization of all that results from communal acting and simultaneously enables the one who is acting to realize thereby the personalistic value of his action. However, this ability is followed by its actualization. Thus the notion of "participation" includes here both that ability and its realization.

4. INDIVIDUALISM AND ANTI-INDIVIDUALISM

The Theoretical and Normative Significance of Participation

The conception of "participation" that we are developing in this study has a theoretical significance. As stated earlier, it is required in our attempt to explain – on the ground of the dynamic correlation of the action with the person – the reality of the social nature of man. The conception is theoretical but it is also empirical in the sense that the theory of participation explains the fact of man's acting as well as his existing together with other men. Moreover, it is apparent that the theory has simultaneously an indirectly normative significance; it not only tells us how the person acting together with others fulfills himself in his acting, that is, how he realizes the personalistic value of his action, but it also points indirectly to certain obligations that are the consequence of the principle of participation. For if in acting "together with others" man can fulfill himself according to this principle, then, on the one hand, everyone ought to strive for that kind of participation which would allow him in acting together with others to realize the personalistic value of his own action. On the other hand, any community of acting, or any human cooperation, should be conducted so as to allow the person remaining within its orbit to realize himself through participation.

Such is the normative content that has emerged so far from our analyses. It is this content that seems to determine the normative – and not only the theoretical – significance of participation. This significance is instilled into the different systems of acting "together with others" by means of the personalistic value, which it strictly corresponds to and relies upon. Since the personalistic value of action is – as we know – the fundamental value conditioning both ethical values and the ethical order, the norm of conduct that issues from it directly must also have a fundamental significance. Such a norm is not, in the strict sense of the term, ethical; it is not the norm of an action performed because of the action's objective content, but one that belongs to the performance itself of the action, to its personal subjectiveness – an "inner" norm concerned with safeguarding the self-determination of the person and so also his efficacy. We earlier discussed these matters in some detail, so that the boundary between the strictly ethical and the personalistic order should now be considered sufficiently defined and distinct.

Individualism and Totalism as the Two Limitations of Participation

At the same time, however, the personalistic value so conditions the whole ethical order in acting and cooperation that the order is also determined by it. The action must be performed not because only then can it have an ethical value – and can that value be assigned to it – but also because the person has the basic and "natural" (i.e., issuing from the fact that he is a person) right to perform actions and to be fulfilled in them. This right of the person attains its full sense and import as a right with respect to acting "together with others." It is then that the normative significance of participation comes into full light and is confirmed. For it is in acting together with others that the performance of actions – the performance that is simultaneously the fulfillment of the person in action, and the performance and fulfillment in which the personalistic value of the action consists – can be limited or definitely thwarted. This may happen in two ways: first, there may be a lack of participation caused by the person as the subject-agent of acting; second, participation may become impossible for reasons external to the person and resulting from defects in the system according to which the entire human community of acting operates.

At this point in our analysis we encounter two systems, the implications of which must be considered, if only in part. One of these is called "individualism"; the other has received different names, more recently "objective totalism," though it could just as well be called "anti-individualism." Since a full-scale discussion of the two systems would lead us away from the chief objectives of this study we will consider only some of their implications. It is necessary to note, however, that they both have an axiological and indirectly an ethical significance.

Individualism sees in the individual the supreme and fundamental good, to which all interests of the community or the society have to be subordinated, while objective totalism relies on the opposite principle and unconditionally subordinates the individual to the community or the society.

Clearly, each of these systems has entirely different visions of the ultimate good and the foundation of norms. Furthermore, each system occurs in a wide range of variations and shades, so much so that their analysis would require comprehensive sociological and historical studies. For these reasons we must put aside the exploration of these momentous problems and even simplify them somewhat; we will restrict our considerations only to those essential trends which according to the formulations just introduced characterize the two systems. We shall concentrate our attention on the implications they may have for the main theme of our present discussion, which is the acting person in all the different situations that may arise in his acting "together with others."

As has been maintained so far, inherent in acting "together with others" is the principle of participation, which is the essential trait of such acting and a special source of the rights and obligations of the person. The person has as his specific attribute the right to perform actions and the obligation to fulfill himself in action. This obligation results from the personalistic value inherent in fulfillment.

Each of the two systems or trends – whether it be individualism or objective totalism – tends in different ways to limit participation either directly, as a possibility or an ability to be actualized in acting "together with others," or indirectly, as that feature which is of the essence of the person and which corresponds to his existing "together with others," his living in a community.

Individualism Implies a Denial of Participation

Individualism limits participation, since it isolates the person from others by conceiving him solely as an individual who concentrates on himself and on his own good; this latter is also regarded in isolation from the good of others and of the community. The good of the individual is then treated as if it were opposed or in contradiction to other individuals and their good; at best, this good, in essence, may be considered as involving self-preservation and self-defense. From the point of view of individualism, to act "together with others," just as to exist "together with others," is a necessity that the individual has to submit to, a necessity that corresponds to none of his very own features or positive properties; neither does the acting and existing together with others serve or develop any of the individual's positive and essential constituents. For the individual the "others" are a source of limitation, they may even appear to represent the opposite pole in a variety of conflicting interests. If a community is formed, its purpose is to protect the good of the individual from the "others." This in broad outline is the essence of individualism, the variations and different shades of which we shall not consider here. We should notice, however, that individualism carries with it an implied denial and rejection of participation in the sense we have given it before; from the individualistic point of view an essentially constituent human property that allows the person to fulfill himself in acting "together with others" simply does not exist.

Totalism as Reversed Individualism

The denial of participation is also implied in totalism or anti-individualism, which may be looked upon as "reversed individualism." The dominant trait of totalism may be characterized as the need to find protection *from* the individual, who is seen as the chief enemy of society and of the common good. Since totalism assumes that inherent in the individual there is only the striving for individual good, that any tendency toward participation or fulfillment in acting and living together with others is totally alien to him, it follows that the "common good" can be attained only by limiting the individual. The good thus advocated by totalism can never correspond to the wishes of the individual, to the good he is capable of choosing independently and freely according to the principles of participation; it is always a good that is incompatible with and a limitation upon the individual. Consequently, the realization of the common good frequently presupposes the use of coercion.

Again, we have presented but a summary outline of the thinking and proceedings characteristic of the system of anti-individualism, in which the principles of individualism are clearly apparent but viewed in reverse and applied to contrary ends. Individualism is concerned with protecting the good of the individual from the community; the objective of totalism, in contrast – and this is confirmed by numerous historical examples – is to protect a specific common good from the individual. Nevertheless, both tendencies, both systems of thinking and proceedings have at their origin the same conception of man.

The Conception of the Human Being Underlying Both Systems

The way of thinking about the human being underlying both systems may be defined as "impersonalistic" or "antipersonalistic," inasmuch as the distinctive characteristic of the personalistic approach is the conviction that to be a person means to be capable of participation. Obviously, if this conviction is to mature it has to find its concretion in reality: it has to be cultivated and developed. It is not only human nature that forces man to exist and to act together with others, but his existing and acting together with other human beings enables him to achieve his own development, that is, the intrinsic development of the person. This is why every human being must have the right to act, which means "freedom in the action," so that the person can fulfill himself in performing the action.

The significance of this right and this freedom is inherent in the belief in the personalistic value of human action. It is on account of this value and because of it that the human being has the right to the total freedom of acting. This leads to the rejection of both individualism and anti-individualism together with all their erroneous implications.

On the one hand, the total freedom of action, which results from its personalistic value, conditions the ethical order and simultaneously determines it. On the other hand, the moral order instills into human actions – in particular, those within the orbit of acting "together with others" – those determinants, and thus also limitations, which are the consequence of purely ethical values and norms. The determinants and the limitations so introduced are not, however, opposed to the personalistic value; for it is only in the "moral good" that the person can fulfill himself, inasmuch as "evil" means always a "nonfulfillment."

There can be no doubt that man has the freedom of acting; he has the right of action, but he has not the right to do wrong. Such is the general trend of the determinant, which while issuing from the rights of man corresponds nevertheless to the personalistic order.

5. PARTICIPATION AND COMMUNITY

Participation as a Constitutive Factor of the Community

We know that individualism and totalism (anti-individualism) grow out of the same soil. Their common root is the conception of man as an individual, according to which he is more or less deprived of the property of participation. This way of thinking is also reflected in the conceptions of social life, in the axiology of the society and in ethics, or, more precisely, in those different axiologies of the society and different social ethics which proceed from the same ground. It is not our intention to examine the details of the many varieties of individualism and anti-individualism, which have been widely studied. We should note, however, that in the thinking about man characteristic of these two tendencies there seems to be no sufficient foundation for any authentic human community.

The notion of "community" expresses the reality that we have been focusing upon in the present chapter, in which "acting and existing together with others" has been repeatedly mentioned. The human community is strictly related to the experience of the person, which we have been tracing from the first but especially at this stage of our discussions. We find in it the reality of participation as that essential of the person which enables him to exist and act "together with others" and thus to reach his own fulfillment. Simultaneously, participation as an essential of the person is a constitutive factor of any human community.

Because of this essential property the person and the community may be said to coalesce together; contrary to the implications manifest in the individualistic and anti-individualistic thinking about man they are neither alien nor mutually opposed to each other.

The Community Is Not the Subject in Acting

In order to grasp more precisely the meaning of "participation" – and this is now our chief aim – we have to look at it from the point of view of the community. Actually, such has been our standpoint from the first, and it is the reason why we have so often used the expression "together with others" in our analyses of the action and the being of the person. The notion of "community" is correlated with this expression while simultaneously it introduces a new plane of action or a new "subjectiveness" in the acting. Indeed, as long as we are speaking of acting or being "together with others" the man-person remains the manifest subject of the acting and being, but once we begin to speak of the *community*, then what so far has been contained in an adverbial sentence, can now be expressed in substantival and abstract terms.

However, we should now speak of a "quasi-subjectiveness," rather than of a proper subject of acting. All the people existing and acting together are obviously exercising a role in a common action but in a different way than when each of them performs an action in its entirety. The new subjectiveness is the share of all the members of a community, or, in a broader sense, of a social group. In fact, it is but a quasi-subjectiveness, because even when the being and acting is realized together with others it is the *man-person who is always its proper subject*. The human individuals constitute, each of them, the basic order of action. The term "community," like "society" or "social group," indicates an order derived from the first one. Being and acting "together with others" does not constitute a new subject of acting but only introduces new relations among the persons who are the real and actual subjects of acting. In all discussions about the community this comment is necessary to avoid misunderstanding. The concept "community," also in its substantival and abstract sense, seems to come very near to the dynamic reality of the person and participation, perhaps even nearer than such notions as "society" or "social group."

Associational Relationship and Community Membership

To analyze the notion of "community" we may and must consider as many – almost indefinitely numerous – facts as in the analysis of the

acting person, a point already stressed in the introductory chapter of
this study. Moreover, in either case it is necessary to apply
methodologically analogical procedures. These remarks confirm once
again the need to adhere to the same approach that we adopted at the
start of these investigations. It is on this level of investigation that we
shall have to analyze the relation existing between participation and
community membership.

Within the community we find the human being, with all his
dynamism, as one of its members. There are different terms and
expressions to denote this membership, suited to the different kinds
of relationships within the community or group. Thus "kinship" tells
us of membership in a family group, a "compatriot" is one who
belongs to a national group, and a "citizen" is a member of a still
broader society represented by the state. These are only examples,
for innumerable other social groups or communities have associated
according to different principles, such as religious and other affiliations. In each of these examples man's associational relationship is
differently constituted.

Sociologists quite rightly point to the semantic difference between
the terms "society" and "community"; "society" objectivizes the
community or a number of mutually complementary communities.
Since in this study our objective is to *disclose the bases or foundations of things*, we are primarily concerned with community membership rather than with the associational relationship of the society.
The examples noted above tell of membership in different kinds of
communities; they not only indicate the principle of membership in a
community but also the different bonds and relations that exist
between men and women belonging to these communities. For instance, words such as *brother* and *sister* stress the family bonds
rather than that membership in a family group denoted by the term
kinship.

In the rich resources of language there are countless words that
stress – like all the terms in the previous examples – the fact of the
community itself, the communal existence of human beings and the
bonds that are formed among them on account of their communal
existence. There are, however, other words that denote first of all
the community of acting rather than the communal existence, the
community of being. For instance, when speaking of an apprentice, an
assistant, or a foreman, we imply that there is a team or group working

together; the stress is then on the community of acting and the bonds thus formed, while communal existence, the community of being, is implied only indirectly.

Associational Relationship Differs from Participation

In the preceding section we saw that man can be a member of different communities, all of which are the product of man existing or acting together with other men. At present we are mainly interested in the "community of acting" because of its closer relation to the dynamic action–person correlation as a basis and a source of cognition. Nevertheless, the "community of being" always conditions the "community of acting," and so the latter cannot be considered apart from the former. The crux of the problem lies, however, in that *membership in any of these communities is not to be identified with participation.* This is perhaps best illustrated by the following example. A team of laborers digging a trench or a group of students attending a lecture are communities of acting; each laborer or student is a member of a definite community of acting. These communities may also be considered from the point of view of the aim that its members are collectively striving for. In the first case, the aim is the trench, which in turn may serve other aims, such as laying foundations for a construction. In the other, the aim is to learn about the problems that are the theme of the lecture, which in turn forms part of a course of studies and thus of the students' curriculum. We also see that all the diggers and all the students have a common goal. This objective unity of goals helps to objectivize the community of acting itself. Hence, in the objective sense, a "community of acting" may be defined according to the aim that brings men to act together; each of them is then a member of an objective community.

From the point of view of the person and the action, however, it is not only the objective community of acting but also its subjective moment, which we have here called "participation," that is important. The question is whether a man belonging to a community of acting, like those mentioned in our examples, is in a position in his communal acting to perform real actions and fulfill himself in them; the possibility of this performance and the fulfillment it brings about are determined by participation. Nevertheless, even when acting "together with others" man can remain outside the community that is constituted by participation.

At this point we are faced with a problem that can never be resolved without at least a cursory look at the question of the so-called "common good." We already know that the moment of participation inheres among others in choice; man chooses what others choose and indeed often because others choose it, but even then he chooses it as his own good and as the end of his own striving. What he thus chooses is his own good in the sense that he as the person can fulfill himself in it. It is participation that enables him to make these choices and to undertake this way of acting "together with others." Perhaps it is only then that such acting deserves to be called "cooperation," inasmuch as acting "together with others" does not by itself necessarily result in cooperation (just as it does not necessarily initiate the moment of participation). Within the sphere of acting, just as within the sphere of existing, a community may remain at the objective level and never pass to the subjective level.

6. PARTICIPATION AND THE COMMON GOOD

The Common Good and the Problem of Community and Participation

We now see that the solution to the problem of the community and participation lies not in the reality itself of acting and existing "together with others," but is to be looked for in the common good, or, more precisely, in the meaning we give to the notion of the "common good." If the meaning of "common good" is for us the same as that of the "good of the community," then we understand it correctly though we run a serious risk of one-sidedness. This one-sidedness threatens in the domain of axiology and is similar to that suggested in anthropology by the conceptions of individualism and anti-individualism. The common good is obviously the good of the community – or, to go even further in the direction of objectivation, the good of the society – but it has still to be clearly defined in the light of the foregoing considerations.[78]

Evidently, the very fact that people act together is sufficient to ascertain the existence of an objective community of acting, as for instance in the cases of the team of laborers digging a trench or of the group of students attending a lecture. In this context the common good as the good of a definite community of acting – and this is always connected with a community of being – may be easily identified with the goal of the community. Thus for the laborers the common good may appear to be solely the completion of the excavation, and for the students the commitment to memory of the information contained in the lecture.

These common goods, however, may also be considered as links in a teleological chain, in which case every one of them is seen as a means to attain another goal that now presents itself as the common good; thus the excavation dug out by the laborers will serve to lay the foundations for a future construction, and the attended lecture is but a link in a long and complex process of learning with examinations as a formal test of the knowledge acquired in that particular field.

Teleological and Personalistic Conceptions of the Common Good

To identify the common good, however, with the goal of common acting by a group of people is manifestly a cursory and superficial simplification. The preceding examples lead to the conclusion that the *goal* of common acting, when understood in a purely objective and "material" way, though it includes some elements of the common good and has reference to it, can never fully and completely constitute it.

This assertion becomes obvious in the light of our previous analyses. It is impossible to define the common good without simultaneously taking into account the subjective moment, that is, the moment of acting in relation to the acting persons. When we consider this moment we see that the common good does not consist solely in the goal of the common acting performed by a community or group; indeed, it also, or even primarily, consists in that which conditions and somehow initiates in the persons acting together their participation, and thereby develops and shapes in them a subjective community of acting.

We can conceive of the common good as being the goal of acting only in that double – subjective *and* objective – sense. Its subjective sense is strictly related to participation as a property of the acting person; it is in this sense that it is possible to say that the common good corresponds to the social nature of man.

In our investigations we have tended to avoid going into the details of that extensive and momentous domain of axiology and ethics which is associated with the notion of the "common good" and determines its full significance. We have concentrated on the common good primarily as the principle of correct participation, which allows the person acting together with other persons to perform authentic actions and to fulfill himself through these actions. Our concern is therefore with the *genuinely personalistic structure of human existence in a community*, that is, in every community that man belongs to.

The common good becomes the good of the community inasmuch as it creates in the axiological sense the conditions for the common existence, which is then followed by acting. If we can say that in the axiological order the community, the social group, or the society are established by the common good, then we can define each of them according to its appropriate common good. Acting is then considered jointly with being, with existing.

The common good, however, belongs primarily to the sphere of being "together with others," while the acting together with others is insufficient to disclose the whole reality of the common good, though it also plays its role in this respect. Even groups that are brought together mainly by their common acting rather than by any social bonds – for instance, a group of laborers excavating a trench or of students together attending a lecture – not only strive through their acting together to attain their goal but also manifest in different ways the appropriate modes of participation of the individual members of a community of acting.

The Common Good as the Foundation of Authentic Human Communities

In groups established on the principle of a temporary community of acting, participation is neither manifested as clearly, nor realized to the same extent, as in communities where their stability is grounded in the fact of being together – for instance, a family, a national group, a religious community, or the citizens of a state. The axiology of these latter communities, which is expressed in the common good, is much deeper. Consequently the foundations of participation are much stronger, while the need of participation is much more acute.

In such communities of being – they have earned the name of natural societies because they inherently correspond to the social nature of man – each of its members expects to be allowed to choose what others choose and because they choose, and that his choice will be *his own good* that serves the fulfillment of *his own* person. At the same time, owing to the same ability of participation, man expects that in communities founded on the common good his own actions will serve the community and help to maintain and enrich it.

Under conditions established according to this axiological pattern he will readily relinquish his individual good and sacrifice it to the welfare of the community. Since such a sacrifice corresponds to the ability of participation inherent in man, and because this ability allows him to fulfill himself, it is not "contrary to nature."

Thus the priority of the common good, its superiority over the partial or individual goods, does not result solely from the quantitative aspect of the society; it does not follow from the fact that the common good concerns a great number or the majority while the individual good concerns only individuals or a minority. It is not the numbers or even the generality in the quantitative sense but the intrinsic character that determines the proper nature of the common good. This treatment of the problem is a continuation of our criticism of individualism and anti-individualism; it follows from our earlier discussion of participation and serves as a further confirmation of the conclusions then reached. We can see how from the reality constituted by "common acting" and "common being," participation emerges as a dynamic factor of the person and the action and also as the basis of every authentic human community.

7. "AUTHENTIC" ATTITUDES

A Pre-ethical Analysis

The discussion of the proper significance of the "common good," that is, of the relation that ought to exist between participation as the essential dynamic spring of a person and the common good, leads us to consider some attitudes that characterize the acting and being "together with others." First, we must distinguish the attitudes of

"solidarity" and of "opposition." We propose that the proper meaning of both "solidarity" and "opposition" emerges from the investigation of the community of acting or being and by reference to
the common good specific for this community. To start with, the
meaning of these terms is associated with a certain qualification
of action that ultimately becomes an ethical qualification. In the present
analysis, however, we will concentrate rather on the personalistic
significance of each of these attitudes and consequently the
qualification itself which we have in mind will remain at a pre-ethical
rather than an ethical level. Our aim remains, indeed, to outline the
structures of human acting and in this connection to underline the
value of the *fulfillment* of an action rather than that type of value of a
performed action which issues from its *relation to ethical norms*. Of
course, we may from this approach pass easily to an ethical analysis,
once we assume the very performance of an action constitutes a good,
which by its immanent value becomes an obligation. Undoubtedly,
the performance itself of the action is a good of the kind that imposes
an obligation on the one who performs it as well as on others, and this
latter is an essential element of social ethics.

Here we intend to continue our interest in the subjective performance of actions and in its immanent value so far as this value is
personalistic. It is in these relations that we can find the key to the
interpretation of the person's appropriate dynamism, also within the
framework of different communities of acting and being. Thus we will
investigate the above-mentioned attitudes, primarily in the personalistic perspective and in this sense pre-ethical. At the same time,
however, we must keep in mind that here, even more than throughout
this study, we are moving upon the territory of ontology and ethics, to
which we are committed by the axiological aspect of action and by
the wealth of values inextricably involved in the ontology of the
person and the action.

The Attitude of Solidarity

The attitude of "solidarity" cannot be dissociated from that of
"opposition," for each is necessary to the understanding of the other.
The attitude of solidarity is, so to speak, the natural consequence of
the fact that human beings live and act together; it is the attitude of a
community, in which the common good properly conditions and

initiates participation, and participation in turn properly serves the common good, fosters it, and furthers its realization. "Solidarity" means a constant readiness to accept and to realize one's share in the community because of one's membership within that particular community. In accepting the attitude of solidarity man does what he is supposed to do not only because of his membership in the group, but because he has the "benefit of the whole" in view: he does it for the "common good." The awareness of the common good makes him look beyond his own share; and this intentional reference allows him to realize essentially his own share. Indeed, to some extent, solidarity prevents trespass upon other people's obligations and duties, and seizing things belonging to others. In this sense solidarity is in harmony with the principle of participation, which from the objective and "material" point of view indicates the presence of "parts" in the communal structure of human acting and being. The attitude of solidarity means respect for all parts that are the share of every member of the community. To take over a part of the duties and obligations that are not mine is intrinsically contrary to participation and to the essence of the community.

Nevertheless, there are situations in social and individual life that make it necessary. In such a situation, to keep strictly to one's own share would mean, in fact, lack of solidarity. Such a possibility indicates that in the attitude of solidarity the reference to the common good must always remain alive: it must dominate to the extent that it allows one to know when it is necessary to take over more than one's usual share in acting and responsibility. That acute sense of the needs of the community which distinguishes the attitude of solidarity emphasizes above any particularism or divisions the mutual complementariness between the members of the solidaristic community; every member of a community has to be ready to "complement" by his action what is done by other members of the community. This mutual complementariness is in a way an intrinsic element in the very nature of participation, which we are now interpreting subjectively, that is, as the dynamic factor of the person, and not just objectively as the "parts" that are the share of every participant in the communal structure of acting and being. It is why we see in the attitude of solidarity an intrinsic manifestation of participation as a feature of the person. It is this attitude that allows man to find the fulfillment of himself in complementing others.

The Attitude of Opposition

As mentioned above, the attitude of solidarity does not contradict the attitude of opposition; opposition is not inconsistent with solidarity. The one who voices his opposition to the general or particular rules or regulations of the community does not thereby reject his membership; he does not withdraw his readiness to act and to work for the common good. Different interpretations of opposition that an individual may adopt with respect to society are of course possible, but here we adopt the one that sees it as essentially an attitude of solidarity; far from rejecting the common good or the need of participation, it consists on the contrary in their confirmation. This opposition aims then at more adequate understanding and, to an even greater degree, the means employed to achieve the common good, especially from the point of view of the possibility of participation. We have experience of innumerably different types of oppositions that have been continually expressed in the course of man's existing and acting "together with others," which show that those who in this way stand up in opposition do not intend thereby to cut themselves off from their community. On the contrary, they seek their own place and a constructive role within the community; they seek for *that* participation and *that* attitude to the common good which would allow them a better, a fuller, and a more effective share of the communal life. It would be too easy to quote endless examples of people who contest – and thus adopt the attitude of opposition – because of their deep concern for the common good (e.g., parents may disagree with the educational system or its methods because their views concerning the education of their children differ from those of the official educational authorities).

It would need a thorough inquiry to show the essence of opposition in all its aspects, whereas we may here only indicate it. The attitude of opposition is relative, on the one hand, to that particular view one takes of the community and of what is good for it, and on the other, it expresses the strong need to participate in the common existing with other men and even more so in the common acting. There can be no doubt that this kind of opposition is essentially constructive; it is a condition of the correct structure of communities and of the correct functioning of their inner system. More precisely, in order for opposition to be constructive, the structure, and beyond it the system of communities of a given society must be such as to allow the opposition that emerges from the soil of solidarity not only to *express* itself within the framework of the given community but also to *operate* for its benefit. The structure of a human community is correct only if it admits not just the presence of a justified opposition but also that practical effectiveness of opposition required by the common good and the right of participation.

The Sense of Dialogue

We thus see that the common good has to be conceived of dynamically and not statically – a fact that has been noted earlier. In fact, it must liberate and support the attitude of solidarity but never to a degree such as to stifle opposition. It seems that the principle of dialogue is very aptly suited to that structure of human communities and participation which satisfies these needs. The notion of "dialogue" has different meanings, but here we are primarily concerned with the one that is operative in the formation and the strengthening of interhuman solidarity also through the attitude of opposition. Undoubtedly opposition may make the cooperation of men less smooth and more difficult, but it should never damage or prevent it. The principle of dialogue allows us to select and bring to light what in controversial situations is right and true, and helps to eliminate any partial, preconceived or subjective views and trends. Such views and inclinations may become the seed of strife and conflict between men, while what is right and true always favors the development of the person and enriches the community. Dialogue, in fact, without evading the strains, the conflicts, or the strife manifest in the life of various human communities takes up what is right and true in these differences, what may become a source of good for men. Consequently, it seems that in a constructive communal life the principle of dialogue has to be adopted regardless of the obstacles and difficulties that it may bring with it along the way.

8. "NONAUTHENTIC" ATTITUDES

Authentic and Nonauthentic Attitudes

All that was said so far about solidarity and opposition as well as our general option of the principle of dialogue (a more detailed justification of this option would require a separate study) has to be constantly verified in juxtaposition with that truth about the action and the person which we have been laboriously striving for throughout this book. Both the attitude of solidarity and that of opposition appear to be intrinsically "authentic." In the first place, each allows the actualization not only of participation but also of the transcendence of the person in the action. (We have submitted to comprehensive analyses this transcendence – the self-determination and the fulfillment of the person.) In the second place, it appears that in either of those attitudes transcendence may play its role. Thus in this sense both attitudes are authentic inasmuch as *each respects the personalistic value of the action.*

Evidently, recognizing the essential role for both attitudes, it has to be kept in mind that in practice they have to be constantly tested as well in the interpretation given to specific situations as in other actual manifestations. Indeed, the lack of discernment may very easily distort the attitude of solidarity as well as that of opposition, changing either of them in concrete situations into nonauthentic attitudes deprived of their true personalistic value. The touchstone for discernment is the *dynamic subordination of action to truth* that is so essential for the person's transcendence in the action. This subordination is reflected in the *righteous conscience*, the ultimate judge of the authenticity of human attitudes. Also, the common good as recognized has to manifest itself in its relation to the righteous conscience, which safeguards its dynamism and the viability of participation.

Speaking of the possible loss of authenticity, which threatens the attitudes of solidarity and opposition, each in a different way and for different reasons, we have to make note of some nonauthentic attitudes, which we shall define here by popular rather than scientific terms. One of these attitudes is currently called a servile "conformism" and the other may be called "noninvolvement"; either may develop when man deviates from the authentic attitudes of solidarity and opposition by depriving them of those inherent elements which are the condition of participation and the personalistic value. The neglect of these elements may gradually change solidarity into conformism and the attitude of opposition into that of noninvolvement. It would, however, be an accidental occurrence, whereas the essential cause of the lack of authenticity in either of these distorted attitudes seems to be of a fundamental nature. It is on this assumption that we will now proceed with our discussion.

Conformism as a Nonauthentic Attitude

The term "conformism" derives from "to conform" and denotes a tendency to comply with the accepted custom and to resemble others, a tendency that in itself is neutral, in many respects positive and constructive or even creative. This constructive and creative assimilation in the community is a confirmation and also a manifestation of human solidarity. But when it begins to sway toward servility, it becomes highly negative. It is this negative tendency that we call "conformism." It evidences not only an intrinsic lack of solidarity but simultaneously an attitude of evading opposition; in short, a noninvolvement. If it still denotes man's assimilation with the other members of a community, it does so only in an external and superficial sense, in a sense devoid of the personal grounds of conviction, decision, and choice. Thus conformism consists primarily in an attitude of compliance or resignation, in a specific form of passivity that makes the man-person to be but the subject of *what happens* instead of being the *actor* or *agent* responsible for building his own attitudes and his own commitment in the community. Man then fails to accept his share in constructing the community and allows himself to be carried with and by the anonymous majority.

Even when the servile attitude of conformism does not become an outright denial or limitation, it always indicates a weakness of personal transcendence of self-determination and choice. It is this weakness that clearly shows the personalistically negative significance of the attitude of conformism. The problem of conformism obviously does not lie solely in the submission to the other members of the community, all the more so as such a submission may very often be a positive symptom. It lies much deeper and consists in a definite renunciation of seeking the fulfillment of oneself in and through acting "together with others." We may say that the man-person complies with his own self being as absorbed by the community. At the same time, however, he himself withdraws from the community.

Conformism in its servile form then becomes a denial of participation in the proper meaning of the term. A mere semblance of participation, a superficial compliance with others, which lacks conviction and authentic engagement, is substituted for real participation. Thus the specifically human ability of shaping creatively his community is dwarfed, annihilated, or perverted. This state of things cannot but have a negative effect on the common good whose dynamism springs from true personal participation. Simultaneously, conformism favors situations marked by indifference toward the common good. We may then look at it as a specific form of individualism leading to an evasion from the community, which is seen as a threat to the good of the individual, accompanied by a need to dissimulate oneself from the community behind a mask of external appearances. Hence conformism brings *uniformity* rather than *unity*. Beneath the uniform surface, however, there lies latent differentiation, and it is the task of the community to provide for the necessary conditions for turning it into personal participation.

Situations of prevailing conformism can never be accepted as satisfactory; for when people adapt themselves to the demands of the community only superficially and when they do so only to gain some immediate advantages or to avoid trouble, the person as well as the community incur irremediable losses.

Noninvolvement as a Nonauthentic Attitude

The attitude, which we have called "noninvolvement," seems to be characterized by a disregard for those appearances of concern for the common good which also characterizes conformism. In spite of the fact that the attitude of conformism evades opposition, that of avoidance evades conformism. This latter does not thereby adopt an authentic feature of opposition, which would consist in both an active concern for the common good and in participation. Noninvolvement is nothing but a withdrawal. It may sometimes manifest a protest, but even then it still lacks the active concern of participation; moreover, it characterizes man's absence from his community. The absent, as the saying goes, are always in the wrong. This is very often found to be true in the case of noninvolvement, though sometimes the attitude is adopted in the hope that absence can be expressive, that it may in certain situations involve taking a position in an argument; noninvolvement then becomes a kind of substitute or compensatory attitude for those who find solidarity too difficult and who do not believe in the sense of opposition. Indeed, it would be impossible to deny that this attitude may result from a deliberate conscious decision and then its essentially personalistic value has to be acknowledged. But even if there are valid reasons to justify its being adopted by the individual these same reasons become an accusation of the community insofar as it has caused it. After all, if participation is a fundamental good of a community, when participation becomes impossible – as in the attitude of noninvolvement when justified by the existing conditions – the functioning and the life of the community must somehow be defective. If the members of a community see the only solution to their personal problems in withdrawal from the communal life, this is a sure sign that the common good in this community is conceived of erroneously.

Nevertheless, for all that may in a way justify noninvolvement as a kind of shrunken compensatory attitude for full-fledged fulfillment, we cannot consider it as authentic. At many points it borders on conformism, not to mention the instances when both attitudes merge into something that might perhaps be defined as a "conformist noninvolvement." The most important, however, is the fact that either attitude causes man to abandon his striving for fulfillment in acting "together with others"; he is convinced of being deprived of his prerogatives to be "himself" by the community and thus tries to save it in isolation. In the case of conformism he attempts to maintain appearances but in that of noninvolvement he no longer seems to care about them. In either case he has been forcibly deprived of something very important: of that dynamic strain of participation unique to the person from which stem actions leading to his authentic fulfillment in the community of being and acting together with others.

9. FELLOW MEMBER AND NEIGHBOR

Two Interrelated Systems of Reference

Thus we are led to an even deeper layer of the reality of the person when his existing and acting is viewed from the standpoint of his membership in a community "together with others." The problem of participation appears to have been discussed sufficiently in contemporary sociological and anthropological studies with respect to the fact that man belongs to various communities simultaneously. His membership in any one of them entails a specific reference system, which the differentiation of a whole range of persons belonging to the same community makes very complex and rich. This reference system of being a "member" of a group is closely related to another one that also plays a very important role in participation and is best designated by the word "neighbor." In spite of the nearness and even some mutual overlapping of these systems of references, they are not identical. The content of the notion of "neighbor" differs essentially from what is contained in the notion "member of a community." Each points toward different possibilities and different tendencies within the personal participation. Each expresses differently the personal and the social nature of man.

If *neighbor* and *member of a community* are then two different notions each representing different forms and different reference systems, it is because to be and to act "together with others" places man within the range of diverse relations. The terms "neighbor" and "member of a community" (society) may help to understand better and more precisely the idea of participation. Indeed, "participation" itself means something else when it refers to a member of a community than when it refers to a neighbor.

To some extent, however, the two notions concur. As a member of a community, man is also another man's neighbor; this brings them closer together and makes them, so to speak, "closer" neighbors. Hence with respect to the membership of the same community the circle of every man's neighbors is either closer or more distant to him. It is natural for us to be closer with our family or our compatriots than with the members of other families or other nations. In this system of reference closer relationships always tend to displace the more distant ones; but of course in interhuman relations there is also alienation or estrangement. The notion of neighbor has, however, a deeper application than closeness (as opposed to alienation) in inter-human relations, and it is thus more fundamental than the notion of membership in a community. Membership of any community presupposes the fact that men are neighbors, but it neither constitutes nor may abolish this fact. People are or become members of different communities; in these communities they either establish close relations or they remain strangers – the latter reflects a lack of the communal spirit – but they are all neighbors and never cease to be neighbors.

The Interrelation of All Men in Humanness

This brings us to the axiological moment of great significance at this stage of our discussion when we are concentrating on the personalistic value in the community of being and acting. The notion of "neighbor" forces us not only to recognize but also to appreciate what in man is independent of his membership in any community whatever; it forces us to observe and appreciate in him something that is far more absolute. The notion of "neighbor" is strictly related to man as such and to the value itself of the person regardless of any of his relations to one or another community or to the society at large. The notion takes into account man's humanness alone, that humanness which is concretized in every man just as much as it is in myself. It thus provides the broadest basis for the community, a basis that reaches deeper than estrangement; it unites human beings, all human beings who are even members in different human communities. Although membership in a community or society presupposes the reality that is referred to in the notion of "neighbor," it also limits and in some respects removes to a more distant plane or even overshadows the broader concept of "neighbor"; it puts into the forefront man's relation and subordination to a given community – while when speaking of a neighbor we stress, on the contrary, only the most fundamental interrelations of all men in their humanness. The notion of "neighbor" refers then to the broadest, commonly shared reality of the human being and also to the broadest foundations of interhuman community. Indeed, it is the community of men, of all men, the community formed by their very humanness that is the basis of all other communities. Any community detached from this fundamental community must unavoidably lose its specifically human character.

From this point of view we have to look again at the problem of participation and try to reach to its ultimate consequences. We have already investigated the significance of participation with respect to the membership of the man-person in different communities, the membership which reveals and confirms his social nature. We now see, however, that the ability to participate has a wider scope and extends over the whole connotation of the notion of "neighbor." The man-person is capable not only of partaking in the life of a community, to be and to act together with others; he is also capable of participating in the *very humanness of others*. It is in this ability to participate in the humanness of every human being that all types of participation in a community are rooted, and it is there that it receives its personal meaning. This is what is ultimately contained in the notion of "neighbor."

Participation Consists in Sharing the Humanness of Every Man

The notion of "neighbor" brings out at last the full significance of that specific reality which from the beginning of this chapter we have been referring to as "participation." At this point it is important to emphasize that in the light of our reflection, any suggestions tending to mutually oppose the notions of "neighbor" and "member of a community" or to separate them from each other appear wholly unwarranted. We mentioned earlier their partial concurrence and now we intend to examine it closer. The basic concurrence of these notions is evidenced by the societal nature of man, even though it is in the relation to this nature that the difference between a neighbor and a member of a community becomes clearly apparent. We are not to assume, moreover, that the system of reference denoted by the term "neighbor" is the basis of all interhuman relations or that "member of a community" refers to the basis of social relations. Such an interpretation would be superficial and insufficient. The two systems of reference overlap and interpenetrate not only in the objective order, which shows every neighbor as belonging to a community and every member of a community as a neighbor, but also in the subjective order of participation. We have presented in this respect participation as a dynamic enactment of the person. Enactment, which is the person's essential feature, is manifested in that performance of actions "together with others," in that cooperation and coexistence which simultaneously serves the fulfillment of the person. Participation is closely associated with both the community and the personalistic value. This is precisely why it cannot be manifested solely by membership in some community but through this membership must reach to the *humanness of every man*. Only because of the share in humanness itself, which is at the roots of the notion of "neighbor," does the dynamic feature of participation attain its personal depth as well as its universal dimension. Only then can we claim that participation serves not just the fulfillment of some individual being, but that it also serves the fulfillment of every person in the community, indeed, because of his membership in the community. We may say this participation serves the fulfillment of persons in *any community* in which they act and exist. The ability to share in the *humanness itself of every man is the very core of all participation and the condition of the personalistic value of all acting and existing "together with others."*

10. THE COMMANDMENT OF LOVE

The Neighbor as the Fundamental System of Reference

In view of the preceding remarks concerning sharing in the humanness of every man it seems appropriate to dedicate the last pages of this book to the evangelical commandment of love. Having repeatedly stressed our intention not to make inroads on the territory of ethics we will not pursue here the purely ethical content of the commandment "Thou shalt love." We will not analyze the entire objective content of this commandment and in particular we will not seek out the ethical significance of love; our aim is only to emphasize the confirmation it contains for our claim that the reference system centered on "thy neighbor" has a crucial significance in any acting and existing "together with others."

In the first place "Thou shalt love" entails the juxtaposition of my neighbor with my own ego: "thy neighbor as thyself." The significance of the system's referring to my own self, that is, everyone's self, to the neighbor, is thereby brought into the fullest light. It appears fundamental because this system underlies any other reference system existing in a human community by its scope, sim-

plicity, and depth. At the same time it tells of a fullness of participation that is not indicated by membership in a community alone.
The relation to the neighbor is then the ultimate point of reference for
any system of reference resulting from the membership in a community. The former is essentially superior to the latter. Such is the
correct hierarchy of values because the system of reference to the
neighbor shows the mutual relation and subordination of all men
according to the principle of their common humanness itself while the
system of reference based on membership in a community is
insufficient to reveal this relation and this subordination. We may also
speak of a sort of transcendence of being a "neighbor" with regard to
being a "member of a community." All this is indirectly contained in
the evangelical commandment of love.

Of course, nothing of what has been said here is to be interpreted
as a depreciation of the communal human acting and being; any such
conclusions would be entirely false. The commandment, "Thou shalt
love," has itself a thoroughly communal character; it tells what is
necessary for a community to be formed, but more than anything else
it brings into prominence what is necessary for *a community to be
truly human.* It also tells what determines the true dimension of
participation. This is why the two reference systems – of the relationship to the neighbor and to the membership of a community –
must be considered jointly and not separately or, indeed, in opposition to each other, even though their distinction is entirely justified.
This also is contained in the evangelical commandment. If we were to
take a different point of view, then unavoidably some mutual limitations would arise; as a member of a community man would limit
himself as a neighbor and vice versa. Such limitations would be a sign
of a fundamental weakness of the person, of an absence of that
dynamic feature in the person which we have defined as participation,
of a serious defect in the social nature of man, etc. Does not the
social nature of man have its roots in this fundamental relation and
consequently in the very humanness of man?

The Commandment of Love Discloses the Roots of Alienation

Thus from the point of view of participation we have to reject any
limitations that either of the two systems of reference may impose on
the other. In acting and being together with others the system of

reference of being a neighbor and the one of being a member of a community must, in part, interpenetrate each other and, in part, remain mutually complementary. Should a separation occur between them in actual practice, it would lead to downright alienation. Nineteenth- and twentieth-century philosophy has rightly interpreted alienation as draining or sifting man from his very own humanness, that is, as depriving him of the value that we have here defined as "personalistic." In the sphere of acting and being "together with others" this danger becomes imminent when participation in the community itself sets constraints and overshadows participation in the humanness of others, when that fundamental subordination of my own good to that of my fellowman which imparts the specifically human quality to any community of men becomes defective. It seems, in fact, that the view sometimes expressed according to which the danger of "dehumanization" of our present-day civilization lies chiefly in the system of things – man's relationship to nature, the system of production and distribution of material goods, the blind pursuit of progress, etc. – is prejudiced and misleading. Though this view cannot be entirely overlooked, it is equally impossible to accept it as the only correct interpretation of the illnesses of the present-day world. Moreover, we have to remember, on the one hand, that although man did not create nature, he is its master; on the other hand, it is man who creates the systems of production, forms of technical civilization, utopias of future progress, programs of social organization of human life, etc. Thus it is up to him to prevent such forms of civilization from developing that would cause a dehumanizing influence and ensuing alienation of the individual. Consequently that alienation of human beings from their fellowmen for which man himself is responsible, is the prime cause of any subsequent alienation resulting from the reference systems of the material arrangements of goods and their distribution in social life. The essence of this alienation appears to be revealed by the commandment "Thou shalt love." Man's alienation from other men stems from a disregard for, or a neglect of, that depth of participation which is indicated in the term "neighbor" and by the neglect of the interrelations and inter-subordinations of men in their humanness expressed by this term, which indicates the most fundamental principle of any real community.[79]

The Commandment of Love as the Rule of Being and Acting
"Together with Others"

The reference systems of the "neighbor" and of the "member in a
community" – let us repeat once again – overlap and interpenetrate in
the objective order of things. They interpenetrate as attitudes taken
by men and rooted within the same individuals. Man's social nature is
expressed by both systems: by the fact that everybody is a member
of a community – even of several communities at once – as well as by
the fact that everybody is a neighbor; it is there that is contained
every man's special relation to himself as a person and to his own
ego. In the light of the hierarchy of the systems outlined here and of
the personalistic implications of the evangelical commandment of
love we must remember in actual-life conduct the necessity of so
coordinating acting and being "together with others" as to protect the
fundamental and privileged position of the "neighbor." This will
afford us the best protection from the dangers of alienation; in order
to avoid this latter our concern must be to make the system of
reference to the neighbor the ultimate criterion in the development of
the coexistence and cooperation of men in the communities and the
societies that are established at different levels and according to
different intracommunal bonds. Any human community that allows
this system of reference to become defective condemns itself to
becoming unfavorable for participation and throws open an unbridgeable gulf between the person and the community. It leads to the
disintegration of the community itself. Such disintegration is not the
result of mere indifference of man toward his fellowman; its destructive causes lie in the threat directed toward the person but
through the person unavoidably extending to the whole community.
How intimate is the union between the person and the community and
what is the essential content in the assertion of the social nature of
man seems to have become clear. But it is also in this perspective that
the neglect of its truth seems to reveal its ominous aspect.

This ominous aspect is not, however, the most significant. The
commandment "Thou shalt love" gives prominence first of all to the
brighter aspects in the reality of man's existing and acting "together
with others." It is on that brighter side that we have kept the analyses
in this last chapter of our study, without losing the focus upon the
acting person. To conclude: The commandment of love is also the

measure of the tasks and demands that have to be faced by all men – all persons and all communities – if the whole good contained in the acting and being "together with others" is to become a reality.

POSTSCRIPT

We have now come to the end of our inquiry concerning person and action, but before we definitely close this theme it seems necessary to comment on some ideas that may have either remained outside entirely or have been abandoned before they were brought to some definite conclusion. The last chapter introduced a new dimension of the experience "man-acts" inasmuch as we concentrated on the type of actions when man acts "together with others" and on some aspects of intersubjectivity accomplished by participation. The present author is well aware that his attempt is incomplete, that it remains but a "sketch" and not a well developed conception. Nevertheless, he thought it necessary to incorporate such a "sketch," if only to draw attention to the need of including the experience of man who acts together with others in the general conception of the acting person. This attempt, however, shows in turn that the whole conception of the acting person awaits rethinking along new lines. Whether such an inquiry would still deal solely with person and action or would shift to the community, intersubjectivity, or to personal interrelations, in which the acting person would reveal himself and confirm or correct our already obtained insights in some other new dimension, is another matter.

The doubt may arise, however, whether the experience of acting "together with others" is, in fact, the basic experience, and if not, whether the conception of the community and intersubjective relations should not be presupposed in any discussion of the acting person. And yet, this author is convinced that no interpretation of the community and interpersonal relations can be laid out correctly unless it rests on some already existing preconception of the acting person, indeed, on a conception that in the experience of "man-acts" adequately discloses the transcendence of the person in the action. Otherwise the interpretation may fail to bring out all that constitutes the person and also what intrinsically conditions as well as defines a community and its interrelations as a community and as an interrelation of persons.

Thus from the point of view of method as well as of substance the correct solution seems to be the one that would recognize the priority of the conception of the person and the action, and at the same time on the basis of this conception would search for an adequate interpretation of the community and interpersonal relations with all their richness and differentiations.

Finally, there is still one more disturbing question that demands some consideration. It concerns man's "existential status," the status of his being or existing, the whole truth about his limitations and his ontic contingency. Is this truth sufficiently built into the analyses of the person and the action? Has man's ontic status been marked with sufficient clarity in these analyses? Our concern in this regard is justified if for no other reason than that the conception of the acting person presented here issues from the experience "man acts" and ought to correspond to the authentic content of this experience. The theme of this study has been the person who reveals himself in and through the action, who reveals himself through all the psychosomatic conditionings that are simultaneously his wealth and his specific limitation. This is why the person manifests not only his transcendence in the action but also his integration appropriate to the action; it is in the integration and not beyond or above it that the dynamic reality of the action is constituted. The person, who manifests himself through the action, so to speak, permeates and simultaneously encompasses the whole psychosomatic structure of his own subject.

Admittedly, the aspect of the integration of the person in the action does not in itself explain sufficiently the ontic status of man, but it does bring us nearer to grasping and understanding man's status so far as this is made possible by the assumptions and the methods adopted in this study. Already in the introduction we stated that our aim was to extract from the experience of the action everything that would shed some light on man as a person, that would help, so to speak, to visualize the person; but our aim was never to build a theory of the person as a being, to develop a metaphysical conception of man. Even so, the vision of man who manifests himself as the person in the way which we have tried to disclose in our analyses seems to confirm sufficiently that his ontic status does not exceed the limits of his contingency – that he is always a being.

Having added these two explanations the author is satisfied that he can now close for the time being this discussion of the acting person.

NOTES

[1] In the phenomenological perspective the conception of experience received its full meaning. Following Husserl, we do not have reason to accept a restrictive interpretation of "experience." Experience should be considered as the source and the basis of all knowledge about objects, but this does not mean that there is one and only one kind of experience and that this experience is the so-called "sense" perception, which may be either "transcendent" or "immanent." In general, for phenomenologists "experience" means immediate givenness or every cognitive act in which the object itself is given directly – "bodily" – or, to use Husserl's phrase, is *leibhaft selbstgegeben*. Opposing the empiricistic reductionism there are, then, many different kinds of experience in which individual objects are given to be taken into account, for instance, the experience of the individual psychical facts of other selves, the aesthetic experience in which works of art are given, and so on.

The problem of experience and a broad range of related methodological questions were a major topic in a discussion of *The Acting Person* among philosophers active in Poland. Cf. *Analecta Cracoviensia*, V–VI (Cracow: Polskie Towarzystwo Teologiczne, 1973–1974) contributions by J. Kalinowski, M. Jaworski, S. Kamiński, T. Styczeń, and K. Kłósak. M. Jaworski, who differed with the position of J. Kalinowski, stressed the specific traits of the experience of man that underlies the understanding of his nature.

[2] This approach seems to go counter to the views of M. Blondel in his classic work *Action* (Paris: F. Alcan, 1963).

[3] It is interesting to note that in authors representing the so-called school of common language analysis in ethics, especially the Anglo-American exponents of this school, anthropological questions are almost entirely disregarded or limited to marginal remarks on the freedom of will and determinism. Cf., e.g., C. L. Stevenson, *Ethics and Language* (New Haven: Yale University Press, 1944) and also Stevenson's chief critic, R. B. Brandt, *Ethical Theory: The Problem of Normative and Critical Ethics* (Englewood Cliffs, N.J.: Prentice-Hall, 1959).

[4] The way this methodic procedure is employed in mathematics seems to illustrate sufficiently well in what sense and for what purpose "placing before brackets" will be used in this study. The aim is to exclude the essentially ethical problems in favor of the anthropological ones. It is to be stressed, however, that this does not entail that the essence is distilled and separated from actual existence, so characteristic for Edmund Husserl's phenomenological *epoché*. Thus this study does not follow the principles of a strictly eidetic method; and yet, throughout these investigations the author's intention has been to understand man as the person, that is, to define the "eidos" of the human being.

[5] Phenomenologists speak of the cognition of what is essential (in this case it would be cognition of the essence inherent in the event "man-acts"). In their opinion this kind of cognition is *a priori*, remains correlative with a specific intuition, and is consequently not to be reached inductively. Ingarden, for instance writes, "Though ... a phenomenologist does not essentially renounce the investigation of facts, the proper

field of his inquiries is located elsewhere. His chief task is the *a priori cognition of the essence of objects"* (*Z badań nad filozofia współczesną*, p. 318, Warsaw: PWN, 1965). This one-sided emphasis is, however, one more reason why it seems absolutely necessary to bring forth again the role of induction as conceived of by Aristotle (in contrast with the conception of induction in the positivists).

[6] The problem of practical knowledge in the Aristotelian and Thomistic approach with reference to Kant and contemporary philosophy has been studied by J. Kalinowski, *Teoria poznania praktycznego* (*Theory of practical knowledge*) (Lublin: Tow Nauk. Kul., 1960). In this study we do not intend to consider questions of practical knowledge as a specific source and the basis of human "praxis," though we will make use of the "praxis" itself as a source of knowledge of the man-person.

[7] This seems to explain not only the ends that in the author's intention this study is to serve but also provides a comment to the previously mentioned question of priorities in the relation between theory and praxis. Indeed, we are also concerned with the sense itself of philosophical and scientific cognition, in which the ambition of this study is to share.

[8] The author has given much thought to the work of M. Scheler, in particular his *Der Formalismus in der Ethik und die materiale Wertethik. Neuer Wersuch der Grundlegung eines ethisches Personalismus* (Bern: Francke, 1966). The critique of Kant contained in that work is of crucial significance for the present considerations and was for this author the occasion for reflection and the cause of a partial acceptance of some of Kantian personalism. This refers specially to the "ethical" personalism expounded in *Grundlegung zur Metaphysik der Sitten* (1785), in Kant, *Gesammelte Schriften, herausgegeben von der Königliche Preussischen Akademie der Wissenschaft* (Berlin, 1903), IV, 387–483.

The discussion between Scheler (*Der Formalismus in der Ethik und die materiale Wertethik*) and Kant was in a way the "starting ground" for the reflection underlying the analyses of the "acting person" contained in this study. The positions of these two philosophers directly referred to the conception of ethics but were inherently concerned with the conception of man, in particular the conception of the person, which philosophy – and theology – owes to Boethius, and thus became a challenge, if not an obligation, to search for a new approach to and a new presentation of the problem. These currents were also in one way or another reflected in the writings of Roman Ingarden. (The Polish edition of *The Acting Person* appeared before Ingarden published his *Über die Verantwortung. Ihre ontischen Fundamente* [Stuttgart: Philipp Reclam, 1970].) Some original writings by Ingarden as well as some major interpretations of his thought have appeared also on several occasions in *Analecta Husserliana, The Yearbook of Phenomenological Research*, ed. A.-T. Tymieniecka (Dordrecht: D. Reidel Publ. Co.). In particular see vol. IV, *Ingardeniana* and the treatise by A.-T. Tymieniecka, 'Beyond Ingarden's Idealism/Realism Controversy with Husserl – The New Contextual Phase of Phenomenology' (pp. 241–418).

[9] While writing this book (in the first, Polish version) the author attended the Second Vatican Council and his participation in the proceedings stimulated and inspired his thinking about the person. It suffices to say that one of the chief documents of the Council, the *Pastoral Constitution on the Church in the Modern World* (*Gaudium et spes*), not only brings to the forefront the person and his calling but also asserts the belief in his transcendent nature. The Constitution asserts, "The role and competence

of the Church being what it is, she must in no way be confused with the political community, nor bound to any political system. For she is at once a sign and a safeguard of the transcendence of the human person." *Gaudium et spes* 76, *The Documents of Vatican II*, ed. Walter M. Abbott, S.J. (New York: Guild Press, 1966).

[10] The original Polish term here used is "*czyn*," which as the author himself stresses, is not the exact equivalent of the Latin *actus*; nor is it the equivalent of the English *act* since its connotations stress deliberateness and purpose in human acting. This is why the translator has tended to render it by the term "action" rather than "act" (translator's note).

[11] See Thomas Aquinas, *Summae Theologiae* I–II, 'De actibus humanis,' qu. VI and fol., also *Summa Theol.* I, qu. LXXVII, 3. Cf. also J. de Finance: *Être et Agir dans la philosophie de Saint Thomas* (Paris: Beauchesne, 1943).

[12] It has often been noted that man manifests himself through actions, through his acting, though these assertions did not necessarily refer to the structure of man as the person. E.g., M. Blondel expresses this in a rather general way when he says, "Le corps de l'action n'est pas seulement un système de mouvements manifestés par la vie organique dans le milieu des phénomènes; il est constitué par la synthèse réelle et plus ou moins harmonisée des tendances multiples où s'expriment notre nature, notre spontanéité, nos habitudes, notre caractère." *L'action* (Paris: Beauchesne, 1963), II, 192–193. The proper perspective for this study is that of the person who discloses himself through the action. In this sense we are dealing with the ontological interpretation of the person through action as the action. By "ontological interpretation" we mean an interpretation that shows what the reality of the person is.

[13] Though *dynamism* is repeatedly mentioned here, its appropriate philosophical interpretation is deferred till it emerges from further considerations.

[14] The conviction that the traditional concept of "*actus humanus*" implicitly contains and, so to speak, conceals the aspect of consciousness, which in this study we are trying to disclose, is reinforced by an even more deeply rooted belief about the essentially continuous and homogeneous character of the whole philosophy of man, regardless of whether it is practiced from the position of the so-called "philosophy of being" or from those of the so-called "philosophy of consciousness." The action, as the keystone in revealing and understanding the reality that the person is, ensures that we reach this reality itself and do not stop at the level of consciousness alone, of absolute consciousness.

[15] The problem of the identity of consciousness, like that of its continuity, recurs constantly in the entire Western philosophical thought from Plato, through Descartes, Kant, Husserl and the contemporary existential thought in its different currents. When in the context of this study we assert the continuity and the identity of consciousness we thereby confirm our earlier assertion that consciousness plays a decisive part in establishing the reality of man as the person. The person is in a way also constituted by and through consciousness (though not "in consciousness" and not only "in consciousness"). The continuity and identity of consciousness reflects and also conditions the continuity and identity of the person.

[16] Even while rejecting the intentional character of consciousness and of its acts this author does not deny that consciousness is always – as stressed by Brentano, Husserl, and generally the phenomenologists – the consciousness of something. E.g., Husserl wrote, "We understood under intentionality the unique peculiarity of experiences 'to be

the consciousness of something'." *Ideas, General Introduction to Pure Phenomenology,* trans. R. Boyce Gibson (London: Allen and Unwin, 1939), p. 242. Nevertheless, this author's concern is at present the acting person from the viewpoint of the *aspect* of consciousness, and thus consciousness seen in a broader perspective; hence the questions he must ask are, *why* (*qua ratione*) and in *what way* (*quo modo*) consciousness is always the consciousness of something. In this connection it seems proper to adopt a different, dynamic concept of the act – the concept associated with the Aristotelian tradition – and consequently also a different concept of intentionality. We thus regard as *acts* in the strict sense of the word only the manifestations of the real powers of the person. Thus when following the manner of speaking widely accepted in phenomenology we refer to "acts of consciousness," the reader has to remember that we are using the phrase only figuratively, for its convenience and not its adequacy. Similarly we understand "intention" as an active directing upon the object; thus strictly speaking consciousness, as here conceived, has no intentionality and so the term, as we use it, has only a secondary and derived meaning owing to the intentional acts of knowledge or self-knowledge as real faculties.

[17] Here the "ego" means the subject having the experience of his subjectiveness and in this aspect it also means the person. The structure of the human person will be submitted to more comprehensive analysis when we come to the personal structure of self-determination. However, it has to be pointed out that the aim of our study is to show the reality of the person in the *aspect of consciousness* and not to analyze consciousness as such.

Because of self-knowledge the person – that is, the ego subjectively constituted by consciousness (self-consciousness) in the sense of the experience had of its own appropriate subjectiveness – has himself given as an object and simultaneously is objectively cognized by himself. This is why we can say of self-knowledge and consciousness that they are mutually consistent or cohesive. M. A. Krąpiec writing from the positions of existential Thomism sees self-knowledge as the knowledge of the existence of the ego. Cf. *"Ja-człowiek": Zarys antropologii filozoficznej ("The Ego-Man": An Outline of Anthropological Philosophy)* (Lublin: Towarzystwo Naukowe Polskiego Uniwersytetu Katolickiego w Lublinie, 1974), p. 109.

[18] The belief that knowledge has a general object springs from the Aristotelian tradition.

In connection with our discussion of self-knowledge it is worth noting that the position taken by J. Nuttin appears to come close to our analysis of self-knowledge. Nuttin wrote, "Cette présence cognitive de l'objet en face du moi implique, pour le moi, une certaine possession cognitive de soi-même, et une possibilité de prendre possession de l'objet comme tel. Une telle perception de l'objet crée la 'distance' nécessaire qui permet à la personnalité de se percevoir comme sujet percevant le monde, sans coincider avec cet acte". *La structure de la personnalité* (Paris: Presses Universitaires de France, 1971), p. 219.

[19] The stream of consciousness is spoken of in philosophy from the times of James and Bergson. Husserl emphasizes the crucial role of the stream of consciousness with respect to the ego. In the Husserlian analysis, especially in *Ideas I* and *Cartesian Meditations*, the structure "stream of consciousness – acts – the ego pole" constitutes the existential foundation of the human being and his life-world.

When speaking of the "vitality" that is peculiar and pertains to consciousness we are not thinking solely of the vitality that manifests itself as the stream of consciousness; what we are trying to achieve is to reach the source itself of the stream.

A. Póttawski, in his essay 'Ethical Action and Consciousness,' *Analecta Husserliana* Vol. VII, *The Human Being in Action* (Dordrecht: D. Reidel, 1978), pp. 115–150, has endeavored in a comprehensive and penetrating manner to compare the conception of consciousness presented in this study with that of the eminent French psychiatrist Henri Ey.

[20] The question may well be asked whether apart from experience – that is, experience of subjectivity, which we have here related to the reflexive function of consciousness – it is at all possible to know that it is the ego who is the subject. In view of what was said before about experience (see Introduction), the answer should be that while the experience of man (as an outer experience) allows us to some extent to ascertain him as the subject of existing and acting, it is the experience of one's own ego – an inner experience – that gives that special manifestation to this conviction and at the same time establishes its new dimension, that is, the dimension of the experienced subjectivity. It seems that according to E. Levinas a kind of "enjoyment" (*jouissance*) belongs to the essence of experience. He writes, "Le monde dont je vis ne se constitue pas simplement au deuxième degré après que la représentation aura tendu devant nous une toile de fond d'une réalité simplement donnée et que des intentions 'axiologiques' aient prêté à ce monde une valeur qui le rende apte à l'habitation. Le 'revirement' du constitué en condition s'accomplit dès que j'ouvre les yeux: je n'ouvre les yeux qu'en jouissant déjà du spectacle." *Totalité et Infini. Essai sur l'extériorité*, 4th ed. (The Hague: Nijhoff, 1971), p. 103. Further: "La sensibilité met en rapport avec une pure qualité sans support, avec l'élément. La sensibilité est jouissance. L'être sensible, le corps, concrétise cette façon d'être qui consiste à trouver une condition en ce qui, par ailleurs, peut apparaître comme object de pensée, comme simplement constitué" (*ibid.*, p. 109). If this position were accepted, then the only possible interpretation of the function of consciousness would be that it *conditions* experience and not that it *constitutes* experience.

[21] This approach has persisted in philosophy from Berkeley through Kant to Husserl, though of course with many subtle modifications.

[22] We could venture to say that as for Bergson "cognition," so here "experience" appears as this definitive and ultimate shape. We may also remark that in this approach consciousness, as the direct condition of having the experience of one's own ego, becomes the essential factor of realism in the conception of man. Here "realism" is used not only in the sense of simply ascertaining the objective "beingness" of man but also of carrying the analysis to the ultimate limits of the possible interpretation of that man in his unique concreteness.

[23] Scheler shows moral values as appearing "*auf dem Rücken*" of volitions directed toward different objective values (*materiale Werte*). Cf. M. Scheler, *Der Formalismus in der Ethik und die materiale Wertethik* (Bern: Francke, 1966), pp. 45–51, particularly the passage, "Der Wert 'gut' erscheint . . . an dem Willensakte. Eben darum kann er nie die Materie dieses Willensaktes sein. Er befindet sich gleichsam 'auf dem Rücken' dieses Aktes, und zwar wesensnotwendig; er kann daher nie in diesem Akte intendiert sein" (pp. 48–49). While it is impossible not to admire the subtlety of Scheler's analysis it is equally impossible to dismiss the suspicion that it somehow relaxes or perhaps

306   NOTES

even disregards the bonds connecting the subject – that is, one's own ego – given in experience as the agent with those very values of which he is the agent and not only the subject. Consequently the moment of a certain "identification" of the subject with the goodness or badness that he himself performed seems to disappear from the experience of morality, in which it plays a crucial role; indeed, it is this moment that determines the thoroughly personal character of these values.

These problems have on various occasions been critically considered by this author, among others in 'The Intentional Act and the Human Act, that is, Act and Experience,' *Analecta Husserliana*, vol. V (Dordrecht: D. Reidel, 1976), pp. 269–80.

[24] In this way we attribute to consciousness, and especially to self-consciousness, a certain function that in the structure of the person consists in the possession of oneself. This view is shared by other writers, among them also Nuttin, who says, "Cette perception et connaissance, ou conscience, de soi est une forme de possession de soi, qui constitue un élément essentiel d'un psychisme personnalisé." *La structure de la personnalité* (Paris: Presses Universitaires de France, 1971), p. 22. The question remains, however, whether "self-consciousness" has the same meaning for Nuttin as it has in this study.

It is on the assumption, according to which possession of oneself and self-control of oneself are in the structure of the human person conditioned by consciousness, that the emotionalization of consciousness is here analyzed. The joint and in a way homogeneous function of consciousness and self-determination – i.e., of will – in the integral structure of the person and the action will become even more evident when in the course of subsequent considerations self-possession or self-control are directly related to self-determination or will (cf. Chap. 3).

[25] Berkeley distinguishes two ways of existing: the *esse* of things is equivalent to *percipi* and the *esse* of spiritual beings is equivalent to *percipere et velle*. When considering the views of different philosophers it is essential to pay careful attention to the meaning each of them gives to the word "consciousness," because sometimes it may simply denote a conscious being.

[26] The sense in which "dynamism" is used here will still emerge in the course of further analyses. The term is related to the Greek "dynamism" and its genesis reaches back to Plato and Aristotle, from whom it passed to medieval philosophy (*potentia*). In modern philosophy dynamism (Leibniz) is opposed to mechanism (Descartes). Dynamism is closely connected with dynamics, which is most often understood as the opposite of statics; it is in this sense that it is used in the context of this study.

[27] Beginning our analysis of the dynamism pertaining to man with the distinction between "man-acts" and "something-happens-in-man" as fundamental structures we reach to what appears to be the most primitive in experience. This distinction is also given in experience and thus appears as directly evident to human cognition. We may add that the differentiation between the two structures seems to have as its equivalent in Aristotelian metaphysics the two separate categories: ποιεῖν-πασχεῖν or παθεῖν; cf. φανερὸν οὖν ὅτι ἐστι μὲν ὡς μία δύναμις τοῦ ποιεῖν καὶ πασχεῖν (δύνατὸν γάρ ἐστι καὶ τῷ ἔχειν αὐτὸ δύναμιν τοῦ παθεῖν καὶ τῷ ἄλλο ὑπ' αὐτοῦ), ἐστι δὲ ὡς ἄλλη *Metaphysics*, IX-θ1, 1046a, 19–22.

The author wonders whether the starting point for the analyses adopted in this study is not in some way close to P. Ricoeur's *Le volontaire et l'involontaire*, Paris: Aubier, 1949.

[28] See, e.g., ἐπεὶ δὲ λέγεται τὸ ὂν τὸ μὲν τὸ τὶ ἢ ποιὸν ἢ ποσόν, τὸ δὲ κατὰ δύναμιν καὶ

ἐντελέχειαν καὶ κατὰ τὸ ἔργον (...) ἐπὶ πλέον γάρ ἐστιν ἡ δύναμις καὶ ἡ ἐνέργεια τῶν μόνου λεγομένων κατὰ κίνηοιν. *Metaphysics*, IX-θ1, 1045b, 34–35; 1046a, 1–2; or *Metaphysics*, XII-(5, 1071a, 4–5 and other passages); *Summ. Theol.* Ia, S. Tomm.: "In uno et eodem, quod exit de potentia in actum, prius sit tempore potentia quam actus, simpliciter tamen actus prior est potentia, quia quod est in potentia, non reducitur in actum nisi per ens actu" (III, 1; III, 8) and "Potentia, secundum illud quod est potentia, ordinatur ad actum. Unde oportet rationem potentiae accipi ex actu ad quem ordinatur" (LXXVII 5).

[29] In connection with this problem R. Ingarden wrote, "In dem Bereich seiner möglichen Verwandlungen ist das Subjekt der Schöpfer seines Selbst. Es gäbe diejenige Gestalt seines Wesens nicht, die sich letzten Endes in seinen Leben realisiert, wenn es seine Taten und Verhaltensweisen in den Beziehungen zu seiner Umwelt nicht gegeben hätte. Unter den Menschen unseres Jahrhunderts hat das zuerst und am konkretensten R. M. Rilke gesehen, nach ihm erst Max Scheler, dann Heidegger und die Existentialisten." *Der Streit um die Existenz der Welt*, II, 2 (Tübingen: Niemeyer, 1965), p. 299, n. 30. This conception of constructing oneself through the action leads to more specific questions about the so-called "auto-creationism" in the philosophy of man. It invites confrontation with the conception of "man as creator" by A.-T. Tymieniecka, summarized in her critical work 'Beyond Ingarden's Idealism/Realism Controversy with Husserl – the New Contextual Phase of Phenomenology,' *Analecta Husserliana*, Vol. IV (Dordrecht: D. Reidel, 1976), pp. 241–418, especially Part 4: 'The Contextual Phase of Phenomenology and its Program. Creativity: Cosmos and Eros.' (Tymieniecka's theory of *creative activity* has been presented in a challenge to the classic phenomenology of "constitution" in her book *Eros et Logos, esquisse de la phénoménologie de l'intériorité créatrice*, Louvain: Nauwelaerts, 1961. Editor's note.) Cf. also by the same author: 'Initial Spontaneity and the Modalities of Human Life,' *Analecta Husserliana*, Vol. V (Dordrecht: D. Reidel, 1976), pp. 15–37.

[30] Cf. J. de Finance, *Être et Agir dans la philosophie de Saint Thomas* (Rome: Presses de l'Université Grégorienne, 1965).

[31] Cf. Boethius, *De duabus naturis et una persona Christi*, Migne, Patrol. Lat., vol. LXIV, 1343 D: "Persona proprie dicitur naturae rationalis individua substantia."

[32] Reaffirming the traditional position that "nature" is the basis for the integrity of the person we have to admit that it would be difficult to disregard that "paradox of freedom and of nature" of which P. Ricoeur wrote: "Derrière ces structures est le paradoxe qui culmine comme paradoxe de la liberté et de la nature. Le paradoxe est, au niveau même de l'existence, le gage du dualisme au niveau de l'objectivité. Il n'y a pas de procédé logique par lequel la nature procède de la liberté, (l'involontaire du volontaire), ou la liberté de la nature. Il n'y a pas de système de la nature et de la liberté.

"Mais comment le paradoxe ne serait-il ruineux, comment la liberté ne serait-elle pas annulée par son excès même, si elle ne réussissait pas à récupérer ses liaisons avec une situation en quelques sorte nourricière? Une ontologie paradoxale n'est possible que secrètement réconciliée. La jointure de l'être est aperçue dans une intuition aveuglée qui se réfléchit en paradoxes; elle n'est jamais ce que je regarde, mais cela à partir de quoi s'articulent les grands contrastes de la liberté et de la nature." *Le volontaire et l'involontaire* (Paris: Aubier, 1949), p. 22.

The integration of the human nature in and through the person has something in common with Ricoeur's "ontologie paradoxale" that "n'est pas possible que secrètement réconciliée" because of the moment of freedom, which is essential and constitutive for the action; and it is the action that in a special way reveals the person.

The treatment of the problem of the person's relation to nature in *The Acting Person* was critically discussed by J. Kalinowski in the previously mentioned discussion published in *Analecta Cracoviensia*.

[33] The notion of the potentiality of man – like the concept of the *actus*, to which it is strictly related – belongs to the heritage of the Aristotelian tradition. On the ground of these conceptions a certain systematization has been obtained of the powers accessible to man (cf. Aristotle, *De anima*, III, 8, 432, and particularly III, 9, 432b; see also S. Thomm., *Summa Theol.*, qu. LXXVII–LXXXIII). In our approach this systematization is omitted; for only what is given as the most primitive element of experience – namely, the difference between the experience of "man-acts" and that of "something-happens-in-man" – appears to have an essential significance for revealing, and thus also for understanding, the reality of the person, of his transcendence as well as his integration in the action.

[34] The need to distinguish between the unconscious and the subconscious was stressed by C. Tresmontant: "Dans l'inconscient de l'homme, il n'y a donc pas seulement ni même d'abord ce que j'ai 'refoulé,' des souvenirs que je me dissimule à moi-même. Il y a d'abord l'inconscient biologique, organisateur, qui opère en moi, dans l'organisme que je suis, sans que je sache comment. C'est un premier niveau de l'inconscient, un premier ordre ou domaine de l'inconscient." *Le probleme de l'âme* (Paris: Seuil, 1971), p. 186. It is to be noted, however, that the unconscious as a structural element of man can be spoken of meaningfully only if we accept man's virtuality and when we are discussing the relation between the virtuality and consciousness. Otherwise the unconscious does not seem to denote anything that would form part of the real structure of the human subject; it is but a negation of consciousness.

[35] The assertion that the threshold of consciousness not only divides but also connects consciousness and subconsciousness may be accepted only so far as we consider them on the ground of their relation to man's virtuality. It is perhaps necessary to ask how this fits in with Freud's conception that "There are two paths by which the contents of the id can penetrate into the ego. The one is direct, the other leads by way of the ego-ideal; which of these two paths they take may, for many mental activities, be of decisive importance.

"The ego develops from perceiving instincts to controlling them, from obeying instincts to curbing them. In this achievement a large share is taken by the ego-ideal which indeed is partly a reaction-formation against the instinctual processes in the id." *The Ego and the Id* (London: Hogarth Press, 1950).

[36] The problem of connecting the existential status of man with time, giving primacy to time, is especially attractive and important for phenomenologists and existential philosophers. E.g., J.-P. Sartre, 'La temporalité,' in *Être et le Néant, Essai d'ontologie phénoménologique* (Paris, 1943), pp. 150–218; D. v. Hildebrand, *Wahre Sittlichkeit und Situations-Ethik* (Düsseldorf: Pathmos, 1957), pp. 103–4; E. Levinas, 'La relation éthique et le temps,' in *Totalité et l'Infini* (The Hague: Nijhoff, 1971), pp. 195–225. Let us recall that the impulse came from Martin Heidegger. The traditional philosophy of man constructed on the ground of the philosophy of being did not occupy itself directly and explicitly with this problem. It was however, implicitly contained in the concept of the "contingency" of beings which referred to the human being as well as to all other derivative (i.e., created) beings.

The author admits that in this study the aspect of the contingency of man has not received sufficient attention and this is all the more true of the historical aspect of man.
[37] In view of the changeability of both man's body and his psyche philosophers have often debated the question of his identity in time. Their answers were of course different depending on the metaphysical position they adopted. Here we may quote, for example, Shoemaker who examined, among others, the causes allowing us to speak of man's identity in time. In this respect he assumes the knowledge (significant solely for men and not for things) that need not make use of any criteria and then goes on to say, "There is noncriterial knowledge of the identity (or persistence) of persons, namely, that expressed in memory statements," and then adds, "... persons are spatiotemporally continuous entities that can know their own pasts without using spatiotemporal continuity (or anything else) as a criterion of identity." *Self-Knowledge and Self-Identity* (Ithaca, 1963), pp. 258–59.

[38] It is necessary to note here the (possible!) ambiguity of the term "self-determination." It may be understood as meaning "I am the one who determines," and then the meaning of "self-determination" would coincide with the freedom of will, with "I may but I need not" (this was discussed in the preceding section). But it may also mean that "I am determined by myself" (this will be discussed in the next section). In the former sense the will manifests itself first of all as a power while in the latter it is a property of the person. We may presume that these two meanings (thus also two paths in the development of the philosophy of the will) derive from two dimensions and also two "moments" of the same experience rather than from two different experiences.

[39] Cf. "... Liberum arbitrium est causa sui motus: quia homo per liberum arbitrium seipsum movet ad agendum." *Summa Theol.* 83, 1 ad 3. For St. Thomas the will appears to be first of all a power, which makes man determine his own actions.

[40] In a sense Kant is the exponent of "the apriorism of freedom." His whole notion of the categorical imperative is constructed so as to allow "pure freedom" (autonomy) to mark its role in man's action, because it is only in "pure freedom" that "pure morality" can be actualized. At the same time it would be difficult to deny that it was Kant who contributed to the personal meaning (and indirectly the personal structure) of self-determination; though perhaps the decisive role in this matter was played by the so-called "second imperative" rather than by his theory of a priori freedom. Cf. "Handle so, dass du die Menscheit sowohl in deiner Person, als in der Person eines jeden andern jederzeit zugleich als Zweck, niemals bloss als Mittel brauchest." *Grundlegung zur Methaphysik der Sitten* (Leipzig: Philipp Reclam, 1904), p. 65. Kant points out that self-determination is a right of the person. A right, however, cannot be suspended in the void, it must have a real structure to correspond to. By means of this structure the person – that is, that which in itself is subjective – becomes his own first object. It is this relation that we have called "self-determination." This author is convinced that it cannot be expressed in terms of the intentionality itself of an act of will (I will something).

[41] This is not transcendence "toward something," transcendence directed toward an object (value or end), but one within the frame of which the subject confirms himself by transgressing (and in a way outgrowing) himself. This kind of transcendence appears to be represented by Kant rather than by Scheler.

[42] Cf. "... quamvis liberum arbitrium nominet quendam actum secundum propriam significationem vocabuli; secundum tamen communem usum loquendi, liberum arbitrium dicimus id quod est huius actus principium, scilicet quo homo libere iudicat.

Principium autem actus in nobis est et potentia et habitus... Oportet ergo quod liberum arbitrium vel sit potentia, vel sit habitus... Quod autem non sit habitus..." Thomas, *Summa* 83, 2c.

[43] According to A.-T. Tymieniecka, "The initial spontaneity makes itself ascertain, within the complete phenomenological framework of inquiry, as the authentic counterpart of the ordering systems in which it represents the *elemental* ground of the primitive forces and the *subliminal* source of man's passions, drives, strivings and nostalgias." 'Initial Spontaneity and the Modalities of Human Life,' in: *Analecta Husserliana* Vol. V (Dordrecht: D. Reidel, 1976), p. 24. Elsewhere she writes, "... 'Brute' Nature could hardly by itself explain in its universally designed progress the *differentiation* of the initial spontaneity as it flows into the act of human experience. ... Once bound into the orchestration of human functions these blind energies of Nature may stir from below its apparatus and supply it with 'forces.' However, it is the intermediate 'territory' of *spontaneity, differentiating, and endowed with specific virtualities* – territory which we call 'subliminal' – that is, postulated in order that the functional progress and its articulation may come about" (*ibid.*, p. 34).

[44] It seems right and correct to draw a distinction, as does Ingarden, between "intention" and "intent." Cf. R. Ingarden, *Studies in Contemporary Philosophy* (Warsaw: PWN, 1963), p. 364, n. 1.

[45] See N. Ach, *Über den Willensakt und das Temperament* (Leipzig, 1910), A. Michotte and N. Prümm, 'Le choix volontaire et ses antécédents immédiats, *Arch. de psych.*, 10 (1910). In Poland the analysis of the will was developed in a similar direction by, e.g., M. Dybowski: *How Execution Depends on the Traits of the Willing Process* (Warsaw, 1926); *On the Types of Will. Experimental Researches* (Lvov–Warsaw, 1928).

[46] When in this study we point to the moment of decision we do so because of previously adopted assumptions; we consider the will primarily as self-determination (personal structure of self-determination) and only, so to speak, secondarily as a power. It is noteworthy that Ricoeur also incorporates the problem of choice (*le choix et les motifs*) into the analysis of decision (*décider* or rather "*se décider*"); cf. *Le volontaire et l'involontaire*, (Paris: Aubier, 1949), p. 37ff.

[47] See also K. Wojtyła, 'Zagadnienie woli w analizie aktu etycznego' ('The problem of will in the analysis of the ethical act'), *Roczniki Filozoficzne*, 5, no. 1 (1955–1957), 111–35, and 'O kierowniczej lub służebnej roli rozumu w etyce. Na tle poglądów Tomasza z Akwinu, Hume 'a i Kanta' ('The directing or subservient role of reason in ethics discussed in relation to Thomas Aquinas, Hume and Kant'), *Roczniki Filozoficzne*, 6, no. 2 (1958), 13–31.

This juxtaposition is meant to reflect the conviction that, in spite of the diametrical difference between metaphysical realism (Thomas) and *a priori* rationalism (Kant), it is still possible to find in the conception of man some common ground for comparison.

[48] The transcendence of the person in the action is thus ultimately constituted as the "transgressing of oneself in truth" rather than "toward truth" (see note 41 above).

[49] Cf. "En pervertissant l'involontaire et le volontaire, la faute altère notre rapport fondamental aux valeurs et ouvre le véritable drame de la morale qui est le drame de l'homme divisé. Un dualisme éthique déchire l'homme par delà tout dualisme d'entendement et d'existence. 'Je ne fais pas le bien que je veux, et je fais le mal que je ne veux pas'." P. Ricoeur, *Le volontaire et l'involontaire*, (Paris: Aubier, 1949), p. 24.

[50] See M. Scheler, *Der Formalismus in der Ethik und die materiale Wertethik*, mainly

Das Apriori-Materiale in der Ethik (p. 99ff.). In this context the assertion that the moment of truth about a good is essential in the experience had of value has meaning primarily so far as it allows us to bring out the personal structure of self-determination and also the transcendence of the person in the action. The author is fully aware that this assertion can be considered only against a broad background of investigations dealing specifically with the theory of value and knowledge (the cognitive experiencing of value). Cf. D. v. Hildebrand, *Ethik*, in *Gesammelte Werke*, vol. 2 (Stuttgart: Habbel-Kohlhammer, 1974), pt. 1, especially 'Die Realität der Werte wider ihre Verächter' and 'Wesentliche Aspecte der Wertsphäre,' pp. 83–174, or the English translation entitled *Christian Ethics* (New York: McKay, 1952). See also N. Hartmann, *Ethik* (Berlin: De Gruyter, 1926), Part 4: 'Vom Wesen der ethischen Werte,' pp. 107–53, especially chap. 16: 'Gnoseologisches Ansichsein der Werte,' pp. 133–35.

[51] There seems to be a strict relation between acknowledging the results of an intransitive action and acknowledging the reality of the goodness or badness – of moral values – within the personal subject that man is. This relation has a crucial significance for the meaningfulness of the whole of our discussion over the relation of self-determination to fulfillment. When in the coming discussions we are using the phrase "man fulfills himself" (or fails to fulfill himself), we are aware that fulfillment itself has in a way an absolute sense. The absolute dimension of the fulfillment of oneself, however, is never mentioned either in this chapter or throughout this book. No concrete action in the terrestrial experience of man can actualize such an absolute dimension. Nevertheless, every action discloses to some extent the structures of personal fulfillment, just as it discloses the structures of personal self-determination. Since in the preceding chapter we inspected the structures of self-determination it is now necessary to examine the structures of personal fulfillment in connection with the action.

The discussion of what is transitive and intransitive in the action must be related to the traditional philosophy of being and acting (*l'être et agir*).

[52] At this point it is perhaps necessary to recall M. Scheler's critique of the Kantian ethics, in which he saw "pure obligation" (*Pflicht aus Pflicht tun*) instead of obligation itself as a specific fact and thus also a specific experience. The important thing about this experience is that it must be adequately rooted in value. Nevertheless, the question remains whether the Kantian imperatives (especially the so-called second imperative) do not in a way presuppose a turn toward values lying at the basis of obligation, or even pertaining to obligation.

In the course of this analysis the author's prime concern is to reveal the roots, from which both the experience of value and obligation develops, so to speak, organically. Values are "normogenic."

[53] The discussion of the interrelation of "truthfulness and consciousness" is strictly connected with the debate in Chapter 1, 'The Acting Person in the Aspect of Consciousness.' The whole process, whereby the person with his constitutive structures is gradually disclosed by the action, forces us to concentrate attention on truthfulness; for consciousness can be identified only in its broad and, so to speak, secondary sense with "moral conscience."

[54] The question refers to the basis of the dynamic structure of self-determination, which is connected with man's fundamental striving to be good and not to be bad. The position taken by Scheler – who maintains that to make moral values the object of

desiring would be a hypocritical attitude – is understandable in the light of his assumptions; for "to want to be good" and "to want to have the experience of being good" are two entirely different things and a dose of hypocrisy may indeed be suspected in the latter. See also this author's 'The Intentional Act and the Human Act, that is, Act and Experience' in *Analecta Husserliana*, Vol. V (Dordrecht: D. Reidel, 1976), pp. 272–73.

In the light of these analyses we become convinced that the role of the will in the structure of the person and the action is to be considered from the point of view of self-determination and not of "intentionality" (see Chap. 3, 'The Personal Structure of Self-determination').

[55] These views about the nature of ethical judgments relate to the metaphysical belief that values have no real existence (evaluational nihilism) or to the epistemological belief that values are not an object of cognition (acognitivism). These beliefs are apparent in the emotivism of A. J. Ayer. Cf. *Language, Truth and Logic* (London: Gollancz, 1936) as well as in the prescriptivism of R. M. Hare, *The Language of Morals* (Oxford: Oxford U.P., 1952). Hare, however, tries to attenuate this extreme emotivism in favor of objectivism in ethical judgments and maintains that moral norms can be justified though this does not consist in demonstrating their truthfulness.

[56] Rom. 12:1.

[57] Ricoeur writes, "... en me réveillant de l'anonymat, je découvre que je n'ai pas d'autres moyens de m'affirmer que mes actes mêmes. 'Je' ne suis qu'un aspect de mes actes, le pôle-sujet de mes actes. (En ce sens Husserl dit que hors de son implication dans ses actes le moi n'est pas 'un objet propre de recherche': 'si l'on fait abstraction de sa façon de se rapporter (Beziehungsweisen) et de se comporter (Verhaltungsweisen), il est absolument dépourvu de composantes eidétiques et n'a même aucun contenu qu'on puisse expliciter; il est en soi et pour soi indescriptible, moi pur et rien de plus (*Ideen*, I, 160). Je n'ai aucun moyen de m'affirmer en marge de mes actes. C'est ce que me révèle le sentiment de responsabilité." *Le volontaire et l'involontaire*, (Paris: Aubier, 1949), p. 56.

[58] It seems that this sort of misconception lies at the root of the so-called "hedonistic calculus" constructed according to the principle of maximum pleasure and minimum pain: see J. Bentham, *Principles of Morals and Legislation* (1789). Too much attention can never be given to the way in which the old Greek concept of *eudaimonia* has been evolving in the course of history: see W. Tatarkiewicz, *Analysis of Happiness* (Warsaw: PWN, 1976). The stand taken in this study has emerged from reflections influenced both by Kant's criticism of Bentham's utilitarianism and by Scheler's analysis of human emotionality: see *Der Formalismus in der Ethik und die materiale Wertethik* (Bern, 1954), pp. 256–67, 341–56.

[59] R. Ingarden in his *Über die Verantwortung (Ihre ontischen Fundamente)* (Stuttgart: Reclam Universal-Bibliothek, 1970) makes the following assertions:

(1) Responsibility presupposes that there is a definite and not some one or other theory of the person. He writes, "Alle Theorien, welche die Person auf Mannigfaltigkeiten reiner Erlebnisse reduzieren, sind für die Klärung der ontischen Fundamente der Verantwortung unzureichend. Nur sofern man den Menschen und insbesondere seine Seele und seine Person für einen realen, in der Zeit verharrenden Gegendstand hält, der eine spezielle, charakteristische Form hat, ist es möglich, die Postulate der Verantwortung zu erfüllen" (p. 66).

(2) He then goes on to stress that among the essential conditions of responsibility

there is the *freedom* of the person performing an action. But freedom itself, he explains, presupposes a definite formal structure of the person and of the real world, in which the person acts. The one and the other must form a relatively isolated system; it is in the notion of such systems that the solution to the so-called problem of freedom has to be sought for.

(3) The relation between responsibility and obligation can be deduced from what Ingarden says about the ontic foundations of responsibility. For him one of these foundations consists of values, of which he says elsewhere that their nature is that of obligation. "Die Existenz der Werte und der zwischen ihnen bestehend Zusammen-hänge ist die erste Bedingung der Möglichkeit sowohl der Idee der Verantwortung als auch des Sinnvollseins des an den Täter gerichteten Postulats, die Verantwortung für seine Tat zu ubernehmen und ihre Forderungen zu erfüllen," *Über die Verantwortung* (Stuttgart: Reclam, 1970), p. 38.

In the discussion on *The Acting Person* published in *Analecta Cracoviensia* (vols. 5–6) some participants pointed to certain methodological analogies between this study and R. Ingarden's *Über die Verantwortung op. cit.* See M. Jaworski, 'Koncepcja antropologii filozoficznej w ujęciu Kardynala Karola Wojtyły' ('The conception of philosophical anthropology in the approach of Cardinal Karol Wojtyła'), pp. 103–4, and T. Styczeń, 'Metoda antropologii filozoficznej w *Osobie i czynie*' ('The method of philosophical anthropology in *The Acting Person*') (Cracow: *Analecta Cracoviensia*, Vols. V–VI, 1973–74), pp. 113–15. Yet the methodological affinity of the two has its source in Scheler.

[60] The analyses of Ingarden seem also to indicate that the "experience of the soul" is given only indirectly and not directly; this experience he sees contained in the "pure ego." Cf. *Der Streit um die Existenz der Welt* (Tübingen: Niemeyer, 1965), pp. 320–322.

[61] The concept of disintegration has been applied in different branches of anthro-pological science. In Poland, for instance, the so-called positive disintegration has been used in attempts to interpret the whole of the psychical phenomena: (see the following by K. Dąbrowski: *La désintégration positive. Problèmes choisis* (Warsaw: Polish Academy of Sciences, 1964); *Personnalité, psychonévroses et santé mentale d'après la théorie de la désintégration positive* (Warsaw: Państwowe Wydawnictwo Naukowe, 1965); *Psychothérapie des névroses et psychonévroses. L'instinct de mort d'après la théorie de la désintégration positive* (Warsaw: Państwowe Wydawnictwo Naukowe, 1965); also other works of same author brought out by the same publishers.

[62] In the above quoted discussion on *The Acting Person* attention was directed to the significance that the philosophical conception of man as the person who "possesses and governs himself" has in psychiatric research and practice: see W. Półtawska, 'Kon-cepcja samoposiadania podstawą psychoterapii obiektvwizującej – w świetle książki Kardynała Karola Wojtyły' ('The concept of self-possession as the basis of objectifying psychotherapy – in the light of the book by Cardinal Karol Wojtyła'), *Analecta Craco-viensia* vols. 5–6, pp. 223–41.

[63] Cf. E. Kretschmer, *Körperbau und Charakter. Untersuchungen zum Konstitution-sproblem und zum Lehre von den Temperamenten*, 24th ed. (Berlin: Springer, 1961).

[64] Luijpen, in criticizing views which treat the body as an object of having (he is of course speaking of "having" in the literal sense of the word), says, "My Body is Not the Object of 'Having.' . . . I 'have' a car, a pen, a book. In this 'having' the object of the 'having' reveals itself as an exteriority. There is a distance between me and what I

'have.' What I 'have' is to a certain extent independent of me. ... My body is not something external to me like my car. I cannot dispose of my body or give it away as I dispose of money. ... All this stems from the fact, that my body is not 'a' body, but *my* body ... in such a way that my body *embodies* me." (*Existential Phenomenology*, 3d ed. (Louvain: E. Nauwelaerts, 1963), p. 188. To explain the relation between the conscious subject and the body Luijpen remarks: "In the supposition that I 'am' my body, I am a thing and wholly immersed in a world of mere things. But then the conscious self is reduced to nothing, and, consequently, also my body as 'mine,' as well as the world as 'mine.' Accordingly, I neither 'am' my body nor 'have' it. My body is precisely mid-way between these two extremes. It constitutes the transition from the conscious self to the worldly object. It is the mysterious reality which grafts me on things, secures my being-in-the-world, involves me in the world, and gives me a standpoint in the world" (*ibid.*, pp. 189–90).

[65] Bergson, on the other hand, is inclined to believe that it is the spirit that uses the body. For instance, he asserts, though in a different context, that "... c'est à dire aussi que la vie de l'esprit ne peut pas être un effet de la vie du corps, que tout se passe au contraire comme si le corps était simplement utilisé par l'esprit, et que dès lors nous n'avons aucune raison de supposer que le corps et l'esprit soient inséparablement liés l'un à l'autre." *L'énergie spirituelle*, 5th ed. (Paris: F. Alcan, 1920), pp. 57–58.

In connection with these different views the present author thinks it necessary to stress that when he affirms, "man *is not* the body, he only has it," this statement is the consequence of the belief that man "is" his own self (i.e., the person) only insofar as he possesses himself; and, in the same sense, if he *has* his body.

[66] We find this expression in D. Hume, *Treatise on Human Nature* and in many other authors subsequent to him. Today it is of virtually universal occurrence in both specialist and popular literature. The expression also presupposes a definite anthropology; it is this line of thinking that we have followed when dealing here with the problem of "integration and the psyche."

[67] In this study the problem of constructing – or rather, of self-constructing – the personal subject has only been sketched in rough outline, but actually it seems to deserve a much more thorough investigation. The distinction drawn between the somatic and the psychical "subjectiveness" within the frame of the integrated personal subjectiveness seems to support the notion of "strata" in the philosophy of man. See N. Hartmann, *Ethik*, 4th ed. (Berlin: de Gruyter, 1962), especially part 3, chap. 2, sect. 71: 'Zur ontologischen Gesetzlichkeit als Basis der Freiheit,' pp. 675–85.

[68] See M. Scheler, "... Wertgefühle ... , (z B. 'Achtungsgefühl' usw) dürfen diese nur darum heissen, weil in der primären Gegebenheit des 'vollen Lebens' die Werte selbst noch unmittelbar gegeben waren, derentwegen allein sie ja den Namen 'Wertgefühle führen'." *Der Formalismus in der Ethik und die materiale Wertethik* (Bern: Francke, 1966), pp. 209–10.

[69] The distinction between the concupiscent and irascible appetite is also to be found in P. Ricoeur, when for instance he says, " 'irascible' ne se révèle empiriquement qu'à travers les passions d'ambition, de domination, de violence, de même que le 'concupiscible' se révèle empiriquement à travers les passions du plaisir et de facilité." *Le volontaire et l'involontaire* (Paris: Aubier, 1949), p. 112.

[70] Cf. M. Scheler, *Der Formalismus in der Ethik und die materiale Wertethik* (Bern: Francke, 1966), especially 'Zur Schichtung des emotionalis Lebens', pp. 331–45.

[71] The position taken here differs from that of M. Scheler (cf. *op. cit.*, especially 'Formalismus und Apriorismus', pp. 82–84). Indeed, it seems necessary to draw a distinction between even the most intimate "proximity" of the subject and with values – this being the function of emotion – and their adequate "cognition."

[72] This belief appears to be also contained in what Aristotle says of the power of the intellect and the will over emotions having a "political" (or "diplomatic") rather than an absolute character (cf. *Politics*, bk. 1, chap. 3; *Nicomachean Ethics*, bk. 4, chaps. 3–5). We may also add that one of the elements of the "political" nature of this power is to know when it is to be exercised in an "absolute" manner.

[73] In the course of the history of philosophy the question of the soul–body relation has been raised time and again and has received many different answers.

[74] This distinction has often been used throughout the history of Christian ethics and ascetics; it derives from St. Paul (cf. Rom. 7:15–24, and 6:6; 1 Cor. 15:47–49).

In the present context the "higher man" refers to the subject who manifests himself in the experience of both transcendence and integration; thus the "lower man" applies to the same subject – if he manifests himself as such – who because of the transcendence appropriate to the actions of a person still requires integration.

[75] The last chapter of this study of the acting person is but a comment to what was said hitherto and must be regarded as such. This comment, however, appears to be indispensable and without it our study would be incomplete. Having begun our discussion with the experience "man-acts" we must at least take note of the circumstance that usually – if not always – he in one way or another acts "together with others." From the point of view of the person this circumstance has many different implications, which it would be impossible to expose here; we intend to concentrate on only one of them, namely, on the one that appears to be historically the most important.

The heading of the chapter is 'Intersubjectivity by Participation.' When Husserl speaks of *Intersubjektivität* he stresses primarily the cognitive dimension of intersubjectivity. In the fifth *Cartesian Meditation* he analyses step by step the way in which consciousness is constituted by means of the *Fremderfahrung* of the community conceived of as the *intermonadologische Gemeinschaft*, the decisive step being apparently the constituting of the intersubjective nature (*die intersubiektive Natur*). (Cf. 'Vorgemeinschaftung der Monaden und die erste Form der Objektivität: Die intersubjektive Natur': E. Husserl, *Cartesianische Meditationen und Pariser Vorträge* (The Hague: Nijhoff, 1963), Meditation 5, sect. 55, p. 149.

In the approach adopted in this study it is the action that serves as the fundamental source for the cognition of man as the person. Since in fact man acts "together with others" it is also necessary to extend on the same basis our knowledge of man in his intersubjectivity. In this way in the place of "intersubjectivity" as a purely cognitive category we have now, so to speak, introduced "participation." We thus have man who in acting *"together with others,"* that is, by *participating*, discloses a new dimension of himself as the person. It is this dimension, which we have here called "participation," that we are now going to submit to a brief analysis. This road, we hope, will bring us to a more complete – or, at any rate, more complementary – understanding of human intersubjectivity.

[76] This and the following section have previously appeared in the *Phenomenology Information Bulletin*, 2 (1978), published by *The World Institute for Advanced Phenomenological Research and Learning*, Belmont, Mass. (Editor's note).

[77] We cannot be too emphatic in stressing the specific sense in which we are here speaking of participation. This is all the more necessary in view of the different meanings, or rather shades of meanings, that this term has had for different traditional and contemporary philosophical schools. In this study participation may be said to emerge at the very beginning of the analysis of man's acting "together with others" as that fundamental experience whereby we are trying to grasp man as the person. The person – as that "man who acts together with others" – is in a certain manner constituted through participation in his own being itself. Thus participation is seen as a specific constituent of the person.

In the discussion published in *Analecta Cracoviensia*, vols. 5–6 (Cracow: Pol. Tow. Teol., 1973–74) this specific meaning of participation was accepted with appreciation but it also aroused some controversy; see L. Kuc, Uczestnictwo w człowieczeństwie "innych" ('Participation in the humanity of "other selves"'). A counterproposition was suggested with regard to both the substantial and the methodic approach in *The Acting Person*. From the position of this counterproposition the essential knowledge of man as the person is the knowledge that emerges in his relations to other persons. While acknowledging the validity of this epistemological position this author – after due consideration to the arguments for and against – still holds that a sound knowledge of the. subject in himself (of the person through the action) opens the way to a deeper understanding of human intersubjectivity; indeed, it would be entirely impossible to establish the right proportion in the understanding of the person and his interrelations with other persons without such categories as self-possession and self-governance.

[78] The discussion that follows is an attempt at a reinterpretation – though still in the form of but a rough sketch or mere outline – of the concept of the "common good." The critical nature of this interpretation (made in a definite historical context) will obtain its specific significance when considered together with the subsequent tentative analysis of authentic and nonauthentic attitudes.

[79] An attempt at a broader interpretation of this problem is to be found in 'Participation or alienation?' *Analecta Husserliana* vol. 6 (Dordrecht: D. Reidel, 1976), pp. 61–73.

We have to emphasize once again that the whole of Chapter 7 is but a comment and no more than an outline of the problem. The analyses it contains have led us to the conclusion that participation as a property of man, who exists and acts "together with others," lies at the roots of two different dimensions of human intersubjectivity. One dimension refers to the "man–other man" (I–you, *soi–autrui*) relation and the other is to be found in the "we" relation (community). Either form of intersubjectivity demands a separate analysis; for participation understood simply as participating, or taking part, in the humanness of others is quite a different thing than participation seen as the correct membership in different communities (societies) in which man's destiny is to exist and act "together with others."

LITERAL TRANSLATION OF CHAPTER SEVEN
PRIOR TO EDITORIAL REVISION:
INTERSUBJECTIVITY BY PARTICIPATION

1. AN INTRODUCTION TO PARTICIPATION*

Man's Acting "Together With Others"

The starting point for the discussions in this study was the conviction that the action marks a special moment in the manifestation of the person, a conviction overtly asserted from the first. In due course we have also unraveled the various aspects of the person's dynamism in the action. The road to an understanding of the person has led us through the action and has simultaneously allowed us to grasp the action; for the action is not only the means or a special basis of the intuition of the person, but it also discloses itself with every step that brings us nearer the person. On this road we have relied throughout on a strict correlation of the person and the action, a correlation of which the person and the action are the two members – or perhaps the two poles; each strictly corresponds to the other, and they also mutually display and explain each other. This correspondence and this correlation gradually reveal the main lines for the interpretation of the acting person.

The present chapter, the last in this study, adds one more element to the whole as given above. This new element, though actually contained in all the previous ones, has not received the attention it deserves and must be more thoroughly examined; thus we will now investigate that aspect of the dynamic correlation of the action with the person which issues from the fact that actions can be performed by people together with other people. Admittedly, the expression "together with other people" lacks the necessary precision and does not describe sufficiently the reality it refers to, but for the moment it is the most appropriate phrase, since it draws attention to the diverse communal or social relations in which human actions are usually

---

* Cf. Note 75 in the definitive version of the text above.

involved. This of course is a direct and natural consequence of the fact that man lives "together with other men": indeed, we may go so far as to say that he exists together with other men. The mark of the communal – or social – trait is firmly imprinted on the human existence itself.

An Interpretation of Cooperation Requires an Understanding of Human Acting

The fact that man lives and exists together with others, as well as the effect this has on his acting, on the action, bring us closer to that reality which we usually designate as *society* or *community*. Nevertheless, our purpose here is not to consider the society; we do not even intend to introduce the assertion that human actions have a social significance, because this would lead our discussion into an entirely new field and away from the plane on which both our subject matter and our methods have been situated so far. On the contrary, our intention is to retain our initial approach and to continue to view the acting person as the major preoccupation and pivot of our investigations. In this chapter we wish only to bring into view that aspect in the dynamic correlation of the action with the person which comes as a consequence of the fact that man lives and acts together with other men; the fact could also be defined as cooperation, though between the two expressions there is a clear semantic difference: *to cooperate* is not the same thing as *to act together with others*. For the time being we may as well use the latter expression, which appears to be more amenable to further differentiations and any subsequent, more precise definitions that may prove to be necessary in this connection.

We know human actions may be performed in various interhuman relations and also in various social relations. When we say they are performed "together with others," we have all these different relations in mind without specifying the details of any particular one. They all form part of that aspect of the action and the dynamic correlation of the action with the person which we have not yet considered in our analyses. The omission was not due to any lack of appreciation but to the inner logic of the problem as a whole; it appears logical that only a thorough understanding of man's acting can lead to a correct interpretation of cooperation, and not the other way round. The dynamic correlation of the action with the person is in itself a fundamental reality and it will still be such a reality in any actions performed together with others. It is only on the basis of this fundamental relation that any fact of acting together with other people assumes its appropriate human significance. Such is the basic sequence, which cannot be reversed or neglected, and it is this sequence we have followed in our inquiries.

The Participatory Aspect in the Person's Acting "Together With Others"

It is only natural that the fact of acting together with other people and the many different relations and reference systems it involves will raise new problems in our discussion. We well know how extensive and how rich is the realm of, for instance, sociology, which by its investigations of societies and social life indirectly shows man as a member of various social groups or communities that in turn influence his acting. But let us stress once again that we are not interested at present in the problems of acting from the point of view of all its complex and extensive sociological implications; in particular we will not consider its specifically sociological significance. Since the acting person is the proper plane for this study we cannot now shift our argument to a totally new level. This approach is further justified by the fact that the dynamic correlation of the action with the person is also the basic and fundamental reality in all the multifarious actings that have a social, communal, or interhuman character. The actions which man performs in all his different social involvements and as a member of different social groups or communities are still the actions of the person. Their social or communal nature is rooted in the nature of the person and not vice versa. On the other hand, it appears that to explain the personal nature of human actions it is absolutely necessary to understand the consequences of the fact that they may be performed "together with others." How does this fact affect the dynamic correlation itself of the action with the person? An answer to this question seems all the more necessary inasmuch as acting "together with others" is frequent and usual, indeed, of universal occurrence.

The answer we are seeking will emerge gradually from the series of discussions in this chapter entitled "Intersubjectivity by Participation." The purpose of such a title is twofold; it is informative about the problems to be considered and it points out the direction in which their solution will be sought. Participation seems to be a trait well suited to the dynamic correlation of the action with the person whenever acting is performed "together with others." An explanation of this fact, however, must be reached step by step.

2. THE "PERSONALISTIC" VALUE OF THE ACTION

The Performance of the Action Is a Value

Before we continue our investigations we must look back upon the whole of the previous analyses in order to recognize the strictly personal content of the action. We notice that the performance itself of an action by the person is a fundamental value, which we may call the *personalistic* – or personal – value of the action. Such a value always differs from those moral values which belong to the performed action and which issue from their reference to a norm. The personalistic value, on the other hand, inheres in the performance itself of the action by the person, in the very fact that man acts in a manner appropriate to himself, that self-determination thus authentically inheres in the nature of his acting, the transcendence of the person being realized through his acting. This, as we know from the two preceding chapters, leads to integration in both the somatic and the psychical sphere of man. The personalistic value, which inheres essentially in the performance itself of the action by the person, comprises a number of values that belong to the profile either of transcendence or of integration, because they all, in their own way, determine the performance of the action and at the same time every one of them is in itself a value. Thus, for instance, every synthesis of action and motion introduces a specific value that differs from that constituted by the synthesis of action and emotion, though the one and the other inhere in the dynamic whole of the performance of the action. Each in its own way conditions and realizes self-determination.

The "personalistic" value of the human action – that is, the personal value – is a special and probably the most fundamental manifestation of the worth of the person himself. Since this study is primarily concerned with the ontology of the person, there is no place here for an examination of his axiology. Even this approach, however, may give some insight into the axiology of the person insofar as a definition both of the value of the person as such and of the different values within the person and the hierarchy of their mutual relations are concerned. Though being is prior to action, and thus the person and his value are prior to and more fundamental than the value of the action, it is in actions that the person manifests himself – a fact we have been stressing from the first. The "personalistic" value of an action, strictly related to the *performing* of the action by the person, is therefore a special source and the basis of the knowledge about the value of the person and also about the values inherent in the person according to their appropriate hierarchy. Essentially the correlation of the action with the person is valid also in the sphere of axiology, similarly as in the sphere of the ontology of the person; but a detailed study of this axiology is not among the aims of our investigations.

The "Personalistic" Value of the Action Conditions Its Ethical Value

The personalistic value of an action – that is, the value that according to the interpretation in Chapter 4 depends on the performance of the action – is essentially to be distinguished from the strictly moral values and those values of the performed action which spring from their reference to norms. The difference between them is clearly apparent; the "personalistic" value is prior to and conditions any ethical values. Obviously, any moral value good or bad, presupposes the performance of the action, indeed, of a full-fledged performance. If the action was not actually performed or if it showed any defects with respect to the authenticity of any of the different aspects of self-determination, then the moral value in it would lose its foundations or, at any rate, lose them partly if not completely. Hence any judgments about moral values, about any merits or demerits attributed to man, have to begin by determining efficacy, self-determination, and responsibility; in other words, we have first to establish whether this particular man-person did or did not perform the action. It is this precondition that all the discussions and differentiations concerning the will and its functions referred to in the traditional approach. We know that the insight reached in these discussions and differentiations is often penetrating and deep.

We do not consider the performance of the action by the person as having a purely ontological significance; on the contrary, we also attribute to it an axiological significance: the performance itself of the action by the person is a value. The value is "personalistic" because the person performing the action also fulfills himself in it. This we sought to explain in the analyses of the particular elements of such self-fulfillment; we also found that self-fulfillment in the action is strictly related to the ethical value, so much so that moral evil may be regarded as the opposite of fulfillment; indeed, it is a nonfulfillment of the self in acting. But we also noted in these analyses that the strict interrelation of ethical and personalistic values did not imply their sameness. The personalistic value consists in the fact that the person actualizes himself in the action, whereby his appropriate structure of self-governance and self-possession is manifested. It is in this actualization, which we have defined as the performance of the action, that ethical value is rooted; it develops on the substratum of the personalistic value, which it permeates but with which it is not to be identified.

The Relation of "Communal Action" to the Personalistic Value of Action

Throughout this study we have been moving in the direct proximity of ethical values, and from time to time we have even, though only indirectly, moved into their territory. Nevertheless, the proper terrain for our investigations is the personalistic value alone. It is this value that allows us to speak – with reference to human actions – of full-fledged performance or of various defects of performance; in this connection it is perhaps worth recalling the traditional teaching on human actions (*de actibus humanis*), which drew a distinction between the perfect and imperfect volitions, the term *volition* referring to the will as the power that actions depend upon. Here the action and performance is related to the person, not in an attempt to deny the traditional approach but in order to supplement it and in a way to rethink it to the end. For does not the will as a power inhere in the person, in that self-determination whereby the person manifests his appropriate structure? It is for this reason that the reduction of the content of volition to will as a power alone may to some extent impoverish the reality contained in the action.

Moreover, the disclosure of the dynamic correlation of the action with the person, coupled with an attempt at its interpretation, should provide us with the shortest and most direct road to the personalistic value of the action. An analysis of human acting at the level of the will as a power seems to reduce the significance of the action with regard to both its ontology and its axiology, and also with regard to "ethical axiology"; in this approach the action appears to have but an instrumental significance relatively to the whole ethical order. On the other hand, the personalistic notion of the action that we have been trying to outline here in its many different aspects supplies convincing evidence of the authenticity of the personalistic value. This value is not yet in itself ethical, but, springing from the dynamic depth of the person, it reveals and confirms ethical values and thus allows us to understand them better in their strict correspondence with the person and with the whole "world of persons."

All this has a fundamental significance in connection with the fact mentioned at the beginning of this chapter that man acts together with other men. We then asked, what were the consequences of this fact for the dynamic correlation itself of the action with the person? Now we have to ask another question that adds precision to the first; what is the relation of acting "together with others" to the personalistic value of the action?

3. A MORE DETAILED DEFINITION OF THE NOTION OF PARTICIPATION

The Person in the Philosophy of Man

The question we just asked leads to many others, whose significance is contained in the previous analyses. How does man, we ask, fulfill himself when acting together with others in the different interhuman or social relations? How does his action then retain that fundamental cohesion with the person which we have defined as the transcendence of the person in the action – which we also defined as the integration of the person in the action? In what way do man's actions preserve within the frame of the acting "together with others" the hierarchy of values that issues from both transcendence and integration?

Such questions as "how" and "in what way" seem to imply no doubt or uncertainty; they only draw attention to the problems that arise when the fact of acting "together with others" is considered. There is no need, however, to dissimulate any doubts, at any rate not when their source has a methodic character. Indeed, doubt permeates through and through the thinking and the mind of contemporary man. In anthropological philosophy this is probably connected with the transition to new positions with attention centered on the person. The traditional philosophy of man, on the other hand – even in its conceptions of the person – tended to underline the role of nature: the nature of man is rational and thus he is the person; but at the same time he has a "social" nature. In this respect the way of thinking about man has evolved, not toward the rejection of the principle itself but rather in search of a better understanding and more comprehensive interpretations. Nobody seems to doubt either that the nature of man is rational or that he also has a "social nature." We have to ask, however, what this means. Our questions here will accordingly refer to the meaning of these assertions from the point of view of acting, that is, of the dynamic correlation of the action with the person.

Our aim is to develop or explicate more fully the actual content of the assertion about the social nature of man in order to advance our knowledge of the human person. With this in mind we must return to the starting point. After all, at the origin of the assertion about the social nature of man there can be nothing but the experience that man exists, lives, and acts together with other men – an experience that we also have to account for in this study. The phrase *social nature* seems to signify primarily that reality of existing and acting "together with others" which is attributed to every human being in, as it were, a consequential way; obviously this attribute is the consequence of the reality itself and not vice versa.

Participation as a Trait of Acting "Together With Others"

In this approach the questions we are discussing are by no means secondary; on the contrary, they are of primary importance. Their aim, let us stress once again, is not to put in doubt the social character of human nature but to explain it at the level of the person and with regard to his whole dynamic portrait, which has emerged in the course of our previous analyses. We have now reached a point propitious for a more precise definition of *participation*, a notion we have introduced together with the problem of cooperation – of acting "together with others." The term is used in its current sense, the one best known and most widely applied, but it also has a distinct philosophical meaning. In current usage *participation* is more or less equivalent to having a share or a part in something. We may speak, for instance, of participating or taking part in a meeting; we then state the fact in the most general and, so to speak, static way without reaching to the essence of participation. On the other hand the philosophical sense of *participation* compels us to look for its inherent essence. In this latter sense the term has a long and eventful history insofar as its philosophical and theological applications are concerned. In our discussions, of course, we follow the philosophical meaning of both the term *participation* and the ideas it expresses; for we are here concerned not so much with a superficial assertion of the fact that a concrete man takes part together with other men in some kind of acting, but rather in reaching to the basis of his role and his share in this acting.

Our task is thus to reach to the foundations inherent in the person. (This will be perhaps the main difference between the notion of participation as conceived of here and the traditional philosophical meaning of the term, which seems to have been more connected with nature.) As conceived of here, participation corresponds to what the person's transcendence in the action consists of when the action is being performed "together with others," when it is performed in different social or interhuman relations. Naturally, once it corresponds to transcendence it also corresponds to the integration of the person in the action because, as we know, the latter is a complementary aspect relatively to the former. The trait of participation thus indicates that man, when he acts together with other men, retains in this acting the personalistic value of his own action and at the same time shares in the realization and the results of communal acting. Reversing this sequence we may say that owing to this share man, when he acts together with others, retains everything that results from the communal acting and simultaneously realizes – *in this very manner* – the personalistic value of his own action.

Participation as a Trait of the Person Acting "Together With Others"

In this last, more comprehensive assertion the stress laid on the words "in this very manner" is important because they show the real nature of the participation that we are considering. First, we see clearly that the idea of participation is used here in order to reach to the very foundation of acting together with other people, to those roots of such acting which inhere in and are appropriate to the person himself. Then, we observe that everything that constitutes the personalistic value of the action – namely, the performance itself of an action and the realization of the transcendence and the integration of the person contained in it – is not only maintained but indeed is realized because of acting together with others.

Participation thus represents a property of the person himself, that inner and homogeneous property which determines that the person existing and acting together with others still exists and acts as the person.* Insofar as acting itself is concerned, participation is responsible for the fact that the person acting together with others performs an action and fulfills himself in it. We see now that participation is the factor that determines the personalistic value of all cooperation. The sort of cooperation – or, more precisely, of acting together with others – in which the element of participation is missing, deprives the actions of the person of their personalistic value. On the other hand, we know from experience that in acting with other people situations may arise which in different ways limit self-determination and thus also the personal transcendence and the integration of acting. Indeed, the limitation of the personalistic value may sometimes go so far that we can hardly speak any more of "acting together with others" in the sense of the "authentic" actions of the person. Under certain conditions "acting" (as the synonym of "action") may change into something that only "happens" to a particular man under the influence of other men. An extreme example of this is so-called "mass psychology," when a large group of men may begin to act in an uncontrolled way and so affect the behavior of individuals.

---

* Cf. Note 77 in the definitive version of the text above.

Participation as the Ability to Make Multiform Interpersonal Relations

All this must be taken into consideration when defining the notion of "participation" in its proper sense. In the diverse relations of acting together with others, participation presents itself as an adaptation to these relations and hence as a multifarious reference of the person to other persons. In explaining, if only in outline, the form and the content of participation, we must examine communal acting in the objective and the subjective sense of the term. In addition, we must undertake some other analyses, although even then we shall not exhaust the essential meaning and the substance of "participation"; as conceived of here it not only applies to the different forms of the reference of the person to "others," of the individual to the society, but it also denotes that very foundation of these forms which inheres in and corresponds to the person.

Participation corresponds to the person's transcendence and integration in the action because it is that property which allows man, when he acts together with other men, to realize thereby, and at once, the authentically personalistic value – the performance of the action and the fulfillment of himself in the action. Acting "together with others" thus corresponds to the person's transcendence and integration in the action, when man chooses what is chosen by others or even *because* it is chosen by others – he then identifies the object of his choice with a value that he sees as in one way or another homogeneous and his own. This is connected with self-determination, for self-determination in the case of acting "together with others" contains and expresses participation.

When we say that "participation" is a property of the person we are not referring to the person in the abstract but to a concrete person in his dynamic correlation with the action. In this correlation "participation" signifies, on the one hand, that ability of acting "together with others" which allows the realization of all that results from communal acting and simultaneously enables the one who is acting to realize thereby the personalistic value of his action. On the other hand, this ability is followed by its actualization. Thus the notion of "participation" includes here both that ability and its realization.

4. INDIVIDUALISM AND ANTI-INDIVIDUALISM

The Theoretical and Normative Significance of Participation

The conception of "participation" that we are developing in this study
has a theoretical significance. As stated earlier, it is required in our
attempt to explain – on the ground of the dynamic correlation of the
action with the person – what is the reality of the social nature of
man. The conception is theoretical, but it is also empirical in the sense
that the theory of participation explains the fact of man's acting as
well as his existing together with other men. Moreover, it is apparent
that the theory has simultaneously an indirectly normative significance; it not only tells us how the person acting together with
others fulfills himself in his acting, that is, how he realizes the
personalistic value of his action, but it also points indirectly to certain
obligations that are the consequence of the principle of participation.
For if in acting "together with others" man can fulfill himself according to this principle, then, on the one hand, everyone ought to strive
for that kind of participation which would allow him in acting
together with others to realize the personalistic value of his own
action. On the other hand, any community of acting, or any human
cooperation, should be conducted so as to allow the person remaining
within its orbit to realize himself through participation.

Such is the normative content that has emerged so far from our
analyses. It is this content that seems to determine the normative –
and not only the theoretical – significance of participation. This
significance is instilled into the different systems of acting "together
with others" by means of the personalistic value, which it strictly
corresponds to and relies upon. Since the personalistic value of the
action is – as we know – the fundamental value conditioning both
ethical values and the ethical order, the norm of conduct that issues
from it directly must also have a fundamental significance. Such a norm
is not, in the strict sense of the term, ethical; it is not the norm of an
action performed because of action's objective content, but one that
belongs to the performance itself of the action, to its personal
subjectiveness – an "inner" norm concerned with safeguarding the
self-determination of the person and so also his efficacy as well as his
transcendence and integration in the action. We earlier discussed these
matters in some detail, so that the boundary between the strictly ethical

APPENDIX 329

and the personalistic order should now be considered sufficiently defined and distinct.

Individualism and Totalism as the Two Limitations of Participation

At the same time, however, the personalistic value so conditions the whole ethical order in acting and cooperation that the order is also determined by it. The action must be performed not because only then can it have an ethical value – and can that value be assigned to it – but also because the person has the basic and "natural" (i.e., issuing from the fact that he is a person) right to perform actions and to be fulfilled in them. This right of the person attains its full sense and import as a right on the basis of the acting "together with others." It is then that the normative significance of participation is confirmed. For it is in acting together with others that the performance of actions in the sense previously defined – the performance that is simultaneously the fulfillment of the person in the action, and the performance and fulfillment in which the personalistic value of the action consists – can be limited or definitely thwarted. This may happen in two ways: first, there may be a lack of participation caused by the person as the subject-agent of acting; second, participation may become impossible for reasons external to the person and resulting from defects in the system according to which the community of acting operates.

At this point in our analysis we encounter two systems, the implications of which must be considered, if only in part. One of these systems is called "individualism"; the other has received different names, more recently "objective totalism," though it could just as well be called "anti-individualism." Since a full-scale discussion of the two systems would lead us away from the chief objectives of this study we will consider only some of their implications. It is necessary to note, however, that they both have an axiological, and indirectly an ethical, significance. Individualism sees in the individual the supreme and fundamental good, to which all interests of the community or the society have to be subordinated, while objective totalism relies on the opposite principle and unconditionally subordinates the individual to the community or the society.

Clearly, each of these systems has entirely different visions of the ultimate good and the foundation of norms. Furthermore, each system occurs in a wide range of variations and shades, so much so that their analysis would require comprehensive sociological and historical studies. For these reasons we must put aside the exploration of these momentous problems and even simplify them somewhat; we will restrict our considerations only to those essential trends which according to the definitions just introduced characterize the two systems. We shall concentrate our attention on the implications they may have for the main theme of our present discussion, which is the acting person in all the different situations that may arise in his acting "together with others."

Inherent in acting "together with others" is the principle of participation, which is the essential trait of such acting and a special source of the rights and obligations of the person. The person has as his special attribute the right to perform actions and the obligation to fulfill himself in the action, an obligation that results from the personalistic value inherent in fulfillment. Each of the two systems or trends – whether it be individualism or objective totalism – tends in different ways to limit participation either directly, as a possibility or an ability to be actualized in acting "together with others," or indirectly, as that property of the person which corresponds to his existing "together with others," his living in a community.

Individualism Implies a Denial of Participation

Individualism limits participation, since it isolates the person who is then conceived of solely as an individual concentrated on himself and on his own good, which is also regarded in isolation from the good of others and of the community. The good of the individual is then treated as if it were opposed or in contradiction to other individuals and their good; at best, this good, in essence, may be considered as involving self-preservation and self-defense. From the point of view of individualism, to act "together with others," just as to exist "together with others," is a necessity that the individual has to submit to, a necessity that corresponds to none of his positive properties; neither does the acting and existing together with others serve or develop any of the individual's positive properties. For the individual, the "others" are a source of limitation: they may even appear to represent the opposite pole in a variety of conflicting interests. If a community is formed, its purpose is to protect the good of the individual from the "others." This in broad outline is the essence of individualism, the variations and different shades of which we shall not consider here. We should notice, however, that individualism carries with it an implied denial and rejection of participation in the sense we have given it before; from the individualistic point of view a property that allows the person to fulfill himself in acting "together with others" simply does not exist.

Totalism as Reversed Individualism

The denial of participation is also implied in totalism or anti-individualism, which may be looked upon as "reversed individualism." The dominant trait of totalism may be characterized as the need to find protection *from* the individual, who is seen as the chief enemy of society and of the common good. Since totalism assumes that inherent in the individual there is only the striving for individual good, that any tendency toward participation or fulfillment in acting and living together with others is totally alien to him, it follows that the "common good" can be attained only by limiting the individual. Totalism presupposes only this significance, this form of the common good. The good thus advocated by totalism can never correspond to the wishes of the individual, to the good he is capable of choosing independently and freely according to the principles of participation; it is always a good that is incompatible with and a limitation upon the individual. Consequently, the realization of the common good frequently presupposes the use of coercion.

Again, we have presented but a summary outline of the thinking and proceedings characteristic of the system of anti-individualism, in which the principles of individualism are clearly apparent but viewed in reverse and applied to contrary ends. Individualism is concerned with protecting the good of the individual from the community; the objective of totalism, in contrast – and this is confirmed by numerous historical examples – is to protect a specific common good from the individual. Nevertheless, both tendencies, both systems of thinking and proceeding have at their origin the same intellectual conception of man.

The Intellectual Conception of Man Underlying Both Systems

The way of thinking about man underlying both systems may be defined as "impersonalistic" or "antipersonalistic," inasmuch as the distinctive trait of the personalistic approach is the conviction that the ability of participation is appropriate to the person. Obviously, if this conviction is to mature it has to be actualized: it has to be cultivated and developed. It is not only man's nature that forces him to exist and to act together with others, but his existing and acting together with other men enables him to achieve his own development, that is, the intrinsic development of the person. This is why every human being must have the right to act, which means "freedom in the action," so that the person can fulfill himself in performing the action.

The significance of this right and this freedom is inherent in the belief in the personalistic value of human action. On the basis of this value, and because of it, man has the right to the total freedom of acting. This leads to the rejection of both individualism and anti-individualism together with all their erroneous implications. The total freedom of action, which results from its personalistic value, conditions the ethical order and simultaneously determines it. On the other hand, the moral order instills into human actions – in particular, those within the orbit of acting "together with others" – those determinants, and thus also limitations, which are the consequence of purely ethical values and norms. The determinants and the limitations so introduced are not, however, opposed to the personalistic value; for it is only in the "moral good" that the person can fulfill himself, inasmuch as "evil" is always a "nonfulfillment." There can be no doubt that man has the freedom of acting; he has the right of action, but he has not the right to do wrong. Such is the general trend of the determinant, which while issuing from the rights of man corresponds nevertheless to the personalistic order.

5. PARTICIPATION AND MEMBERSHIP IN THE COMMUNITY

Participation as a Constitutive Factor of the Community

We know that individualism and totalism (anti-individualism) grow out of the same soil. Their common root is the conception of man as an individual, according to which he is more or less deprived of the property of participation. This way of thinking is also reflected in the conceptions of social life, in the axiology of the society and in ethics, or, more precisely, in those different axiologies of the society and different social ethics which grow out of this same soil. It is not our intention to examine the details of the many varieties of individualism and anti-individualism, which have been widely studied. We should note, however, that in the thinking about man characteristic of these two tendencies there seems to be no sufficient ground for any authentic human community.

The notion of "community" expresses the reality that we have been focusing upon in the present chapter, in which "acting and existing together with others" has been repeatedly mentioned. The human community is strictly related to the experience of the person, which we have been tracing from the first but especially at this stage of our discussions. We find in it the reality of participation as that property of the person which enables him to exist and act "together with others" and thus to reach his own fulfillment. Simultaneously, participation as a property of the person is a constitutive factor of any human community. Because of this property the person and the community may be said to coalesce together; contrary to the implications manifest in the individualistic and anti-individualistic thinking about man, they are neither alien nor mutually opposed to each other.

The Community Is Not the Substantial Subject in Acting

In order to define still more precisely the meaning of "participation" – and this is now our chief aim – we have to look at it from the point of view of the community. Actually, such has been our standpoint from the first, and it is the reason why we have so often used the phrase "together with others" in our analyses of the action and the being of the person. The notion of "community" corresponds to this phrase while simultaneously it introduces a new plane or a new "subjectiveness." This is so because as long as we are speaking of acting or being "together with others" the man-person remains the manifest subject of the acting and being, but once we begin to speak of the *community*, then what so far has been contained in an adverbial phrase, can now be expressed in substantival and abstract terms.

We can, however, now speak of a "quasi-subjectiveness," which is constituted by all the people existing and acting together. The new subjectiveness is the share of a community, or, in a broader sense, of a social group. In fact, it is but a quasi-subjectiveness, because even when the being and acting is realized together with others it is the *man-person who is always its proper substantial subject.* The terms "community," like "society" or "social group," are indicative of the accidental order. Being and acting "together with others" does not constitute a new subject of acting but only introduces new relations among the persons who are the real and actual subjects of acting. In all discussions about the community this comment is necessary to avoid misunderstanding. The concept "community," also in its substantival and abstract sense, seems to come very near to the dynamic reality of the person and participation, perhaps even nearer than such notions as "society" or "social group."

Associational Relationship and Community Membership

To analyze the notion of "community" we may and must consider as many – almost indefinitely numerous – facts as in the analysis of the acting person, a point already stressed in the introductory chapter of this study. Moreover, in either case it is necessary to apply methodologically analogical procedures. These remarks confirm once again the need to adhere to the same reasoning that we adopted at the start of these investigations. It is on this plane that we shall have to analyze the relation existing between participation and community membership.

Within the framework of a community we see man, with all his appropriate dynamism, as one of its members. There are different terms and expressions to denote this membership, which are suited to the different kinds of relationships within the community or group. Thus "kinship" tells us of membership in a family group, a "compatriot" is one who belongs to a national group, and a "citizen" is a member of a still broader society represented by the state. These are only examples, for innumerable other social groups or communities have associated according to different principles, such as religious and other affiliations. In each of these examples man's associational relationship is differently defined.

Sociologists quite rightly point to the semantic difference between the terms "society" and "community"; "society" objectivizes the community or a number of mutually complementary communities. Since in this study our objective is to *disclose the bases or foundations of things*, we are primarily concerned with community membership rather than with associational relationship of the society. The examples noted above tell of membership in different kinds of communities; they not only define the principle of membership in a community but also the different bonds and relations that exist between men belonging to these communities. For instance, words such as "brother" and "sister" stress the family bonds rather than that membership in a family group denoted by the term "kinship."

In the rich resources of language there are countless words that stress – like all the terms in the previous examples – the fact of the community itself, the communal existence of men and the bonds that are formed among them because of their communal existence. There are, however, other words that denote first of all the community of acting rather than the communal existence, the community of being. For instance, when speaking of an apprentice, an assistant, or a foreman we imply that there is a team or group working together; the stress is then on the community of acting and the bonds thus formed, while communal existence, the community of being, is implied only indirectly.

Associational Relationship Differs from Participation

In the preceding section we saw that man can be a member of different communities, all of which are the product of man existing or acting together with other men. At present we are mainly interested in the "community of acting" because of its closer relation to the dynamic action-person correlation as a basis and a source of cognition. Nevertheless, the "community of being" always conditions the "community of acting," and so the latter cannot be considered apart from the former. The crux of the problem lies, however, in that membership in any of these communities is not to be identified with participation. This is perhaps best illustrated by the following example. A team of laborers digging a trench or a group of students attending a lecture are communities of acting; each laborer or student is a member of a definite community of acting. These communities may also be considered from the point of view of the aim that its members are collectively striving for. In the first case, the aim is the trench, which in turn may serve other aims, such as laying foundations for a construction. In the other, it is to learn about the problems that are the theme of the lecture, which in turn forms part of a course and thus of the students' curriculum. We also see that all the diggers and all the students have in each case a common goal. This objective unity of goals helps to objectivize the community of acting itself. Hence, in the objective sense, a "community of acting" may be defined according to the aim that brings men to act together; each of them is then a member of an objective community.

From the point of view of the person and the action, however, it is not only the objective community of acting but also its subjective moment, which we have here called "participation," that is important. The question is whether a man belonging to a community of acting, like those mentioned in our examples, can in his communal acting perform real actions and fulfill himself in them; this performance and the fulfillment it brings are determined by participation. Nevertheless, even when acting "together with others" man can remain outside the community that is constituted by participation.

At this point we are faced with a problem that can never be resolved without at least a cursory look at the question of the so-called "common good." We already know that the moment of participation inheres among others in choice; man chooses what others choose and indeed often because others choose it, but even then he chooses it as his own good and as the end of his own striving. What he thus chooses is his own good in the sense that he as the person can fulfill himself in it. It is participation that enables him to make these choices and to undertake this way of acting "together with others." Perhaps it is only then that such acting deserves to be called "cooperation," inasmuch as acting "together with others" does not by itself necessarily result in cooperation (just as it does not necessarily initiate the moment of participation). Within the sphere of acting, just as within the sphere of existing, a community may remain at the objective level and never pass to the subjective level.

6. PARTICIPATION AND THE COMMON GOOD

The Common Good and the Problem of Community and Participation

We now see that the solution to the problem of the community and participation lies not in the reality itself of acting and existing "together with others," but is to be looked for in the common good, or, more precisely, in the meaning we give to the notion of the "common good." If the meaning of "common good" is for us the same as that of the "good of the community," then we understand it correctly though we run a serious risk of one-sidedness. This one-sidedness threatens in the domain of axiology and is similar to that suggested in anthropology by the conceptions of individualism and anti-individualism. The common good is obviously the good of the community – or, to go even further in the direction of objectivation, the good of the society – but it still has to be clearly defined in the light of the foregoing considerations.*

Evidently, the very fact that people act together is sufficient to ascertain the existence of an objective community of acting, as for instance in the cases of the team of laborers digging a trench or of the group of students attending a lecture. In this context the common good as the good of a definite community of acting – and this is always connected with a community of being – may be easily identified with the goal of the community. Thus for the laborers the common good may appear to be solely the completion of the excavation, and for the students the commitment to memory of the information contained in the lecture.

These common goods, however, may also be considered as links in a teleological chain, in which case every one of them is seen as a means to attain another goal that now presents itself as the common good; thus the excavation dug out by the laborers will serve to lay the foundations for a future construction, and the attended lecture is but a link in a long and complex process of learning, with examinations as a formal test of the knowledge acquired in that particular field.

---

* Cf. Note 78 in the definitive version of the text above.

Teleological and Personalistic Conceptions of the Common Good

To identify the common good, however, with the goal of common acting by a group of people is manifestly a cursory and superficial simplification. The preceding examples lead to the conclusion that the *goal* of common acting, when understood in a purely objective and "material" way, though it includes some elements of the common good and has reference to it, can never fully and completely constitute it.

This assertion becomes obvious in the light of our previous analyses. It is impossible to define the common good without simultaneously taking into account the subjective moment, that is, the moment of acting in relation to the acting persons. When we consider this moment we see that the common good does not consist solely in the goal of the common acting performed by a community or group; indeed, it also, or even primarily, consists in that which conditions and somehow initiates in the persons acting together their participation, and thereby develops and shapes in them a subjective community of acting. We can conceive of the common good as being the goal of acting only in that double – subjective *and* objective – sense. Its subjective sense is strictly related to participation as a property of the acting person; it is in this sense that it is possible to say that the common good corresponds to the social nature of man.

In our investigations we have tended to avoid going into the details of that extensive and momentous domain of axiology and ethics which is associated with the notion of the "common good" and determines its full significance. We have concentrated on the common good primarily as the principle of correct participation, which allows the person acting together with other persons to perform authentic actions and to fulfill himself through these actions. Our concern is therefore with the genuinely personalistic structure of human existence in a community, that is, in every community that man belongs to.

The common good becomes the good of the community inasmuch as it creates in the axiological sense the conditions for common existence, which is then followed by acting. If we can say that in the axiological order the community, the social group, or the society are established by the common good, then we can define each of them according to its appropriate common good. Acting is then considered jointly with being, with existing.

The common good, however, belongs primarily to the sphere of being "together with others," while the acting together with others is insufficient to disclose the whole reality of the common good, though it also plays its role in this respect. Even groups that are brought together mainly by their common acting rather than by any social bonds – for instance, a group of laborers excavating a trench or of students together attending a lecture – not only strive through their acting together to attain their goal but they also manifest in different ways the participation appropriate to the individual members of a community of acting.

The Common Good as the Foundation of Authentic Human Communities

In groups established on the principle of a temporary community of acting, participation is neither manifested as clearly, nor realized to the same extent, as in communities where their stability is the fact of being together – for instance, a family, a national group, a religious community, or the citizens of a state. The axiology of these communities, which is expressed in the common good, is much deeper. Consequently the foundations of participation are much stronger, while the need of participation is much more acute. Everybody expects that such communities of being – they have earned the name of natural societies because they inherently correspond to the social nature of man – will allow one to choose what others choose and because they choose it, and that his choice will be *his own good* that serves the fulfillment of *his own* person. At the same time, owing to the same ability of participation, man expects that in communities founded on the common good his own actions will serve the community and help to maintain and enrich it. Under conditions established according to this axiological pattern he will readily relinquish his individual good and sacrifice it to the welfare of the community. Since such a sacrifice corresponds to the ability of participation inherent in man, and because this ability allows him to fulfill himself, it is not "contrary to nature."

Thus the priority of the common good, its superiority over the partial or individual goods, does not result solely from the quantitative aspect of the society; it does not follow from the fact that the common good concerns a great number or the majority while the individual good concerns only individuals or a minority. It is not the numbers or even the generality in the quantitative sense but the intrinsicalness that determines the proper nature of the common good. This treatment of the problem is a continuation of our criticism of individualism and anti-individualism; it follows from our earlier discussion of participation and serves as a further confirmation of the conclusions then reached. We can see how from the reality constituted by "common acting" and "common being," participation emerges as a property of the person and the action and also as the basis of every authentic human community.

7. AN ANALYSIS OF ATTITUDES: AUTHENTIC ATTITUDES

The Pre-ethical Significance of this Analysis

The discussion of the proper significance of the common good, that is, of the relation that ought to exist between participation as a property of the person and the common good, makes necessary an analysis of some attitudes that distinguish the acting and being "together with others." First, there are the attitudes of solidarity and of opposition. The proper meaning of both *solidarity* and *opposition* is established in connection with a community of acting or being, and by virtue of this community with the common good. This we shall now try to explain. The meaning of the term is associated with a certain qualification that ultimately becomes an ethical qualification. In the present analysis we will, however, concentrate on the personalistic significance of each of these attitudes, and consequently the qualification itself will have a pre-ethical rather than an ethical significance. The reason is that our aim continues to be an outline of the structures of human acting and in this connection to underline the value of the fulfillment itself of an action rather than that value of a performed action which issues from its relation to ethical norms. Of course the whole reasoning can be very easily converted to an ethical analysis, once we assume that the very performance of an action constitutes a good, which by its immanent value becomes an obligation. Indeed, this is beyond question; the performance itself of the action is a good of the kind that imposes an obligation on the one who performs it as well as on others. The latter obligation is an essential element of social ethics.

If we were to pass to the domain of ethics, we would have to treat the value of the performance of an action as an object of the performed actions and also as their normative basis. This, however, is not the approach that we have adopted here; we intend to continue our interest in the subjective performance of actions and in its immanent value so far as this value is personalistic. It is in these relations that we can find the key to the interpretation of the person's appropriate dynamism within the framework of different communities of acting and being. Thus the qualification of the attitudes, which we will analyze, is primarily personalistic and in this sense in a way pre-ethical. At the same time, however, we must remember that here, even more than throughout this study, we are moving on the terrain of ontology and ethics, to which we are confined by the axiological aspect – by the wealth of values inextricably involved in the ontology of the person and the action.

The Attitude of Solidarity

Our analysis deals with the attitude of solidarity together with that of opposition, for each is necessary to the understanding of the other. The attitude of solidarity is, so to speak, the natural consequence of the fact that human beings live and act together; it is the attitude of a community, in which the common good properly conditions and initiates participation and participation in turn properly serves the common good, fosters it, and furthers its realization. Solidarity signifies a constant readiness to accept and to realize one's share in the community – what is one's share because of one's membership in a particular community. In accepting the attitude of solidarity man does what he is supposed to do not only because of his membership in the group, but because he has the "benefit of the whole" in view: he does it for the common good. The awareness of the common good leads him to look beyond his particular share in the community, though this intentional reference allows him to realize essentially his own share. Indeed, solidarity is to some extent a restraint from trespassing upon other people's obligations and duties or from taking over as one's own the part that belongs to others. So conceived, solidarity is in harmony with the principle of participation, which from the objective and "material" point of view indicates the presence of parts in the communal structure of human acting and being. The attitude of solidarity pays due regard to the parts that are the share of every member of the community. To take over a part of the duties and obligations that are not mine is intrinsically contrary to participation and to the essence of the community.

Nevertheless, there are situations that make even this necessary. In such situations to keep strictly to one's own share would signify and confirm a lack of solidarity. This proves indirectly that in the attitude of solidarity the reference to the common good must always remain alive, that it must dominate to the extent which allows one to know when it is necessary to take over more than one's usual share in acting and responsibility. That acute sense of the needs of the community which distinguishes the attitude of solidarity brings out over and above any particularism or divisions its trait of complementarity; this consists in the readiness of every member of a community to "complement" by his action what is done by other members of the community. The trait of complementarity is in a way an intrinsic element in the very nature of participation, which we are now interpreting subjectively, that is, as the property of the person, and not just objectively as the parts that are the share of every participant in the communal structure of acting and being. Complementarity helps explain why we see in the attitude of solidarity an intrinsic manifestation of participation as a property of the person. It is this attitude that allows man to find the fulfillment of himself in complementing others.

The Attitude of Opposition

It is important to note, however, that the attitude of solidarity is not contradictory to the attitude of opposition; opposition is not intrinsically inconsistent with solidarity. The one who voices his opposition does not thereby reject his membership in the community; he does not withdraw his readiness to act and to work for the common good. Of course, different interpretations of opposition are possible, but we have here adopted the one that sees it as essentially an attitude of solidarity; it then consists not in rejecting the common good or the need of participation, but on the contrary in their confirmation. The matters to which this kind of opposition refers are solely the way of understanding and, to an even greater degree, the means employed to achieve the common good, especially from the point of view of the possibility of participation. The experience of innumerably different oppositions that have been continually express-ed in the course of human existing and acting "together with others" shows that those who stand up in opposition do not intend thereby to cut themselves off from their community. On the contrary, they seek their own place within the community, they seek for that participation and that attitude to the common good which would allow them a better, a fuller, and a more effective share in the community. It would be easy to quote endless examples of people who contest – and thus adopt the attitude of opposition – because of their deep concern for the common good; for instance, parents may disagree because they have at heart the education of their children, and rival politicians contend because of different opinions concerning the welfare of the nation and the state.

These examples are perhaps insufficient to show the essence of opposition in all its aspects but at any rate they lead us up to it. The attitude of opposition is a function, on the one hand, of that particular view one takes of the community and of what is good for it, and on the other, of the strong need to participate in the common existing and even more so in the common acting. There can be no doubt that this kind of opposition is essentially constructive; it is a condition of the correct structure of communities and of the correct functioning of their inner system. This condition, however, must be defined more precisely: the structure, the system of communities, must be such as to allow the opposition that grows out of the soil of solidarity not only to express itself within the framework of the community but also to operate for the benefit of the community – to be constructive. The structure of a human community is correct only if it admits not just the presence of a justified opposition but also that effectiveness of opposition which is required by the common good and the right of participation.

The Sense of Dialogue

We thus see that the common good has to be conceived of dynamic-ally and not statically – a fact that has been briefly noted earlier.

Essentially it must liberate and support the attitude of solidarity but never so as to stifle and shut itself off from opposition. It seems that the principle of dialogue is very aptly suited to that structure of human communities and participation which satisfies these needs. The notion of *dialogue* has different meanings; here we are primarily concerned with one, namely, the one that may be applied to the formation and the strengthening of interhuman solidarity through the attitude of opposition. Admittedly opposition may make the coexistence and cooperation of men more difficult, but it should never damage or prevent them. The principle of dialogue seems to be best suited to select and bring out what in controversial situations is right and true, and to eliminate any partial, preconceived, or subjective views and attitudes. Such views and attitudes may become the seed of strife and conflict between men while what is right and true always favors the development of the person and enriches the community. All this confirms the value of the principle of dialogue, which without evading the strains, the conflicts, or the strife manifest in the life of various human communities takes up what is right and true in these differences, what may become a source of a good for men. The principle of dialogue has to be adopted regardless of the obstacles and difficulties that may appear on the road to its realization.

8. AN ANALYSIS OF ATTITUDES: NONAUTHENTIC ATTITUDES

Authentic and Nonauthentic Attitudes

What we have stated previously concerning solidarity and opposition, as well as our general approval of the principle of dialogue (a more detailed justification of this approval would require a separate study), must be constantly verified in juxtaposition with that truth about the action and the person which we have been laboriously striving for throughout this book. Both the attitude of solidarity and that of opposition appear to be intrinsically authentic. At any rate each allows the realization not only of participation but also of the transcendence of the person in the action. We have submitted to comprehensive analyses this transcendence – the self-determination and the fulfillment of the person; now it appears that in either of those attitudes the functions of transcendence may play their role. Thus in this sense both attitudes are authentic inasmuch as each respects the personalistic value of the action.

Evidently, in spite of the general and essential approval for both attitudes, they have to be constantly tested with regard to their particular elements and actual manifestations. Indeed, it is very easy to distort the attitude of solidarity as well as that of opposition by changing either of them in concrete situations into nonauthentic attitudes deprived of their true personalistic value. The touchstone in this case is the dynamic subordination to truth that is so essential to the person's transcendence in the action. This subordination is reflected in the righteous conscience, which is the ultimate judge of the authenticity of human attitudes in what concerns the being and acting "together with others." In addition, the common good has to find its manifestation in the righteous conscience, which safeguards the dynamism of the common good and the viability of participation.

Speaking of the possible loss of authenticity, which threatens the attitudes of solidarity and opposition, each in a different way and for different reasons, we must make note of some nonauthentic attitudes, which we shall define here by popular rather than by scientific terms. These attitudes are on the one hand a servile *conformism* and on the other avoidance; either may be reached by deviating from the authentic attitudes of solidarity and opposition when they are deprived of those inherent elements which are the condition of participation and the personalistic value. The rejection of these elements may gradually change solidarity into conformism and the attitude of opposition into that of avoidance. These distortions, however, would then be but accidental. Actually, the cause of the lack of authenticity in either of these distorted attitudes seems to be fundamental and not merely a deformation of solidarity and opposition. It is on this assumption that we will now proceed with our discussion.

Conformism as a Nonauthentic Attitude

The term *conformism* derives from *to conform* and denotes a tendency to comply with the accepted custom and to resemble others, a tendency that is in itself natural, in many respects positive and constructive or even creative. This contructive and creative assimilation in the community is a confirmation and also a manifestation of human solidarity. But when it begins to sway toward servility, it becomes a highly negative tendency. It is this negative tendency that we call *conformism*, which evidences an inherent lack of solidarity and simultaneously an attitude of evading opposition; if it still denotes man's assimilation with the other members of a community, it does so only in an external and superficial sense, in a sense devoid of personal grounds of conviction and choice. Thus conformism consists primarily in an attitude of compliance or resignation, in a specific form of passiveness that makes the man-person to be but the subject of *what happens* instead of being the actor or agent responsible for building his own attitudes and his own commitment in the community. He then fails to accept his share in constructing the community and allows himself to be carried with and by the multitude. Even when the servile attitude of conformism does not become an outright denial or limitation, it always indicates a weakness of personal transcendence, of self-determination and choice. It is this weakness that clearly shows the personalistically negative significance of the attitude of conformism. The problem obviously does not consist solely in the submission to the other members of the community, all the more so as such a submission may very often be a positive symptom. It lies much deeper and consists in a definite resignation from seeking the fulfillment of oneself in and through acting "together with others." We may say that the man-person complies with his own self being annexed by the community.

At the same time, however, he himself withdraws from the community. Conformism in its servile form then becomes a denial of participation in the proper sense of the term. A mere semblance of participation, a superficial compliance with others, which lacks conviction and authentic engagement, is substituted for real participation. Thus the ability appropriate to man of creatively shaping the community is arrested or indeed falsified. This state of things cannot but have a negative effect on the common good whose dynamism springs from true participation. Simultaneously, conformism has the opposite effect inasmuch as it favors situations marked by indifference toward the common good. We may also look at it as a specific form of individualism; it then becomes an evasion from the community, which is seen as a threat to the good of the individual, accompanied by a need to dissimulate oneself from the community behind a mask of external appearances. Hence conformism brings uniformity rather than unity. Beneath the uniform surface, however, there is a latent differentiation that it is the task of the community to provide with the necessary conditions of participation. Situations of prevailing conformism must never be accepted as satisfactory; for when people adapt themselves to the demands of the community only superficially and when they do so only to gain some immediate advantages or to avoid trouble, the person as well as the community incur irremediable losses.

Avoidance as a Nonauthentic Attitude

The attitude, which we have called avoidance, seems to be characterized by a disregard for those appearances of concern for the common good which are the distinguishing trait of conformism. In a sense it is perhaps more authentic, but in fact it also suffers from defective authenticity. The attitude of conformism evades opposition while that of avoidance evades conformism, though it does not thereby change into an authentic attitude of opposition, which would consist in both an active concern for the common good and participation. Avoidance is nothing but a withdrawal, sometimes to manifest a protest, but even then it still lacks the active concern of participation; it consists in a lack of participation and in being absent from the community. The absent, as the saying goes, are always in the wrong. This is very often found to be true in the case of avoidance, though sometimes the attitude is adopted in the hope that even absence can be telling, that it may in certain situations become an argument; avoidance then becomes a kind of substitute or compensatory attitude for those who find solidarity too difficult and who do not believe in the sense of opposition. Indeed, it would be impossible to deny that this attitude may result from conscious choice and then its essentially personalistic value has to be acknowledged. But even if there are valid reasons to justify it, these same reasons become an accusation of the community. After all, we know participation to be a fundamental good of a community, so when participation becomes impossible – as evidenced by the attitude of avoidance when justified by the existing conditions – the functioning and the life of the community must somehow be defective. If the members of a community see the only solution to their problems in withdrawal, then this is a sure sign that the common good in this community is erroneously conceived.

Nevertheless, for all that may in a way justify avoidance as a kind of compensatory attitude, it is impossible to ascribe to it the traits of authenticity within the frame of being and acting "together with others." At many points it borders on conformism, not to mention the instances when both attitudes merge into something that might perhaps be defined as a "conformist avoidance." The most important, however, is the fact that either attitude causes man to abandon this striving for fulfillment in acting "together with others"; he is convinced of being deprived of himself by the community and thus tries to withdraw from it. In the case of conformism he tries to keep up appearances but in that of avoidance he no longer seems to care about them. In either case he has been forcibly deprived of something very important. He is deprived of that dynamic trait of participation appropriate to the person which allows him to perform actions and thereby to fulfill himself authentically in the community of being and acting together with others.

9. FELLOW MEMBER AND NEIGHBOR

Two Interrelated Systems of Reference

The analysis of participation conducted here leads us to what is an even deeper layer of the reality that is constituted by the person when his existing and acting is viewed from the standpoint of his membership in a community "together with others." The problem of participation appears to have been discussed sufficiently in connection with the fact that man belongs to different communities. His membership in any one of them is like a specific reference system, which the possibility of participation by every person belonging to the community makes very complex and rich. This reference system is closely related to another one that also plays a very important role in participation and is best designated by the word *neighbor*. In spite of the nearness and even some mutual overlapping of these systems, they are not identical. The content of the notion of *neighbor* differs essentially from what is contained in the notion *member of a community*. Each points toward different possibilities and different tendencies within personal participation. Each expresses differently the personal and the social nature of man.

Neighbor and *member of a community* are two different notions each representing different forms or even different reference systems, because to be and to act "together with others" places man within the range of diverse relations. The terms *neighbor* and *member of a community* (the society) may help to bring order into these relations or reference systems and thereby to understand better and more precisely the idea of participation. Indeed, participation itself means something else when it refers to a member of a community than when it refers to a neighbor.

To some extent, however, the two notions concur. As a member of a community a man has other men for neighbors; this brings them closer together and makes them, so to speak, "nearer" neighbors. Hence with respect to the membership of the same community the circle of every man's neighbors is either nearer or more distant to him. It is natural for us to be closer with our family or our compatriots than with the members of other families or other nations. In this system of reference closer relationships always tend to displace the more distant ones, but of course in interhuman relations there is also alienation or strangeness. The notion of neighbor has, however, a deeper application than closeness or alienation in interhuman relations and it is thus more fundamental than the notion of membership in a community. Membership of any community presupposes the fact that men are neighbors, but it neither constitutes nor abolishes this fact. People are, or become, members of different communities; and in these communities they either establish close and even friendly relations or they remain strangers – the latter reflects a lack of the communal spirit – but they are all neighbors and never cease to be neighbors.

The Interrelation of All Men in Humanness

This brings us to the axiological moment of great significance at this stage of our discussion, when we are concentrating on the personalistic value in the community of being and acting. The notion of *neighbor* forces us not only to recognize but also to appreciate what in man is independent of his membership in any community whatever; it forces us to observe and appreciate in him something that is far more absolute. The notion of neighbor is strictly related to man as such and to the value itself of the person regardless of any of his relations to one or another community or to the society. The notion takes into account man's humanness alone – that humanness which is the possession of every man just as much as it is my own. It thus provides the broadest basis for the community, a basis that extends beyond any strangeness or foreignness, as well as beyond the strangeness that results from membership in different human communities. Membership in a community or society in a way presupposes the reality that is referred to in the notion of neighbor, but it also limits and in some respects removes to a more distant plane or even overshadows the broader concept of neighbor. In the forefront we then have man's relation and subordination to a given community, while when speaking of neighbors we stress only the most fundamental interrelations and the intersubordination of all men in their humanness. Thus the notion of neighbor refers to the broadest, the most common reality, and also to the broadest foundations of inter-human community. Indeed, it is the community of men, of all men, the community formed by their very humanness that is the basis of all other communities. Any community becoming detached from this fundamental community must unavoidably lose its human character.

From this point of view we have to look again at the problem of participation and try to reach to its ultimate consequences. We have already investigated the significance of participation with respect to the membership of the man-person in different communities, the membership which reveals and confirms his social nature. We now see, however, that the ability of participation has a wider scope and extends over the whole range of the notion of neighbor. The man-person is capable not only of partaking in the life of a community, of being and acting together with others, but he is also capable of participating in the humanness of others. It is on this ability to participate in the humanness of every human being that all participation in a community is based and it is there that it receives its personal sense. This is what is ultimately contained in the notion of neighbor.

Participation Consists in Sharing in the Humanness of Every Man

The analysis of the notion of neighbor brings out the full significance of that specific reality which from the beginning of this chapter we have been referring to as participation. At this point it is important to note that any suggestions tending to mutually oppose the notions of *neighbor* and *member of a community* or even to separate them from each other are wholly unwarranted. We mentioned earlier their partial concurrence and now we intend to examine it closer. The basic concurrence of these notions is evidenced by the societal nature of man, even though it is in the relation to this nature that the difference between a neighbor and a member of a community becomes clearly apparent. We are not to assume, moreover, that the system of reference denoted by the term *neighbor* is the basis of all interhuman relations or that *member of a community* refers to the basis of social relations. Such an interpretation would be superficial and insufficient. The two systems of reference do not overlap and interpenetrate only in the objective order, which shows every neighbor as belonging to a community and every member of a community as a neighbor.

More important than the objective order is, however, the interpenetration in the subjective order of participation. We have here presented participation as a dynamic property of the person. This property is manifested in that performance of actions "together with others," in that cooperation and coexistence which simultaneously serves the fulfillment of the person. Participation is closely associated with both the community and the personalistic value. This is precisely why it cannot be manifested solely by membership in some community but through membership must reach to the humanness of every man. Only because of the share in humanness itself, which is indicated in the notion of neighbor, does the dynamic property of participation attain its personal depth as well as universal dimension. Only then can we claim that participation serves not just the fulfillment of some individual person, but also serves the fulfillment of every person in the community, indeed, *because* of his membership in the community. We may also say that this participation serves the fulfillment of persons in any community in which men act and exist. The ability to share in the humanness itself of every man is the very core of all participation and the condition of the personalistic value of all acting and existing "together with others."

10. THE SENSE OF THE COMMANDMENT OF LOVE

The Neighbor as the Fundamental System of Reference

In view of what we have just said concerning each man's sharing in the humanness of all, it seems proper to dedicate the last pages of this book to the evangelical commandment of love. Having stressed time and again our intention not to make inroads on the territory of ethics we will not pursue the purely ethical content of the commandment, "Thou shalt love." We will not analyze all the objective content of this commandment and in particular we will not seek out the ethical significance of love; our aim is only to note that it very strongly and very consistently confirms that the reference system centered on "thy neighbor" has a crucial significance in any acting and existing "together with others." This is achieved by the juxtaposition of the neighbor with one's own ego: "thy neighbor as thyself." The significance of the system referring to the neighbor is fundamental because this system surpasses any other reference system existing in a human community by its scope, simplicity, and depth. At the same time it tells of a fullness of participation that is not indicated by membership in a community alone. The relation to the neighbor brings to its ultimate consequences any system of reference resulting from the membership in a community. The former is essentially superior to the latter. Such is the correct hierarchy of values, because the system of reference to the neighbor shows the mutual relation and subordination of all men according to the principle of humanness itself while the system of reference based on membership in a community is insufficient to reveal this relation and this subordination. Moreover, we may also speak of a sort of transcendence of "neighbor" with regard to "member of a community." All this is indirectly contained in the evangelical commandment of love.

Of course, nothing of what has been said here is to be interpreted as a depreciation of the communal human acting and being; any such conclusions would be entirely false. The commandment, "Thou shalt love," has a thoroughly communal character; it is an expression of what is necessary for a community to be formed, but more than anything else it brings into prominence what is necessary for a community to be really human. It also discloses what determines the true dimension of participation. This is why the two reference systems – to the neighbor and to the membership of a community – have to be considered jointly and not separately or, indeed, in opposition to each other, even though their distinction is entirely justified. This is also contained in the evangelical commandment. If we were to take a different point of view, then unavoidably some mutual limitations would arise; as a member of a community man would limit himself as a neighbor and vice versa. Any such limitations would be a sign of a fundamental weakness of the person, of an absence of that property in the person which we have defined as participation, of a serious defect in the social nature of man. Is it not that the social nature of man has its roots in the fundamental relation and subordination that is the consequence of the very humanness of man?

The Commandment of Love Discloses the Roots of Alienation

Thus from the point of view of participation we have to reject any limitations that either of the two systems of reference may impose on the other. In the acting and being together with others the system of reference of the neighbor and that of the membership of a community have to interpenetrate each other and become mutually complementary. Any separation between them is inadmissible and dangerous because it leads to downright alienation. Nineteenth- and twentieth-century philosophy has interpreted alienation as the isolation or separation of man from humanness, his deprivation of the value that we have here defined as personalistic. In the sphere of acting and being "together with others" this danger becomes most imminent when participation in the community itself limits and overshadows participation in the humanness of others, when that fundamental relation and subordination which imparts the human quality to any community of men becomes defective. It seems that the view, sometimes expressed, according to which the danger of dehumanization lies chiefly in the system of things – nature, the system of production, civilization – is prejudiced and misleading. Though it would be impossible to reject this view entirely it is equally impossible to accept it as the only correct interpretation. Moreover, we have to remember that though man did not create nature, he is its master; on the other hand, it is man who creates the systems of production or civilizations. Thus it lies in his power to prevent civilization from exerting a dehumanizing influence and causing alienation. This is why we must assume that the alienation for which man himself is responsible is the prime cause of any alienation resulting from the reference systems based on things. The real essence of this alienation appears to be revealed by the commandment, "Thou shalt love." Man's alienation from other men stems from a disregard for, or a neglect of, that real depth of participation which is indicated in the word *neighbor* and by the related notion of interrelation and intersubordination of men in their humanness, that most fundamental principle of any real community.*

The Commandment of Love as the Rule of Being and Acting "Together With Others"

The reference systems of the neighbor and of the membership in a community – let us repeat – overlap and interpenetrate in the objective order. They interpenetrate because they are the property of the same people. Man's social nature is expressed by both systems – by the fact that everybody is a member of a community and of different communities as well as by the fact that everybody is a neighbor; it is there that is contained every man's special relation to the person, to his own ego. Considering the hierarchy of the systems outlined here and keeping to the personalistic implications of the evangelical commandment of love we must, however, recall the necessity of coordinating the acting and the being "together with others" in order to protect the fundamental and privileged position of the reference system to the neighbor. This will protect us from the dangers of alienation; for our concern must be to make the system of reference to the neighbor the ultimate criterion in the development of the coexistence and cooperation of men in those communities and societies that are established at different levels and according to different intracommunal bonds. Any human community that allows this system of reference to become defective condemns itself to a deficiency of participation and fixes an unbridgeable gulf between the person and the community. Such disintegration is not the result of mere indifference; indeed, its causes are destructive, the destruction threatening first the person rather than the community, but through

* Cf. Note 79 in the definitive version of the text above.

the person unavoidably extending to the whole community. Now we see how intimate is the union between the person and the community and what truth is contained in the assertion of the social nature of man. It is also here that this truth seems to reveal its ominous aspect.

This ominous aspect is not, however, the most significant. The commandment "Thou shalt love" gives prominence first of all to the brighter aspects in the reality of man's existing and acting "together with others." It is on that brighter side that we have concentrated, though only cursorily, the analyses in this last chapter of our study, the main theme of which has been the acting person. But the commandment of love is also the measure of the tasks and demands that have to be faced by all men – all persons and all communities – if the whole good contained in the acting and being "together with others" is to become a reality.

POSTSCRIPT

We have now come to the end of our researches concerning the acting person, but before we definitely leave this theme it seems necessary to comment on some ideas and thoughts that may appear to have been either omitted entirely or interrupted before they were brought to a definite conclusion. The last chapter introduced a new dimension to the experience "man-acts" inasmuch as we concentrated on (1) those actions which occur when man acts "together with others" and (2) on some aspects of intersubjectivity by participation in an attempt at interpreting this new dimension of experience. The author is aware that his attempt is incomplete, that it remains but a "sketch" and not a well-developed conception. Nevertheless, he thought it necessary to incorporate such a "sketch" if only to draw attention to the need of including the experience of man who acts together with others in the general conception of the acting person. This in turn shows that the whole conception of the acting person awaits rethinking along new lines. Whether such an inquiry would still deal solely with the person and the action or would shift to the community or to personal interrelations, in which the acting person would reveal and confirm himself in some other new dimension, is another matter.

The question may arise, however, whether the experience of acting "together with others" was not the fundamental experience, and if so, whether the conception of the community and intersubjective relations should not be presupposed in any discussion on the acting person. This author is convinced, however, that no interpretation of the community and interpersonal relations can be laid out correctly if it does not rest on some already existing conception of the acting person, indeed, on a conception that in the experience of "man acts" adequately discloses the transcendence of the person in the action. Otherwise the interpretation may fail to bring out all that constitutes the person and also what intrinsically conditions as well as defines a community and its interrelations as a community and as an interrelation of persons. Thus from the point of view of method as well as of substance the correct solution seems to be the one that would recognize the priority of the conception of the person and the action, and at the same time on the basis of this conception would search for an adequate interpretation of the community and of interpersonal relations with all their richness and differentiations.

Finally, there is still one more disturbing question that demands consideration. It concerns man's "existential status," the status of his being or existing, the whole truth about his limitations and his ontic contingency. Is this truth sufficiently built into the analyses of the person and the action? Has man's ontic status been marked with sufficient clarity in these analyses? Our concern in this regard is justified if for no other reason than that the conception of the acting person presented here issues from the experience "man acts" and ought to correspond to the authentic content of this experience. The theme of this study has been the person who reveals himself in and through the action, who reveals himself through all the psychosomatic conditionings that are simultaneously his wealth and his specific limitation. This is why the person manifests not only his transcendence in the action but also his integration appropriate to the action; it is in the integration and not beyond or above it that the dynamic reality of the action is constituted. The person, who manifests himself through the action, so to speak, permeates and simultaneously encompasses the whole psychosomatic structure of his own subject.

Admittedly, the aspect of the integration of the person in the action does not in itself explain sufficiently the ontic status of man, but it does bring us nearer to grasping and understanding man's status insofar as this is made possible by the assumptions and the methods adopted in this study. In the introduction we stated that our aim was to extract from the experience of the action everything that would shed some light on man as the person, that would help, so to speak, to visualize the person; but our aim was never to build a theory of the person as a being, to develop a metaphysical conception of man. Even so, the vision of man who manifests himself as the person in the way which we have tried to disclose in our analyses, seems to confirm sufficiently that his ontic status does not exceed the limits of his contingency – that he is always a being.

Having added these two explanations the author is satisfied that he can now close for the time being this discussion of the acting person.

INDEX OF NAMES

Abbott, W. M. 303
Ach, N. 126, 310
Adler, A. 92
Aquinas, St. Thomas xiii, xxi, 25, 235,
    251, 303, 307, 309, 310
Aristotle viii, xiii, xx, xxi, 14, 25, 63,
    67, 129, 157, 202, 204, 205, 244, 302,
    306, 308, 315
Ayer, A. J. 312

Bentham, J. 312
Bergson, H. 304, 305, 314
Berkeley, G. 305, 306
Blondel, M. 301, 303
Boethius 73, 302, 307
Boyce Gibson, R. 304
Brandt, R. B. 301
Brentano, F. xx, 303

Dąbrowski, K. 313
Descartes, R. vii, 303, 306
Dordick, W. xxii
Dybowski, M. 310
Dziewanowski, M. K. xiv
Dziwisz, S. xxii

Ey, H. 305

Finance, J. de 303, 307
Fink, E. xx
Freud, S. 92

Hallett, G. xxii
Hare, R. M. 312
Hartmann, N. 311, 314
Heidegger, M. 307
Hildebrand, D. von 308, 311
Hume, D. 310, 314
Husserl, E. xiii, 145, 301–305, 307, 312,
    315

Ingarden, R. xxi, 301, 302, 307, 308,
    310, 312, 313

James, W. 304
Jaworski, M. 301, 313
Jung, C. G. 92

Kalinowski, J. 301, 302, 308
Kamiński, S. 301
Kant, I. xiii, xiv, xxi, xxii, 165, 243, 244,
    250, 302, 303, 305, 309, 310, 312
Kłósak, K. 301
Krąpiec, M. A. 304
Kretschmer, E. 313
Kuc, L. 316

Leibniz, G. W. von 135, 306
Levinas, E. 305, 308
Luijpen, W. A. 314

Michotte, A. 126, 310
Mill, J. S. 14

Nuttin, J. 304, 306

Paul, St. 166, 315
Plato 202, 205, 303, 306
Półtawska, W. 313
Półtawski, A. 305
Potocki, A. iii, ix, xxii
Prümm, N. 310

Ricoeur, P. 306, 307, 310, 312, 314
Rilke, R. M. 307
Rumian, E. xxii

Sartre, J.-P. 12, 308
Scheler, M. viii, xiii, xiv, xx, xxi, 178,
    233, 239, 244, 302, 305, 307, 309–
    315

Shoemaker, S. 309
Stevenson, C. L. 301
Styczeń, T. 301, 313

Tatarkiewicz, W. 312

Tresmontant, C. 308
Tymieniecka, A.-T. ii, iii, viii, ix, x, xiii,
    xiv, xxiii, 302, 307, 310

Wojtyła, K. iii, vi, ix, xix, xx, 310, 313

ANALYTICAL TABLE OF CONTENTS

action (*see also* human action)
  activation *vs.* 69
  communal 266
  existence priority over 82
  insight into person by 10
  ontological basis of 72
  performance of, as value 264
activation
  action *vs.* 69
activeness
  basis of 61
activity
  potentiality of man and 87
actus humanus see human action
affectivity
  disintegration and 243
  human, stir of emotion in 239
alienation
  roots of 296
anthropology
  ethics and 13
appetite
  concupiscent and irascible 234
  intendedness, intentionality, and 125
  transcendence *vs.* 124
attitude
  authentic 283
  nonauthentic 288

beauty
  person's transcendence in relation to 155
becoming
  being and human action in relation to 96
  development, potentiality, and 97
behavior
  definition 254
  person's integration in action and 255
being

becoming and human action in relation to 96
body
  human, as person's means of expression 204
  consciousness of, feeling and 228
  dynamism of 206
  inaction 205
  outerness and innerness of 200
  reactivity and vitality of 209
  subjectivity of 210
  soul and, integration and transcendence in relation to 256
  -soul relation, current and hylomorphic meaning of 257

causality
  of nature 80
choice
  decision and 130
  motivation of 129
cognition
  as condition of act of will 140
  dynamic structure of object and 135
  human, self-knowledge and 39
  objectifying, government of will by 113
common good
  community, participation, and 280
  foundation of human communities 282
  personalistic and teleological conceptions of 281
community
  member of 292
  membership of 277
  participation in 276
complexity
  of man-person 183
comprehension
  sequence of 182
conduct

definition 254
person's integration in action and 255
conformism 289
conscience
  action, moral goodness, and 154
  as inner normative reality 156
  creative rôle of 165
  fulfillment of person conditioned by 157
  man's self-responsibility in 173
consciousness 19
  autonomous subject 33
  definition 31ff
  dynamism and 60
  ego, self-knowledge, and 36
  emotionalization of 52
  emotion and 50
  experience of action and 48
  experience of ego by 43
  feelings and, in personal dynamism 230
  feelings, sensitivity, and 231
  in human act 28ff
  potentiality and 90
  psychic, delimitations of 91
  psychoemotive potentiality and 88
  self-determination and 112
  self-knowledge and 35
  self-, self-knowledge and 38
  somatic, delimitations of 91
  somato-vegetative potentiality and 89
  subconsciousness and 94
  subjective experience and 41
  truthfulness of, transcendence and 159
  voluntariness and 27
cooperation
  human action and 262

decision
  choice and 130
  judgement and 146
  moral, acts of will and 133
  truth, will, and 136
  will and 126
development
  becoming, potentiality, and 97
dialogue 287
disintegration

affectivity and 243
  as defect of self-governance and self-possession 193
  integration of person in action revealed by 194
  meanings of 192
duty
  personal fulfillment and 163
  truth and; normative power as 161
dynamism
  act conjugate, potency, and 63
  consciousness and 60
  emotive, as concentrator of experiences 226
  of body and man 206
  personal; consciousness precedence over feelings in 230
  psychical and somatic 199
  somatic, reactivity of 207, 208
  subconsciousness and 93

efficacy
  consciousness, emotivity, and 246
  definition 66
  experience of 67, 68, 69
  freedom and 100
  obligation, responsibility, and 169
  of person 80
  personal; emotion, will, and 246
  subjectiveness vs. 71, 74
  tension between emotivity and 244
ego
  as object 108
    in self-determination 112
  as subject 45
  consciousness, self-knowledge, and 36
  experience of 43
  in field of experience 5
  objectification of, in structure of freedom 120
  subjective, emotional content of 245
  understanding man using 49
elation
  excitement vs. 237
emotion
  consciousness and 50
  content of; values and 248

differentiation between excitement
    and 241
emotive content of 242
etymology of 223
human experience and 247
in subjective ego 245
richness of 240
stirring, as core of human affectivity
    239
    excitement *vs.* 238
will and 246
emotionalization
    consciousness and 52, 54
emotivity
    conscious efficacy and 246
    conscious response of will and 225
    etymology of 223
    reactivity and 225
    tension between efficacy and 244
empiricism
    phenomenalism and 8
ethics
    anthropology and 13
ethos
    basis of human 69
excitability 237
    as constituent of instincts 238
excitement
    as emotive fact 235
    differentiation between emotion and
        241
    elation *vs.* 237
    stirring emotions *vs.* 238
existence
    personal, dynamic cohesion of man
        and 83
    priority over action 82
experience
    as basis of knowledge of man 4
    comprehension and 6
    consciousness, emotionalization, and
        54
    ego and man in field of 5
    emotive dynamism as concentrator of
        226
    human spirituality and 47
    of acting and happening 65, 66

of action; consciousness and 48
of efficacy 66
of ego 43
of man's acting 10
of man; cognition of person and 8
    inner and outer aspects of 7
    meaning of 3
    reduction and 14
subjective; consciousness and 41

feeling
    consciousness of body and 228
    consciousness precedence over, in
        personal dynamism 230
    psychical and somatic subjectivity in
        relation to 228
    self- 229
felicity
    as part of personal structure 176
    in relation to others 175
    intrapersonal profile of 176
    pleasure *vs.* 177
    (= self-fulfillment) 174
    truth and freedom as sources of 174
freedom
    basis of man's bad and good 99
    efficacy and 100
    instinct of, meaning of 122
    personal aspects of 115
    structure of, ego objectification and
        120
    truth and, as sources of felicity 174
free will *see* will, free
fulfillment
    in human action 149
    of person in action, duty and 163
    of self; action, morality, and 150
        in action 167

good
    person's transcendence in relation to
        155

human action
    ambiguity in concept of 65
    bad and good in 98
    becoming and being in relation to 96

body in 205
causal relation of person and 67
conjugate; potency and 63
consciousness in 28ff
cooperative 262
ethical and personalistic value of 265
experience of; consciousness and 48
fulfillment and 149
fulfillment in; duty and 163
immanent; person and 114
inner and outer transitive effects of 149
instinctive; meaning of 123
integration of person in 194
    conduct and behavior in relation to
      255
interpretation of, traditional 25
man's transcendence of 68
moral goodness, conscience, and 154
morality, self-fulfillment, and 150
moral modality of 11
nature as determinant of 77
participatory 261, 263
personal 26
phenomenological basis of 9
pleasure, displeasure, and 178
self-fulfillment in 167
    moral dimensions of 152
subjective basis of 76
synthesis of motion and 212
transcendence and 179
transcendence in; spirituality and 181
transcendence of person revealed in 111
human being
  impersonalistic concept of 275
human efficacy
  analysis of 59
humanness 293
human praxis
  theory 16
hylomorphism 203

immanence
  of spiritual element in man 181
independence
  conditioning of 120
individualism
  as denial of participation 273

as limitation of participation 272
  reversed (= totalism) 274
induction
  meaning and 14
instinct
  complex nature of 215
  excitability as constituent of 238
  interpretation of 219
  self-determination vs. 116
  self-preservation 217
  sex and reproductive 218
  somatic reality in relation to 216
integration
  complex unity of 191
  dynamic unity of action and 198
  human complexity revealed in 255
  of person 20
  soul as principle of 257
  transcendence and 189
    soul and body in relation to 256
intention
  appetite, intentionality, and 125
intentionality
  appetite, intention, and 125
  of volition; objectification and 109
interpretation
  adequate 17
  of object 18
  reduction and; in theory of human
      praxis 16
intuition
  perception of values and 147
  phenomenological 183

judgement
  decision and 146
  thought and 144

knowledge
  of man; experience as basis of 4

love
  commandment of 296, 298

man
  corporeal, spirituality of 185
  dynamic cohesion of 83

dynamism of 206
experience of; cognition of person and
    8
  inner and outer aspects of 7
  meaning of 3
  reduction and 15
in field of experience 5
knowledge of; experience as basis of 4
ontic complexity of 185
ontological foundation of action in 73
psychosomatic integrity of 201
spiritual element and spiritual
    potentiality of 184
subjectivity of 18
understanding, ego, and 49
meaning
  induction and 14
mind
  truth and 158
moral decision
  spontaneous attraction or repulsion
    and 251
morality
  action, conscience, and 154
  action, self-fulfillment, and 150
  of fulfillment in action 152
  truthfulness and 163
moral proficiency
  function of 253
moral value
  insight into person and 12
  of human action 11
  subject's responsibility for 171
  truth and 139
motion
  human, somatic constitution and 214
    synthesis of action and 212
motivation
  definition of 128
  of choice and simple willing 129

nature
  as determinant of manner of acting 77
  causality of 80
  person and 79, 84, 85
  person vs. 76, 78
neighbor 292

as system of reference 295
noninvolvement 290

object
  determination of; free will and 132
  dynamic structure of 135
  ego as; in self-determination 108, 112
    in structure of freedom 120
  independence of; truth, will, and 138
  intentional, of volition 120
  interpretation and understanding of 18
objectification
  integral dynamism of will and 114
  intentionality of volition and 109
obligation
  efficacy, responsibility, and 169
  transition to, from value 166
  value and; person's transcendence
    evidenced in 168
opposition 286ff

participation 261ff, 294
  as constitutive factor of community
    276
  associational relationship vs. 279
  as trait of acting 268, 269
  denied by individualism 273
  individualism and totalism as limitations
    of 272
  interpersonal relations and 270
  significance of 271
passiveness
  basis of 61
passivity
  potentiality of man and 87
person
  acting; psychosomatic unity of 196
  -action unity; psychosomatic
    complexity and 196
  appeal of values, act of will, and 134
  causal relation of actions and 67
  cognition of; experience of man and 8
  efficacy of 80
  human nature and 84
  immanent act and 114
  in philosophy of man 267
  insight into, action as 10

moral value and 12
integration of 20
nature and 79, 85
nature *vs.* 76, 78
pleasure, displeasure and 178
problems of, significance of 21
self-dependence of; free will and 117
somatic constitution and 203
transcendence of 20
  meaning of 119
  revealed in action 111
phenomenalism
empiricism and 8
pleasure
displeasure and; person and action in
  relation to 178
felicity *vs.* 177
potency
act conjugate and 63
potentiality
activity, passivity, and 87
becoming, development and 97
consciousness and 90
dynamism, subconsciousness and 93
of man-subject 85
psychoemotive; consciousness and 88
somato-vegetative; consciousness and
  89
subject and 86
psyche 220
definition 221
somatic constitution and 222

reactivity
emotivity and 225
reduction
experience of man and 15
interpretation and, in theory of human
  praxis 16
responsibility
efficacy, obligation, and 169
personal authority in relation to 172

self-determination
as basis for subjective moral values 171
ego as object in 108, 112
independence and 120

instinct *vs.* 116
personal aspects of freedom in 115
self-governance, self-possession and 106
spontaneity and 243
  tensions between 249
volition and 110
will and 105
will used in 121
self-fulfillment (*see also* felicity) 174
self-governance
disintegration as defect of 193
presupposition of self-possession in 107
self-determination, self-possession, and
  106
self-knowledge
consciousness and 35
consciousness, ego, and 36
human cognition and 39
self-consciousness and 38
self-possession
disintegration as defect of 193
presupposition of, in self-governance
  107
self-determination, self-governance,
  and 106
sensitivity
consciousness of feelings and 231
experience of values and 232
skill
in action–motion synthesis 213
solidarity 284ff
soul
as principle of transcendence and
  integration 257
body and; integration and transcendence
  in relation to 256
–body relation; current and hylomorphic meaning of 257
experience of 186
spiritual element
spiritual potentiality and 184
spirituality
human; ego and 47
of corporeal man 185
transcendence in action and 181
spiritual potentiality
spiritual element and 184

spontaneity
  self-determination and 243
    tensions between 249
stimulus
  motor; affective and 227
subconscious 92
  consciousness and 94
  dynamism and 93
subject
  ego as 45
  moral value of, basis of 171
  ontological basis of action 72
  potentiality and 86
  thought and efficacy of 143
subjectification
  efficacy *vs.* 71, 74
  integral dynamism of will and 114
subjectivism
  subjectivity and 56
  subjectivity *vs.* 58
subjectivity
  inherent in acting person 56
  psychical and somatic; feeling and 228
  subjectivism and 56
  subjectivism *vs.* 58

thought
  efficacy of subject and 143
  judgement and 144
totalism
  as limit of participation 272
  individualism reversed as 274
transcendence
  appetite *vs.* 124
  definitions of 179

  experience of acting and 179
  human complexity revealed in 255
  in action; spirituality and 181
  integration and 189
  integration and; soul and body in
    relation to 256
  of person 20
    good, truth, and beauty in relation
      to 155
    obligation, value, and 168
    truthfulness of conscience and 159
  soul as principle of 257

truth
  axiological and practical 142
  decision, will, and 136
  duty and; normative power of 161
  freedom and; as sources of felicity 174
  good, and experience of values in 141
  moral norms and 163
  moral value and 139
  normative power of 158
  object, will, and 138
  person's transcendence in relation to
    155

unity
  of man-person; phenomenological
    intuition and 183

value
  attraction and repulsion in spontaneous
    reference to 250
  emotion content refers to 248
  ethical, of action 265
  experience of, sensitivity and 232
    truth, good, and 141
  obligation and; person's transcendence
    evidenced in 168
  perception of; thought and 147
  performance of action as 264
  personalistic, of action 265
  responsibility for, and responsiveness
    to 170
  spontaneous experience of 249
  transition of, to obligation 166
virtue
  function of 253
volition
  objectification and 109
  self-determination and 110
  striving for good and 127
  transcendence of person revealed by
    111
voluntariness
  consciousness and 27

will
  act of; moral determinism and 133
    value appeal and 134

(will)
cognition and 140
conscious response of; emotivity
and 225
decision and 126
dynamic structure of object and 135
emotion and 246
free; object determination and 132

self-dependence of person and 117
government of, by cognition 113
integral dynamism of 114
motivation and 139
motivation of simple 129
object, truth, and 138
self-determination and 105, 121
truth, decision, and 136

ANALECTA HUSSERLIANA

The Yearbook of Phenomenological Research

Editor

ANNA-TERESA TYMIENIECKA

1. *Analecta Husserliana.* 1971, ix + 207 pp.

2. *The Later Husserl and the Idea of Phenomenology.* 1972, vii + 374 pp.

3. *The Phenomenological Realism of the Possible Worlds.* 1974, vii + 386 pp.

4. *Ingardeniana.* 1976, x + 438 pp.

*5. *The Crisis of Culture.* 1976, vii + 383 pp.

*6. *The Self and the Other.* 1977, xi + 186 pp.

*7. *The Human Being in Action.* 1978, xvii + 261 pp.

8. *Japanese Phenomenology.* 1979, xi + 291 pp.

*9. *The Teleologies in Husserlian Phenomenology.* 1979 (forthcoming).

*Indicates the volumes to which Karol Wojtyła has contributed.